BRITAIN'S GURKHAS

BY CHRISTOPHER BULLOCK

THIRD MILLENNIUM
PUBLISHING, LONDON

BRITAIN'S GURKHAS
Text copyright ©The Gurkha Museum
Design copyright © Third Millennium Information Ltd 2009

NOTE: All royalty income from sales of this book will be divided equally
between **The Gurkha Museum**, Peninsula Barracks, Romsey Road,
Winchester, SO23 8TS and **The Gurkha Welfare Trust**, P.O. Box 2170,
22 Queen Street, Salisbury, SP2 2EX

First published in 2009 by Third Millennium Publishing Limited,
a subsidiary of Third Millennium Information Limited.

2–5 Benjamin Street
London
United Kingdom
EC1M 5QL
www.tmiltd.com

ISBN: 978 1 906507 27 5 HB
ISBN: 978 1 906507 28 2 PB

British Library Cataloguing in Publication Data
A CIP catalogue record for this book is available from the British Library.

Designed by Susan Pugsley and Matt Wilson
Production by Bonnie Murray

Reprographics by Studio Fasoli, Italy
Printed in Slovenia by Gorenjski Tisk

FRONTISPIECE: Image: from a painting by Brigadier R.S. Hunt (HQ
Brigade of Gurkhas). Text: from the poem *Epilogue*, in *New Collected
Poems* by Stephen Spender ©2004. Reprinted by kind permission of
the Estate of Stephen Spender.

CONTENTS

FOREWORD

GENERAL SIR DAVID RICHARDS
KCB CBE DSO ADC GEN
COLONEL COMMANDANT BRIGADE OF GURKHAS

The history of the Gurkhas who have served in the British and Indian Armies is a noble and valiant one. It is a story of outstanding bravery and endurance, matchless discipline and loyalty – but also of humour and good nature. It is a story which reflects the character of the Gurkha himself.

From the far-off battles of the British Raj in India, through the World Wars of the early 20th century, and the post–Imperial conflicts in Malaya and Borneo, to the campaigns of the present day in Iraq and Afghanistan, Nepal and her gallant sons have stood steadfast with Britain in every crisis. The Gurkhas have come forward – and continue to come forward – in great numbers to fight alongside us. Over 95,000 Gurkhas served in the First World War, over 130,000 in the Second. The Brigade of Gurkhas today is a good deal smaller, totalling around 3,000 all ranks, but the desire to serve in it remains strong – there were some 17,000 applicants for 230 places in the most recent annual recruiting exercise. The pride and martial spirit of the Gurkhas is maintained and reinvigorated as generation succeeds generation, and the close comradeship between Briton and Gurkha endures, founded on mutual respect and affection.

Many fine writers and historians have turned their attention to the history of the Britain's Gurkhas, but surely none have been better qualified to address the subject than Brigadier Christopher Bullock. He knows the Brigade in all weathers, and from many points of view. As a young company commander he was awarded the Military Cross leading Gurkhas in daring clandestine raids across the Indonesian border during the Borneo Confrontation, and later commanded a Gurkha battalion with great distinction. As Brigadier Brigade of Gurkhas – the professional head of the Brigade – in the early 1990s, he was intimately involved with many of the difficult and sensitive politico-strategic considerations over the Brigade's future which he covers in this book. And finally as Curator of the Gurkha Museum at Winchester, from 1995 to 2002, and later as Chairman of its Trustees, Brigadier Bullock has immersed himself in all aspects of Gurkha history. He writes, therefore, with unsurpassed authority – and with a very warm but informed regard for Gurkhas.

The whole panorama is here. The Nepal Wars when the British first encountered the gallantry and fighting power of the Gurkhas. The heroism on Delhi Ridge during the Indian Mutiny, as Gurkhas and British Riflemen fought side by side against daunting odds. The fights on the North-West and North-East Frontiers of India. The horrors of the Western Front, Gallipoli and the Middle East in the Great War, into which the regiments of the old Indian Army were plunged. The defeats and then victories in the deserts, hills and jungles of the Second World War. And all the post-war operations, right up to today's deployment in Afghanistan (with all the resonance that country has for Gurkhas). Interwoven are accounts of the individual Gurkhas who have won the Victoria Cross, illustrations of the highest form of valour. Yet Brigadier Bullock does not seek to avoid the controversial areas – the Amritsar massacre of 1919, for instance, or the Hawaii incident in 1986 – but deals with them with objectivity and insight. He also gives us just the right amount of historical background, particularly covering events in Nepal, so that readers who may be unfamiliar with the context of some of these 'battles long ago' are not left perplexed. Overall, there is an excellent balance of detail, analysis and anecdote.

As Colonel Commandant Brigade of Gurkhas, I have been proud to see at first hand the courage, resilience and skill of Gurkhas on operations, and their unquenchable cheerfulness and generosity. I wholeheartedly commend Brigadier Bullock's book as our authorized history to anyone who wishes to know more about our splendid soldiers. You will be left in no doubt that Britain is fortunate indeed to have the Gurkhas as our friends and comrades.

General Sir David Richards KCB CBE DSO ADC Gen
Colonel Commandant Brigade of Gurkhas. (By kind
permission of Headquarters Brigade of Gurkhas)

ACKNOWLEDGEMENTS

CHRISTOPHER BULLOCK

Writing a history of the Brigade of Gurkhas was always going to be a demanding task and so it proved to be. In retrospect it would not have been possible without the help of many others. Foremost amongst these helpers must be Field Marshal Sir John Chapple, Colonel Denis Wood and Colonel Richard Cawthorne, all accomplished historians and authors themselves. Scrupulously checking every chapter they ensured total accuracy and balance and redirected me when I strayed on so many occasions. In any claim that *Britain's Gurkhas* represents an authoritative history it is because of their scholarship.

It really goes without saying that without the help and unflagging enthusiasm of Major Gerald Davies, the Gurkha Museum Curator, I could not have progressed very far and the same goes for Gavin Edgerley-Harris, our gifted Archivist, who expertly found suitable images for the text and endlessly ferreted out supporting references. Also grateful thanks to all the others of the staff of the Gurkha Museum, both British and Gurkha, who became involved in this project in one way and another – not least my fellow Trustee Lieutenant Colonel Mike Barrett, whose expert help on the medal illustrations was invaluable.

I also wish to acknowledge the support of The Gurkha Museum Vice-Patrons and Trustees and, of course, in particular General Sir David Richards, Colonel Commandant Brigade of Gurkhas for kindly agreeing to write the Foreword. Mention must be made as well of his most supportive staff at Headquarters Brigade of Gurkhas for their help and patience, in particular Simon Lord for his expert comment and guidance. Grateful thanks too for the generous support of The Friends of The Gurkha Museum who so kindly provided the start–up loan for this project and to The Director and staff of The Gurkha Welfare Trust for publicizing this work. Thanks also to all those people, too numerous to mention, who in different ways gave advice, encouragement and helpful criticism.

Finding a publisher who would do justice to this unique story was likely to be a challenge so we counted ourselves extremely lucky to have found Dr Joel Burden and his great team from Third Millennium, Chris Fagg, the Publisher, Matthew Wilson, the illustrator, designer Susan Pugsley and publicist Michael Jackson, not forgetting Randal Gray for his expert vetting, and David Harding for his timely help with the index and text. Perfectionists themselves, there was never going to be any worries over the quality of this production.

Finally thanks to my long-suffering wife Liz to whom the term 'completely retired' has in my case assumed an entirely different meaning!

(Photo by kind permission of Colonel B.M. Niven)

MAPS

PHYSICAL FEATURES

	Sea / Lake
Jumna	River
	Principal land
	Other land
	Land elevation (non-specific gradation)
Chunuk Bair 850ft ▲	Mountain / Hill elevation (specific)
	Forest / Woodland
	Marsh / Swamp
7	Buildings
	Boundary lines

MILITARY

MALAUN ✗	Battle / Battlefield / Landing
	Allied advance
	Enemy advance
ORAKZAI	Tribes

COMMUNICATIONS

	Principal road
	Other road
	Track
	Railway
✈	Airfield / Landing strip

ADMINISTRATION

	International boundary
	Internal boundary
Shutargarjan Pass	Mountain pass
BHUTAN	Country name
SIRMOOR	Administrative area name

SETTLEMENTS

KATHMANDU ●	Captial city
Annapurna ●	Principal city / Town
Pokhara ●	Town / Village
	Urban area

Following pages: Gurkhas attacking; probably at the battle to break into the Mareth Line in 1943 during the desert campaign. (Gurkha Museum)

(Photo opposite by kind permission of C. Schulze)

CHAPTER ONE

NEPAL
AND THE
GURKHAS

Although it would probably be correct to say that all Gurkhas were Nepalese, it certainly would not be right to say that all Nepalese were Gurkhas. To appreciate the difference it is necessary to go back some way into the history of Nepal.

Most visitors to Nepal arrive by air into Kathmandu the capital. In Nepalese folklore the mountain-encircled valley of Kathmandu (meaning literally 'wooden temple') was once a huge lake, which the Hindu god Vishnu hacked with a mighty sword, letting out the water and revealing the future site of the capital. Actually the valley was probably the crater of a volcano and it was the volcanic ash that made the soil so rich and productive. Either way, here was an incredibly fertile valley with the impregnable rampart of the highest peaks in the world to the north and surrounded by their foothills and irrigated by the melting snow waters. It was a perfect place for human settlement.

The first recorded habitation was that of the Newar dynasty, whose craftsmen (in wood) prompted the name of the city. Outside the valley, pastoral tribes of Tibeto-Burman origin peopled the steep mountainsides, eking out a precarious existence hunting and subsistence farming.

However, events far to the south were unfurling that were to have dramatic effects on Nepal. Here around AD 1300 the Moguls, originating from Central Asia, began the first of their many invasions of India. The Moguls were Muslims, the Indians were Hindus; thus the bitter fighting was not just over territory but about which religion should prevail. At that time, among the foremost fighting men of India were the Rajputs, who bitterly resisted the Mogul invasion. The bloody warfare ebbed and flowed, until by AD 1500 the Rajput resistance started to crack and groups began to flee north to Nepal to escape the Moguls. Because of its protected and favourable location many headed for Kathmandu, where by force and intermarriage they soon replaced the Newars as the dominant faction.

Elsewhere, Rajput groups started settlements above the malarial border forests of the Terai where they came into contact with the mountain tribes. Unlike the Rajput occupation of Kathmandu, Rajput assimilation by the mountain tribes was relatively peaceful. If these proud newcomers were to survive and prosper in their adopted land, they needed to intermarry with the tribal women. The women were content to marry them but only on condition that resulting children should enjoy all the religious privileges of their high-born Rajput Hindu lovers. In fact, the religious constraints of the Rajputs forbade this, but such was their need to cohabit that they did it anyhow! Thus there grew outside and to the west of Kathmandu new local dynasties (or kingships) controlled by the offspring of Rajputs and tribal girls; these dynasties were known as the Chaubisia, or the

Hanuman Dhoka temple Kathmandu by John Mole. By kind permission of John Mole.

Twenty-Four Kingships. To the east of Kathmandu on the precipitous slopes of the Himalayas, the warlike eastern tribes of the Kiranti remained virtually untouched and unaffected by the Rajput incursion.

Inevitably, as time went on, the Twenty-Four Kingships, when not fighting among themselves, cast envious glances on the huge wealth and prosperity of the Kathmandu valley, by now split into four separate principalities, physically separated but generally regarded as forming a single entity, Kathmandu. Had these four principalities cooperated they would have been easily able to repulse any assaults by groupings from the Chaubisia. Indeed such assaults had been made and bloodily repulsed by the individual much better-armed and organized forces of the four Kathmandu principalities. Unfortunately, continuous bickering and petty warfare among themselves made the principalities increasingly vulnerable to outside interference.

In 1742, Prithwi Narayan Shah, at 20 years old, became ruler of the Kingdom of Gorkha, situated some 50 miles due west of Kathmandu. Not being one of the kingdoms of the Chaubisia,

Gorkha was nominally under the control of the capital, Kathmandu. However, Prithwi Narayan's father had successfully thrown off the yoke of the four principalities, leaving Gorkha as an independent state outside the Chaubisia.

As a youth, Prithwi Narayan had travelled widely in Nepal and India, and had seen at first hand the slow but sure spread of British power through its surrogate East India Company. He interested himself in its weaponry and brought back flintlock muskets, then the latest in firearms.

At exactly what stage the young ruler decided to conquer Nepal is difficult to gauge, but he did so decide and began to gather an army. Looking back, his task smacks of 'mission impossible', involving as it did three major challenges. First he had to gain dominance over the Chaubisia, for it was in part its manpower of tough Gurung and Magar tribesmen that he would need to augment his army; then he had to invade and conquer the hitherto invincible four principalities of the Kathmandu valley and, finally, he had to push east out of Kathmandu and subdue the warlike eastern tribes of the Kiranti in their mountain

NEPAL AND INDIA

A picture of a Nepalese nobleman, posssibly Prithi Narayan Shah clearly showing his Rajput ancestry in his features. (Gurkha Museum)

fastness. Only a man of supreme self-confidence, courage and total indifference to reverses, suffering or hardship could have any chance of success. Prithwi Narayan was just such a man – one who combined all these attributes with political cunning, duplicity and total ruthlessness.

In fact the first task proved relatively simple. Rather than the Chaubisia fighting each other and Gorkha for the sparse spoils available, an attack on the four principalities of the Kathmandu valley, with their fabled riches, was an attractive option. It was rather akin to a Third Division football team having a crack at the Premiership, glittering success unlikely but worth trying for! Not all the states of the Chaubisia joined Gorkha, but those that did not came to regret it as Prithwi Narayan settled with them at his leisure once his main objective was achieved.

Today, Prithwi Narayan's mountain fort of Gorkha is a National Monument and as you climb up to it on huge rock steps, the massive peaks of the Himalaya tower above you, while to the west and east the rolling foothills and cleft mountain passes stretch as far as the eye can see. Only to the south are the hills lower, forming a final mountain barrier before they drop down towards the great Gangetic plain.

Standing on the red-painted terraces of the fort, one can imagine the sight of troops of mountain warriors armed with swords, kukris and spears wending their way towards Gorkha, where Prithwi Narayan's battle standard fluttered in the mountain

This photo of the ancient fort of Goorkha in the western hills of Nepal is where Prithi Narayan Shah raised his Gurkha army and from where they took their name. (Gurkha Museum)

breeze. Since Prithwi Narayan's army gathered at Gorkha, his warriors came to be known as Gurkhas. Written in *nagri*, the written language of Nepal, the word Gurkha would appear to most of us as a line of incomprehensible squiggles. However when it is romanized or turned into our lettering it reads 'Gurkha'. So the historic name of Gurkha came into being. Originally it described only those western tribal warriors who joined Prithwi Narayan at Gorkha but, as we shall see, it eventually came to include the eastern warriors of the Kiranti.

As his army gathered, Prithwi Narayan was busy sowing dissension among the four principalities of the Kathmandu valley. It was essential they should not unite against him as otherwise he would be crushed. Here he was fortunate: the principalities were busy squabbling among themselves and, moreover, the important but separate Kingdom of Nawarkot, just to the west of the capital, was willing to sell out to him. With Nawarkot in the bag he felt confident enough to attack and his army debouched out of the mountain passes and into the Kathmandu valley, centring their attack in 1749 on the mainly Newar principality of Kirtipur. Here he had the shock of his life: the Newaris fought like wildcats, and although they got precious little help from the three uncommitted principalities, they managed to hurl the Gurkha

The ancient Patan district of Kathmandu centre of religious devotion and now a UNESCO World Heritage site. (Gurkha Museum)

army out of the Kathmandu valley in defeat and confusion. Many were for giving up but, back at Gorkha, as his Gurkhas licked their wounds, Prithwi Narayan was planning again.

In between planning he met a beautiful princess from the neighbouring kingship of Makwanpur, site of the holiest of provincial temples. Her father and his ministers rejected him as a

This picture 'Assemblage of Ghookhas' is evocative of the raising of Prithwi Narayan Shah's army at Gorkha. (Gurkha Museum)

suitable match and laughed him out of court. Prithwi Narayan returned with his army, imprisoned the king, married the princess and flayed the chief ministers alive. People were discovering that it was dangerous to cross the King of Gorkha!

Prithwi Narayan's next plan was to starve out the four principalities. Again using the buffer state of Nawarkot as a sally port, he surrounded Kathmandu and besieged it in 1765. Despite great hunger and privation, the four principalities refused to give in. Prithwi Narayan tightened the siege, hanging anybody found carrying any goods into the valley of Kathmandu. Soon corpses were to be seen hanging from every tree – but still the principalities would not give in. His army growing restless and the Chaubisia threatening his base, Prithwi decided on another attack on Kirtipur – but despite hunger and disease the Newars still held out, and he returned to Gorkha a second time unsuccessful.

While Gorkha's ruler had been away, the powerful state of Lamjung, a neighbour to his west, had declared against him and now Prithwi turned his frustrated army on them, swiftly bringing them to heel before going on to totally subjugate his wife's home state of Makwanpur. These little local difficulties resolved, the

King of Gorkha turned his attention back to his main objective, the four principalities of the valley: Kathmandu, Patan, Bhatgaon and the unvanquished Kirtipur.

This time Prithwi Narayan trusted in traitors whom he had suborned within Kirtipur. When he attacked again in 1767 the gates were open and his Gurkha army made much better headway, in spite of the other three principalities coming to Kirtipur's aid. In vain did the Prince of Bhatgaon implore the aid of the British: the Honourable East India Company sent a small detachment but it got lost in the jungle of the Terai and never arrived! Despite desperate resistance, Kirtipur was doomed; Prithwi Narayan offered terms, the Newars reluctantly agreed and surrendered. Once Kirtipur was in his power, Prithwi Narayan ordered that the lips and noses of every male over six be cut off and brought to him. The weight of the cut-off features exceeded 40 kilos. Henceforth Kirtipur was known as Naskatipur, city of cut-off noses! Threatened with the same treatment, with the additional loss of their right hands, the people of Bhatgaon and Patan gave in; only Kathmandu fought on to a bitter end. Prithwi Narayan became master of the capital on 29 September 1768.

Leaving his lieutenants to complete the victory, the King of Gorkha took the main part of his army east, where the formidable Kiranti awaited him. Desperate were the battles between Prithwi Narayan's Western highlanders and the Eastern highlanders of the Kiranti. Eventually, superior weaponry in the form of flintlocks and better tactics won the day, and the Chieftain of the Kiranti lay dying on the field of battle.

Unlike his treatment of the four principalities, Prithwi Narayan treated the defeated Kiranti with clemency and sensitivity, erecting a tomb to their fallen chieftain and allowing them to disperse peacefully to their remote mountain fastnesses. After all they were now Gurkhas, ruled by the King of Gorkha, now King of Nepal! His dream, so bloodily and tenaciously pursued, had been realized and he ruled over a unified state roughly comparative in size and configuration to modern Nepal. It had been an amazing achievement.

Prithwi Narayan died aged 45 in 1775. At first his unique legacy would be squandered but, later, similarly powerful characters would take up the baton and confront the most formidable enemy yet: the British!

A Gurkha family group in traditional western Gurkha hill dress. (Gurkha Museum)

The picture 'Eight Gurkhas' from the William Fraser collection in the Gurkha Museum shows the type of soldier that made up Prithwi Narayan Shah's Gurkha army. Bought by Friends of the Gurkha Museum, The Victoria and Albert Purchase Fund and The Art Fund.

CHAPTER TWO

WAR
WITH THE
BRITISH

Because Prithwi Narayan died relatively young, he was unable to ensure stability of succession. His eldest son reigned only a further two years before dying himself. The grandson was but an infant and there followed a period of court strife involving the Queen Mother, the Regent and later the adolescent boy himself. However the wonderfully efficient army created by Prithwi Narayan continued under its own volition to expand Nepal's borders by making war on its neighbours.

To the north-east, it invaded Sikkim and then went on to invade Tibet. China could not stand by and allow Tibet to be conquered so, gathering together an army of 70,000 with cannon, it eventually drove the hardy mountaineers out in 1792 – but not before they had gutted the rich monasteries of all the loot they could carry. More serious perhaps were their forays to the south-west in 1793–94, where they defeated and occupied the rich areas of Kumaon, Sirmoor and Garhwal and pushed down as far as the Punjab. These territorial acquisitions began to concern the British, especially as they were made by a country which appeared to have no effective government with which to negotiate.

At this point let us examine what the British were doing in India and why. Like the Portuguese and French before them, the British originally came to India to trade. They sought the silks and spices of India, which they traded for manufactured goods and firearms. In London a trading company, The Honourable East India

This picture from the William Fraser collection shows a typical Gurkha soldier in Amar Singh's army. Bought by Friends of the Gurkha Museum, The Victoria and Albert Purchase Fund and The Art Fund.

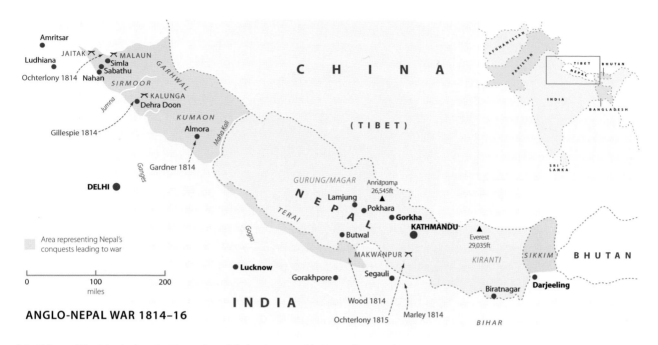

A detailed map of Nepal showing its territorial expansion and the invasion routes of the Honourable East India Company armies in 1814 and 1815.

Company, was set up in 1600 to develop and exploit trade with India. While the Portuguese were Britain's oldest ally in Europe, France was its traditional enemy and whereas Portugal had come primarily to trade, France had imperial ambitions. Either France or Britain was to be the dominant power in India, and the then Colonel Robert Clive gave Britain a crucial lead by gaining control of Bengal at the Battle of Plassey in 1757. Thereafter Britain, working through the Honourable East India Company, started to extend its power throughout the huge landmass of India.

The Company's army, well equipped and armed, was more than a match for the smaller princely states; one by one these gradually came under the Company's control, each being forced to accept a British Resident, who ensured that in exchange for the Company's protection, the state and its ruler did as they were told. In the case of larger states or tribal groupings such as the Sikhs in the Punjab, or the Maratha Confederacy, the Company watched and waited its opportunity.

At this stage the British in India became intermingled with those they had conquered and it was considered quite usual for them to intermarry. Indeed, Major General Sir David Ochterlony, who was later to defeat the Nepalese, had at least six children by two or more Indian wives. Fighting in India also became a test of military prowess: the then Major General Arthur Wellesley made his name fighting the Maratha Confederacy, before becoming the victor of the Peninsular Campaign and Waterloo as Duke of Wellington.

Nepal represented a concern for the East India Company. Here was an aggressive military state on India's borders that was attacking

and seizing large tracts of territory under British protection. Moreover, it refused to abide by any treaty, rejected any suggestion of accepting a Resident and remained totally unpredictable in its future territorial ambitions. A clash was inevitable.

In Kathmandu, Ranbahadur, the grandson of Prithwi Narayan, had grown into a monster of cruelty and depravity. While his generals invaded other countries, along with areas of India under British protection, the King scandalized polite society by abandoning his aristocratic Rajput wife for a slave girl by whom he had several children. Frequently spending long periods of time in the Indian city of Benares (now Varanasi), he installed a mistress there by whom he had a child. Critics of his behaviour were invariably imprisoned or murdered, and he became universally hated. Sensing the feelings against him he fled to his mistress in Benares and took on the religious role of a *swami* or Holy One, a role for which he was singularly unfitted. However, in his absence civil war broke out between the Kathmandu-based Pande clan and the Thapa clan of the Western hills. Sensing an opportunity to retake power, he hurried back to Nepal and, ruling as both a temporal and spiritual king, sided with the Thapa clan, appointing their powerful Chief Bhim Sen as his Prime Minister.

For a while Ranbahadur seemed secure, but hatred for him remained. He quarrelled bitterly with his half-brother, who in a public argument at court whipped out his sword and cut down Ranbahadur, only to be cut down in turn by Balnar Singh Konwar, father of the great Jangbahadur whom we shall meet in the next chapter. As he lay dying, Ranbahadur nominated as his heir the son of his Benares mistress. Bhim Sen acted ruthlessly and swiftly, using the authority of his recently slain master. Rounding up all court and political opponents he slaughtered the lot. He forced Ranbahadur's slave girl queen to burn herself to death on her husband's funeral pyre, and installed the rightful but childless Queen as a figurehead, retaining all power himself.

Bhim Sen acknowledged the son of Ranbahadur by the high-born Benares mistress as heir apparent but made sure he was powerless. The year was 1806. It was not until 1950 that a king of Nepal regained any power. In the intermediate years a succession of hereditary prime ministers wielded all power in Nepal, successive monarchs being simply figureheads.

Having disposed of all opposition satisfactorily, Bhim Sen now busied himself with territorial expansion at the expense of the British East India Company. His generals warned him that he might be taking on too much but he disregarded them. As well as capturing large tracts of land in Garhwal and Kumaon to the west of Nepal, Bhim Sen started to encroach due south by the simple expedient of capturing East India Company customs posts by armed attack, then occupying land beyond and refusing to withdraw.

The sorely tested patience of the East India Company finally snapped: on 1 November 1814 the Governor-General formally declared war on Nepal after a month of military preparations. In so doing the British were aware that it was going to be a tough fight. Nepal was a martial state whose army was highly efficient and used to operating in mountainous and inhospitable terrain on very light scales of equipment and supplies.

Conversely, the East India Company Bengal Army, although well armed and equipped, had hitherto operated on the plains of Northern India and was used to moving with a host of camp-followers and servants who did all the menial tasks for officers and men.

An army of some 30,000 troops, 60 guns, 12,000 Indian auxiliaries, 1,113 elephants and 3,682 camels had assembled, comprising a mixture of the Honourable East India Company sepoy units officered by Company officers, along with native other ranks and purely British King's regiments. For the times this was a formidable force which was split into four columns. The columns of Major Generals Bennet Marley and John Wood were to attack from the south through the heavily jungled Terai towards Butwal, while the columns of Major Generals Rollo Gillespie and David Ochterlony moved into the territories of Kumaon and Garhwal, previously captured and occupied by the Gurkhas.

Marley's and Wood's columns were confronted by numerically much smaller Gurkha forces but nevertheless were roughly handled on their way to Butwal and, after General Marley had given up and gone home, having suffered a nervous breakdown, the rest of the force remained inactive, simply defending itself

and making no effort either to press the Gurkhas or force its way into Butwal.

Fortunately the column commanders operating to the far west against Garhwal and Kumaon were made of sterner stuff. The redoubtable Gillespie thrust deep into Garhwal while Colonels William Gardner and Jasper Nicholls, with two smaller columns, advanced into Kumaon and cut off the main Gurkha force from its supplies and withdrawal route to Nepal. Despite determined opposition in the form of barricaded defences, Gillespie managed to secure the important area of Dehra Doon before being finally halted before the well-defended hill fort of Kalunga. Although the Gurkhas had only 650 men to Gillespie's 4,000 they refused to surrender and successfully beat off the first attack. After subjecting the fort to a 10-cannon pounding Gillespie attacked again on 31 October 1814, but was again repulsed, with the loss of his own life and that of many of his men. He was shot through the heart 30 yards from the Gurkha palisade leading a dismounted party of his old regiment, The 8th, or King's Royal Irish, Light Dragoons (later the 8th Hussars), and collapsed dead into the arms of his ADC, one Lieutenant Frederick Young (about whom we will hear a good deal more). The British force then brought up siege artillery (arrived from Delhi) and subjected the fort to savage bombardment, the defenders, including women and children, suffering terrible casualties.

As the siege raged, a lone Gurkha suddenly appeared through the gun smoke holding his jaw shattered by a bullet and asked for medical treatment, which he was given. Now bandaged up, he requested permission to return to the fort to carry on fighting the British! By now the Gurkha defenders of Kalunga had lost 520 of their original 650 with many wounded. Realizing further resistance was hopeless, Balbahadur Singh, the able Gurkha commander, took the remaining 70 fit Gurkhas and slipped away out of the fort during the night of 1 December leaving the dead, along with the wounded, women and children to the advancing British.

The British had also suffered severely, losing 31 officers and 520 men, casualties that today would be regarded as a national calamity but which were then taken as a matter of course. Some time after occupying the shattered shell of Kalunga, the British erected two monuments. One to the fallen British dead and one to the fallen Gurkhas '… their gallant adversaries … who fought in fair conflict like men and in the intervals between actual conflict showed us liberal courtesy.'

To the far west in Garhwal, General Ochterlony was operating against the Gurkha main force of some 3,000, commanded by the senior Gurkha general Amar Singh Thapa. Both commanders

General Sir David Ochterlony, the skilful and compassionate victor of the Anglo-Nepal War 1814–16. Painted by A. W. Devis. (National Gallery of Scotland)

were well matched in experience, skill and determination, but the half-Scottish, half-American Ochterlony was to prove the more able. Meanwhile Major General Gabriel Martindell, who had succeeded the heroic Gillespie, came up to assist Ochterlony by attacking Amar Singh's son Ranjur, who had slowly withdrawn onto the strong mountain fortress of Jaithak. There was only one approach to Jaithak – up a steep spur which led to the fort. Despite heavy artillery support the attack could make no headway and, having lost a third of his men, Martindell pulled back and asked Ochterlony for assistance.

Ochterlony was in no position to help, but wisely realized that victory over Amar Singh would make Jaithak untenable, so pushed on against his opponent who was slowly withdrawing through a series of stoutly defended villages onto the formidable fortress of Malaun. The Gurkha general defended with great skill, forcing Ochterlony to fight every step of the way. Ochterlony responded by cutting new roads and bringing up guns to blast Amar Singh out of his well-defended delaying positions. When artillery would not work, the British general would stage a series of short hooking manoeuvres which unbalanced Amar Singh and forced him to withdraw. Amar Singh still remained formidable: one such hooking manoeuvre outrunning its artillery support was savagely attacked by the Gurkhas, who killed over a hundred men in this one counterstroke. However, even as Amar Singh's skilfully managed retreat continued he began to lose the support of the local chieftains, who could see that the British were driving the Gurkha army back.

If Amar Singh was to succeed in holding Malaun it was essential that he should also strongly occupy a succession of mountain peaks that dominated it. This he neglected to do, leaving two unguarded. Ochterlony was just too good a general with whom to take such risks and, too late, on 15 April 1815 Amar Singh found two British battalions dug in on top of the two vital ridges with two 6-pounder cannon. He immediately organized a counter-attack using over 2,000 of his force. Caught on a bare slope they lost over a quarter of their number in fatal casualties alone, and Bhakti Thapa, his faithful lieutenant, was killed. Reluctantly, Amar Singh withdrew into the fort of Malaun. Unfortunately, the Gurkha general's remaining 200 battleworthy men were far too few to hold a huge fort like Malaun properly, and both he and Ochterlony knew it. With no prospect of success, Amar Singh sued for terms, and so Malaun and Jaithak fell to the British.

Ochterlony granted generous terms to Amar Singh. He could leave Malaun with arms and accoutrements, colours flying and two guns while his son Ranjur could leave Jaithak in the same

Amar Singh, the able Gurkha commander who opposed the British East India Company army. (Buddhiman Gurung)

A portrait of General Frederick Young (1786–1864), who raised and commanded The Sirmoor Battalion (later 2nd Gurkhas). By J. P. Beadle. (Gurkha Museum)

manner but with one gun! They were free to join up once over the Kali river, which was to be the new border for Nepal. The territorial terms Ochterlony imposed were less congenial. All Nepal's conquests in the west – Sirmoor, Garhwal and Kumaon – were to be given up, as was Sikkim in the north-east. Worse, far worse, Nepal was to give up vast tracts of its fertile southern Terai, its own territory. Most vexatious of all, Kathmandu was to be forced to accept a British Resident. Everybody knew what that meant. Once arrived the Resident would become all powerful and if opposed would simply call upon the East India Company to enforce his will.

If they were to avoid being disarmed and made prisoner, Amar Singh and his son had to agree these harsh terms, but back in Kathmandu Bhim Sen, when he heard of the terms, refused to ratify them and prevaricated.

He was encouraged by news coming in that the East India Company's army might soon be engaged by the Sikhs and the Maratha Confederacy. Bhim Sen reasoned that, if he waited, the East India Company might get so bogged down elsewhere that they

This picture shows the signing of the Treaty of Segauli after the defeat of the Nepalese army.

would lose interest in Nepal and back off from their demands rather than fight another war. Also, having not fought the British himself he tended to discount his general's advice on how formidable they were. His hardy highlanders had conquered every other adversary; why not the British? Here he severely miscalculated.

Most impressed with Gurkha fighting abilities, Ochterony had found time to address the Commander-in-Chief on the advisability of recruiting Gurkhas into the East India Company's army. Permission granted, Ochterlony started recruiting Gurkhas from the many prisoners and deserters he had taken. Many of the men he enlisted came from areas subjugated by Nepal and were perfectly willing to change sides, having no great affection for their conquerors. However, Ochterlony was really after the incredibly tough hard-core *parbatyas* (hillmen) of the Nepalese army, but most of these were either dead or had withdrawn with Amar Singh and Ranjur. Inevitably, knowing no better, and unable to distinguish one group from another, the British recruited much riff-raff.

Lieutenant Frederick Young, Gillespie's ADC, in whose arms he had died, was put in charge of some 2,000 such dubious characters and ordered to clear the area of stay-behind parties left by Amar Singh to keep a foothold in Kumaon. Encountering a force of 200 of these, Young's men fled, never to be seen again. Laughingly the Gurkhas made him prisoner asking why he had not run like his men. Young replied that he had not come so far in order to run away. 'We could serve under men like you!' they

replied. Young spent a good deal of time as their prisoner. Well treated, he learned their language and customs and became their friend. He also discovered how to differentiate between his previous faithless rabble and true Gurkhas, who he had always known were soldiers of superb quality. He determined to raise a corps of them for British service.

In April 1815, two months before Wellington and Blücher were to defeat Napoleon at Waterloo, the East India Company agreed that four regiments of Gurkhas, just under 5,000 men in total, should be raised. These were two battalions of the 'Nusseeree' (perhaps from *Nasiri*, a Hindi word meaning 'friendly'. Of these two battalions one was disbanded and the other later became the 1st Gurkhas). There was also raised one battalion of the 'Sirmoor' or 2nd Gurkhas and one battalion of the 'Kumaon' or 3rd Gurkhas. The numerical appellations came later. Frederick Young, now released, was on hand to make sure they recruited exactly the right type of true Gurkha.

However, the war with Nepal was far from over and, since their terms had been rejected, the British prepared for another campaign under the able Ochterlony. For this campaign he had 14,000 regular troops, many of them King's regiments, 4,000 irregulars and 83 guns. In January 1816 he advanced, objective Nepal's capital Kathmandu.

Ranjur, who had held Jaithak so ably, faced Ochterlony and determined to make him fight for every ridge, from when he

The fighting was desperate and casualties horrific, especially on the Gurkha side as Ochterlony's 83 guns got to work. Shipp again '… the bodies astonished me, it was scarcely possible to walk without stepping on them.'

Makwanpur was abandoned, Ranjur pulled back with the remnant of his force. Bhim Sen signed the Treaty of Segauli on 4 March 1816, conceding all British demands – even the Resident. 'Accept either a Resident or war!' demanded Ochterlony, now Major General Sir David Ochterlony. Actually, the Residents turned out to be better than expected – especially the third, Brian Hodgson. A highly intelligent, sensitive man, he became an expert on Nepalese culture and customs, language and religion, and was much loved by the Nepalese. It was his advice that encouraged the Honourable East India Company to expand the recruitment of Gurkhas: 'In my humble opinion they are far the best soldiers in India.'

Certainly they had given the British the hardest fight they had so far experienced on the subcontinent.

The Treaty of Segauli had been difficult for Bhim Sen to accept, but at least it had not included the occupation of Kathmandu, the holy capital – unless one counted the Resident!

The Makwanpur Wine Cooler given to General Sir David Ochterlony on the successful conclusion of the Anglo-Nepal War by the commander of the escort to the first British Resident of Kathmandu. Bought by The Friends of The Gurkha Museum, The Victoria and Albert Purchase Fund and The Art Fund.

emerged from the flat jungles of the Terai to when, if ever, he got to the mountain kingdom. Ochterlony was equally determined not to get bogged down in this sort of warfare, which was intended to delay him until the onset of the monsoon in late May or early June, after which offensive operations would be rendered impracticable and he would have to withdraw back to India. Discovering a steep, almost impassable, smugglers' track that led behind the main Gurkha defence position, Ochterlony made a moonlit night approach with 3,000 infantry taking only two guns carried by elephant. It was a daring but very risky manoeuvre – and it paid off.

Come the dawn Ranjur was amazed to find Ochterlony's force drawn up and preparing to turn the flank of his carefully prepared defensive positions. He had no alternative but to fall back on the strong fortress of Makwanpur. Here the fighting was intense. Lieutenant John Shipp of the 87th Foot (the Royal Irish Fusiliers) reported of the Gurkha enemy '… I never saw more steadiness or more bravery exhibited by any set of men in my life. Run they would not and of death they seemed to have no fear, though their comrades were falling thick around them, for we were so near that every shot told.'

Medal struck for Anglo-Nepal War 1814–16. (Gurkha Museum)

CHAPTER THREE

ESTABLISHING A REPUTATION
AND
THE GREAT SEPOY MUTINY

After their formation as 'local' corps in 1815, three of the four Gurkha corps or battalions – Nusseree (later 1st Gurkhas), Sirmoor (later 2nd Gurkhas), Kumaon (later 3rd Gurkhas) – were located in the provinces of Sirmoor, Garhwal and Kumaon, a region recently occupied by the Nepalese army and the scene of heavy fighting. Their officers were keen that they should participate, but General Ochterlony, as wise and compassionate as he was militarily able, forbade it, saying it was unnatural that they should be required to fight against those who until recently had been their own kith and kin.

Typical Gurkha kukri with bone handle and scabbard; the traditional fighting weapon of the Gurkha. (Gurkha Museum)

This illustration of the battle of Koonja shows The Sirmoor Battalion smashing down Koonja's gates with their battering ram from which they received their insignia of a ram's head. (Gurkha Museum)

Coming under the direction of the senior East India Company local official, the newly formed Gurkha battalions were soon involved in pacifying the area overrun by terrorist gangs called 'dacoits' who, well-armed and ruthless, were terrorizing the local population. In 1824 one such 800-strong gang was assaulted in its seemingly impregnable fort of Koonja by 350 men of The Sirmoor Battalion who, after marching 36 miles in 12 hours, succeeded in breaking into the fort and destroying the gang, killing 173 of them in close-quarter fighting, using the traditional short hacking weapon of Nepal, the kukri. The men of The Sirmoor Battalion, led by Captain Frederick Young, showed great powers of improvisation when they felled a tree and, using it as a battering ram, smashed in the huge entry gate, thus gaining access to this incredibly strong bastion. Thereafter the Ram's Head formed a prominent feature of their accoutrements; indeed nearly 200 years later it is still included on the silver whistle chain boss of officers' pouch belts in The Royal Gurkha Rifles. An early version of the

Ram's Head from officers' cross belt.

crossbelt and a replica of the battering ram can be seen in the Gurkha Museum, Winchester.

A depiction at the time shows their uniform as a green embroidered jacket and light-coloured trousers, local shoes and a close fitting cap. They were armed with a short musket, a bayonet and their traditional kukri – on which a few words would not be out of place.

This crooked knife is about 20 inches long with the heavier part of the blade in the tip. The handle is generally of buffalo horn or occasionally of native hardwood such as sal and is secured by a metal shank which is a continuation of the blade. Immediately below the handle is a half-moon indentation said to stop blood from an adversary or animal flowing onto the handle and making it slippery. The half-moon indentation is bisected by a minute prong, giving it the same shape as the half-moon design on the national flag of Nepal, itself of religious significance. Some hold that the shape is the same as the cloven foot of a cow, reminding the user that in Hindu religion the cow is sacred and its blood must not be shed. This latter theory seems rather unlikely as the kukri is routinely used to slaughter water buffalo and deer, both of which have cloven hooves. In Eastern Nepal the hill tribes tend to decorate both handles and blades much more ornately than in the West. In the hands of an expert the kukri is both a lethal weapon and a vital tool to a country man or boy living on the wild hills of Nepal. It is used to cut wood, strip bamboo, butcher meat, clear scrub and thorn and, of course, for self-defence.

A Gurkha will easily decapitate a goat with one blow of a kukri, and when felling a tree will skilfully place each successive blow into the same notch. In the hands of anybody else the kukri will be no more effective than a billhook! The kukri scabbard is made of buffalo skin and integral to it are two small knives, one a sharp skinning knife and one a blunt knife that, used with wayside flint, will make fire when struck into dried moss, and can also serve as a sharpener for the kukri blade. The metal used to make kukris is strong but relatively soft, which means it will not shatter, but on the other hand does not hold its cutting edge for long and needs continual re-sharpening.

Myths abound about the kukri. The favourite one is that every time the kukri is drawn it has to shed blood; if true, it would lead to widespread septicemia! The Gurkha himself rather enjoys such mythical interpretations and makes little effort to contradict them.

In the hills of Nepal girls and women do not carry kukris but instead a curved knife called an ansi, which is secured in a round wooden carrier on a cord or belt, the blade protruding underneath. These wooden carriers are often highly decorated and elaborately carved. An ansi in its carrier bobbing up and down on a well-rounded thigh is often an ingredient in hill love songs! The ansi knife itself is generally used for cutting ears of wheat, barley and millet on the steep hill terraces.

★★★

For the next decade the four battalions of Gurkhas led a fairly peaceable existence. From time to time they were called out to suppress gangs in aid of the Civil Power, but otherwise busied themselves improving their barracks and enjoying the lovely area to which they had brought peace and plenty. Situated at 2,500 feet on the slopes of the eternal snows, the area was cool and exhilarating even in the unbearable heat of the Indian summer. The wooded hills and lush valleys abounded with game and to keen Gurkha *shikaris* (hunters) it represented a sporting paradise. Originally the summer retreat of the bodyguard of the Governor-General, it had been unused for several years and pleas were made to cede the land to the Gurkha battalions. Eventually successful in their appeal, the three surviving Gurkha regiments became possessed of superb regimental homes in, respectively, Dharamsala, Dehra Doon and Almora.

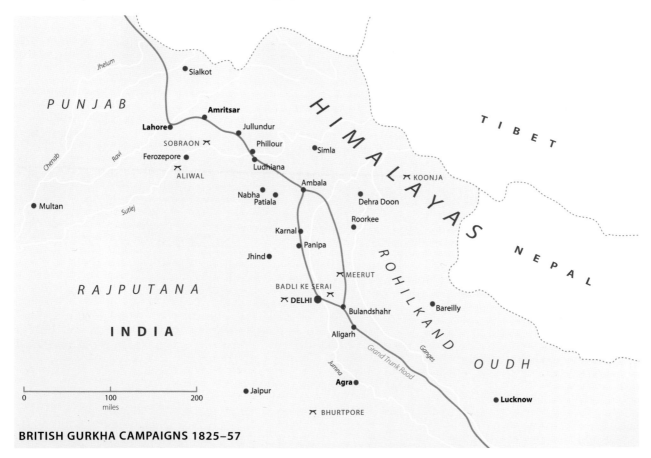

BRITISH GURKHA CAMPAIGNS 1825–57

An incident during the first Sikh wars.(Gurkha Museum)

Another call to arms came in 1825. The causes were familiar. The old ruler of Bhurtpore, a native state near Agra, died. While he had recognized the British, his successor did not and started to cause problems. The wily General Ochterlony, scenting trouble, rapidly raised an army and marched on Bhurtpore. Unfortunately, Lord Amherst, the Governor-General, took a more conciliatory approach and ordered Ochterlony to pull back and disperse his army. In typical military fashion what earlier could have easily been dealt with by Ochterlony now became a major problem, with the army of the rebellious state shutting itself up in the immensely strong fortress of Bhurtpore and from there defying the British.

Finally, Lord Combermere, the Commander-in-Chief, was obliged to raise an army of 27,000 and take every artillery piece in Northern India to lay siege to Bhurtpore. Among the troops gathered were 200 men each from The Nusseree and Sirmoor Battalions who acquitted themselves with great distinction in preliminary actions and the final assault, made after a mine containing 10,000 pounds of explosive was detonated under the walls, lifting them several feet in the air! No fewer than 13,000 rebels were killed in the action for a loss of 1,100. A huge amount of treasure was found and in the Gurkha Museum there are some fine examples of silverware taken by The Sirmoor Battalion.

More fighting was to follow with the powerful Sikh nation in the Punjab which in 1845 crossed over its natural boundary, the Sutlej river, and attacked provinces of the East India Company. The Sikhs were among the most powerful of Indian ethnic groupings and their attack represented a major challenge for the East India Company. The Sirmoor Battalion was rushed to the key town of Ludhiana where the Sikhs were busy burning down European residences and barracks. The Gurkhas promptly drove them off, thus saving the situation. This however was only a skirmish, the main, immensely strong, Sikh army being drawn up for battle at Aliwal at a convenient bend of the Sutlej river.

Battle joined, The Nusseree and Sirmoor Battalions were soon in the thick of it. Advancing with the left wing of the army they were involved in hand-to-hand fighting with ferocious Sikh swordsmen. At one stage The Sirmoor Battalion lost its colour but a Gurkha havildar (sergeant) sprang forward and recovered it, lashing left and right with his kukri. Casualties were heavy, 49 dead and wounded in The Sirmoor Battalion alone, and 6 killed and 16 wounded in The Nusseree Battalion.

The Sikh army withdrew across the Sutlej with heavy casualties but stood again ready, 13 days later, for battle at Sobraon. If the battle at Aliwal had been hard, that at Sobraon, was doubly so. This time the Sikhs fought from a heavily fortified encampment, its fortifications resting on the edge of the flooded river Sutlej: 35,000 Sikhs and 70 cannon opposed the 20,000 British. Having received additional reinforcements, the British subjected the Sikhs to a heavy bombardment before assaulting their fortifications. Soon both Gurkha battalions were heavily involved in hand-to-hand fighting. Captain John Fisher, Commandant of The Sirmoor Battalion was killed leading his men and Gurkha casualties in The Sirmoor Battalion were 145 out of a total of 610, a terribly high price. The Nusseree Battalion also suffered heavily with 7 killed and 77 wounded.

An exciting diorama in the Gurkha Museum depicts Gurkha and Sikh locked in mortal combat.

After the battle and the defeat of the Sikhs, the veteran army commander Lieutenant General Sir Hugh Gough wrote in his dispatch of 13 February 1846:

> I must pause in this narrative especially to notice the determined hardihood and bravery with which our two battalions of Ghoorkhas(sic), The Sirmoor and Nusseree, met the Sikhs, wherever they were opposed to them. Soldiers of small stature but indomitable spirit they vied in ardent courage with The Grenadiers of our own nation, and, armed with the short

Bahadur Shah Zafar, the last Mogul King of Delhi and reluctant figurehead of the Mutiny.

> weapons of their mountains, were a terror to the Sikhs throughout this great combat.

In a separate dispatch he referred in these words to the deceased Captain Fisher, Commandant of The Sirmoor Battalion: 'Who fell at the head of his valiant men being much respected and lamented by the whole army.'

★★★

Although the powerful Sikh nation was eventually defeated, a much more potent and potentially disastrous threat was gathering, largely undetected and unacknowledged by the East India Company and its army. Gurkhas first became aware of it early in 1857 when a contingent was sent to the newly formed musketry school at Amballa to learn about the recently issued Enfield rifled musket. There Gurkhas found that contingents from Indian regiments were refusing to handle the cartridges of the new weapon since they maintained they were greased with either pork or beef fat. Pig is unclean to Muslims and cow is sacred to Hindus, so here was a double abomination – especially as the end of the greased cartridge had to be bitten off before pushing it down the barrel. The Gurkha contingent soon became aware of such mutinous feelings and, reporting them to the British Commandant, asked that their tents be pitched with the British troops as they wished to have nothing to do with the potentially mutinous Indians. They then asked to be issued with the cartridges to show that they had no qualms about using them.

Unfortunately this vexed matter of the greased cartridges was but one indication of the forthcoming insurrection led by the Bengal Army. With time the British had drifted further away from the Indians. The previous mutual respect had, on the British side, been replaced by arrogance and inept administration. Mixed marriages were now disapproved of and British clergy were allowed free rein to convert Muslim and Hindu alike. Officers and men of the native regiments of the Bengal Army who had served so gallantly now saw their food allowances cut and their religion threatened. For the most part high-class Brahmins and Rajputs, their pride was hurt and they were angry and frightened. Their British officers had become slack and uninterested, and the best had been creamed off by the burgeoning civil service.

Strange signs and portents circulated; night runners delivered small cakes far and wide, signifying impending revolt. Signs and portents there were for those that could read them, but the East India Company remained oblivious – anyway there was no

figurehead to whom any insurrection could rally! Had they forgotten the elderly poet Shah Zafar, last of the great Mogul Emperors, seemingly powerless in his exquisite Delhi palace?

For Gurkhas the issue was more straightforward. On 14 May, three days after the mutiny had broken out at Meerut, a messenger arrived at Dehra Doon with orders for the Gurkhas to deploy. The Sirmoor Battalion was ordered to march on Meerut as quickly as possible to help subdue the mutiny which was spreading by the hour. With no time available to pack tentage and stores, Major Charles Reid, Commandant of The Sirmoor

Battalion, marched off his Gurkhas with 60 rounds of ammunition a man and two elephants carrying the ammunition reserve. Meerut was over a hundred miles away!

No sooner than they had started they were confronted by mutinous Indian soldiers begging the Gurkhas to join them and reminding them that they were Hindus. The Gurkhas took no

Below: A panorama picture of Delhi before the siege clearly showing the entrances into Delhi and the high ground to the right on which stood the Hindu Rao's House. (By kind permission of W.J.C. Meath-Baker Esq)

Jang Bahadur Rana, the Prime Minister of Nepal who came to the aid of the British during The Indian Mutiny. (Gurkha Museum)

notice, strung up a few Brahmins who had stolen government stores and pressed on amid scenes of revolt, carnage and destruction. Since Brahmins were notionally inviolate this action gave a clear indication to the mutineers that they could expect no wavering from Gurkhas.

The Bengal Army was now deserting in droves and heading for the ancient capital of Delhi. Diverted to Delhi, the 500-strong Sirmoor Battalion joined Lieutenant General Sir Henry Barnard's force, where they found their tents already pitched for them and covered by the guns of the artillery in case they mutinied. Actions spoke louder than words, and in the battle with the mutineers the next day at Badli-ki-Serai, the Gurkhas of The Sirmoor Battalion were so effective that no further doubts as to their loyalty were entertained. Here they fought alongside the 60th Rifles with whom they were to forge a close and lasting friendship.

The mutineers, beaten, withdrew onto the huge fortifications of the ancient capital of Delhi, which allowed General Barnard's force to occupy the ridge above Delhi overlooking the city. It soon became apparent that Delhi was to become the centre of the mutiny and Shah Zafar its reluctant figurehead.

Mutineers poured into the city and soon vastly outnumbered General Barnard's 3,500 troops who were hard pressed to hold their ridgeline against incessant artillery pounding and infantry attack. The whole British grip on northern India swayed in the balance as, aghast, the British saw themselves opposed or, worse, besieged and massacred in a score of cities. Actual British troops were thin on the ground, reinforcements months away by sea and lately embroiled in the Crimean War. It all depended on how many native regiments remained loyal and how well they fought.

There was, however, another unexpected but welcome ally to the north: Nepal. Here the powerful Prime Minister Jang Bahadur

HM 1/60th Rifles and The Sirmoor Battalion launching a counter attack from the Hindu Rao's House during the siege. By Jason Askew. (The Royal Gurkha Rifles)

Gurkhas at the time of the Mutiny. (Gurkha Museum)

had recently visited England and been mightily impressed. Besides meeting Queen Victoria, the Duke of Wellington and other high dignitaries, he saw, like Peter the Great of Russia before him, the huge industrial potential and latent power of Britain, and determined to be her friend and ally himself with her – without in any way sacrificing his country's independence. Hearing of the mutiny, Jang Bahadur immediately offered 6,000 men from his own army.

The East India Company initially declined the offer on the basis that that, if Nepalese troops were to become involved, it might encourage wavering Indian states to believe the Company could not cope on its own. More mature judgement eventually prevailed and the troops were gratefully accepted. Once they deployed they soon showed their worth clearing the rebels from the key Bareilly area of Northern India. The King of Nepal, who seemed to have moved from homicidal mania in youth to early senile dementia in a remarkably short period, was at no stage deemed worthy of consultation.

Back in Garhwal and Kumaon, the 66th or Goorkha Regiment (the new designation for the surviving Nusseree Battalion) deployed to meet a vastly superior force of mutineers intent on wresting the provinces from the British. Despite their inferiority in numbers and artillery, these Gurkhas immediately attacked and, after a hard-fought battle, drove off the mutineers, thus saving these vital provinces to the Crown. Lieutenant John Tytler, their Adjutant, wounded in three places and at the very forefront on horseback, was awarded the first Gurkha officer Victoria Cross. Gurkhas themselves were not to become eligible for this supreme award until 1911, after the visit of King George V to India. The Indian Army equivalent was the Indian Order of Merit, and Gurkhas were to be frequently decorated with this award in the coming desperate months.

Meanwhile, back at Delhi it was hard pounding as the rebels threw in everything to get the British off the ridge. However, the 60th Rifles, Sirmoor Battalion and the Corps of Guides had no intention of giving an inch no matter what was thrown at them. Aided by the guns of Scott's battery and Major Tombs' troop, but with the greatest difficulty and mounting casualties they managed to keep the mutineers off the ridge and out of their key point of Hindu Rao's House.

British Artillery from the centre battery firing on Delhi at night with a Sirmoor Battalion Gurkha sentry to the left. By Jason Askew. (By kind permission of Major G.L. Davies)

Cholera too now added to their precarious position, killing not only officers and men but also the commanding general, Barnard, who was replaced by Brigadier General Archdale Wilson. The latter, said to suffer from bouts of depression, showed no little skill in the handling of his much inferior force but it was only because of the stoical endurance of the troops involved that, despite 26 separate rebel attacks, the vital ridge was held. In Major Reid the Gurkhas had a fine commander: his shot-shattered telescope and bone-handled kukri are displayed in the Gurkha Museum.

In Delhi itself the huge army of mutineers were experiencing their own problems, the main one being shortage of food. Unless they could take the ridge and break the siege they were going to starve. The elderly King of Delhi, more used to exchanging rhyming couplets with fellow poets, gloomily watched while cavalry mounts were watered at his celestial fountains and mired his scented flower beds. Occasionally he was wheeled out to watch

a grand attack guaranteed to take the accursed ridge, but he always returned disappointed. He put 10 rupees reward on the head of each Gurkha taken, the same as for a European, but even that failed to improve matters.

On the ridge, in burning heat, the besiegers were preparing to turn from the defensive to the attack. The 'Lion of Punjab' – Ulsterman Brigadier General John Nicholson – had arrived five days ahead of his reinforcements of guns and 4,200 men on 14 August.

The Sirmoor Battalion, having lost half its number, was reinforced by 90 men. Meanwhile The Kumaon Battalion, which had arrived with the siege train in early August, was readied to assault the Kashmir Gate together with the 52nd Light Infantry of Waterloo fame. A final rebel attack was beaten off, and then on 14 September, the men on the ridge moved forward in four columns to storm the city. The rebels resisted furiously, mortally wounding John Nicholson, but, despite fearful casualties, feats of incredible valour – such as the blowing of the Kashmir Gate – got the besiegers into the city, and once in there was no stopping them. Amid six days of slaughter and vengeful bestiality the mutineer defence collapsed, the King was made prisoner, three of his sons were later shot out of hand. Delhi had fallen and the Gurkhas had established a reputation for courage, loyalty, élan and stoical endurance against overwhelming odds.

Of the three Gurkha battalions, perhaps The Sirmoor Battalion had established the reputation of Gurkhas most positively. They and the 60th Rifles had fought side by side together for three months in conditions of quite unspeakable horror and privation. Both regiments had lost well over half their number through violent death, suppurating wounds or cholera. Not once did they fail to answer the call of duty, and between these two totally diverse races arose quite spontaneously a mutual feeling of trust and affection based on observed conduct, since they had no common language with which to communicate. What they shared was mutual respect and the sure knowledge that the one would rather die than let the other down. It was something unique that only they could understand and that their uncomprehending officers could only profoundly admire. After Delhi, The Sirmoor Battalion became Riflemen like the 60th; no longer sepoys, they were allowed to take on the scarlet facings of the 60th and were accorded a third colour to commemorate Delhi. In fact this led to a tricky contradiction because traditionally rifle regiments did not carry colours. Hearing of the Gurkhas' predicament, Queen Victoria personally devised a Truncheon of intricate design commemorating their gallant service at Delhi, a Truncheon that is still carried today by their successor regiment The Royal Gurkha Rifles. In all this one could discern the hand of the 60th Rifles.

Unfortunately, when it comes to medals for gallantry each regiment is on its own. Sadly, the wounded and promoted Colonel

HM 52nd Light Infantry and The Kumaon Battalion (later 3rd Gurkhas) taking the Kashmir Gate. By Jason Askew. (Gurkha Museum)

Reid, The Sirmoor Battalion's commander, wrote his citations during the siege in pencil. General Lord Clyde, the Commander-in-Chief, declined to accept them in this form. Later, written in ink and in fair copper plate handwriting they were deemed too late and rejected – *plus ça change…*!

When Delhi fell the Mutiny was mortally struck but desultorily continued for another year. Slowly the mutineers gave up their awful gains. The starved and desperate defenders of Lucknow heard the skirl of Major General Sir Henry Havelock's Scottish pipers on the morning breeze.

Jang Bahadur was following up with 10,000 Nepalese rather slowly as there was a lot of loot to get on board! Shah Zafar gazed vacantly in his Burmese captivity dreaming of what might have been, while his followers were hanged or blown from the cannon's mouth by the vengeful British. Whenever a sensitive soul cried 'Stop!' the cry went up 'Remember the Massacre at Cawnpore!' and the slaughter went on. Occasionally a man dragged to the gibbet or the gun was the orderly of the executing officer and then,

sometimes, try as he would, the officer could not remember Cawnpore but only remember the man's thoughtful and loving service to him and his family, and how much he had been trusted until that fateful day when the little unleavened cakes arrived.

When the Mutiny was finally suppressed huge changes were inaugurated. The Honourable East India Company ceased to exist; India was now ruled directly by Britain through a Viceroy, and recognized as the finest Jewel in the Imperial Crown. The Army, too, was totally reorganized and the number of resident British formations significantly increased. All new weaponry went to British units; in each infantry brigade of three battalions one was always British; all heavy artillery was British. In the Mutiny one British regiment had been surprised in church without its weapons: as a result, all garrison churches were thenceforward furnished with rifle racks.

The Gurkhas emerged from the Mutiny with a very high reputation; during the Mutiny another two regiments, to become the 4th and 5th, were raised. Soon others, hitherto mixed, were

Left: The gallant survivors of The Sirmoor Battalion (later 2nd Gurkhas) in front of Hindu Rao's house on Delhi Ridge which they, and the 60th Rifles and the Guides had held for three months in the face of continual attacks by the mutineers. (Gurkha Museum)

Right: The Queen's Truncheon awarded to the 2nd Gurkhas by Queen Victoria in recognition of their gallant service during the Mutiny. (Gurkha Museum)

loyalty and timely help had been rewarded by giving him back a slice of the rich southern Terai originally confiscated at the end of the Nepal War – but he was not in too much hurry to let the British Raj take his finest fighting men!

In an account such as this it would burden the reader to trace in detail how each of the ten Gurkha regiments came into being, but by the first decade of the twentieth century all were now in place, constituting a form of elite infantry corps within the new British-Indian Army.

The 6th and the 8th recruited from the Western highlands of Nepal, and the 10th and their offshoot the 7th from the warlike Kiranti Eastern tribes of Rai and Limbu. The 9th, originally a Bengali regiment, was subsequently designated a Gurkha regiment and, uniquely, recruited a large number of Chhetris, the original high-caste warriors or *Kshatriya* (see glossary), but augmented their numbers with Magars from the Western hills.

So by a slow process in 1908 we have the recognizable Gurkha Brigade of ten regiments, each of two battalions, some 20,000 intrepid warriors. As we shall see in post-Mutiny India there were no shortage of opportunities to use them.

reformed as purely Gurkha. In the 42nd Gurkha Light Infantry (earlier Assam Local Light Infantry, later to become 6th Gurkhas) long arguments over many a restoring *chota peg* were sustained on whether to retain Sikhs or Gurkhas. Both ethnic groups were excellent soldiers and both had remained loyal in the Mutiny. After tortured discussions the 42nd decided to become all Gurkha and so eventually did most of the other mixed regiments which had hitherto included only a proportion of Gurkhas.

As the regiments became all Gurkha so their composition was decided. The original four had drawn their men from Western Nepal, Garhwal and Kumaon; now they were to come exclusively from the Western highlands of Nepal and the newly raised 4th followed suit. The 5th, originally the Hazara Goorkha Battalion, came next, centralizing all Gurkhas within the elite Punjab Frontier Force into a single Gurkha battalion. Recruiting the fighting highlanders of Western Nepal was difficult: Jang Bahadur was not minded to be particularly helpful. During the Mutiny his

Indian Mutiny Medal 1857–58.

Chapter Four

THE
TROUBLED FRONTIERS

Well before the Mutiny British India had experienced great difficulty in maintaining control of its north-western and north-eastern boundaries. In the north west the hardy and rebellious Pathan tribesmen were disinclined to admit of British control and behaved accordingly. Isolated British garrisons were continually being attacked, while relieving columns were harried incessantly by Pathan marksmen, whose natural shooting and fieldcraft skills made them formidable foes. This continual fighting was further complicated by the presence of the vital buffer state of Afghanistan further to the west.

With some reason Britain feared that Russia would gain control of Afghanistan and use it as a gateway to attack British India. To avoid this, Britain tried to ensure that Afghanistan was pro-British, even to the extent of political interference in the internal workings of governance and royal succession. This interference was bitterly resented and led on several occasions to outright war, in which Britain suffered a number of reverses: indeed, on one infamous occasion an occupying British force trying to extricate itself from Kabul back to India was totally wiped out. This political and military manoeuvring between British India and Russia, with Afghanistan as the prize, was known as the 'Great Game' and gave rise to a host of Kipling's stories and ballads. We will see that Gurkhas played a significant part in this deadly game.

To the east, in Burma, the mountain tribes resented the assumed domination of Britain over their tribal lands and reacted by attacking newly established tea-growing plantations and ambushing relieving troops as they arrived. Here the terrain was

A Pathan from one of the warring frontier tribes who proved such formidable opponents throughout the history of British India and in the form of the Taliban continue to do so today. (Gurkha Museum)

The 42nd Goorkha Light Infantry (later 6th Gurkhas) on the North East Frontier with their light guns 'Bubble and Squeak'. (Gurkha Museum)

entirely different: great swathes of thick jungle cloaked the precipitous hills, making the going at best difficult and at times impossible. It was a terrain that Allied troops would become all too familiar with in the Second World War.

To the far north, beyond Nepal and the vast wall of the Himalayas, lay Tibet and China, areas that could easily become hostile and threaten British India.

These frontiers had to be defended and in so far as possible pacified, and – as we shall see – it was on this unending and often thankless task that the forming Gurkha regiments were to be continually employed. One regiment, the 5th, became part of the permanent Punjab Frontier Force, which spent its whole time on the North-West Frontier. It was a brigade-sized force consisting of mountain artillery, cavalry and infantry, and had an enviable reputation for efficiency and skill. The Corps of Guides, whom we have already met fighting shoulder to shoulder with the 60th and The Sirmoor Battalion of Gurkhas on Delhi Ridge, formed a large khaki-clad cavalry and infantry component of the Frontier Force. Composed of a high proportion of Sikhs and including Pathans, they knew the country intimately. It was a great accolade to Gurkha fighting ability that a battalion of them should form a

permanent part of this élite force. Other Gurkha battalions took their turn as campaigns developed on both frontiers.

In the north east we see Gurkha battalions being raised specifically to cope with the hostile tribes such as Nagas, Abors, Lushai and Manipuri who disputed what they regarded as the invasion of their tribal territories by British India. The 6th, 8th and 10th were all raised for this specific purpose. The 6th underwent many changes of title which reflected its transformation from a mixed to a purely Gurkha regiment.

It would be nice to believe that British policy was just and enlightened. Unfortunately, often this was not the case and the forceful grabbing of large tracts of land for tea plantations and the installation of British District Officers infuriated the mountain tribes and forced them into bloody revolt. Although indifferently armed, the tribes knew the terrain intimately. In 1858 the Abors broke the fragile peace in upper Assam. The 1st Assam Light Infantry, later to become the 6th Gurkhas, at first met with little success, mainly because of lack of cooperation between the battalion commander and the District Officer. A year later, a much better organized and coordinated attack was carried out. Nevertheless the furious Abor defence of their defended villages

AFGHANISTAN AND INDIA'S NW FRONTIER SHOWING TRIBAL AREAS AND MAJOR BATTLES

inflicted some 45 casualties before they were defeated, which gives a feel for the intensity of the fighting.

In the war against the Lushai in 1871–2 five Gurkha Regiments were involved: the 2nd (previously Sirmoor), the 4th, the 42nd (later 6th), 43rd (later 2nd Battalion 8th Gurkhas) and 44th (later 1st Battalion 8th Gurkhas). They were deployed in two separate columns which converged on the main enemy objective, a strongly defended fort surrounded by high palisades and defended by a surrounding band of *panjis* or sharpened bamboos. These columns had to make their way through appalling terrain to reach their objective. When they did reach it they were met by an immense volume of fire and immediately started taking casualties. The situation was further complicated because the Lushais started burning an adjoining village, the smoke from which obliterated everything and made coordination between the two columns

virtually impossible. Fortunately, Major Donald Macintyre of 2nd Gurkhas managed to use the cover of the smoke to get over a three metre-high stockade into the fort with a few Gurkhas. Their appearance in the midst of the Lushais led to panic and the collapse of the Lushai defence. For his gallant conduct Major Macintyre was awarded the Victoria Cross.

Perhaps the campaign that gives the best feel for the extent and ferocity of this fighting on the North-East Frontier was the Manipur campaign. This was to involve five Gurkha battalions: the 2nd, 4th, 6th and 8th (in two battalions still called 43rd and 44th). In March 1891 a revolution broke out in the little Assamese state of Manipur where the maharajah was ousted by his two brothers, one of whom became ruler and the other deputy, or 'Jubraj' in local parlance. The British refused to recognize the new rulers and decided to send their representative to make the British position

**INDIA'S NE FRONTIER AND
BURMA SHOWING TRIBAL AREAS**

per man (instead of the full 170), ammunition soon ran low and the defenders realized they would have to break out. In the early afternoon the two remaining British officers, one British female nurse and 150 riflemen succeeded in getting out of the Residency and fighting their way down the track up which they knew a supporting column of about 200 Gurkhas from the 43rd was coming. Having succeeded in meeting with them, and given the sorry state of the Residency defenders, together the combined parties continued slowly to withdraw.

One person who was not cautiously withdrawing was Lieutenant Charles Grant, who commanded a detachment of the 43rd (later 2/8th Gurkhas) some 50 miles away at Tamu on the Assam/Burma border, who, hearing of the fighting at Imphal, and having telegraphed for approval, collected what extra men there were in the vicinity plus three elephants to carry stores and advanced into Manipur. His force, numbering 80, were blocked at Lang Thobal some 15 miles from Imphal by 800 Manipuri soldiers dug in behind a river. Undeterred, Grant ordered his mainly Gurkha force to fix bayonets and advance across the river. The Manipuris, amazed, withdrew, only to return in greater force and repeatedly counter-attacked, aided by two field guns. Grant's little force beat off all these attacks and withdrew only after ten days on receipt of orders from higher up. Unsurprisingly, Grant was awarded the Victoria Cross and every survivor of his men the Indian Order of Merit. There is a splendid little diorama of Charles Grant's action in the Gurkha Museum.

Clearly this was behaviour up with which British India declined to put! A Manipur relief column of some 5,000 men was hastily assembled, consisting mainly of Gurkhas from the 4th, 42nd, 43rd, and 44th Gurkha Battalions. On the convergence of this powerful force in three columns, the Jubraj fled and, after a brief resistance, the Manipuris submitted five weeks after the original Gurkhas marched into their capital.

As the hill tribes were slowly pacified, a further Gurkha battalion was formed from 1887. Initially called the Kubo Valley Military Police Battalion and with some Gurkhas in it, this unit was charged with keeping the peace close to Manipur in that frontier valley of Burma (which was fully annexed to the British Empire after the Third Anglo-Burmese War ended that year). In 1890 this police battalion was merged with the old 10th Madras Native Infantry became a rifle regiment in 1892 and a fully Gurkha unit three years later. Close proximity in Burma in 1895 to the famous and oldest Scottish regiment, the Royal Scots, led to the 10th Gurkhas adopting the Hunting Stewart tartan and learning to play the bagpipes! In 1901 its title finally became 10th Gurkha Rifles.

Let us now return to the North-West Frontier and Afghanistan. While intermittent local hostilities prevailed almost

clear and to arrest the Jubraj and deport him – in itself a pretty tall order. The British Commissioner for Assam was escorted by the Commanding Officer of the 42nd and 454 Gurkhas, drawn equally from the 42nd and 44th at Kohima.

Arriving at Manipur's capital, Imphal, the Commissioner called a durbar (or conference) without actually making clear his real intention of arresting the Jubraj. At first the Manipuris made everyone welcome and allocated areas for the soldiers to pitch their tents. Meanwhile further reinforcements arrived in the form of a detachment of 100 men from the 43rd. Suspecting the British, the Jubraj kept delaying the conference.

The Commanding Officer, with a small group of the 42nd, then tried to seize the Jubraj in his palace by force; this failed, and soon fighting broke out. Before long the greatly outnumbered British force were penned into the residency compound overlooked by the city walls from which came a torrent of artillery and small arms fire. Realizing the position was grim, a deputation of six, which included the British Commissioner and the Commanding Officer, went out to 'parley' with the Manipuris and were promptly beheaded. In the meantime the beleaguered force in the Residency fought on against increasingly desperate odds, all the while taking casualties. As there were only 40 rifle cartridges

The 5th Gurkha Rifles in action on the NW Frontier 1888.

continually on the North-West Frontier, hostilities with Afghanistan consisted of three major wars, 1839–42, 1878–81 and 1919. The first of these wars was very much caused by Britain's wish to keep the buffer state of Afghanistan within her sphere of interest.

Dost Mohammed, the popular and strong ruler of Afghanistan (ruled 1826–63), was suspected of conniving with the Russians to the detriment and danger of British India and, moreover, of claiming British territory in the form of the city of Peshawar. In retrospect one can see that the Russian threat was not all that serious and that the claim on Peshawar was never likely to succeed given its strategic value to British India. Nevertheless at the time both threats were taken very seriously and it was decided to replace Dost Mohammed, from the Baraksai tribe, with Shah Shuja from a different tribe, the Sadozai, as ruler of Afghanistan.

A captured Manipuri leader with his Gurkha guards following the war of 1891.
(Gurkha Museum)

To do this the British would have to invade Afghanistan and defeat and depose the popular Dost Mohammed; quite an undertaking!

Although the Honourable East India Company's army would do most of the fighting, it was felt that Britain's nominee Shah Shuja should have an army of his own, so 6,000 troops were raised for him using the same methods of recruiting as for the Company's own army. Among the regiments raised was a Gurkha unit. There were additionally Gurkhas in Captain George Broadfoot's Sappers and Miners, also part of Shah Shuja's army.

After some very bitter fighting, Dost Mohammed was defeated and fled; Shah Shuja was installed as ruler with an occupying British army to safeguard him in Kabul. Unfortunately Shah Shuja was disliked by the Afghans, and the British army of occupation reviled as an affront to national sovereignty. The situation was exacerbated by the fact that British officers and soldiers were sleeping with Afghan women – an insult to personal and Muslim susceptibilities. Soon the situation began to deteriorate and the threat to the British military garrison became more overt.

The Bala Hissar in Kabul, scene of so much fighting during the Afghan wars. (Gurkha Museum)

An energetic and capable commander could probably have nipped the insurrection in the bud, but Major General William Elphinstone was an elderly ditherer who kept changing his mind, while his second in command took a delight in seeing his chief get everything wrong. As supplies dwindled the situation in Kabul and outlying districts got more threatening. Up-country British outposts began to come under sustained attack. One of them, at Charikar, was manned by the Gurkha Regiment of Shah Shuja's army. Afghans loyal to Dost Mohammed besieged the town. When the water supply failed the garrison tried to break out and fight their way to Kabul, but it was a hopeless endeavour and only two British officers and one Gurkha from the whole garrison succeeded in getting to Kabul.

Left: 5th Gurkhas and Seaforth Highlanders at the battle of Peiwar Kotal by Vereker Hamilton. (National Army Museum)

Another detachment of Shah Shuja's Gurkhas managed to hold out at the nearby Bamiyan, the site of the amazing Buddhist statuary blown up by the Taliban in 2001, but now being restored.

In Kabul itself the garrison belatedly decided its position was untenable and decided to retreat to India, despite it being in the middle of the winter of 1841/42 and being encumbered with baggage, families and 12,000 male camp-followers. The result was one of the greatest military disasters ever to befall the British-Indian Army. Apart from the women and children whom the Afghans spared, and General Elphinstone, the rest of the retreating 4,500-strong garrison were systematically destroyed in a 90-mile, week-long snowbound retreat across mountain passes, despite many hopeless acts of valour. Only the wounded Assistant Surgeon William Brydon managed to escape captivity to ride into Jalalabad to tell the awful tale on 15 January 1842. The Afghans invested Jalalabad but, largely through the drive and ingenuity of Captain

The Battle of Kandahar showing a 2nd Gurkha rifleman capturing an Afghan gun. From a painting by Colonel E.A.P. Hobday. (Gurkha Museum)

Broadfoot and his Sappers and Miners, many of whom were Gurkhas, the city was successfully defended until relieved.

British and East India Company prestige demanded instant retribution and in the hard-fought campaign to return to Kabul, Captain Broadfoot's gallant Gurkhas again distinguished themselves. Successfully back in Kabul by September, the British carried out a punitive policy of destruction and revenge, rescuing many hostages, and then left. Maintaining a large permanent garrison in Kabul was simply beyond their military or financial means. Peace of a sort was established.

The circumstances of the Second Afghan War of 1878–81 bore remarkable similarities to the first. Sher Ali, the ruler of Afghanistan who had succeeded his father Dost Mohammed in 1863, had also been coerced by the Russians into accepting a Russian envoy. The British, hearing about this, insisted on sending their own diplomatic mission. Sher Ali said that he did not want a British diplomatic mission, but Major Louis Cavagnari was sent nonetheless. Unsurprisingly the Afghans would not allow him to

enter the country; as a result, the British invaded the country in late November 1878 with the ultimate aim of detaching some of the western border provinces of Afghanistan and bringing them under permanent British administration.

By this time there were five Gurkha regiments in being, all of which were to be involved. The invasion force consisted of three columns advancing on the Peshawar, Kurram valley and Kandahar routes. Although Kandahar fell fairly easily to the British, they subsequently found themselves involved in some very heavy fighting as the Afghans slowly withdrew on Jalalabad, which eventually fell to the invaders. Meanwhile Colonel Frederick Roberts VC's 3,200-strong force and 13 field guns which included the 5th Gurkha Regiment (they became Rifles in 1891) advanced from India and occupied the vital Kurram valley. However, they found that the head of the valley at Peiwar Kotal was blocked by the bulk of the Afghan army, some 18,000 men with 18 artillery pieces, all in well-prepared defences along the heavily wooded mountainside.

An initial reconnaissance in force was repelled, so Roberts, who had known and admired Gurkhas ever since his days as a lieutenant on Delhi Ridge in 1857, carried out a night march to try and turn the Afghan left flank. The force he selected to carry out this operation included the 5th Gurkha Regiment and the 72nd (later Seaforth) Highlanders. Just before sunrise these two regiments rushed the Afghan position at Peiwar Kotal and succeeded in capturing it. This allowed Roberts to push on the rest of his force into a frontal attack which finally dislodged the Afghans. During the flank attack, Captain John Cook of the 5th Gurkhas saved the life of a fellow officer and drove off a force of Afghans attempting to recover one of their guns. He was subsequently awarded the Victoria Cross, while five Gurkhas received the Indian Order of Merit, a decoration dating to the first year of Queen Victoria's reign.

Without doubt the successful attack by the Seaforths and 5th Gurkhas was the turning point of the battle, and a superb painting by Vereker Hamilton, which now hangs in the National Army Museum, shows Highlanders and Gurkhas charging up the wooded hillside in the face of terrific Afghan fire. Vereker Hamilton was renowned for the accuracy of his paintings, and it is interesting to note that the post-Mutiny policy of giving only British troops the latest weaponry is reflected by the fact that the Seaforths are carrying the new Martini-Henry rifle whereas 5th Gurkhas are carrying the older Snider. The 5th Gurkhas always ascribed their light casualties to the fact that most of the Afghan small arms fire went over their heads. The Seaforths, also mountain-dwellers but taller, were not so lucky; again the painting well illustrates this.

Although there was severe fighting ahead, the Battle of Peiwar Kotal ensured that British troops marched again into Kabul. Sher Ali had fled north, soon to die at Mazar-i-Sharif. Cavagnari was installed as British Resident in July 1879 to the new Amir, Yakub Khan, rebellious son of Sher Ali, who had already signed a peace treaty with the British envoy (knighted for this achievement).

The new Amir was not popular and the presence of the British Resident and his small escort of 77 Guides was resented. The Afghan regular regiments from distant Herat who had not been involved in the recent war came into Kabul to collect their back pay for three months, but were only given one month's worth. They then attacked the British Embassy in overwhelming numbers, backed by two guns. The now Sir Louis Cavagnari and his devoted Guides had no chance, yet made a 12-hour last stand on 3 September. When the recently promoted Major General Sir Frederick Roberts heard of the disaster he immediately started putting together the Kabul Field Force of 7,500 troops to restore the situation and avenge Cavagnari and his men.

At first both the British and the Afghans subscribed to the charade that the British force was coming to assist the Amir, Yakub Khan, to restore order. Indeed, when Roberts had advanced as far as the vital Shutargardan Pass he received an embarrassing visit from the Amir himself, thanking him for his wish to assist but attempting to reassure him that such assistance was not required. When Roberts remained obdurate the veil dropped and an Afghan army of some 14,000 deployed to block Roberts's way at Charasiah.

Roberts repeated the tactics of Peiwar Kotal. The cavalry, 22 guns and one battalion of Highlanders secured the camp and then made as if to attack the Afghan army while 5th Gurkha Regiment and 72nd (Seaforth) Highlanders carried out a flanking attack across the mountain tops. The concerted plan was again successful. On 6 October the Afghans fled with the loss of much of their force and 20 guns. Four days later Roberts was in Kabul and virtually ruler of Afghanistan, as the Amir soon abdicated and was deported to India. To mark the valiant contribution of 5th Gurkhas and 72nd (Seaforth) Highlanders Roberts included a depiction of soldiers from both regiments on his family crest when he was elevated to the peerage.

Once in control of Kabul, Roberts, on instructions from the Viceroy, began a controversial policy of retribution against those who had killed Cavagnari, hanging the ringleaders and imposing martial law as well as exacting fines. This had the effect of infuriating the Afghans. The huge arsenal inside the fortress of the Bala Hissar blew up in mysterious circumstances. As it began to burn, the guards were quickly withdrawn to avoid being blown up – except the 5th Gurkha guard who refused to leave their post until properly relieved! In the explosion the 5th Gurkhas lost all their greatcoats. The 72nd (Seaforth Highlanders) subsequently insisted on loaning their own so that the Gurkhas should not suffer in the increasing cold.

***

Although the regular Afghan army had been defeated, the call for a Jihad against the invaders was answered by a massive uprising which threatened to overwhelm Roberts's force.

He hastily barricaded his 7,000 men, up to a fifth of them Gurkhas (4th and 5th), in the British fortified camp of Sherpur just outside Kabul. This camp had originally been made by Elphinstone's men in 1839 and then used by the Afghan Army, but Roberts had wisely strengthened its defences and laid in plentiful supplies in case he needed to defend it. So although the situation bore some similarities to that of Elphinstone 40 years before, Roberts was in fact in a much stronger position and in addition, significantly, he was, unlike Elphinstone, unencumbered by families and all the trappings of a peacetime garrison. Most importantly, 'Little Bobs' himself was an able and energetic commander, well respected and trusted throughout his command.

Detail from a painting by Vereker Hamilton of The Gordons and 2nd Gurkhas at the battle of Dargai. Piper Findlater, although shot in both legs, plays 'Cock o' The North' as the attack goes in for which he subsequently received the Victoria Cross. (Original painting in possession of the Gordon Highlanders Museum, Aberdeen)

Among the vital preparations had been to wheel in all the 85 captured Afghan artillery pieces into Sherpur's ditches and thus render them unusable by the Afghans.

When the Afghan assault came at dawn in the snows of 23 December not only were the attackers in numbers up to 50,000 but they were fired with religious fervour, fanned to fever pitch by a 90-year-old preacher or Imam with the unlikely title of 'Perfume of the Universe'. However brave and fanatical the Afghans, their ancient Jezails (long muskets) and Afghan knives were no match for breechloaders, 22 guns firing case shot, and two Gatling machine guns. The attacks petered out by noon with 3,000 casualties (33 to the defenders) and the Afghans rapidly dispersed. Roberts could re-occupy the city for the winter and on Christmas Day was joined by a brigade that included 2nd Goorkhas.

Fortunately, by next spring Lieutenant General Sir Donald Stewart was steadily moving up on Kabul from Kandahar with 7,200 troops and a large supply convoy. An estimated 15,000 Afghans fell upon the advance guard of this column from higher ground at the Battle of Ahmed Khel (19 April 1880). At a very critical moment the seemingly invincible 2,000 Afghan cavalry were mainly stopped by 3rd Gurkhas who, having drawn themselves up in four-deep company squares fought off every attack.

Joined by Stewart, Roberts was once again secure in Kabul. However the situation was far from satisfactory, as the claimant for the throne of Afghanistan, Ayub Khan, took the field and in a disastrous day for British arms destroyed a brigade-sized force at the Battle of Maiwand (27 July 1880) and then besieged the survivors in the nearby British-held fortress of Kandahar.

Roberts, collecting 10,000 troops, including three Gurkha battalions, 18 mountain guns and 8,000 supply-animals, advanced out of Kabul and headed for Kandahar. They covered 280 miles in 20 days in this world-famous march. At Kandahar he found that the siege had been lifted and Ayub Khan's 25,000-strong army had taken up a very strong position on the heights overlooking the city. The garrison itself was still in dire danger so Roberts had arrived only just in time. After a very careful reconnaissance in force on 31 August, Roberts decided to hook behind the main Afghan position next day, using his picked 1st Brigade consisting of 92nd (Gordon) Highlanders, 2nd Goorkhas (the regiment retained this previous spelling throughout its long and glorious history), 23rd Pioneers and 24th Punjab Infantry. After 4th Gurkhas had cleared the Afghans from the start-line the 92nd and 2nd Goorkhas stormed the first objective which was a heavily fortified village.

Colonel Arthur Battye, Commandant of 2nd Goorkhas, led his men towards the southern edge of the village while the Gordons hooked round from the right. Heavy and accurate supporting artillery fire enabled them to get to the outskirts of the village relatively unscathed but, once in its restricted confines in close-quarter combat, casualties started to mount. However, eventually the village was captured and the Gordons and two companies of 2nd Goorkhas pressed on to the plain beyond. Here they were confronted by large numbers of Afghans who charged towards them.

At this stage of the battle they were joined by 23rd Pioneers and the rest of 2nd Goorkhas whom Roberts had sent up to assist. Together they charged, and were irresistible: the Afghans broke and fled, the battle was won. A young 2nd Goorkha rifleman, Indebir Lama, reaching the two Afghan guns jumped up on one reputedly shouting 'This gun belongs to my regiment – 2nd Goorkhas. Prince of Wales!' He then thrust his cap down its muzzle to ensure ownership! This title had previously been conferred during the Prince of Wales's ceremonial visit in 1876, and the 2nd Goorkha cap badge from then on was the Prince of Wales feathers. Thereafter, an exact replica of the Afghan gun stood outside the Officers' Mess and now stands outside the Quarter Guard of The Royal Gurkha Rifles Barracks in Shorncliffe, Kent.

The Battle of Kandahar brought a successful military end to the Second Afghan War (although withdrawal operations lasted until April 1881), but the political objectives still remained elusive despite the deaths of 140 British officers and 50,000 casualties overall, mainly from cholera and dysentery. In addition the cost had been ruinous to the British Indian treasury. Fortunately the new Amir, Abder-er-Rahman, proved strong, ruthless and wise. He defeated Ayub Khan, unified the country and pursued a generally pro-British policy which ensured peace until the Third Afghan War in 1919.

The five Gurkha regiments involved had greatly distinguished themselves, and their proven combat-effectiveness paved the way for them to raise second battalions (with a nucleus of 85 Gurkha all ranks each coming from the first battalions) in 1886 under Roberts as Commander-in-Chief India, and eventually for expansion to ten regiments.

Although the Afghan wars fell into definite timescales, the fighting against the Pathan Frontier tribes of Mahsuds, Gilzai, Afridi, Mohmand et al was virtually continuous from when the British occupied the Punjab in 1849 until they left India very nearly a century later.

These tribes took no cognizance of national borders or the governments that purported to control them. Entirely free spirits, they raided, fought and looted at will and continually attacked British outposts and detachments. To steal a modern breech-loading rifle was a universal ambition! They bitterly resented any effort to control or discipline them and those who attempted to do so did so at their peril. Uniquely they have lived until this day as independent entities unadministered and untaxed. British India, continually nervous at Russian encroachment into Afghanistan did all it could to control these warlike tribes, but with less than total success and occasionally disastrous and bloody failure, reflected in casualty returns that would horrify today's public, but then remained largely unreported.

The Punjab Frontier Force, of which 5th Gurkhas was a part, was originally set up specifically to deal with the Pathan tribes, but in 1902 Lord Kitchener, then Commander-in-Chief of the Indian Army, reorganized it so that every infantry battalion should have the capacity to operate on the North-West Frontier.

Although probably a sensible and necessary step, there was considerable criticism along the lines that the knowledge and effectiveness of the unique Frontier Force was being lost. As a sop to the original Punjab Frontier Force units they were allowed to put Frontier Force (FF) in brackets after their title so that after the First World War 5th Gurkhas became 5th Royal Gurkha Rifles (FF), the 'Royal' being accorded them in recognition of their gallant conduct in 1914–18.

Let us now look at an example of a notable campaign that Gurkhas were involved in on the frontier (in fact, they were involved in virtually all of them).

In describing the Pathan as an enemy one has to visualize a man able to cover the most difficult hillside at top speed knowing every yard of the way, probably carrying only a rifle, a knife and perhaps 50 rounds of ammunition. He was physically virtually tireless, as fresh at the end of a battle as when it started. This fitness was allied to a keen natural tactician's eye for ground and an innate ability to strike hard and fast when his enemy dropped their guard. Then it was a murderous dash in and out inflicting half a dozen dead before going off with all the slain's modern rifles and ammunition. When the comrades of the stricken found them they were invariably mutilated. No wonder Kipling, who knew his Frontier, advocated keeping the last bullet for yourself!

The problem was how to deal with these formidable men. Day-to-day matters in the tribal areas were dealt with by Indian Government political officers who through a series of measures, including targeted bribes and threats, maintained some kind of order. Frequently such measures failed and the Pathans, ignoring the political officers, continued to attack isolated military posts, harry vulnerable supply columns and terrorize innocent Indians whose duty it was the Government of India's to protect. When this occurred the army was called in and a force would be sent to the tribal areas in question to destroy villages, burn crops and impose fines (usually in confiscated rifles and livestock); hostages against further good behaviour would also be taken.

Confronted by a show of superior force the Pathans would generally concede, but occasionally they would fight it out and major clashes would take place with quite heavy casualties on both sides. The normal tactic for advancing into hostile tribal territory was for an advance guard to picket all the high ground on either side of the route and for a rearguard to collect in all the pickets as they passed. In the middle, closely guarded, would be all the vulnerable pack animals and stores. This was a slow and exhausting process needing at least a brigade-sized unit of some 4,000 troops including mountain artillery, engineers and of course vitally and most importantly two or more battalions of infantry either British or Indian Army. Once scouts had fixed the position of the Pathan force the commander would try to execute a pincer movement to trap the Pathan and then destroy him by a combination of infantry assault supported by artillery and cut-offs. The Pathan was generally too clever to be thus trapped and, once he realized there was a danger of this, his force would melt away to fight another day. Occasionally however there would be a general uprising of several tribes together, very often religiously inspired by their mullahs or religious teachers.

One such major uprising resulted in the Tirah campaign of 1897–8. Two powerful tribes, the Afridi and the Orakzai, had risen and in great numbers had attacked and taken several military posts, raiding deep and destructively into large swathes of British India. To restore the situation a large force of 44,000 men was gathered, grouped into two infantry divisions, each of two brigades with an additional four infantry battalions to escort the cumbersome supply column of over 60,000 mules, camels and oxen and their often unwilling civilian drivers. Their first objective was to take the Afridi village of Dargai (now in Pakistan) and this was to result in one of the bloodiest battles of Frontier history – and one in which Gurkhas were to be very much involved.

Dargai could only be reached by a precipitous track which debouched into a steep open glacis leading up to the village. Two brigades were used for this operation, one approaching directly and the other hooking round the back, the classic frontier manoeuvre. The brigade doing the hook soon got into difficulties as the path was too narrow to bring up mountain artillery or essential supplies and these had to be sent back under escort. Nevertheless the brigade approaching directly managed, despite desultory sniping, to approach the village. An attack by 3rd Gurkhas and the King's Own Scottish Borderers took the village with few casualties and the defending Orakzai tribesmen disappeared. At 3pm the assaulting brigade and the cut-off brigade met up at Dargai village. Instead of holding the village in strength the decision was made, a disastrous one, to pull back to their camp. The reasons subsequently given were that there were no supplies or water available and that they were vulnerable to night attack by the tribesmen. One night's comfort and a day of preparations would have to be paid for in blood.

Next day at 4.30am on 20 October 1897 the 2nd Goorkhas advanced to reoccupy the village. During the night however

India General Service Medal 1859–95.

hundreds of well-armed Afridi tribesmen had taken up position in the village and on the dominating heights behind. They had constructed strong *sangars* virtually impervious to mountain artillery shells and shrapnel.

At first the 2nd Goorkhas made good progress and the Dorsets who were supporting them joined them in line for a final assault across the bare glacis. As they advanced they were met with a veritable maelstrom of rifle fire; at such a short range nearly every bullet found its billet; men fell literally in heaps and the stony slope was covered in killed and wounded. In the three days of Dargai operations, 2nd Goorkhas lost 17 killed and 48 wounded and 3rd Gurkhas 17 killed and 46 wounded.

As the 2nd Goorkha regimental history graphically records: 'Baffled and astounded, those who had not yet crossed staggered before the hail of bullets which churned up the ground into spurts of gravel and dust, scattering splinters of rock and lead in all directions'.

The Dorsets behind them tried to attack but were met with the same withering fire. The 2nd Goorkhas, gallantly holding the meagre gains made, heard the sound of pipes above the shot and shell, their old comrades of many campaigns were coming! The pipes playing 'Cock o' The North' heralded a charge by the Gordons and joined by Dorsets, 2nd Goorkhas, Derbyshires and 3rd Sikhs, covered by every piece of mountain artillery available; this swung the day, and the Afridis pulled out, pursued by the light trigger fingers of the 5th Gurkha snipers.

In the Gordons' museum in Scotland a wonderful painting by Vereker Hamilton, totally accurate in depiction, shows Piper Findlater shot through both ankles playing on the Gordons as they and 2nd Goorkhas charge forward. Accurate as ever, one can see 2nd Goorkhas still equipped with the old one-shot Martini-Henry rifles while the Gordons have the more modern magazine-fed rifles.

Weapon comparison might be invidious but compassion was general as the Gordons helped carry down the numerous 2nd Goorkha wounded from the blood-stained glacis.

The Frontier remained a very dangerous place to be until the British left India in 1947. The Gurkhas were there at the bitter end, as always uncomplainingly paying the ultimate price with that cheerful insouciance that has always been their trademark.

2nd Afghan War Medal 1878–80.

India General Service Medal 1895–1902.

CHAPTER FIVE

THE FIRST WORLD WAR: FRANCE AND FLANDERS 1914–1915

The British-Indian Army was organized and equipped to safeguard Imperial India's frontiers. With the outbreak of war in August 1914 the Viceroy of India, advised by the Secretary of State for War in Britain, made it clear that he did not feel there was a likelihood that the army would be required outside India. Fortunately his Commander-in-Chief thought otherwise and readied two divisions and a cavalry brigade for possible deployment. By this time there were 10 regiments of Gurkhas, each of two battalions, six battalions of which were part of the two divisions put on stand-by. Each Gurkha battalion was about 1000 strong at war establishment.

In so far as the British Government had planned for the war its thoughts had been that its main task would be a Royal Naval one, keeping the sea routes open and blockading Germany. The Army would provide a small but well-equipped Expeditionary Force (the BEF) to help France, otherwise it would concentrate on the security of the far-flung Empire. It was assumed that France would be mainly responsible for fighting the land battle on the Western Front and Russia on the Eastern. Crushed between the invincible French Army and the Russian 'steamroller' the Germans were thought unlikely to hold out beyond Christmas; one had to enlist quickly otherwise one might miss out on the 'fun'.

It was a hopelessly optimistic attitude and failed to remember the Franco-Prussian War (1870–1) in which Germany had virtually crushed France in a single battle. Germany, unlike 'The Allies', knew exactly what she was about. There had been no need to go to war on behalf of the tottering Austro-Hungarian Empire just because Archduke Francis Ferdinand had been murdered by Balkan extremists in Sarajevo. Serbia did all it could short of renouncing its independence to placate Austria, but Austria knew that Germany was willing and ready behind it. So when war came with awful inevitability as alliances were implemented, Germany had her plan. It was the Schlieffen Plan, a huge turning movement through neutral Belgium with the sickle point pointed at Paris. 'Keep the right strong!' implored Field Marshal Alfred von Schlieffen on his deathbed the year before the outbreak of war.

Fortunately for the Allies, his successors slightly watered down his blueprint and the sickle point reached only to the Marne before General Joseph Joffre was able to halt it and save Paris. Nevertheless, most of Belgium and large swathes of France were in German hands and the small BEF was in tatters. On the Eastern Front the Russians, gallantly advancing into East Prussia, had been decisively defeated at Tannenberg and were retreating. It was clear that not only would the war not be over by Christmas but that unless the French were massively reinforced by Britain, the Allies would be defeated.

Field Marshal Lord Kitchener, now War Minister, started to raise the vast citizen army that would be needed to redress the

balance, but this would all take time, especially as he decided to raise his new army from scratch instead of using the Territorial Army organization. Definitely a great man, Kitchener had his blind spots. As Lady Astor famously observed: 'Lord Kitchener is like a lighthouse, long periods of darkness punctuated by blinding flashes of light!' One thing, however, was very clear to him and that was that the BEF needed reinforcement very urgently. There was only one place such reinforcement could come from – India.

Lord Kitchener had been Commander-in-Chief of the Indian Army and as such had been responsible for its major reorganization to make it operationally much more flexible. The first of the stand-by divisions had been deployed to Mesopotamia (Iraq) to Basra (as of early 2009 the British Army has been deployed there for another six years) in order to secure a port from which to begin operations against Turkey, whose somewhat ramshackle empire embraced the entire Middle East. On the first division's departure another division had been put on stand-by, so when the call to sail for France came it was the Lahore (3rd) and Meerut (7th) Divisions, along with a cavalry brigade, that were deployed. Each division consisted of three infantry brigades, each of four battalions, one of which was always British. So for instance the

Dehra Dun Brigade of the Meerut Division consisted of 1st Seaforth Highlanders, 1/9th Gurkhas , 2/2nd Gurkhas and 6th Jat Light Infantry. In all there were four Gurkha battalions in the Meerut Division: 1/9th Gurkhas, 2/2nd Gurkhas, 2/3rd Gurkhas, 2/8th Gurkhas, and two in the Lahore Division – 1/1st Gurkhas and 1/4th Gurkhas – which made them the largest ethnic grouping within (and a quarter of) the infantry of the Indian Corps as it was known.

Each Gurkha battalion would have on average 12 British officers; the Commanding Officer, a lieutenant colonel, a senior major as second in command, sometimes an adjutant, four company commanders, up to four company officers, a quartermaster and an officer in charge of the machine guns. These would be backed by a larger number of Gurkha or Viceroy Commissioned Officers, the senior being the Subedar Major who was the Commanding Officer's adviser and confidant on all matters Gurkha. In theory junior to the most junior British officer, in practice he and the Commanding Officer ran the battalion and it would be a very stupid British officer who crossed him! In each of the four companies (100 men per company) there would be a Gurkha officer as second in command and three Gurkha platoon commanders (each platoon 27 to 30 men), plus perhaps one or two additional Gurkha officers in the machine-gun detachment and headquarters company.

In fact in the original organization that came from India a system of double companies was worked but this was abandoned in favour of the normal British Army organization. In terms of equipment and clothing the Indian Army was on considerably lighter scales than the British Army. They had only two machine guns as opposed to four or more in British units, they had an earlier mark of rifle, they had no wool serge uniforms, their equipment was leather rather than durable web fabric and their artillery support in medium and heavy guns was less than the British equivalent.

Gurkhas had already served outside India, Burma and Afghanistan. In 1875 the 1st Gurkhas had fought in Perak in Malaya against a rebellious sultan, the 2nd had very briefly served in Cyprus and Malta (1878), the 4th had seen action in China during the Boxer Rebellion, while in 1904 the 8th had fought at 19,000 feet in Tibet – but this was the first time they had served in mainland Europe. There were complications: few if any Gurkhas spoke any English, let alone French. Arriving at the port of Marseilles they received a rapturous welcome from the French locals; one battalion, newly issued with woollen vests and long johns, caused much excitement among the female population by wearing them on the outside of their cotton

uniforms. Horses and carts were issued without any drivers. In the absence of any equine experience, chaos ensued as diminutive Gurkha drivers held on for dear life as their charges trampled over tents and baggage.

However, despite all these excitements in a totally strange and new environment, the 30,000 troops of the Indian Corps arrived at their area of operations just south of Ypres, where the Belgian and French borders joined. Here near Givenchy, the scent-making town, the 2nd Cavalry Division (now dismounted and fighting as infantry) of the BEF was desperately trying to hold a continuing German onslaught. Lieutenant General Sir James Willcocks, commander of the Indian Corps, wanted his formation deployed as a whole but the situation was too dire and his units were just fed into the exhausted 2nd Cavalry Division as they arrived. Unfortunately the area occupied by the BEF cavalrymen was an infantryman's nightmare, flat, waterlogged, intersected by drainage ditches and overlooked by the Germans on the Aubers Ridge. It had never been chosen for defence, being simply where the tide of battle had left the line; indeed it was not even continuous, there being frequent gaps. The trenches were makeshift in the extreme and the protecting barbed wire had gaps supplemented inadequately by cattle fencing taken from the nearby fields.

**WESTERN FRONT
NOV 1914–NOV 1915**

Gurkhas training for an attack on German trenches. (Gurkha Museum)

The 2/8th Gurkhas, the only Gurkha battalion of the Bareilly Brigade, inherited a wide drainage ditch – too wide, since the Germans were able to drop trench mortar bombs and later artillery shells in it with some accuracy. Arriving in the middle of the night on 29 October 1914 they tried desperately to improve their position and raise the firing positions so they could see over the top of the flimsy parapet, being that much shorter in height than their British predecessors.

Soon they were being heavily shelled and mortared, followed by German 13th Division probing attacks which they beat off. On the next morning (30 October) the Germans opened a tremendous artillery bombardment followed by infantry attacks; soon casualties mounted and more and more men from the reserve company had to be fed into the line to hold it in sufficient strength. By early afternoon there were no reserves left, the whole battalion was in the firing line and rifle ammunition was running low. The trenches on the right of the 2/8th Gurkhas where they joined up with the Devons had collapsed and men were fighting out in the open and being cut down in swathes. Nine British officers were dead, wounded or missing and there were 212 Gurkha casualties. Despite a desperate resistance, the Germans had managed to drive a wedge between the 2/8th and the Devons. An immediate

Pipers of 2/3rd Gurkhas entertain their comrades during a period out of the trenches. (Gurkha Museum)

counter-attack of the remnants of 2/8th and other British and Indian units managed to retake some lost trenches and a further, better-coordinated counter-attack by the equivalent of three infantry battalions got back most of the rest. It had been a desperate battle. The loss of 2/8th's British officers was particularly damaging as it was they who traditionally led by example and inspired the Gurkhas in a war that at times they found difficult to comprehend. After all, remove a German's spiked helmet and he looked very like an Englishman.

Three days later it was 2/2nd Gurkhas' turn to bear the brunt of German attack. The battalion mustered 529 all ranks in positions directly in front of the village of Neuve Chapelle which had changed hands several times; on their left were the Irish Connaughts and on their right 1/9th Gurkhas. They had laboured furiously to improve their position, but when the bombardment came, concentrated on their right-hand company, the trenches simply collapsed and the position became compressed to the left; the Germans then seized their opportunity and advanced into the remains of the vacant trenches. The 1/9th, seeing what was happening, launched an immediate attack to restore the situation but were stopped by German fire. A 2/2nd British officer and the Subedar Major, leading a desperate platoon counter-attack with bayonet and kukri, managed to halt the Germans for a while but were both killed, and the 10 survivors were forced back.

Lieutenant Colonel Charles Norie, the Commanding Officer, a veteran of Manipur 1891 who had already lost one arm to wounds received on the North-West Frontier, now prevailed on his friend Lieutenant Colonel Charles Swanston to allow his dismounted cavalry unit, The Poona Horse, to join the remainder of 2/2nd in a counter-attack to regain the lost trenches which they duly did, Colonel Swanston being killed. The attack got within 150 yards of the lost trenches but could get no further. Colonel Norie then used his last 2/2nd Gurkha reserves and bits and pieces from other units and, personally leading them, made one last effort to regain the lost trenches, but the Germans were too strong. His battalion's casualties were grim, 7 British officers, 4 Gurkha officers and 33 men killed and 99 Gurkhas wounded and missing.

It was not over for 1/9th Gurkhas, relieved by 2/2nd Gurkhas; a company was switched to support a 13 November night raid by 200 men of 2/3rd Gurkhas in the nearby Richebourg area which failed with heavy casualties, the 1/9th going out into no-man's land to help recover their fellow countrymen.

Gallantry and courage simply could not be enough to deal with the massive numbers and excellent weaponry of the Germans. They had plentiful ammunition, much better and more modern artillery, very efficient and destructive trench mortars,

Detail from a montage by David Rowlands showing 2/2nd Gurkhas assaulting German positions in the battle of Neuve Chapelle 1915.

Gurkhas in France, a group photo.
(Gurkha Museum)

stick hand grenades and large numbers of machine guns; they were also very brave and determined. For our part we had no trench mortars, no hand grenades, limited ammunition and resurrected heavier guns shot smooth from the Boer War. The 9th Gurkha Regimental history notes that they finally got woollen serge uniforms and British Army-issue greatcoats just before Christmas; up until then they had been in cotton tunics and shorts. If the BEF as a whole was lamentably inferior to the German Army in terms of equipment and weaponry, then the Indian Corps was doubly so. Nevertheless their arrival had come at a critical time for the BEF and swelled its strength by a third.

★★★

Let us now briefly turn to Nepal, because without the help of its prime minister and effective ruler since 1901, Maharajah Chandra Shamsher Jang Bahadur Rana (1863–1929), the appalling losses being suffered by Gurkha regiments in France could not have been

made up or additional battalions formed; nor indeed could India, now devoid of much of its army, be garrisoned.

Chandra Shamsher, like his uncle and predecessor, the great Jang Bahadur, had visited Britain (1908) and became a great ally and supporter. A friend of King Edward VII, Chandra Shamsher was made a British Major General, made honorary Colonel of the 4th Gurkhas, showered with honours and treated with considerable respect and deference as the wise and capable ruler he was. On the outbreak of the Great War, Chandra wrote to the British Resident in Kathmandu as follows:'I have come to request you to inform His Excellency The Viceroy, and through him the King Emperor that the whole military resources of Nepal are at His Majesty's disposal. We shall be proud if we can be of any service, however little that may…'. In fact from a small country of at that time some five million, the help that came was wholly disproportionate. Manpower to replace those lost in battle, manpower to form 13 extra wartime battalions, and almost 16,000 men from his own national army to guard the North–West Frontier and other sensitive areas, thereby releasing men from the Indian Army to fight in France, the Dardanelles, Egypt, Palestine, Persia, Aden, Macedonia, East Africa and Mesopotamia. Some 95,265 Gurkhas fought under the British Crown in the First World War; it was an amazing contribution. Today, in 2009, Britain with a population of over 60 million is hard pressed to maintain a similarly volunteer professional army of 100,000. Of course circumstances are very different, but it does give a certain perspective.

Chandra Shamsher also arranged for a dispensation from the extensive Hindu purification procedures attendant on return to Nepal after crossing the oceans or 'kalo pani' (literally 'black water'). These purification rites were taken very seriously and failure to observe them could lead to the equivalent of excommunication. Chandra Shamsher's dispensation was therefore of considerable importance in terms of reassuring the Gurkhas' religious conscience.

After a comparatively quiet period in March 1915, it was decided to try and re-take the village of Neuve Chapelle. It had been a key objective ever since the Indian Corps had been forced out of it the previous autumn. It needed to be recaptured as it formed a dangerous salient jutting into the British lines. The attack was personally ordered by the Commander-in-Chief, General Sir John French, in an effort to try and regain the initiative and reassure General Joffre, his French counterpart, that the British were not simply content to sit on the defensive. It was to involve elements of four British Corps and the Indian Corps, a total of four infantry divisions. The plan was not limited to retaking Neuve Chapelle but in a second phase it was hoped to push on and capture the vital Aubers Ridge that overlooked the British lines.

The plan was for a two-pronged attack, one prong involving the Meerut Division. Its Garhwal Brigade, which included 2/3rd Gurkhas, would assault first, followed up by the Dehra Dun Brigade, which included 2/2nd Gurkhas and 1/9th Gurkhas. Since this was to be the first major offensive of the BEF since the retreat from Mons it was coordinated with meticulous care. The Royal Flying Corps dominated the sky above the intended area of attack, preventing German reconnaissance planes getting any early warning and also sending back a continual stream of information on German preparedness or lack of it. On the morning of the attack, 420 guns delivered the heaviest British barrage of the war so far, catching the Germans unprepared and stunning them with its 35 minutes of ferocity.

At 8.05am on 10 March 1915 the Garhwal Brigade, consisting of 2nd Battalion The Leicestershire Regiment, 39th Garhwalis and 2/3rd Gurkhas surged out of their trenches across no-man's land and

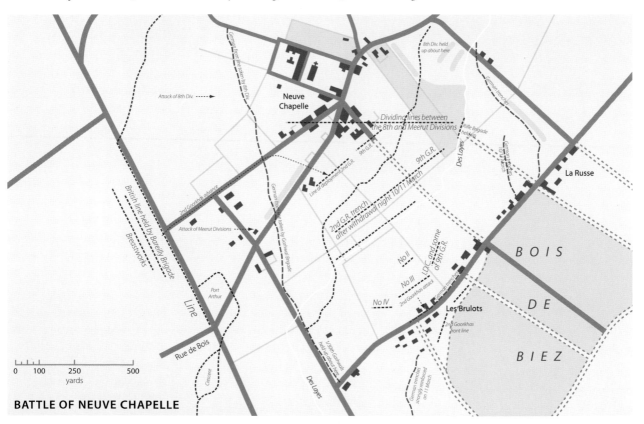

BATTLE OF NEUVE CHAPELLE

Photo of Gurkha Havildar in World War One uniform and equipment holding a Lee Enfield rifle. (Gurkha Museum)

Naik Kulbir Thapa 2/3rd Gurkhas was awarded the Victoria Cross for repeatedly crawling forward into no mans land to rescue wounded British and Gurkha comrades whilst continually under heavy German fire. (Gurkha Museum)

with bayonet and kukri rushed the German trenches before the Germans could recover from the artillery barrage. Having taken the trenches killing and capturing large numbers, the attackers pushed on to the village of Neuve Chapelle. Rifleman Gane Gurung of 2/3rd Gurkhas, tiring of the rather slow, stereotyped methods of house-clearing taught in training, rushed one house alone and after a breath-catching pause emerged prodding seven German prisoners with his bayonet to the rapturous applause of the 2nd Rifle Brigade, the nearest unit of the British division forming the other wing of the attack. The attack was a brilliant success and for amazingly light casualties Neuve Chapelle had been taken and the German line broken.

It was now the moment for the Dehra Dun Brigade to surge through and take Aubers Ridge before the Germans could recover. Sadly the bugbear of appalling communications, as so often in

1914–18, now exerted its malign influence. Communications were reliant on thin telephone wire run between forward units and rear headquarters. This was frequently smashed by enemy shellfire. When this happened messages had to be sent by hand of runners. Very often they too were killed or wounded or simply got lost or seriously delayed.

Because of such delays, when 2/2nd and 1/9th Gurkhas eventually advanced the Germans had recovered from the artillery barrage and were ready and waiting, having been reinforced. Nevertheless, with great gallantry and suffering casualties all the time, the Gurkhas managed to cross the vital Layes brook, which because of heavy rain had become a major water obstacle. Unfortunately, it was getting dark; 2/2nd and 1/9th Gurkhas were ordered to pull back to the west bank of the Layes brook. Next day, confused orders led them to believe they had been ordered to retire rather than attack again. In fact the intention had been for them to hold their positions while a fresh brigade were passed through them to attack the Germans but just as the relieving brigade were forming up, 16,000 Germans attacked trying to cross the Layes brook. They offered a perfect target for the waiting soldiers who poured rifle and machine-gun fire into them, halting the attack and causing an estimated 3,000 casualties.

If at that critical moment additional follow-up troops had been available Aubers Ridge might well have been taken. However, there was a long delay during which time the Germans frantically strengthened their position on the far bank and the opportunity was lost. Despite this, the Indian Corps had successfully captured Neuve Chapelle, taken 629 prisoners, pinched out the German salient and advanced over 1,000 yards. It represented a major British trench-warfare achievement and silenced French criticism of British inactivity. But it had been achieved at a cost of 4,200 men to the Indian Corps which by now had lost a third of its original strength in killed and wounded.

Sir Douglas Haig, the First Army commander, never the most imaginative of generals, continued to launch attack after attack that spring to gain the Aubers Ridge, regardless of the fact that the Germans had now been heavily reinforced. Using all three of his Corps, including the Indian Corps, he launched a massive three-pronged attack on the Aubers Ridge in mud and rain on 9 May, but despite a 40-minute preliminary artillery barrage much of the German wire remained uncut and the German machine guns were ready and waiting. Although 2/2nd Gurkhas got as far as the German trenches they suffered heavily, losing all their British officers yet again and many of their best Gurkha officers and non-commissioned officers. The follow-up Bareilly Brigade then attacked, but still could not break into the German trenches. In a single day the Indian Corps had lost 2,000 men.

In this and subsequent carnage there were great acts of individual gallantry, such as that of Rifleman Dhanraj Thapa, 2/8th Gurkhas, who while awaiting urgent casualty evacuation with a shattered hand crawled out into no-man's land amid shot and shell to recover a dead British officer. In subsequent attacks 1/1st, 1/4th and 2/3rd Gurkhas were all involved, 1/1st Gurkhas actually getting into the German trenches but, unsupported they were, after a desperate resistance with bayonet and kukri, finally pushed out.

During the similar autumn Battle of Loos, Rifleman Kulbir Thapa of 2/3rd Gurkhas was awarded the Victoria Cross for crawling out into no-man's land under heavy enemy fire on 25 and 26 September to rescue three wounded British and Gurkha soldiers with no thought for his own wound or the novel poisonous gas conditions. He was the first Gurkha non-officer to receive the VC, for which Gurkha soldiers had only become eligible in 1911. Up until that time native soldiers of the Indian Army received their highest gallantry award, the Indian Order of Merit. This was given in three classes for the first and subsequent acts of gallantry. When they became eligible for the Victoria Cross, the Indian Order of Merit, now reduced to two classes, remained, so many Gurkhas were awarded this medal rather than a VC.

By now units in the Indian Corps had become so depleted as to be ineffective without reorganization and reinforcement. While this was going on demands for Gurkha troops to fight at Gallipoli were being received from General Sir Ian Hamilton, a protégé of the late Lord Roberts (who had died on the Western Front during a November 1914 visit to the Indian Corps); so 1/4th Gurkhas were redeployed to the Gallipoli peninsula. Gurkhas had established a tremendous reputation in France, being assessed by their Corps commander as his best infantry. These young hillmen from the calm foothills of the Himalaya had poured out their life blood in the carnage of the Western Front and in the process had left an enduring memory among friend and foe for courage and stoical endurance laced by humour even in the most appalling conditions. So we must leave France now and follow other Gurkha battalions to Gallipoli.

The 1914 Star.

CHAPTER SIX

THE FIRST WORLD WAR: THE TURKISH FRONTS 1914–1918

THE DARDENELLES

In retrospect, it was not inevitable that Britain should have gone to war with Turkey as well as Germany and the Austro-Hungarian Empire. A series of British diplomatic misappreciations drove Turkey into the arms of Germany which, by clever diplomacy and material aid, induced her to enter the war as an ally.

Britain's occupation of Egypt in 1882, then part of the Ottoman (Turkish) Empire, was the first of many affronts to Turkey. The final and fatal insult was in 1914 when the last-minute confiscation of two Turkish battleships, being built in British yards and already paid for, incensed the Turks and convinced them to throw in their lot with Germany. In the event, Turkey did not declare war until the end of October 1914 when it seemed as if Germany might well triumph.

Britain's high-handed and insensitive dealings with Turkey reflected the commonly held view of Turkey as the 'Sick Man of Europe' and her ramshackle Empire as ripe for dissolution. For many years this had been the case, but all had changed in 1908 when a group of mainly young Turkish officers, incensed at the despoliation of Turkey's empire and her waning influence, seized power from her weak and ineffectual rulers, the Sultan and his government (generally referred to as the Sublime Porte) in Constantinople. Known as 'The Young Turks', prominent among whom were Enver Pasha and Mustapha Kemal (later Atatürk), they

GALLIPOLI

Gurkha stretcher bearers carrying a casualty at Gallipoli. (Gurkha Museum)

soon started to rejuvenate Turkey. As part of this process they set about strengthening Turkey's already firm ties with Imperial Germany and its Kaiser, Wilhelm II. Before long their army was being reorganized by efficient and experienced German officers and rearmed with modern German weaponry. These far-reaching organizational changes, embracing a much more efficient system of mobilizing reserves, enabled them to put 800,000 troops into action in a short space of time.

In British military thinking the Turkish Army was still considered to be much inferior to their allies, the Germans. This assumption was to prove woefully mistaken. The Turkish soldier was naturally hardy and brave and when efficiently led, well organized and properly armed could be formidable, sharing many characteristics with the Gurkha soldier.

After the Allied defeats of 1914 in France and Belgium and the ensuing unproductive trench warfare, Winston Churchill, who was then First Lord of the Admiralty (Naval Minister), advocated the idea of pushing a battle fleet through the Dardanelles. Once through these narrow straits and into the Sea of Marmara, it would be able to bombard the Turkish capital of Constantinople (Istanbul), as well as opening up an alternative ice-free supply route to Russia through the Black Sea to Odessa. This would strengthen Russia's ability to continue the war with Germany, Austria and Turkey, despite her defeats in East Prussia and Poland. There was also the hope that a naval bombardment of Constantinople might in itself lead to the Turks suing for peace given their perceived weakness. The Royal Navy was dubious, but eventually went along with Churchill and using elderly battleships

tried to force the Dardanelles. The Turks, more by good luck than good judgement, had mined the narrow waterway with floating mines haphazardly floated down with the tide. Nevertheless six British and French battleships were sunk or damaged with the loss of many sailors drowned. The Royal Navy now became nervous and eventually refused to make any further attempt until the Army had cleared the Gallipoli Peninsula of Turks. Thus the first of three golden opportunities was lost.

General Sir Ian Hamilton (brother of the talented artist Vereker Hamilton) was appointed commander of the invasion force, which consisted of the ANZAC Corps of one Australian and one New Zealand division and the British 29th Division. Almost immediately, on 25 March 1915, he wrote to Lord Kitchener asking for Gurkhas to be added to his force:

> *I am very anxious, if possible, to get a Brigade of Gurkhas, so as to complete the New Zealand divisional organization with a type of man who will, I am certain, be most valuable on the Gallipoli Peninsula. The scrubby hillsides on the southwest face of the plateau are just the sort of terrain where these fellows are at their brilliant best … each little Gurkha may be worth his full weight in gold at Gallipoli …*

As a result of this plea, on 1 May 1915 1st Battalion 6th Gurkha Rifles arrived from the Suez Canal, where as part of 29th Indian Infantry Brigade it had been involved in warding off Turkish attempts to cut this vital waterway. By the time 1/6th Gurkhas disembarked the initial landings were six days old. The 29th British Division,

Men of the 2/10th Gurkhas at Gallipoli – note the white arm bands to distinguish them to their own artillery. (Gurkha Museum)

comprised of India-based British units, had landed in the Cape Helles area and the second golden opportunity had been lost by failing to push on up to the vital high ground before Turkish resistance had stiffened. Now 29th Division was pinned down near the landing beaches, while the ANZAC divisions were pinned further up the coast at the foot of the vital Sari Bair feature; all divisions having suffered very heavy casualties.

General Liman von Sanders, the German coordinator of the Turkish defence, had fed three additional divisions into the battle and the Allies, despite the advantage of naval gunfire support, were unable to break out of their beach-heads to which they clung with the greatest difficulty. On 9 May the 1/6th Gurkhas now took up position on the far left of the Allied position at Helles where, after suffering a steady stream of casualties from Turkish artillery fire, they were given the task of taking a steep hill or bluff on the far right of the Turkish position. Two attempts had already been made to take this important feature and both had failed with heavy casualties. The Commanding Officer of 1/6th Gurkhas, Lieutenant Colonel the Honourable Charles Bruce, made a plan based on information from an officer who had surveyed the objective from the light cruiser HMS *Talbot* and from the results of a daring land reconnaissance carried out by Subedar Gambirsing Pun, of whom we shall hear more.

Prevailing upon the adjacent unit to divert the Turks by a furious fusillade of fire, and using naval gunfire to suppress the deadly Turkish machine guns that commanded the wide ravine at the bottom of the bluff, 1/6th Gurkhas managed to get across relatively unscathed and, being natural hillmen, rapidly ascended

the steep sides of the bluff during the night of 12 May to find the crest only lightly defended. They had achieved almost total surprise and gained a very important feature. The Turks, realizing what had happened, counter-attacked strongly but were severely mauled by naval bombardment and could make no headway. It was a brilliantly planned and executed attack and vindicated General Sir Ian Hamilton's faith in Gurkhas. The initial attack incurred 60 Gurkha casualties, but further attempts to enlarge the gains were more costly. At one stage, 1/6th Gurkhas were required to recover trenches lost by a unit sent up to support them, which they did at heavy cost to themselves.

Liman von Sanders now realized how dangerous were the gains made by 1/6th Gurkhas and ordered the Turks to carry out continual if very costly counter-attacks. Hamilton for his part was determined to enlarge the area already gained round Gurkha Bluff, as it was now known in honour of 1/6th Gurkhas' achievement. Using additional troops and all of 29th Indian Brigade, which now comprised 1/5th, 1/6th and 2/10th Gurkhas, he launched an attack to the north of Gurkha Bluff to try and seize an important feature called Achi Baba from which the Turks dominated the vulnerable beaches. The 1/6th Gurkhas were involved in the first attack which, despite heavy preliminary naval and artillery support, failed to cut the Turkish wire on which the subsequent attack foundered with heavy casualties. Later in the day, 1/5th Gurkhas attacked repeatedly with great bravery but again suffered very heavy casualties for very little to show. Men, however courageous, could not breach unbroken wire covered by machine guns. Even when they did reach the Turkish trenches, the lack of hand grenades made it difficult to clear the Turkish trenches, a task for which grenades were the best weapon. The Turks had plenty of highly effective factory-made grenades, whereas Allied troops had to make do with converted jam tins! As 6th Gurkha regimental history rather plaintively makes clear: '... the supply was strictly limited and to a certain extent depended on the amount of jam consumed by the troops'.

In a separate and highly successful operation 2/10th Gurkhas showed what could be done when surprise could be gained and the Gurkha ability to quickly traverse steep and seemingly impassable terrain utilized. In a battle begun on 28 June, to be called Gully Ravine, the 794-strong 2/10th Gurkhas stuck in closely behind the initial bombardment and then slipped behind a cliff before the Turks could register their machine guns on them. Scaling the cliff, which the Turks felt to be impassable, they

suddenly emerged, completely surprising the Turks and driving them back some 1,000 yards. It was probably one of the most successful attacks of the whole campaign and levered the Turks out of a strong defensive position, but the ground thus gained had then to be defended for another three days and nights.

Continually in action the three Gurkha battalions had by now lost heavily in dead and wounded. For instance, since arriving, 1/6th Gurkhas had suffered 96 killed and 383 wounded, the Commanding Officer being among the wounded, as was also the case in 1/5th Gurkhas. It was therefore decided to move all three battered battalions back to the island of Imbros, where they could rest and be reinforced with replacement officers and men.

While on Imbros, the Gurkha battalions learned that they would soon be involved in a major offensive in the ANZAC area of

This painting by Terence Cuneo shows 1/6th Gurkhas attacking the Turkish trenches on the crest of the vital Sari Bair feature, Major Allanson leading. In the background ships of the Royal Navy are giving fire support. Red roundels are painted on the backs of the attacking Gurkhas to distinguish them as friendly troops to the Royal Navy gun crews. (The Royal Gurkha Rifles)

Above: The Quartermaster's store 1/4th Gurkhas Gallipoli. (Gurkha Museum)

Left: Gurkhas using a home made periscope in the trenches. (Gurkha Museum)

Right: Two Gurkha soldiers in a trench at Gallipoli. (Gurkha Museum)

operations. Three fresh divisions were to be employed in a new landing further up the coast at Suvla Bay, combined with a major thrust out of the cramped ANZAC beach-head towards the main central massif of Sari Bair. It was hoped that by so doing it would be possible to cut off all the Turkish troops operating against the landings in Helles and then to force the Turks back up the Gallipoli peninsula towards Constantinople. The 29th Indian Brigade (with 4th Australian Brigade) were to be part of the left flank of the two-pronged night attack that, it was planned, would push up the two major valleys leading to the crest of Sari Bair, the ultimate objective.

The attack on 6 August by 29th Indian Brigade took the Turks by surprise and secured major features, but the right-hand column met strong Turkish resistance so that by the following morning the attacking force was still some way short of the ridgeline. At this stage 1/5th Gurkhas and 1/6th Gurkhas were ordered to swing right to assist the right-hand column but such was the difficulty of the terrain that they could not reach its main body. However, independently, they made considerable gains which brought them close to the Sari Bair ridgeline. A further coordinated attack was ordered for dawn the next day – 8 August. Fighting went on all day as Turkish resistance stiffened and gains of only a few yards were made at the cost of mounting casualties. The 1/6th Gurkhas were reinforced by two companies from the Staffordshire Regiment and one from the Warwickshire Regiment, one of whose officers, Lieutenant William Slim, later Field Marshal Lord Slim, was to take away a life-long admiration for Gurkhas from his experiences that day – an engagement which left him grievously wounded.

Since the complementary attack from the Suvla Bay landings had failed to materialize, it was decided to renew the ANZAC attack the next day after a heavy naval bombardment. The attack that had been supposed to gain the Sari Bair Ridge in one night had now gone on for three days of bitter fighting. The naval

bombardment turned out to be very effective according to the 6th Gurkhas' regimental history: 'Shells of all descriptions were absolutely hurled on the Turkish position which was a mass of smoke, dust and flying clods of earth.'

At exactly 5.23am on 9 August, Major Cecil Allanson led 1/6th Gurkhas and two companies of the South Lancashires into the assault. In the words of General Hamilton who watched the attack:'And now under that fine leader Major C. J. L. Allanson, the 6th Gurkhas of the 29th Indian Brigade pressed up the slopes of Sari Bair … reached the crest and began to attack down the far side of it'.

This was indeed a brilliant success and as they crested Sari Bair 6th Gurkhas' history again takes up the story:

> At the top of the ridge the Turks were met. [Lieutenant] Le Marchant fell, a bayonet through his heart. Major Allanson was also wounded by a bayonet thrust in the thigh. For ten minutes hand-to-hand fighting of the most bitter character ensued …. Then the Turks turned and fled. The key of the whole Peninsula was in the hands of the Battalion.

It was now that the third golden opportunity of the Gallipoli campaign was lost and with it the chance of victory. The 250-odd 1/6th Gurkhas were supposed to be attacking, not almost on their own, but with two complete brigades' worth of infantry. But these had all become lost in the maze of ravines during the previous night's approach march and were too far away to help. As 1/6th Gurkhas pressed on down the hill after the retreating Turks, they and the Turks realized that they were completely unsupported. The Turks turned and counter-attacked under covering artillery bombardment and 1/6th Gurkhas were pushed back step by step, with mounting casualties. Finally, after a fourth 24 hours virtually without sleep or rations, they were forced off the summit which was never again to be reached.

It was left to the Subedar Major, the indefatigable Gambirsing Pun, to withdraw the battalion, every British infantry officer being either dead or wounded, only the medical officer, Captain Edward Phipson, was still on his feet. He translated for Gambirsing when orders emanated from above.

With the failure of this attack the campaign bogged down in trench warfare, and, as autumn turned to winter, the weather conditions became grim, with torrential rain followed by sleet and snow. At one stage the trenches became so flooded that friend and foe perched on the lips of them without shooting at each other. The 1/4th Gurkhas recently arrived from France coped better, being used to surviving in similar conditions, but those who had fought through the long hot Aegean summer suffered terribly from disease and exposure.

A stocky Gurkha and a tall Highlander in Mesopotamia. (Gurkha Museum)

In this kind of warfare, when the Turkish artillery could reach virtually all the Allied positions, reserve trenches were as lethal as front-line ones and the four Gurkha battalions suffered a continual toll of casualties. In mid-November, Field Marshal Lord Kitchener arrived to see for himself. His practised eye told him that without massive reinforcement the deadlock could not be broken, the Turks were just too strong. Britain could not spare any more troops: it needed all it had and more on the Western Front. He decided on a complete evacuation, sacked General Hamilton and appointed General Sir Charles Monro who, on the nights of 18/19 December 1915 and 8/9 January 1916, conducted an almost bloodless final withdrawal covered by naval gunfire. It was some time before the Turks realized that the Allies had gone. If only some of the other operations had been planned as well!

The Gurkhas had yet again left a tremendous name for courage and fighting ability, but at a heavy cost of 755 officers and men killed and a large number of wounded, many of whom would be maimed for life. Later General Hamilton was to write:'It is Sir Ian Hamilton's most cherished conviction that had he been given more Gurkhas in the Dardanelles then he would never have been held up by the Turks.' Valid or not, what can never be disputed was that it was a Gurkha battalion on top of Sari Bair that brought him as near to victory as he ever got. That moment is commemorated by a superb painting by Terence Cuneo on which an exciting and evocative diorama in the Gurkha Museum is based.

EGYPT, PALESTINE AND MESOPOTAMIA

Very early after Turkey's entry into the war, her forces in Palestine made an attempt to cut the Suez Canal, appreciating its vital strategic importance to the British. Before they were redeployed to the Dardanelles and Gallipoli, 1/6th Gurkhas and 2/10th Gurkhas were both involved in the February 1915 defensive actions to safeguard the canal. Fortunately the defenders were able to call upon massive naval gunfire support from Allied warships moored in the canal, and a combination of naval bombardment and strong land defences kept the Turks off.

The 2/7th Gurkhas deployed in the area were involved later that same month in attacking a large Arab force whose intention was also to infiltrate into the canal area and block it. Following a seaborne night approach in the cruiser HMS *Minerva*, 2/7th Gurkhas attacked, gaining surprise and completely dispersing the much larger Arab force with 194 casualties for the loss of only one Gurkha soldier. His funeral ceremony assumed a high profile with ships in the canal flying their flags at half mast and a Royal Marine band in attendance. As 7th Gurkha history wryly noted: 'It is improbable that any Gurkha Rifleman has ever been, or ever will be again, attended to his grave with so much honour.'

Meanwhile in Mesopotamia, a region encompassing modern Iraq, Britain was becoming very nervous about her brand-new oil

refinery on Abadan Island in Persia. This was just across the Shatt-al-Arab waterway from the Turkish-controlled city of Basra. The Royal Navy was in the process of converting from coal-fired ships to the much more efficient oil-fired vessels, so Abadan assumed a vital strategic interest.

Until hostilities with Turkey became imminent, the Turks allowed British tankers going to pick up crude oil from Abadan safe passage up the Shatt-al-Arab waterway, providing that they remained on the Persian side of the channel. However, the Turks now started to threaten British ships in the waterway . Britain responded by sending brigades of the stand-by 6th Indian (Poona) Division from India under naval escort to safeguard rights of passage and the oil supplies. If war broke out with Turkey, the division was to occupy Basra. Despite a determined Turkish defence, this was achieved by a brilliant and daring joint naval and army attack which in a few days of November 1914 virtually destroyed a whole defending Turkish infantry division for very little loss.

Encouraged by this seemingly easy victory, the Poona Division, now at full strength, started to push on up-river out of Basra with the full encouragement of the Viceroy of India who had assumed responsibility for this theatre of operations. Turkish resistance stiffened and, although 12,000 Turks were defeated at

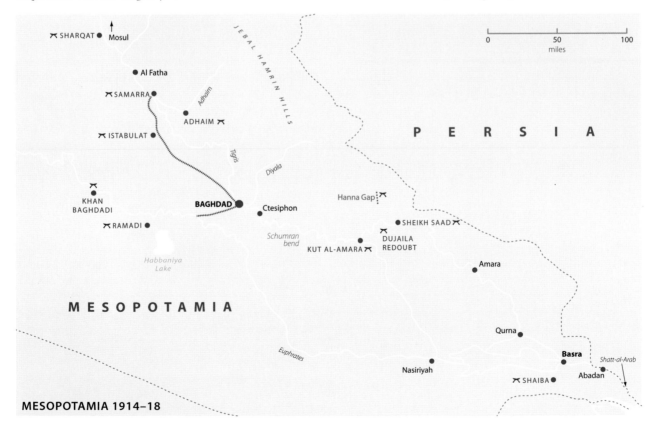

MESOPOTAMIA 1914–18

Shaiba, south-west of Basra, in the first Gurkha battle honour of the campaign, it was a battle which hung in the balance until the very end. Nevertheless it was decided to push on up both the rivers Tigris and Euphrates towards the next Turkish strongpoints of Amara and Nasiriyah respectively.

Major General Charles Townshend, now commanding 6th Division, was given the task of taking Amara on the Tigris and, by a skilful use of a carefully assembled flotilla of small boats, he managed to unbalance the Turkish defence to such an extent as to be able to take Amara with comparatively light casualties.

Nasiriyah, near the ancient Ur of the Chaldees, proved a much tougher proposition for Major General George Gorringe's 12th Division, newly arrived from India. The whole area around Nasiriyah was flooded and any attempt to outflank the Turkish position needed to be partly by boat. The Turks, appreciating this, had laid a huge barrier across the Euphrates which had first to be destroyed and its protecting gunboats silenced. Once this was done, a major turning movement through myriad water channels was necessary to reach the main Turkish defence position six miles south of Nasiriyah. The waterlogged area was swarming with mosquitoes and the troops, which included 2/7th Gurkhas, were suffering terribly from malaria and waterborne diseases. The battalion's effective strength had been reduced from 750 to 380.

Nevertheless, despite generally unhelpful changes of plan by General Gorringe, the two brigades pushed on and assaulted the main Turkish position which was strongly defended, and the July 1915 battle swayed in the balance for several days. It was 2/7th Gurkhas' success in getting into the Turkish trench system with kukri and bayonet that did much to save the day after the main attack seemed to have faltered. The Turks then retreated and Nasiriyah was secured.

General Sir John Nixon, the overall commander, backed by the Viceroy of India, then ordered General Townshend on with a combined force of two divisions for Kut-al-Amara (Kut) at the join of the great rivers Tigris and Shatt-al-Hai (which on maps linked the Tigris with the Euphrates) and a hundred miles short of Baghdad, which was already exerting a magnetic influence. The Turks held a position to the east of Kut which Townshend determined to outflank. Despite daytime temperatures of over 40 degrees Celsius, he manoeuvred his troops so skilfully as to give the impression that his main approach would be west of the Tigris, whereas after nightfall he switched over to the east of the river and hooked round behind the Turks who, outflanked, outmanoeuvred and outnumbered, fell back, allowing Kut to be taken on 28 September. Despite appalling heat and humidity, Townshend's force had achieved a great victory.

Kut had all the appearances of being of strategic importance, which made it strange that the Turks had not defended it more stubbornly; perhaps this should have rung alarm bells but it clearly did not. On the contrary, it seemed as if the Turks were on the run and, again backed by the Viceroy of India, General Nixon ordered Townshend on to Baghdad. The field commander himself was doubtful, feeling he had not sufficient men to go beyond Kut. 'Charlie' Townshend was however overruled, at the same time being reassured that two more divisions, the Meerut and Lahore Divisions from France, were on their way, regardless of the fact that they could not possibly reach him in time to play any part in the forthcoming battle.

For forthcoming battle there was to be, since Townshend's aerial and land reconnaissance had revealed a strong Turkish blocking position at the site of the ancient city of Ctesiphon, 22 miles south-east of Baghdad. All that remained of it now was a broken palace archway and a series of large mounds which the Turks had turned into strong defensive positions. Unbeknown to Townshend, strong Turkish reinforcements, some from Gallipoli, had reached Ctesiphon, and the overall coordination of the Turkish forces was now in the hands of the able German Field Marshal Baron Kolmar von der Goltz. Some 18,000 Turkish troops were at or near Ctesiphon against the 13,000 British and Indian troops intending to attack it. Despite numerical inferiority on the first day (23 November), General Townshend's troops managed to break into the Turkish first-line defences, but instead of methodically rolling up the first line they went straight on to attacking the second line on which they foundered. The Turks then counter-attacked strongly and despite furious resistance Townshend's division was driven back. The stand made by 2/7th Gurkhas was particularly epic. Three hundred of them and about a hundred soldiers from 24th Punjab Regiment occupied one of the raised mounds and held on despite repeated Turkish attacks. Eventually, after suffering heavy casualties, the Turks gave up; their military historian recorded the action as follows: 'I must confess to a deep hidden feeling of appreciation of the deed of that brave self-sacrificing enemy detachment which for [nine] hours, only 400 strong, opposed and finally drove back thousands of riflemen of the 35th Division.'

Gurkha Mound (as it would be named) was certainly a magnificent effort and as night drew on Generals Nixon and Townshend fervently hoped that the Turks would retreat during the night after the severe casualties they had taken. But when dawn came they were not only still in position but had been reinforced. Townshend's troops were exhausted; he had committed them all and had no reserves. With Nixon's agreement, he ordered a withdrawal back to Kut and thus started one of the British Army's most agonizing retreats.

In vicious heat, short of water and continually harried by the triumphant Turks, Townshend's battered division trudged the 80 or

Gurkhas guarding Turkish prisoners in Mesopotamia. (Gurkha Museum)

so miles back to Kut. If you were fit it was bad enough, but if you were wounded (194 were Gurkhas) and bumped around in agony in an unsprung ox-cart it was hell on earth. In those days there were few pain-killers available and because of the insanitary conditions many died of blood poisoning. The administrative and medical back-ups had always been inadequate and were now close to breaking down completely. Nevertheless, Townshend's men did reach Kut intact, covered by the small naval river flotilla whose guns kept the Turks from closing up and which ferried the wounded back to Basra in towed barges. Kut itself was a small dirty town unprepared to host a battered army. On the other hand, bounded by the mighty Tigris on three sides, it was eminently defensible. Supplies of food were sufficient for a two-month siege and there was no shortage of ammunition.

Before the Turks could close the land route, Nixon prevailed upon Townshend to send out the cavalry and boats, but when Townshend suggested he get out his whole army while there was time, Nixon vetoed it, insisting he would be relieved inside two months. Shortly after, on 5 December 1915, the Turks encircled Kut and its 13,000-strong garrison, including just over 400 fit men of 2/7th Gurkhas, were besieged.

History has treated General Townshend rather harshly, perhaps his widely publicized utterance that he would defend Kut as he had famously defended Chitral on the North-West Frontier in 1895 has resonated painfully in view of the subsequent disaster. Nevertheless, up until then he had been very successful and shown much dash and drive, qualities that were·felt to be lacking among certain senior officers at Gallipoli.

With the arrival of the Lahore and Meerut Divisions from France, Nixon was able to assemble a force of three divisions for the relief of Kut. Some Gurkha battalions such as 1/9th Gurkhas went straight on to fight in Mesopotamia, whereas others like 2/2nd Gurkhas were replaced by their sister battalions from India. The relieving Tigris Corps was put under the command of Lieutenant General Sir Fenton Aylmer VC who, ironically, had been in the relieving force at Chitral on the North-West Frontier when Captain Townshend was defending that fort.

In early January 1916 General Aylmer's force was successful in getting the Turks to withdraw from an intermediate blocking position at Sheikh Saad, but suffered very heavy casualties in the process. Pressing on, his force encountered a further Turkish position at a feature known as the Hanna gap. The 1/1st and 1/9th Gurkhas were heavily involved in this battle which successfully ejected the Turks from the gap. Again, medical arrangements were totally inadequate, with wounded men lying in the open for up to six hours without being picked up. The 1/9th Gurkhas were

Gurkhas in pith helmets in Mesopotamia. (Gurkha Museum)

brought back up to strength by using the reinforcements destined for 2/7th Gurkhas shut up in Kut.

On 16 February 1916 the War Office in London took over the running of the campaign in Mesopotamia from the Government of India. British Empire forces had been ejected from Gallipoli and now were on the verge of losing Kut. It was not a good start to 1916. Major General Stanley Maude's British 13th Division, one of the last out of Gallipoli, was being sent as a reinforcement. General Sir Percy Lake had taken overall command from an ailing General Nixon. Lake did all he could to push an increasingly querulous Aylmer on to Kut, where supplies were fast running out and horses and mules were already being shot for food. The Turks had mounted one major attack on Kut which had been bloodily repulsed. They now contented themselves with long-distance shelling and sniping, with the object of starving it out.

★★★

Aylmer closed his force up to the main Turkish blocking position around the so-called Dujaila Redoubt, just seven miles short of Kut. His plan was to hold the Turks with an attacking force and then, while they were fully engaged, hook round their rear while Townshend sortied out from Kut to support him.

Aylmer's 23,000 men and 68 guns moving at night achieved complete surprise, finding the Turkish trenches and main position in the redoubt barely occupied when they arrived before dawn on 8 March. Had an immediate attack been mounted, as urged by the brigade commanders, it would have succeeded and Kut could have been relieved. As it was Aylmer insisted the whole attacking force wait until he had carried out an artillery bombardment. The artillery alerted the Turks who came pouring back into their trenches and defeated subsequent infantry attacks. The hooking movement was far too shallow and Townshend's sortie never took place. The 9th Gurkha history succinctly sums up the disaster:

Protests by the Brigade Commanders overruled and the attack delayed until 10am. Meanwhile strong enemy forces had occupied the trenches and the Redoubt. Throughout the day attacks were pressed with great gallantry but only heavy losses suffered without any appreciable advance. It had been a disastrous day and a costly one for the battalion with 31 killed and 107 wounded ... Thus ended a brilliantly planned move which achieved total surprise, but failed because the higher command gave in to their counsels of fear and delayed to allow artillery bombardment. This costly failure sealed the fate of the beleagured garrison at Kut.

Aylmer had no option but to withdraw his force which had lost 3,574 men. He was replaced by General Gorringe two days later. Time was running out, but Gorringe determined on one last try. Unfortunately, following Aylmer's defeat, the whole army had been obliged to fall back to the Hanna gap which the Turks had again occupied, so Gorringe had once more to remove them, before alternating advances on both sides of the Tigris to try and unbalance the enemy. The 1/1st and 1/9th Gurkhas were prominent in this very successful attack getting into the Turkish trenches with bomb and kukri until the Turks broke and started to pull back.

Despite this successful engagement the Turks, having delayed Gorringe, then took up their previous strong position at Dujaila Redoubt, from which the Tigris Corps was again repulsed with heavy loss. The weather now deteriorated into torrential rain and floods and, given the weather, heavy casualties and battle exhaustion, Gorringe's men could do no more. It was left to Royal Navy volunteers to make the final effort. Lieutenant Commander Charles Cowley RNVR in the paddle steamer *Julna*, carrying 270 tons of vital supplies, made a final desperate attempt to get through by river, but the Turks had erected a bar across the Tigris on which *Julna* foundered. Most of the crew were killed and Cowley captured and executed.

On 26 April the garrison started to destroy their guns and throw their ammunition into the river. Causing shock waves throughout the British Empire, on 29 April Townshend surrendered with 13,309 men, of whom 10,000 or so were combatants. Some wounded were exchanged but the rest, forcibly separated from their officers, had to march to Baghdad and then on by cattle truck to Anatolia where over 4,250 died in the appalling conditions of Turkish prison camps. Many young Gurkhas never returned to the little crofts and hamlets of Eastern Nepal although, generally by sticking firmly to a disciplined hierarchical system under three outstanding NCOs, 2/7th Gurkhas survived better than most. Townshend himself was treated most courteously and travelled to Constantinople in comfort with von der Goltz's body, the latter dying ten days before the moment of his victory.

Within four months of Kut's capitulation General Maude left command of 13th Division, headed the Tigris Corps and then took overall command of the army in Mesopotamia. Although orders from London did not authorize aggressive action, once he had sorted out the chaotic administration, 'Systematic Joe' Maude had no intention of sitting on the defensive with 150,000 men and started to push back towards Kut.

Maude now had under command I Indian Corps, III British Corps and a cavalry division. In his army there were six Gurkha regiments, indeed no fewer than 15 battalions served in Mesopotamia and Palestine, making this the largest Gurkha deployment in 1914–18. We will however concentrate on 1/2nd and 2/9th Gurkhas, which by this stage had relieved their sister battalions which had fought so gallantly in France and, in 1/9th Gurkhas' case, in Mesopotamia as well.

That under General Maude things had changed administratively much for the better is well reflected in the following excerpt from the 9th Gurkhas' regimental history reflecting the arrival of their 2nd Battalion in theatre:

> *The conditions had undergone a radical change at Basra and logistics improved to adequately handle six divisions fighting a major overseas campaign … construction of roads and railway lines had revitalized communications, shore depots, hospitals and rest camps had been established.*

General Maude's plan of attack had to take into account that the Turks were strongly entrenched on both sides of the Tigris and that their positions were sited in considerable depth in front of and around Kut. He intended first of all to attack the Turks on the west bank and then having pushed them back to switch his main strength over to the east of the Tigris where the Turks were most strongly entrenched.

His campaign, bitterly fought, ran from December 1916 to February 1917 before the major breakthrough came. After heavy fighting, his troops managed to clear the west bank far enough to mount a very daring, mainly Gurkha, operation. The operation was planned to cross the Tigris at its Shumran bend and then attack into the rear of the main Turkish position on the eastern bank. This position formed on a series of well-fortified redoubts had hitherto defied all attacks to break into it.

Three crossing places were selected and each given as an infantry battalion task as follows:

No. 1 Crossing (west) – 2nd Battalion The Norfolk Regiment
No. 2 Crossing (middle) – 2nd Battalion 9th Gurkhas
No. 3 Crossing (east) – 1st Battalion 2nd Goorkhas

The Norfolks would row themselves whereas the two Gurkha battalions would be rowed by 1st/4th Hampshire Regiment, a Territorial battalion, many of whom were in civilian life wherrymen and lightermen from Southampton docks. In addition, there were some Sappers and Miners. Unfortunately the Tigris was in flood and flowing very fast.

The 2/9th Gurkhas' first wave of 13 boats under Major George Wheeler crossed at 5.30am on 23 February 1917 and were immediately engaged by a fierce fire from the enemy bank, as a result of which only ten of the boats reached their destination. As soon as they had landed, Major Wheeler led a rush on the Turkish positions and after fierce hand-to-hand fighting with bayonet, kukri and bomb, secured a tenuous foothold on the enemy bank.

The 1/2nd Gurkhas were if anything more exposed to enemy fire than 2/9th Gurkhas and suffered heavy casualties crossing, boatloads of dead and wounded helplessly drifting downstream. However, Lieutenant C. G. Toogood and 56 men made it to the enemy bank much helped by his setting up a lantern to guide in successive boats. After desperate fighting they, too, managed to establish a precarious foothold.

At 9.30 am the order came to switch to the Norfolks' crossing point which was not so exposed, so the remainder of 1/2nd and 2/9th Gurkhas crossed there and, fighting step by step, linked up with their beleaguered comrades and together enlarged the lodgement in spite of increasingly desperate Turkish attempts to drive them into the river. By late afternoon a boat bridge was completed across the Tigris over which streamed two brigades and together the whole force, which now included 2/4th Gurkhas, attacked into the rear of the main Turkish defence position. The Turks, assailed in front and in their rear, started to withdraw towards Baghdad, abandoning Kut but desperately trying to keep their line of withdrawal clear. Maude was equally determined to prevent this and, using the pontoon bridge, deployed cavalry and infantry to cut the Turks off from withdrawing successfully. The 1/5th Buffs and 2/4th Gurkhas were involved in desperate fighting as the written record of Sergeant Farnol of 1/5th Buffs makes clear:

The Gurkha at my left elbow was shot stone dead the bullet having caught him straight between the eyes. As he dropped the Gurkha on my right turned round as though he intended seeing to his dead

The crossing of the Tigris painted by Lionel Edwards, showing 1/2nd Gurkhas seizing a landing place and setting up a lantern to guide in the boats behind. (Gurkha Museum)

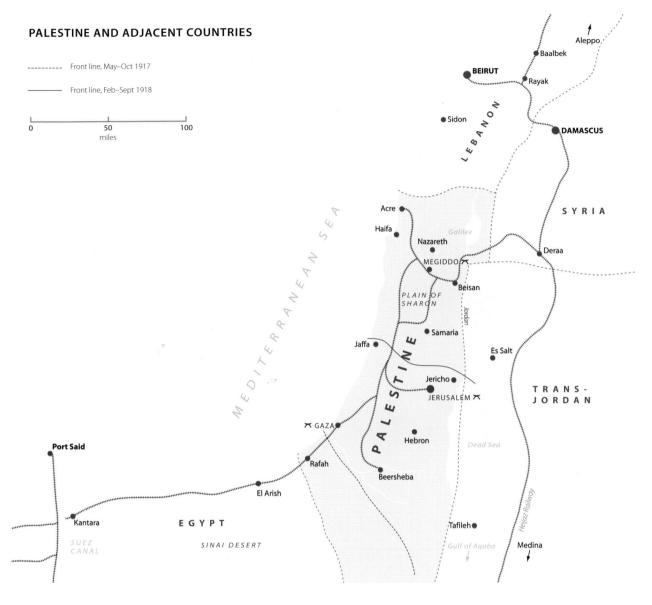

PALESTINE AND ADJACENT COUNTRIES

---------- Front line, May–Oct 1917

————— Front line, Feb–Sept 1918

0   50   100
        miles

comrade but dropped as he turned. We examined him and found he had 'stopped' a dum dum bullet [tip cut to cause severer wound] in his side which had inflicted a dreadful wound. We bandaged him up as best we could. He was still alive when we went forward that evening and actually singing a little Nepalese song.

Despite all efforts to cut them off, the Turks managed to withdraw towards Baghdad more or less intact. Nevertheless it had been a brilliant victory and not only avenged the siege of Kut but, although not realized at the time, spelled the beginning of the end for Turkish resistance in Mesopotamia. General Maude was the first to recognize the key importance of the daring and successful river crossing when he wrote:

By nightfall, as a result of this day's operations, our troops by unconquerable valour and determination forced a passage across a river 340 yards wide in face of heavy opposition and had secured a position 1,000 yards in depth covering our bridgehead.

The cost in 1/2nd and 2/9th Gurkhas had been high; 98 killed (80 in 1/2 Gurkhas) and 132 wounded, and of course many others in 2/4th Gurkhas.

***

In the McDonald Gallery of the Gurkha Museum in Winchester there is a splendid picture by the celebrated artist Lionel Edwards showing the crossing of the Tigris by 1/2nd Gurkhas. In the main

Men of the 3/3rd Gurkhas manning a Lewis gun in Palestine 1917. (Gurkha Museum)

gallery of the museum there is an exciting diorama showing Major Wheeler and his D Company of 2/9th Gurkhas attacking the Turkish bank positions, an action for which he subsequently received the Victoria Cross.

The Turks stood again about 14 miles south of Baghdad in a strong natural defensive position where the river Diyala joins the Tigris. Once Maude's troops were across the Diyala the Turks in danger of being outflanked withdrew and, despite the urging of the Germans, abandoned Baghdad, which Maude's army entered on 11 March 1917. The 2/4th Gurkhas was among the first units into the city, where the first task was to restore order, which had broken down with the departure of the Turks.

It is at Baghdad that the rivers Tigris and Euphrates come very close, and on the Euphrates axis the Turks were still strongly entrenched, while on the Tigris route the railway running along the river up north to Samarra enabled them to deploy troops quickly. On the Tigris route, a link-up was achieved with the Russians who were advancing through Persia from the Caspian. The Turks confronting the Russians were supposed to be a beaten force, but this turned out to be far from correct, and it was the Russians who, thrown into chaos by their two 1917 Revolutions, eventually stopped fighting.

There was some debate as to whether to push on north out of Baghdad or stay put, but the requirement to keep up the pressure to help the Russians prevailed, and General Maude pushed his forces up both rivers. Now some of the fiercest fighting took place

for the railway stations of Istabulat and Samarra, another five miles up the track, which the Turks were determined to hold. The 1/8th Gurkhas were prominent in the battle for Istabulat, which changed hands repeatedly until the Turks withdrew to Samarra, where the whole process had to be gone through again.

The next battle centred on the River Adhaim and the village of the same name. The Turks intended Adhaim as a junction between their Corps on the Tigris and the Corps slowly withdrawing before Russian pressure from Persia. The Adhaim, a major tributary of the Tigris, formed a natural barrier on its eastern bank. The 1/2nd, 2/4th and 2/9th Gurkhas were all involved in this bitter battle (30 April 1917), the last before hostilities stopped by mutual consent with the onset of hot weather. The first phase, capturing Adhaim village, went comparatively easily, but just as 2/9th Gurkhas were about to attack a key feature called the 'boot', a sandstorm blew up and under its cover the whole of the crack Turkish 2nd 'Anatolian' Division fiercely counter-attacked, pushing all before it, recapturing seven guns, releasing 400 Turkish prisoners and taking British ones. The 1/9th and 2/4th Gurkhas were hurled into bloody but unsuccessful counter-attacks, while 1/2nd Gurkhas desperately sought to cross the huge Adhaim river to try and outflank the Turks. The night was spent trying to locate dead and wounded, and digging in with the expectation of another Turkish attack next morning. When dawn came the exhausted soldiers saw with huge relief that the Turks had gone and were heading for the far Jebel Hamrin hills.

For the many Gurkha battalions deployed, the long hot summer meant reorganization and endless guard and fatigue duties on the by now very long lines of communication running back to Basra. These were particularly vulnerable to marauding Arabs. The 2nd Gurkha regimental history recounts just how quickly the Gurkhas learned the art of railway construction! Much reorganization took place which included the raising of an additional Gurkha regiment, the 11th of four battalions. Much officer cross-posting had to take place. Lieutenant Colonel Frank Coningham famously commanded 2/9th Gurkhas at the Tigris crossing battle, 1/8th Gurkhas at the hard-fought Istabulat railway station battle and 1/10th Gurkhas at the Battle of Sharqat, of which more later.

In June 1917 General Sir Edmund Allenby took over command of all British troops in Egypt and started to plan the invasion of Palestine, in conjunction with the efforts of officers such as the then Captain T. E. Lawrence (Lawrence of Arabia) supporting the year-old Arab Revolt on the Turks' desert flank. Allenby was a cavalry general and was to use his cavalry to great effect in Palestine. In theory cavalry should have been able to take advantage of the open flanks of warfare in Mesopotamia, but the arid and waterless nature of the land mitigated against this, as did General Maude's inability to understand the use and limitations of cavalry. Being at daggers drawn with his cavalry division commander did not help either!

In September the heat had sufficiently moderated for General Maude to order the renewed advance up both the Tigris and Euphrates rivers. On the Euphrates, 42nd Brigade, consisting of 1st/4th Dorsets, 1/5th Gurkhas, 2/5th Gurkhas and 2/6th Gurkhas, were to see some very hard fighting at the Battle of Ramadi where the 4,100 Turks had a strong defensive position that had withstood a previous attempt to subdue it by a force which had included the re-raised 2/7th Gurkhas. This time the plan was for 42nd Brigade to hotly engage the Turks frontally while 12th Brigade attacked their right flank and the cavalry hooked round their left flank and cut off their retreat up river. The enemy position hinged on the Euphrates and made use of large humps in the ground or knolls, as well as man-made obstacles such as a canal, villages and walled gardens. The first phase carried out by night by the mainly Gurkha 42nd Brigade involved some hard fighting but succeeded in getting round the Turks' flanks and engaging their centre.

Daylight brought a swift response by the Turks who counter-attacked, repeatedly bringing up reserves. At this stage 12th Brigade attacked on their right acting as the hammer on 42nd Brigade's anvil. Despite vigorous attempts to break out, the Turks were trapped, efforts to escape being cut off by the cavalry. In spite of some confusion among the two brigades as to central planning, the Turks had been totally outmanoeuvred: soon white flags appeared and they surrendered on 29 September. Later, their commander admitted that he had been totally convinced that the main attack was that of 42nd Brigade, so when 12th Brigade attacked his right flank he was left with insufficient forces to repel them. The three Gurkha battalions had played a key part in this major two-day battle.

For 12th and 42nd Brigades there was to be a period of consolidation after Ramadi where all three Gurkha battalions had sustained many casualties although, thankfully, comparatively few actual fatalities.

That autumn two major events occurred, one individual and one national. On 18 November 1917 General Maude died of cholera in Baghdad. The circumstances were somewhat suspicious. Invited to an Arab Shakespearean production he was served coffee in the interval and the milk was said to have contained cholera

Rifleman Karanbahadur Rana VC 2/3rd Gurkhas.

bacilli. His death was a great blow as he had transformed the administrative support of the army from deplorable to exemplary and shown himself a capable and determined commander with strategic and tactical flair. His death was mourned throughout his army, which admired and respected him.

The other major and this time national occurrence was the Bolshevik October Revolution in Russia, the declared aim of which was peace with Germany at any price. As a result, almost overnight, the majority of Russian forces engaged stopped fighting the Germans and Turks and prepared to fight each other in a civil war. In March 1918 the Russians signed the humiliating Treaty of Brest-Litovsk, which ceded huge swathes of Russia to Germany, thus releasing most of the German army on the Eastern Front for a deadly last-throw offensive on the Western Front. Turkey, relieved of the Russian attacks in Armenia and Persia, was encouraged to stiffen her resistance.

Nevertheless, in the spring of 1918 British forces continued to press up the Euphrates, passing through several well-prepared Turkish entrenchments, in the event not contested, until they arrived at Khan Baghdadi, where they encountered a strong Turkish position. The battle-hardened 42nd Brigade, still the 1st/4th Dorsets, 2/5th Gurkhas, 2/6th Gurkhas with 1/5th Gurkhas in reserve, attacked with their normal élan supported by a very heavy artillery barrage. The Turkish resistance collapsed on 27 March. Over 5,200 surrendered including two Turkish generals, two senior German advisers and numerous German soldiers. It became apparent that the Turks were becoming thoroughly fed up with the war and it was only unrelenting German pressure that kept them in it.

However the Russian collapse, as with the defeat of the Allies at Gallipoli, released large numbers of Turks to fight for their tottering empire, so General Allenby in Palestine and Lieutenant General Sir William Marshall (Maude's designated successor) in Mesopotamia were confronted with a considerable task as British units were stripped from other theatres of war to try to stem the German 'Ludendorff' offensives (so called after General Ludendorff, their architect) in France.

General Allenby, who had started his campaign in Palestine (then the area which now comprises Israel, Palestine, the Lebanon and large bits of Jordan and Syria) with mainly British and ANZAC troops, became very reliant on Indian Army units, including five Gurkha battalions which had been brought from fighting north of Baghdad. In Palestine the Turks had built the Hejaz Railway from Damascus to Medina, which allowed them to transport troops and supplies down the length of the country.

By promising them large chunks of the Turkish Empire, including Palestine, Lawrence was able to persuade Prince Feisal and his Bedouin to fight for the British. They did this by

continually cutting and sabotaging the railway, severely disrupting the Turks. Allenby meanwhile advanced north up Palestine during late 1917 and after very hard fighting at Gaza captured Jerusalem by Christmas. His tactics were to pin the main Turkish forces frontally whilst he swung his cavalry round their open flank and got in behind them. Central and northern Palestine were much better watered than Mesopotamia so the cavalry were able to act more effectively and flexibly without being continually hampered by lack of water. Also, in Allenby they had a cavalry general who knew how to use them. There was, however, some very hard fighting for the infantry, especially as they pushed further north towards the Plain of Sharon. Here Rifleman Karanbahadur Rana of 2/3rd Gurkhas, a Lewis machine gunner, was awarded the Victoria Cross for advancing on 10 April 1918 through very heavy enemy fire to silence a German machine-gun position that was inflicting heavy casualties and holding up the advance. Despite his group's commander being killed, Karanbahadur took over the machine gun and, notwithstanding intense enemy fire, including grenades, eliminated the German machine-gun crew and covered the subsequent withdrawal.

1914–15 Star.

Even in the face of the withdrawal of many of his formations to France, Allenby's autumn 1918 campaign was brilliantly conducted, much of it relying on the ability of the infantry to keep marching fast enough to exploit the successful attacks of the cavalry and Lawrence's Arabs (with whom 30 Gurkha volunteers served, mastering the art of riding camels).

In these tactics Allenby's six Gurkha battalions (1/1st, 2/3rd, 3/3rd, 2/7th, 1/8th and 4/11th Gurkhas) never failed, especially at the Battles of Megiddo, where for a time the infantry fought and marched far from their support and supplies to ensure the Turks could not reform. After the victories of Megiddo the Turks began to break and, before the war finally ended, Allenby was at Aleppo on the border of Turkey proper.

Just as Megiddo had spelt the end for the Turks in Palestine, so the Battle of Sharqat (28–30 October 1918) on the Tigris on the way to Mosul spelt the end for the Turks in Mesopotamia. The 1/7th Gurkhas managed to keep up with the cavalry flanking movement, marching 36 miles in 26 hours, while 1/10th Gurkhas, fighting in the main body, overcame frantic Turkish resistance to push the Turks back. Cut off from their line of retreat, they surrendered at the cost of 11,320 men and 51 guns.

When, that same day, Turkey signed an armistice, she had lost almost all her Empire. Relieving her of it had cost the British Empire over 264,000 casualties, among them many Gurkhas, who were not even subjects of the British Empire. Nevertheless they had fought with an uncomplaining cheerful courage through thick and thin to the admiration of friend and foe alike. Even the end of the war with Germany did not spell an end to the fighting for three Gurkha battalions: 1/2nd, 1/4th and 2/6th Gurkhas were all involved on the Black Sea and the Caspian trying to aid General Anton Denikin's White Russian army in their bloody civil war with the Bolsheviks. The 1/2nd Gurkhas did not return from North Persia to their depot in Dehra Dun in India until June 1921!

Thus ended Gurkha involvement in the Great War that had taken them so far from their mountain homes to fight for a country most had never seen, an Empire of which they were not a part and for a cause few of them began to understand. Theirs was an amazing achievement which they would begin to repeat just 21 years later.

1914–20 War Medal.

1914–19 Victory Medal.

CHAPTER SEVEN

PEACE OF A SORT

As we have seen, Armistice Day on the 11th day of November 1918 at the eleventh hour did not mean peace for everybody. Gurkha battalions were to remain in the Caucasus and Salonika, in some cases for nearly three years after the Armistice was signed, in conditions of great uncertainty and confusion. Reds and Whites were locked in increasingly bitter civil war in Russia as with grim brutality the Bolsheviks strove to protect their revolution: in July 1918 they murdered the Tsar and his family together with all members of the aristocracy who did not get out fast enough.

In defeated Germany, the harsh terms of the Versailles Treaty fuelled hatred and resentment and opened the door for Hitler and his Nazis. In France, political chaos, coupled with a determination to extract every last mark from a prostrate Germany, simply sowed the seeds for future conflict. Only in Britain did a semblance of pre-war normality return, but in reality things could never be the same again, as the General Strike of 1926 dramatically demonstrated. Throughout Britain's far-flung Empire (and Commonwealth from 1931) times were changing as well, and nowhere more so than India. Soldiers of the Indian Army had served with supreme loyalty in France, Flanders, the Dardanelles, Egypt, Palestine, Aden, Mesopotamia, Persia, North-West Frontier and Russia. Even so, they had sensed the growing feelings for national independence in places where they had served and on returning to India had seen

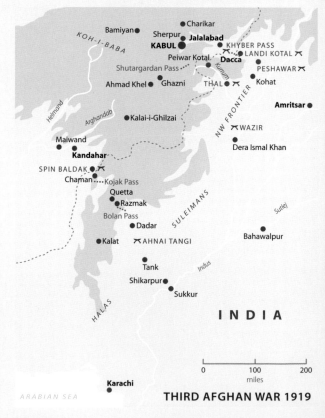

THIRD AFGHAN WAR 1919

Gurkha machine gunners, North-West Frontier. (Gurkha Museum)

those feelings embodied by the political preaching of Mahatma Gandhi. Britain's reactions to increasing demands for self-determination were slow and uncertain: indeed in some cases they were even retrogressive, desperately attempting to return to the *status quo ante*.

In India, during March and April 1919, nationalist-inspired rioting became widespread, especially in the Punjab. One of the main causes was the provisions of the so-called Rowlatt Acts, named after the judge who recommended their adoption. The acts were originally intended as a response to anarchists and terrorists and, in certain circumstances, provided for internment without trial and trial without jury. Indian nationalists managed to stir up considerable outrage about these acts by suggesting that they included a medical examination of couples before marriage, the prohibition of religious processions and even the forcible confiscation of plough oxen. Government installations, including railway stations, were attacked. The situation in Amritsar became particularly threatening, with Europeans being assaulted and killed and banks and government buildings being torched. Amritsar had a population of about 160,000 and was the principal city of the mainly Sikh Punjab. Its Golden Temple was and is the Sikhs' holiest shrine and, since this was the Baisakhi religious festival, the

indigenous population was swollen by many thousands of pilgrims and visitors.

Brigadier General Reginald Dyer, who was in temporary command of the nearby 16th Division, was called upon by the provincial governor to restore order and given wide powers to open fire on civilian mobs if their behaviour in his judgement so merited it.

Arriving in the city, and assessing the situation as threatening, Dyer augmented the forces at his disposal by taking 260 men of the 9th Gurkhas off a passing train halted by the disturbances. These troops had been moving from their depot in the hills of Dehra Dun to their 1st Battalion at Peshawar. The Gurkhas included one or two British officers and a number of instructors and newly trained recruits at the end of their training. Since, apart from their kukris, they had no weapons, Dyer armed 100 of them with rifles from the Amritsar armoury . Clearly the rifles were *unzeroed* (not test-fired for accuracy), but in the event they were to open fire at such close range that they could not miss. Learning that a crowd of some 5,000–6,000 had gathered at an open space surrounded by walls and buildings called the Jallianwala Bagh on 13 April, in defiance of a prohibition on public meetings, Dyer personally led a force of 25 men of 9th Gurkhas and 25 men from the 54th

Sikhs and 59th Scinde Rifles (Pathans) into the Bagh and opened fire. Since the Bagh was surrounded by walls and buildings with only a few narrow exits the crowd could not escape. An estimated 379 were killed, including women and children, and probably about 1,200 wounded.

Dyer's action stopped the threatening insurrection but sent shock waves through India and the British Empire. He was alternatively hailed as a saviour or a beast. As for the 9th Gurkhas involved, they had no particular affinity for Indians, or desi as they somewhat dismissively referred to them. They were simply doing as ordered; probably the Pathans from the Scinde Rifles had a similar attitude. Perhaps that was why Dyer included these two units, one from Nepal and one from the North-West Frontier tribes.

***

In terms of the numbers killed that fateful day, they pale into insignificance when compared to the bloodbath that accompanied Partition in 1947. Nevertheless they were inflicted by the British on unarmed civilians and as such had far-reaching repercussions on how the British were regarded in India and how they regarded themselves in Britain. These wider issues aside, this episode does serve to illustrate the unique position of the Gurkha Brigade. Because Nepal was virtually a closed country, British officers did not know the Gurkha homeland and Gurkhas did not know Britain. They just knew each other and what they knew they, with few exceptions, liked and admired. India was not their country and so unlike the rest of the Indian Army they did not identify with it to the same extent. They were a separate entity among themselves, a band of brothers, the Gurkha Brigade *contra mundum* ('against the world') and this attitude was to provide a constant thread through their history.

While Britain was agonizing about what had happened at the Jallianwala Bagh, others were watching and drawing conclusions. One such observer was Amir Amanullah Khan, the new ruler of Afghanistan. His murdered father, Amir Habibullah, had favoured a peaceful policy during the First World War, refusing to be coerced by Germans, Turks or elements in Afghanistan who wanted him to attack British India while its army was deployed elsewhere. Amanullah, who had skilfully manoeuvred his two elder brothers out of the succession, saw the Gandhi-inspired nationalist uprising in India and interpreted the Amritsar Massacre, as it became known, as a final act of desperation by a decadent Britain. He was unhappy that Britain still thought it could influence his country's foreign policy and restrict with whom he could or could not have foreign relations. The whole world appeared to be changing and only the British seemed reluctant to change with it. The Amir decided to act. On 3 May 1919 a body of Afghan regular troops crossed the Afghan–Indian border near the Khyber Pass and occupied the Indian village of Bagh and cut its water supply from a nearby natural spring, as well as occupying the pumping station which supplied water to the small garrison of Landi Kotal. A number of Indian workers in the pumping station were killed.

This outbreak of hostilities could not have caught the Indian Army at a worse time. Although India was full of soldiers, they were mostly at the depots awaiting demobilization or actually in their villages on leave. Many British troops, mostly Territorials, were on the point of returning to Britain and of what ready troops there were most were deployed on internal security roles. Nevertheless, with Afghanistan invading and all the imponderables of a national uprising in India, as well as a probable attack in unison by the Frontier tribes, something needed to be done and quickly. Indignant Territorials were hauled off ships and re-embodied for service, leave men were recalled and demobilization halted. Arsenals and warehouses were opened and out poured the accumulated weaponry and machinery of the recent war. Lewis machine guns, trench mortars, hand grenades, wireless sets, lorries, armoured cars, aircraft. Soon the assembling fighting men were equipped and mobile as never before.

Immediately a convoy of 57 lorries carrying a battalion of British infantry and a mountain battery of artillery set off to relieve the little garrison of Landi Kotal. At the same time the Afghan Army was preparing to invade India through the traditional invasion routes of the Khyber and Kurram passes, with a third prong through the Bolan Pass against the mountain town of Quetta in Baluchistan. Concurrently, the Amir's agents were stirring up trouble in the border towns, most notably Peshawar, where 7,000 Pathans were armed and ready for murder, destruction, loot and rapine. Fortunately, the British also had their agents, and while the murderous Pathans were taking a restoring afternoon siesta, prior to an evening's mayhem, British forces silently converged on the city, efficiently blocked all entrances and arrested some of the ringleaders. They then threatened that, unless the remaining ringleaders were given up, the water supply would be cut off. After Amritsar nobody was going to try and call the British bluff.

At Landi Kotal the British attacked the besieging Afghan forces, one of the assaulting units being 2/1st Gurkhas, but too many troops had been detached in flank protection and the assault failed to shift the Afghans. More troops arrived, including 1st and 2nd Battalions of 11th Gurkhas, and in a well-coordinated attack, in which 2/11th Gurkhas smashed through the Afghan centre and captured their artillery and 1/11th Gurkhas retook Bagh village, the Afghans were defeated and driven off. At Dacca on the border, the Afghan army was caught by Royal Air Force planes distributing thousands of rifles and supplies to Pathan tribesmen to use against the British. The Afghan army men ran for cover and on emerging found the Pathans had taken all the weapons and supplies but were nowhere to be seen!

Following up this incident a British infantry brigade crossed the border from Dacca and set up pickets on the Khyber Pass. Unfortunately the brigade base camp from which the pickets were mounted was poorly sited, being within range and overlooked by the surrounding hills. This vulnerability was quickly seized upon by the Afghans. A cavalry charge in the nick of time extracted the artillery back into the perimeter which was then attacked by the Afghans. Because it was badly sited there were heavy casualties, not only to men but to mules and horses, as the Afghans continued to shell and snipe throughout the night. Next morning two infantry battalions, one of which was 1/9th Gurkhas, attacked the nearest overlooking hills. The Afghans waited until the attackers were almost at the crest before opening a devastating fire, one battalion recoiled and sought cover retreating through 1/9th Gurkhas who held on and renewed the attack, getting to within 25 yards of the crest of the hill before heavy fire pinned them down. They had by now suffered many casualties and were without supporting artillery fire as the guns had run out of ammunition. As a result they could not advance further. Further ammunition arriving as well as reinforcements, including 2/1st Gurkhas, the advance was resumed and the Afghans driven off.

Despite these setbacks Amir Amanullah persisted with his plans to invade India. Having incited the Pathans of the frontier to rebellion, they had succeeded in tying down the best part of a British division on the Khyber. Soon Afghan forces in the central area had obliged the British to give up most of Waziristan, where local tribal levies had turned against their officers and in some

India General Service Medal 1908–35.

cases shot them. Superior Afghan forces had bottled up a small garrison of four battalions, including the 3/9th Gurkhas at a place called Thal from where a light railway ran to the important city of Peshawar. By a bold march through apparently impassable hills, the Afghans managed to assemble considerable artillery on the heights above Thal and proceeded to bombard it with great intensity. This bombardment set fire to trucks and rolling stock and induced the men of the armed Frontier Constabulary to bolt, allowing the Afghans to capture the garrison's water supply which the Constabulary were supposed to be guarding. The situation for the garrison looked dire. Shrapnel or bullets shredded the lanyard holding up the Union Flag which fluttered to the ground. A young 3/9th Gurkha rifleman, heedless of shells and bullets, grabbed a hammer, shinned up the flag post and fixed the Union Flag back!

The General Officer Commanding then turned to Brigadier General Dyer, so recently and controversially involved at Amritsar, and implored him to relieve Thal before it fell. Dyer with great energy and dispatch commandeered every truck he could lay his hands on and personally leading a brigade set off for Thal,

A contemporary drawing of the battle of Spin Baldak. (ILN Picture Library)

gathering up stray units and guns and adding them to his force as he went. He towed the guns behind his trucks and carried their crews and ammunition inside. Those trucks that were not towing guns towed tree trunks to look like guns or branches which threw up dust and gave the impression of a far larger force.

Arriving some miles short of Thal, Dyer personally led his force up towards the junction of two wings of the Afghan forces. Appearing to threaten one, he turned his whole force on the other and routed it. Having relieved Thal early next morning, he set off with four battalions including the 3/9th Gurkhas only to meet an emissary from the Afghans telling him an Armistice had been declared. Telling the emissary that his guns would give an immediate answer while his Commander-in-Chief would give a more considered one, Dyer prepared to attack! The reference to guns was well made because, as Dyer's force of real and simulated guns deployed, the Afghan commander was heard to complain that every gun in India was arrayed against him. The 3/9th Gurkhas was the left assault battalion which moved in close under the covering artillery bombardment, only to find the Afghan army, 19,000 strong, had fled. Without doubt Dyer's prompt and determined action had saved Thal, but there was no hero's welcome on return. Instead, he faced the Hunter Inquiry into the Jallianwala Bagh shootings. To the astonishment of some and the satisfaction of others, he was found culpable and was obliged to retire from the Army.

Further south the British attacked the strong Afghan fortress of Spin Baldak, using six infantry battalions, including two Gurkha ones. The attack got off to a shaky start when Royal Air Force bombers bombed one of the Indian battalions (22nd Punjabis) in error causing casualties. Then a British Territorial battalion, not keen to seek a foreign grave so near repatriation, went to ground on coming under fire. The 1st Battalion The Duke of Wellington's Regiment went to its assistance and got the unit moving again as the artillery poured shellfire into the fort. Nearing the fort, the assault party erected scaling ladders which were found to be too short! However, the Gurkhas managed to scramble up the walls somehow and stormed the fort. Fighting went on inside for some time until the remnant of the garrison fled, escaping between two groups of cavalry each believing the other to be responsible for blocking them.

Amir Amanullah, realizing that the British were determined to resist invasion and that the Indian population were not going to rise up spontaneously, decided to negotiate peace before British heavy bombers flattened Kabul and other major Afghan conurbations. Negotiations dragged on endlessly but the war stopped. As we have seen from recent deployments against the Taliban, it was not the last time British and Gurkha troops were to fight in that inhospitable terrain, but it was the final war against Afghanistan for the old British-Indian Army.

Although the Amir had been unsuccessful in getting the Indian population to rise up against the British in sympathy with his

Detail from a montage by David Rowlands showing 2/2nd Gurkhas on the North West Frontier.

their Commanding Officer had personally led a bayonet charge in which he was killed at the head of his men. An Indian battalion, 76th Punjabis, was sent up to help 2/5th Gurkhas whose position was made critical by lack of ammunition. The 76th Punjabis themselves suffering heavy casualties were able to do little to help. When all seemed lost, a company of 2/9th Gurkhas fought their way through to their beleaguered countrymen, two further companies arriving later. The Mahsuds mounted four further major attacks which were beaten off only after hand-to-hand fighting with bombs, bayonets and kukris. As the force pushed into the Mahsud homeland, resistance became more and more desperate and both 4/3rd Gurkhas and 3/11th Gurkhas saw some hard fighting, the latter sustaining heavy casualties. The decision was made to occupy Waziristan and to this end roads and forts were built.

Although the Pathan tribes were to continue to give trouble it was never quite on the same scale and with a measure of relief the British-Indian Government started the long delayed demobilization. Most Gurkha regiments had raised at least one extra wartime battalion, one had raised two, these were now disbanded some of their men taking service with the two regular battalions of each regiment while others were discharged to Nepal. All four battalions of the wartime 11th Gurkha Rifles were disbanded and the men returned to their parent battalions. The

invasion, he had been successful in precipitating a major uprising of the Pathan frontier tribes in Waziristan, especially among the warlike Mahsuds. By the end of 1919 so bad had the situation become that a striking force of two brigades was dispatched to subdue the Mahsuds and restore government authority. This striking force included four Gurkha battalions (4/3rd, 2/5th, 2/9th and 3/11th). The first essential of the campaign was to clear the vital Ahnai Tangi Pass which would allow the striking force to get into the Mahsud heartland. Three unsuccessful attempts were made until a night attack in pouring rain dislodged the tribesmen. Because of an administrative failure, overcoats and blankets failed to reach the exhausted and sodden troops before nightfall; and many succumbed to pneumonia on the freezing mountainside.

The striking force was now confronted by three heavily defended Mahsud positions, all mutually supporting. The 2/5th Gurkhas, reaching the left-hand position of the enemy, were attacked in overwhelming numbers, but managed to hang on after

Mahsud and Waziri tribesmen with a variety of weapons. (Gurkha Museum)

A Gurkha battalion leading, probably, a brigade-size frontier reinforcement or relief column. (Gurkha Museum)

11th Gurkhas was not re-raised until after Indian Independence in 1947.

Far away in defeated Germany in September 1919 an ex-Imperial German Army Corporal with the Iron Cross First Class, one Adolf Hitler, helped found the National Socialist German Workers' Party or Nazi Party as it came to be known.

Back in the subcontinent, at long last soldiers could go back to their regimental homes and their families and enjoy again a relatively peaceful and orderly existence between spells on the North-West Frontier that were, as always, dangerous and physically demanding. British officers could once again enjoy their polo and pig sticking and the Gurkhas their football and *khud* (steep hillside) racing, a sport in which the Gurkhas with their mountaineers' physique excelled. To see them run like mountain goats up almost sheer slopes and come down again, leaping from rock to rock, is an awe-inspiring sight. Their strong thigh muscles spring them seemingly effortlessly from crag to rock and back again.

As a result of deficiencies revealed by the widespread overseas deployment of the Indian Army in the recent war, General Lord Rawlinson headed a committee to improve administrative and medical support as well as collective training for the Army. It was, therefore, planned for each Gurkha regiment to set up its own training wing at its regimental depot. Up until that time Gurkha battalions had trained their own recruits. The Indian Government, having limited its peacetime establishment to 20 Gurkha battalions, was unwilling to lose any by setting up battalions specifically for training and this measure took a very long time to implement. Another innovation was for each battalion to concentrate its specialists, such as machine gunners, mortar men, wireless operators, drivers, cooks, in a new company known as Headquarters Wing which was to be commanded by the battalion second in command.

In 1921, 5th Gurkha Rifles was accorded the extra title 'Royal' in recognition of its services in the First World War, thus becoming 5th Royal Gurkha Rifles (Frontier Force). That year the monthly pay of a Gurkha rifleman was finally increased from 11 to 16 rupees.

Meanwhile, the discharged soldiers came home to Nepal, its countryside so long deserted by its young men and its fields tilled and tended by old men, women and boys. Some had lost limbs, many bore scars, lasting evidence of all they had endured. They climbed up the steep rocky paths to their remote mountain villages and returned to their simple, harsh, but peaceful lives. In the warmth of the evening sunlight looking out over the everlasting snows they sipped their *rakshi* (home-brewed spirit) and held respectful audiences spellbound with tales of the greatest war yet known to man, and all they had endured since they set out to answer the call of the British *sarkar* (British Raj). Little did the young men listening in rapt silence realize that their own turn was coming very soon.

In 1929 the great ruler of Nepal, the wise and astute Chandra Shamsher Rana died. A staunch friend of Britain, he had been loaded with honours in thanks for all his small but warlike nation had done to aid Britain in her hour of need. His brother, Commander-in-Chief of Nepal's army, Bhim Shamsher succeeded, but lived only two years before dying himself. He was succeeded by Judha Shamsher, the youngest brother, who was to be the last ruler of the Rana dynasty to exercise absolute power. After him his successors were obliged to concede much to nationalist pressure groups. Temperamental and emotional, Judha Shamsher was to face tremendous pressures that in the end neither he nor his successors could control. The wind of change was blowing through the Indian subcontinent and, try as he might, he could not insulate Nepal against it. He was however to remain a true friend of Britain throughout the next world war. During the Rana dynasty the Kings of Nepal had been kept virtually powerless, although among the population of Nepal they were regarded as semi-divine as a sort of living embodiment of Vishnu. This gave the then king, Tribhuvana, considerable spiritual status which he was not slow to utilize when an opportunity occurred.

Gurkhas off duty wearing Regimental civilian clothes or mufti. (Gurkha Museum)

3rd Gurkhas on the Northwest Frontier. (Gurkha Museum)

A plot to blow up Judha Shamsher and all his family was hatched by India-based Nepalese revolutionaries and received at least tacit support from the king. It was uncovered in the nick of time, the revolutionaries hanged or jailed and the king exposed. Claiming ill-health he fled to India, where he became a natural focus for all who wanted to get rid of the Ranas.

In Quetta, now part of Pakistan and capital of the Baluchistan part of the North-West Frontier, a massive earthquake struck in 1935 almost demolishing the city. A battalion of 8th Gurkhas was garrisoning it and immediately set out to rescue thousands of inhabitants trapped under the wreckage. A young Gurkha with particularly sensitive hearing was able to locate and rescue many who would otherwise never have been found. He subsequently received the Empire Gallantry Medal, one of two awarded to 8th Gurkhas. An example of this rare medal is in the Gurkha Museum as well as the George Cross of the other 8th Gurkha who survived until 1940, when holders of the Empire Gallantry Medal were able to exchange their Empire Gallantry Medals for the newly instituted George Cross.

In Nepal, too, there was a huge earthquake which devastated many hill villages in remote areas of the east. Permission had been given earlier for a plane to fly over Mount Everest and the earthquake was ascribed to the displeasure of the gods at this happening. All permission for flights over Nepal was then unilaterally withdrawn.

Empire Gallantry Medal, which was superseded by the George Cross in 1940.

Meanwhile in India the occupation of Waziristan was proving to be an onerous task and the occupying forces became a natural target for repeated attacks by Pathans living in the area. The construction of roads and small forts occupied large numbers of troops so that the majority of the 20 Gurkha battalions were regularly involved in frontier fighting. This intensified in the spring of 1937 as, no doubt encouraged by the deteriorating situation in Europe, the Fakir of Ipi openly declared against the British. Under Hitler, a rearming and belligerent Germany had reoccupied the Rhineland the year before in direct contravention of the Versailles Treaty, without Britain or France raising a finger. Additionally under Mussolini, Italy, an ally in the First World War, had now gone over to Germany.

It was decided that the warlike moves of the Fakir of Ipi could only be countered by physically occupying the remote area of Damdil near Bannu. A brigade-sized formation was sent to do the job, consisting of three Gurkha battalions (2/5th, 1/6th and 2/6th Gurkhas). On the night of 20/21 March 1937, the Pathans of the Fakir made a massive effort to take out one of the pickets of 2/5th

Gurkhas. The post was manned by a *naik* (corporal) and seven men armed with rifles, and protected by a high stone parapet or *sangar*. The Pathans managed to isolate the post and from dusk to dawn staged furious attacks on it, all of which were repulsed by this incredibly brave little group of Gurkhas, two of whom were killed and the rest seriously wounded. When dawn came relieving troops found the six survivors still holding the picket surrounded by dead Afghans. The Gurkha Museum has a superb and lifelike representation of the battle of No. 11 picket at Damdil, as well as a comprehensive and exciting display of the three Afghan Wars and the North-West Frontier.

In Europe the situation continued to deteriorate. In March 1938, Hitler occupied Austria and in October much of Czechoslovakia; Spring 1939 saw Hitler occupy the remainder of Czechoslovakia as Britain and France did nothing. Next, Hitler secured his eastern flank by concluding the Nazi-Soviet non-aggression pact in August 1939, which would allow him to invade Poland without Soviet opposition. Incredulously, Britain found itself drifting towards war and very belatedly began to prepare.

4th Gurkha Rifles, picket action. By Major (later Brigadier General) A.C. Lovett, CB, CBE. (The National Army Museum)

Right: 6th Gurkha Rifles. By Major (later Brigadier General) A.C. Lovett, CB, CBE. (The National Army Museum)

The First Battalion in the Malakand and the Second Battalion in Abbotabad carried on much as before. Officers wore mess dress or evening dress, the bands played 'Retreat' and sweet music for club dances, swords and medals were worn. Officers on leave in England came hurrying back. The year slipped quietly to its close and it was hard to realize that the whole world was engaged in the first phase of the catastrophic struggle which all but destroyed civilization as we knew it.

At the time of the Munich Crisis, Judha Shamsher had offered eight battalions of the Nepalese Army to help garrison India in the event of war. The Foreign Office thanked him but said the time was not right to accept. Unlike Nepal, in that first year of the war India seemed to do little or nothing to prepare for the Armageddon that was to come.

Gurkhas in action on a picket on the North West Frontier. (Gurkha Museum)

Much encouraged by these developments, the Indian nationalists did their best to discomfort the British by sustained rioting, especially in Calcutta, as well as nationwide strikes. The burden of maintaining order for much of this fell on the Indian Army and of course the Gurkha Brigade. They remained staunch.

The declaration of war on Germany by Britain in September 1939 after Hitler's invasion of Poland was shortly followed by a declaration of war by the Viceroy of India on behalf of India. This he was quite entitled to do, but his failure to discuss his intention led to howls of protest from Indian nationalists and widespread rioting and strikes. Fortunately emergency wartime legislation made it much easier to suppress riots and to jail Indian nationalists.

Rather strangely the start of another world war seemed to have little if any immediate effect on the Indian Army in general or the Gurkha Brigade in particular as 6th Gurkhas' regimental history makes plain:

India General Service Medal 1936–39.

CHAPTER EIGHT

THE SECOND WORLD WAR: THE MIDDLE EAST, NORTH AFRICA AND THE MEDITERRANEAN

A lthough British India was prompt in declaring war, thereafter not very much happened, while Britain itself reeled from one disaster to another. Failing to aid Poland, Britain watched as that country was gobbled up by Germany and Russia. British intervention in Norway was forestalled by Germany, while in May 1940 France was invaded. The British Army was forced to evacuate the continent – mostly through Dunkirk, and minus most of its equipment. Three weeks later France capitulated and Germany controlled Western Europe. The situation appeared grim.

It was therefore not a very propitious time for the British to approach Judha Shamsher, the ruler of Nepal, asking for permission to deploy Gurkhas overseas and to raise additional Gurkha units. The offer of eight Nepalese battalions to help garrison India had already been eagerly accepted, but would these additional requests be agreed in the light of Britain's apparently hopeless position?

To the British envoy's surprise, Judha Shamsher never hesitated, despite the opposition of his own ministers:

> *'Do you let your friend down in a time of need?' Judha asked.*
> *'No Sir.' The envoy replied. 'But there is often a difference between countries and individuals.'*
> *'There should not be.' Judha responded: 'If you win, we will win with you. If you lose we will lose with you.'*

Sketch by Harry Sheldon of a Gurkha boy soldier in the 8th Gurkhas. (Gurkha Museum)

The Gurkhas were in! The priests would raise no objection to them crossing the *kala pani* ('black water'). Soon the steady stream of wheaten-skinned warriors with their strange curved knives would become a flood, furnishing some 130,000 men and manning 46 battalions, including two parachute and two garrison battalions. Desperately the Gurkha Brigade grappled with the problem of training and equipping thousands of young hill men who arrived with nothing except their kukris and a huge smile. The Indian Government authorized the raising of third battalions for each of the ten Gurkha regiments in October 1940 and fourth battalions early the following year; this entailed the transfer of British and Gurkha officers and non-commissioned officers from the existing two battalions of each regiment. For British officers their places were taken by Emergency Commissioned Officers straight from officer training; most of these had never seen a Gurkha before, let alone spoke Urdu or Gurkhali. It was going to be a very steep learning curve! As far as Gurkhas were concerned those officers recently retired were called back while those about to retire were retained.

There was also the problem of equipping these new battalions. In India generally there was an absolute dearth of weapons and equipment. Everything produced in Britain was being used to re-equip the expanding British Army and replace what had been lost at Dunkirk. Soon the Indian armament factories were producing small arms in increasing quantities, but there was an acute shortage of motor transport, guns and armoured vehicles and the petrol necessary to move

them. Gurkha units on exercises were often required to carry petrol in ox carts and only use it on the final phase of any exercise.

As in the previous war, the first deployment outside India was to Basra in Iraq to secure the oil supplies from Abadan in Persia. Both Iraq and Persia had shown themselves friendly towards the Germans, who had sent technicians to help develop oil production. Loss of Persian oil would be disastrous for Britain; it had to be made secure, and so 10th Indian Division under Major General Slim, whom we have already encountered at Gallipoli and who had served seven years with two Gurkha regiments between the wars, was sent from India in May 1941. The division included four Gurkha battalions (1/2nd, 2/4th, 2/7th and 2/10th).

Fortunately the Germans had not established themselves in any strength and in any case were just about to invade Russia, their erstwhile ally, so the Iraqis and then the Persians were brought to order fairly quickly despite a limited Luftwaffe intervention.

The European war scene had now changed dramatically. By mid-September 1940 the German Air Force had failed to subdue Royal Air Force Fighter Command. Without air superiority Germany could not invade Britain, but she could hope to starve her out by unrestricted submarine warfare. Britain for her part was rapidly re-equipping and expanding her army, and was already sending reinforcements to General Sir Archibald Wavell's desert army, which had defeated the Italian army that had invaded Egypt from Cyrenaica (the eastern half of Libya). Wavell was now pushing deep into Italian colonial Africa. Italian efforts to attack Greece through Albania had also failed and been driven back by the Greeks. Spain, dismayed by Italian defeats, refused to join Germany and Italy.

NORTH AFRICA

While they were only fighting the Italians, Wavell's troops were very successful, but as soon as the Germans under Lieutenant General Erwin Rommel arrived on 7 February 1941 things began to deteriorate rapidly. Too much was being required of Wavell. In early 1941 he was being pressed to drive the Italians out of Abyssinia (Ethiopia), continue his offensive in North Africa, prepare to assist Greece in repelling the Italian invasion through Albania and the German one through Bulgaria – and to be prepared to fight the Vichy French in Syria!

The 4th and 5th Indian Divisions had formed the bulk of the British forces that defeated the Italians in Abyssinia and they now became involved in the desert campaign and Syria.

Throughout the spring of 1941 Rommel's force in the desert was being strengthened, especially in armour, as well as by German fighters and bombers. In April the Germans invaded Yugoslavia and in a lightning campaign subdued it.

At the same time from airfields in Italy and the Mediterranean islands, the German Air Force obtained air superiority over most of the area. Wavell was now being required to send more and more units to help the Greeks as the Germans attacked through Bulgaria and tried to take Salonika.

Against this darkening scene, units of 5th Indian Division were being moved to the Western Desert after their victory in Eritrea, others were being moved from Iraq, Syria and Persia where the situation was no longer threatening. The 2/4th Gurkhas was one of those units that now found themselves hurrying towards a major clash of arms and we will follow their progress.

In May 1941, 2/4th Gurkhas arrived in Iraq from India as part of 10th Indian Division and two companies were airlifted into the Royal Air Force base of Habbaniyah to defend it against the pro-German Iraqi army attacking it. The remainder, helped by the Royal Navy, were deployed clearing hostile Iraqis out of the Basra area. That successfully completed, they then joined the two companies in Habbaniyah, at which point the Iraqi army withdrew. Next, 10th Division advanced on Baghdad and the Iraqis sued for peace. The 2/4th Gurkhas were then flown into Mosul which until the day before had been used by the German Air Force.

Handing over to 2/8th Gurkhas, the 2/4th then pushed into Syria from the east. There the Vichy French, supporting the Germans, were determined to hold their colony against any attempt on it by General Charles de Gaulle's Free French supported by the British. Possessing air superiority, the Vichy French made things very hot for the motorized invading force and 2/4th Gurkhas suffered casualties from air attack. As the invasion from Iraq was beginning to falter, General Slim altered his tactics and ordered a very deep cut-off movement to isolate the main French force at Deir-ez-Zor on the Euphrates. The 2/10th Gurkhas were involved in this daring move which demoralized the 2,000-strong enemy and caused them to withdraw from their fortifications on 3 July, minus 100 prisoners and nine guns. The 2/4th Gurkhas were part of the follow-up force which, despite inadequate maps, managed to get through trackless country and follow the enemy to Raqqa, closer to the Turkish border. Their detractors said this feat of navigation was only made possible by

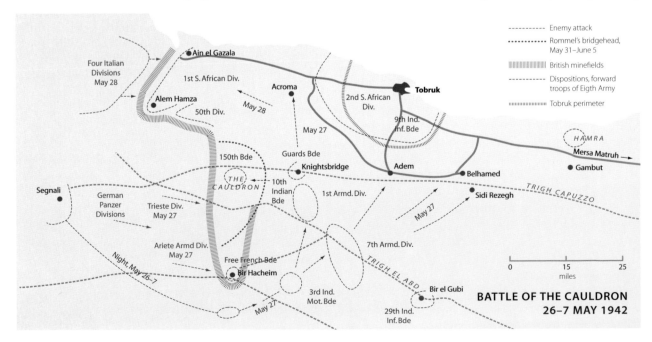

**BATTLE OF THE CAULDRON
26–7 MAY 1942**

Survivors from 2/7th Gurkhas who successfully escaped back to the 8th Army after the fall of Tobruk. (Gurkha Museum)

following a trail of empty wine bottles! After more fighting at Raqqa, where the French and their Arab allies were strongly supported by fighter ground–attack aircraft, the Vichy French collapsed and sued for peace on 11 July.

As autumn 1941 turned to winter, it became clear that the Soviet Union was going to hold the German invasion, despite horrific casualties and massive loss of territory. On the other hand, Greece and Yugoslavia, as well as Crete, had fallen to the Axis powers. British losses had been very severe in both Greece and Crete. Churchill had replaced Wavell by General Sir Claude Auchinleck, previously Commander–in–Chief India; in fact they simply swapped jobs.

Despite Churchill's urging, Auchinleck declined to start his attack to clear the Germans from the Egyptian border and relieve Tobruk until he was ready, which was not until 18 November 1941. Operation 'Crusader', as it was called, was a desperately fought battle by the newly named Eighth Army which swayed in the balance for several days but finally ended in a German/Italian (Axis) withdrawal and the relief of Tobruk. However, by the end of 1941 things had taken a turn for the worse.

In a series of naval disasters, the Royal Navy had temporarily lost control of the Eastern Mediterranean, and the diversion of a complete air corps from the Russian Front meant that the Germans had air superiority in North Africa as well as over the Mediterranean. However, such setbacks paled into insignificance compared with the staggering impact of the Japanese attack on the American Pacific Fleet at Pearl Harbor on 7 December 1941. With the United States in the war there would be ultimate victory, however hard and long the journey.

Into this bewilderingly complex mixture of circumstance, after refitting in Iraq, 2/4th Gurkhas found themselves pitchforked into the Western Desert in March 1942 just as Rommel, heavily reinforced and with local air superiority, was preparing to go over to the offensive. The 2/4th Gurkhas were required to move so quickly that they were obliged to leave detachments behind in Iraq, including signallers employed at the divisional concert party! It turned out that they were the lucky ones.

At this time Eighth Army held a line from in the north Gazala to Bir Hacheim in the south, the latter garrisoned by the Free French Brigade. Behind this line and on the coast was the fortress of Tobruk which had successfully resisted all Rommel's previous efforts to take it. The front from Gazala to Bir Hacheim consisted of six brigade-sized defensive 'boxes' which, sheltering behind a minefield, were intended to hold any German armoured onslaught until British armour arrived to destroy it. The 2/4th Gurkhas were sent to a 'box' called the 'Kennels' at Hamra, some way behind the front line and roughly astride the Libya/Egypt border. In this 'box' was 10th Indian Brigade with 2nd Battalion The Highland Light Infantry and 4/10th Baluch Regiment plus of course normal levels of brigade artillery and other support.

With Rommel's attack imminent, 2/4th Gurkhas and the rest of 10th Indian Brigade were ordered to move to help protect Eighth Army Advanced Headquarters at Gambut which was nearer the coast, east of Tobruk. On 26 May Rommel attacked, sweeping round the left flank of Eighth Army below Bir Hacheim and into the main defensive position.

However, the defensive 'boxes' held firm and forced Rommel to alter his line of attack by cutting through the minefield. Again the 'boxes' held firm and armoured counter-attacks drove the enemy back. Morale was high and 2/4th Gurkhas were told that Eighth Army was now going over to the offensive and that their brigade was to move forward to the west of Tobruk to be ready to take part. Moving all day they had reached their appointed destination by evening when their Commanding Officer was called away to 10th Brigade Headquarters. The next day the whole brigade was ordered to move south-west towards 'Knightsbridge', a 'box' manned by the Guards which had seen much fighting. Moving fast and unguided, 10th Indian Brigade became badly scattered and by nightfall 2/4th Gurkhas were still not concentrated.

Contrary to optimistic reports Rommel was far from beaten and on 1 June he suddenly attacked one of the most forward brigade boxes (150th Brigade) and completely overwhelmed it, taking 3,000 prisoners. The 10th Indian Brigade was ordered that night to advance to a point just short of where 150th Brigade had been destroyed and secure it. Accordingly its units set off in the middle of the night, bombed intermittently by the Germans.

On arrival in a sandstorm they were told that the plan had been changed and that they were now to go many miles south-east and secure gaps through the minefield belt called 'Peter and Paul' although nobody seemed to know which was which! Next day 2/4th Gurkhas arrived at their new location and were eventually joined by the rest of 10th Indian Brigade. Although exhausted and very short of sleep they were immediately at work preparing a defensive position and sending out patrols.

The area immediately to the west of 10th Indian Brigade was known as the 'Cauldron' and numbers of Rommel's tanks were believed to be trapped there between the minefield and Eighth

Army. Accordingly an attack was planned on the area where 150th Brigade had been destroyed and 10th Indian Brigade, supported by tanks, would head the attack at 0300 the next morning. Having got into formation ready to attack, a tricky task in the middle of the night, the Brigadier ordered a delay as increasing numbers of German armoured vehicles were entering the area where the attack was forming up. Eventually the attack went in and secured its objective without much opposition. However, come the dawn large numbers of German tanks attacked the Highland Light Infantry, which without armoured support, was forced to withdraw. The 22nd Armoured Brigade was in the vicinity, but for some reason failed to intervene. At first 2/4th Gurkhas was given orders to move to assist the Highland Light Infantry. Given the presence of German armour this was impracticable, and they were later ordered to dig in and form a defensive box supported by 28th Regiment Royal Artillery with 25-pounders. In fact the ground was rocky and digging was very difficult. The senior brigade Royal Engineer officer visited and promised to come back with a bulldozer and mechanical drills but he never returned. As 4th Gurkha regimental history chillingly puts it: 'It was some time before we realised that no one who left our position ever did return.'

There was no reply to their signals and although they could not understand it at the time that was because their brigade commander and his staff had been overrun and taken prisoner, as had divisional headquarters. The 2/4th Gurkhas were totally surrounded and cut off. The Germans coming through the gap they had made in the minefield had easily avoided the British attack and then struck hard themselves, destroying 1st Battalion The Duke of Cornwall's Light Infantry, which had only just arrived as a reinforcement, and then destroyed brigade and divisional headquarters.

The 2/4th Gurkhas dug in desperately through the night. At dawn the Germans attacked and, by 10 o'clock in the morning, the Gurkhas could see that the nearest battalion, 4/10th Baluchis, had been overwhelmed. Next, the Jats from another brigade were overrun, some of their artillery seeking refuge in the 2/4th Gurkhas' 'box'. Now it was their turn as the German armour closed up. Their 2-pounder anti-tank guns proved useless, shells simply bouncing off the German tanks. Only the artillery's 25-pounders firing over open sights had any effect and, unprotected, these were gradually picked off.

All the time they were subjected to intense enemy artillery fire. As the fire support of their own artillery diminished, the German tanks came right onto the position spraying the slit trenches with machine-gun fire; behind them came the German infantry cautiously mopping up. The Gurkhas fought on through that long day (6 June 1942), having been without food or sleep

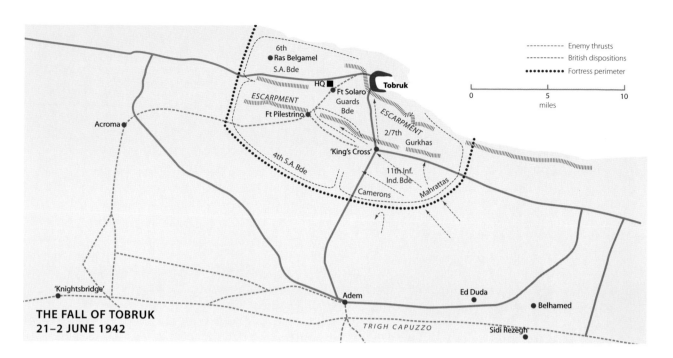

THE FALL OF TOBRUK
21–2 JUNE 1942

for 48 hours but in the end they could do no more. As the 4th Gurkha history describes: 'As the sun went down we were lined up to be led off into captivity, the British separated from the Gurkhas and the Gurkhas from the rest. The darkness descended upon us – a prelude and a presage of the months and years of tribulation to come.'

A few years ago there was a poignant sequel to this disaster. An elderly man brought a kukri into the Gurkha Museum. He had been in 1st Duke of Cornwall's Light Infantry who had been trucked in to the 'Cauldron' battle from Iraq as last-minute reinforcements. As they arrived in the middle of the battle they were overrun by German tanks almost as they got out of their trucks. Having been taken prisoner, trudging along, he picked up a kukri from the now deserted 2/4th Gurkha position and amazingly managed to conceal it from the Germans. Transported to mainland Italy, he was let out from the prisoner-of-war camp when Italy changed sides and joined the Italian partisans where his kukri came in very handy.

* * *

With his victory at the 'Cauldron', the way to Tobruk was now open to Rommel. Wasting no time, he scattered British light forces screening Tobruk and by 19 June was closed up to the perimeter itself.

It had been an Australian division that had so successfully defended Tobruk the previous year, but, at its government's insistence, it had been withdrawn, being replaced by two South African brigades, a Guards brigade and 11th Indian Infantry

Brigade of which 2/7th Gurkha Rifles were a part along with a battalion of Cameron Highlanders and a battalion of Mahratta Light Infantry. The whole garrison was commanded by a South African, Major General Hendrik Klopper. Because Rommel had originally been driven right back to the Italian Cyrenaica border, Tobruk's defences had been allowed to deteriorate somewhat. Sand had filled up the anti-tank ditch, some of the wire was incomplete, as were the minefields, which had become thickly covered in drifting sand; all in all the fortress was not as strong as it had been. On the other hand Tobruk still contained a mass of stores and equipment, sufficient to sustain 30,000 men for at least three months.

On 21 June Rommel swung his German-Italian Afrika Korps round to the east of Tobruk and attacked 11th Indian Brigade on a narrow front, the blow landing on the 2/5th Mahrattas' position. Because the attack was accompanied by incessant Stuka dive-bomber attacks and artillery fire, neither 2/7th Gurkhas nor the Camerons were able to intervene and had to watch helplessly while the Maharattas were destroyed company by company. Through this gap Rommel poured his armour and soon they were right in the centre of the garrison. The 2/7th Gurkhas continued fighting throughout the day, hurling back attack after attack, despite battalion headquarters being overrun and having to seek refuge in a rifle company area. With ammunition running low, the South Africans already surrendering and, completely surrounded, 2/7th Gurkhas' defence was gradually ground down in attacks for a further six hours by three Axis battalions. Morale remained incredibly high to the end but the end was inevitable and, for the second time in their history, 2/7th Gurkhas went into captivity.

With the fall of Tobruk Rommel captured not only its 32,000-strong garrison, but additionally a mass of supplies and much needed fuel. It was a huge Axis victory and a major propaganda coup as well. General Auchinleck desperately tried to hold Rommel at Mersa Matruh (where 275 men of 2/7th Gurkhas were to be liberated in November) half way from the frontier to Cairo, but Rommel was too strong. Extricating the New Zealand Division, which fought its way out at the point of the bayonet, Auchinleck withdrew to the natural defensive position at Alamein where in a 27-day battle he managed to halt Rommel and throw him back on the defensive. It was a battle Auchinleck had to win; failure to hold would have seen Rommel in Alexandria and Cairo.

Despite his brilliant generalship in this the First Battle of Alamein, in August Auchinleck was replaced by a combination of Lieutenant General Sir Harold Alexander as Commander-in-Chief Middle East and Lieutenant General Bernard Montgomery as Commander Eighth Army.

Let us now follow the fortunes of 1/2nd Gurkhas which had been sent from Iraq to garrison Cyprus in April 1942. This was a repeat of history, as they had garrisoned the island in 1878 when Russia was the threat. After four months they moved from garrisoning Cyprus to Egypt. Almost immediately the battalion was struck by an appalling disaster. While at the Mena reception camp, near Cairo, officers and men of Headquarters Company were being instructed on 28 August in how to arm and lay mines. The Royal Engineer instructor under the impression he was dealing with a dummy mine detonated a live one. No fewer than 68 Gurkha officers and men were killed outright and 85 wounded, a number being blinded or losing limbs. The stricken included a high percentage of vital specialists such as signallers, mortar men, anti-tank gunners and carrier drivers. The Commanding Officer had been due to attend but was delayed elsewhere which probably saved his life. It was an appalling blow and, in addition to the human costs, removed at a stroke months of specialist training.

The 1/2nd Gurkhas then found themselves manning a defensive position on the Ruweisat Ridge, a key defensive area continually under German artillery and air attack. The 4th Indian Division, of which 1/2nd Gurkhas formed a part, was not part of the main attack force in the Second Battle of Alamein.

General Montgomery commanding 8th Army flanked by General Horrocks examining a Gurkha's kukri. (Gurkha Museum)

Bren gun carrier platoon of 7th Gurkhas with their carriers. (Gurkha Museum)

Nevertheless it had the important task of pinning the Axis forces in front to ensure they did not join in any counter-attack.

Major General Francis Tuker, the able and gifted commander of 4th Indian Division and also an erstwhile Commanding Officer of 1/2nd Gurkhas who had obtained his old battalion for his division, was determined that not a single enemy unit should move. On the night of the 23/24 October General Montgomery's long planned and prepared counter-offensive went in after an intense artillery barrage. The 1/2nd Gurkhas for their part mounted a raid on the enemy Point 62 strongpoint, a long-time thorn in their sides. After a most determined attack, using three Bren-gun carriers with grapnels to pull away the barbed-wire defences, they were beaten off, but not until the Gurkhas had got among the terrified enemy with their kukris. The officer who led the attack was severely wounded and captured, and 22 Gurkhas were missing or wounded.

However, this diversion had helped ensure that no enemy was able to move away to reinforce Rommel's main force which by this time was involved in a desperate battle to the north. This was to last for 12 days of bitter fighting until the Axis forces turned back in headlong retreat.

Soon 1/2nd Gurkhas were following up the retreating Axis forces after their armour had been smashed in the fierce tank battles on 2–3 November. A roving column under Lieutenant Colonel Osmond Lovett, 1/2nd Gurkhas' Commandant, encountered a long line of Italian infantry withdrawing. Driving off the six escorting light tanks with their carriers, 1/2nd Gurkhas managed to capture 100 Italian officers including the Brescia Divisional Commander and over 2,100 men. Four German tanks trying to intervene were driven off by the anti-tank platoon. It was a good indication of the scale of Rommel's defeat.

Now the Eighth Army pursued the retreating Germans back down the agonizing way they had retreated themselves. Mersa Matruh, Tobruk, Gazala and Benghazi all fell quickly to Montgomery's troops until, outrunning their supplies, they were temporarily forced to halt. On 3 February 1943 General Alexander was able to report to Winston Churchill as follows:

> *Sir, The orders you gave me on 10th August 1942 have been fulfilled, His Majesty's enemies, together with their impedimenta, have been completely eliminated from Egypt, Cyrenaica, Libya and Tripolitania. I now await your further instructions.*

By now, Operation 'Torch', the landing of an Anglo-American army in Algeria and Morocco, had taken place on 8 November 1942, in spite of Vichy French resistance. Hitler however reacted violently to these landings and started to reinforce Tunisia. Rommel's shattered Afrika Korps was meanwhile slowly

Major General 'Gertie' Tuker commanding 4th Indian Division plans the assault on Wadi Akarit with his principal staff officers and Brigadier 'Oz' Lovett commanding 7th Indian Brigade. Painted by Anthony Goss. (Imperial War Museum)

withdrawing back to the Tunisian border, so it was inevitable that the next major battle should be for Tunisia. Allied forces moving in on Tunisia from Algeria got a very bloody nose from a much reinforced Rommel at the Battle of the Kasserine Pass. Rommel then turned his attention to Eighth Army. On the Russian Front, the Germans had just sustained a massive annihilation at Stalingrad. In France, the Germans had occupied 'unoccupied' France, thus much weakening the authority of Vichy.

★★★

Into this rapidly changing scene let us follow 1/2nd Gurkhas and 1/9th Gurkhas, both of which were destined to play key roles in the coming weeks. Rommel's March 1943 attack on Eighth Army had been repulsed and, accepting he could not break through Montgomery's formidable anti-tank defences, he himself went on the defensive (before secretly leaving Africa due to ill-health, handing over to Colonel General Jürgen von Arnim) behind the naturally strong Mareth Line. This was a highly defended zone originally constructed by the French to protect Tunisia against a possible Italian attack from Tripolitania. Now it was being defended by the Germans and Italians against the British!

Initially General Montgomery had planned to try and break his way through on the coastal road: this was just what Rommel's army-level successor General Giovanni Messe intended him to do, as that was where the Axis was strongest. Fortunately, having got a bloody nose trying to break through on the coast road, Montgomery used a left-hook attack to break into the Mareth Line from an unexpected direction, deploying 4th Indian Division on the far left to scale the Matmata Hills and break in behind the enemy. General Tuker, commanding 4th Indian Division, used his two Gurkha battalions (1/2nd and 1/9th) for this task. Unfortunately a well-placed enemy minefield and conflicting orders from above delayed the attack, so that when it did eventually go in on 28 March, it was discovered that the armour had already broken in further to the right.

Right: A painting by the war artist Harry Sheldon of the action in which Subedar Lalbahadur Thapa received the Victoria Cross. (Gurkha Museum)

Next page: Subedar Lalbahadur Thapa 1/2nd Gurkhas recounting the action that won him the Victoria Cross. Painted by Anthony Goss. (Imperial War Museum)

Anthony Gross 1943

Messe, thus edged out of the Mareth Line, now took up an equally strong position 20 miles further back at Wadi Akarit, where he again obliged Montgomery either to try to break through along the heavily defended coastal strip or swing left and try to attack through the seemingly impassable mountains of Fatnassa. Montgomery's original plan was for a major assault on the coastal plain and a comparatively shallow hook by 4th Indian Division over the low hills that covered the centre and near right of the Axis position.

General Tuker was not happy with this plan for two reasons. He felt first that Montgomery was doing what the Axis expected, and second that his division would pay the price for so doing. With considerable moral courage, Tuker made his reservations known and strongly pressed for his division to be allowed to try to storm the Fatnassa heights on the enemy's extreme right flank. These heights were generally supposed to be impassable by both sides. As a result Messe had guarded them with Italian units, albeit backed by Germans. General Tuker knew the mountain warfare capabilities of the men in his division, especially his Gurkhas, and he was confident that they could do it. Later he said to a friend 'It is now in the lap of the gods. Only one thing worries me. Perhaps I have asked too much of them and have set them a task beyond human accomplishment.'

The 1/2nd Gurkhas prepared in great detail for the attack using a large sand map to brief right down to corporal level so that the plan was fully understood. The assault was preceded by a three-mile approach march. The approach march was guided by previously laid white tapes; thereafter each company lined up visually on the peak that was their objective. At 2330 hours on 5 April they moved silently forward. An enemy sentry shouted the alarm moments before a kukri cut off his lifeblood and all hell broke loose. The four rifle companies hugging the ground were soon among the Italians with kukri and bayonet, despite a furious defensive fire.

D Company now raced forward on the key task of securing a steep and narrow chimney-shaped crevasse that came out in the middle of the enemy position. Subedar Lalbahadur Thapa at the head of 16 Platoon led the way, enemy sentries tried to stop them but were overwhelmed and went down under the kukris of the Gurkhas. A machine gun opened up on them and casualties mounted, but still Subedar Lalbahadur kept his men going and took out the machine gun and then at the top of the chimney fell upon another machine-gun crew with his kukri.

In this amazing fashion Subedar Lalbahadur and his platoon secured the vital entrance through which poured the rest of D Company, fanning out to attack the terrified defenders. So it

Gurkhas attacking; probably at the Mareth line battle. (Gurkha Museum)

Gurkhas firing an anti-tank gun. (Gurkha Museum)

was that, two hours before Montgomery's main assault was due to go in, 1/2nd Gurkhas had seized the key point of the enemy's defence line.

Unfortunately higher command was slow to exploit this incredible success, and all through the next day, 1/2nd Gurkhas were counter-attacked by German back-up forces and heavily shelled as the enemy sought to regain the vital ground they had lost. Frequent vicious hand-to-hand battles punctuated 6 April as 1/2nd Gurkhas, without support, fought determinedly to hang on to what they had so brilliantly gained. On their right, in the easier going, 1/9th Gurkhas were fighting hard too, trying to keep up the momentum of the attack against increasingly heavy counter-attacks which included German armour.

Success on the coastal strip and in the centre released increasing artillery support for 4th Indian Division, which once it came into action, greatly eased the situation for 1/2nd Gurkhas still clinging desperately to their cliffs and crags. With his flank turned and heavily attacked elsewhere, Messe was forced to pull

A Gurkha kukri charge, possibly during the battle to break through the Mareth line. (Gurkha Museum)

Following Operation Torch, newly arrived Americans examine a Gurkha kukri. (Gurkha Museum)

back all the way to the shelter of the Tunisian mountain block which stood in a ring 60 miles deep around the city of Tunis and the Gulf of Carthage.

For his incredible bravery and leadership that day Subedar Lalbahadur Thapa was awarded the Victoria Cross, the first of 12 won by Gurkhas in the Second World War.

Under General Dwight D. Eisenhower, the British–American force that had landed on Operation 'Torch' was now given the task of destroying the Axis, mainly German, army penned in close to the Bay of Carthage in Tunisia. General Montgomery and Eighth Army were given the subsidiary task of holding their present position and ensuring there was no enemy breakout. However, playing second fiddle was never much to Montgomery's liking and he determined to interpret his orders flexibly. His intelligence told

him that the mountainous area of the Djebel Garci to his front was comparatively lightly held and, remembering 4th Indian Division's amazing success at Wadi Akarit, decided to use it again in an attempt to break through the ring of mountains and into the main enemy defensive position which would serve to open up the coastal corridor for his armour.

Given the task of taking Djebel Garci, 5th Indian Brigade started to patrol against the enemy defence high up on a long mountain ridgeline. The 1/9th Gurkha patrols, contrary to 8th Army intelligence, found the area strongly held and the enemy very alert. One of their patrols was caught in a minefield and all killed save one man who, desperately wounded, managed to crawl out.

The 5th Brigade's attack plan was for 1/4th Essex Regiment to capture a small hill at the base of the Djebel Garci mountain, then

Colonel General Jürgen von Arnim's pistol. (Gurkha Museum)

4/6th Rajpatana Rifles would move through and capture the first ridgeline, then 1/9th Gurkhas would move through to capture the next ridgeline . Finally, the 1/4th Essex would come forward and join 1/9th Gurkhas for a final assault on the crest of Djebel Garci.

At 2000 hours on 18 April 1943, 1/4th Essex went in and captured the first objective. However, when it came to the 4/6th Rajputana Rifles' attack, the enemy resisted violently and the Raj Rifs as they were known started to receive very heavy casualties including all their British officers. Seeing them desperately engaged on the bare mountainside, 1/9th Gurkhas swung round them and headed for their own objective realizing that unless they could take it by dawn they would be sitting ducks for the enemy artillery.

Captain Peter Jones led D Company forward and was almost immediately engaged with the enemy fighting the 4/6th Rajputana Rifles. Here the Gurkhas met the enemy in hand-to-hand fighting, kukris chopping like demons. As the battle swayed, Captain Denis Donovan arrived with A Company and together they forced the Germans back leaving 44 dead behind them. As they reorganized, Jemedar Dewansing Basnet scouted forward. Being challenged by a German sentry he immediately jumped into the enemy trench and started to lash out with his kukri cutting down five Germans before he was overpowered. Thankfully his platoon arrived seconds after and, throwing grenades, attacked and released him. Bleeding from a dozen wounds, he reassumed command of his platoon. The 1/9th Gurkhas had achieved their objective and held it against successive enemy attacks for three days until withdrawn.

Montgomery, dismayed by mounting casualties and the strength of enemy resistance, decided to leave the final defeat of the Axis to the Americans and the British First Army as originally ordered. The 1/9th Gurkhas suffered 30 killed, 91 wounded and 13 missing believed dead in this hard-fought action. Captain Jones lost an eye but served on to command 2/2nd Gurkhas in 1961.

For the final assault on the Germans, 4th Indian Division was transferred from Eighth Army to First Army. The attack was preceded and accompanied by the biggest Allied air attacks yet seen, which not only totally destroyed the Luftwaffe in the area but prevented any reinforcement by sea or air. The Germans were in a hopeless position and, although fighting with their customary courage and skill, were beaten inexorably by British, American and Free French forces. Soon they started surrendering. The 1/2nd Gurkhas, scouting forward as was their wont, succeeded in capturing Colonel General Jürgen von Arnim himself. His pistol is on display in the Gurkha Museum.

Not far short of 250,000 Germans and Italians surrendered in Tunisia, making it a comparable victory to Stalingrad, a victory in the achievement of which Gurkhas had played a valuable part. We now follow them to their next theatre of operations – Italy.

The Africa Star.

CHAPTER NINE

THE SECOND WORLD WAR:
ITALY AND GREECE

Even while fighting in Tunisia was going on, formations and units were being prepared for the attack on Sicily, known as Operation 'Husky'. On 10 July 1943 a joint US/UK seaborne and airborne armada landed on Sicily, in all some 160,000 men. There was some very hard fighting, especially against troops of the German Parachute Division; additional British and American divisions were needed until, after 38 days, the island was in Allied hands. Unfortunately the bulk of the German forces managed to escape over the narrow Straits of Messina and lived to fight another day. The loss of Sicily led to the fall of Mussolini and almost immediately Italy started to explore peace terms, although these were not finalized until September. If Italy was quitting, Germany certainly was not and soon German formations were streaming into the peninsula. To try to forestall them, US VI Corps and British X Corps were landed at the Bay of Salerno just south of Naples where they met fierce German opposition. Eighth Army, struggling up the western coast to meet them, was also having a difficult time. Let us now see what 1/5th Gurkhas, the first Gurkha battalion into Italy, was up to.

The 1/5th Gurkhas had arrived as part of 8th Indian Division in October and with them were soon in action on the east coast of Italy where the Germans were tenaciously holding successive west-east flowing river lines. In November, in appalling weather conditions far removed from the image of sunny Italy, they were

ITALY 1943–5

Gurkhas crossing a major Italian river, possibly the Sangro. (Gurkha Museum)

across the River Trigno and pressing towards the River Sinella, having suffered some casualties from mortar fire and jumping mines. Crossing the river they came under very heavy artillery and mortar fire, losing their Commanding Officer and three officers wounded. Led by the battalion second-in-command, 1/5th Gurkhas were then directed on the key village of Atessa, part of the very strongly defended River Sangro, forming the forward edge of the formidable defence line from which the Germans intended to hold up the Allies' east coast advance.

By careful patrolling they were able to pinpoint most of the German machine-gun posts, so their silent night attack with kukri and bayonet achieved immediate and devastating success. An immediate German counter-attack was very roughly handled, but later that night a much heavier counter-attack fell on the isolated 15 Platoon, at the same time communications with the artillery failed. Fighting without artillery support, 15 Platoon soon found itself running out of ammunition. The 5th Gurkha history graphically describes the next few moments:

> Then, as ever in times of crisis the Gurkha rose to the occasion.
> Lance Naik Bhagtabahadur Gurung, his section down to almost
> the last round, allowed the Germans to within about twenty yards
> of his post, then with drawn kukris leaped with his section to meet
> them. Hand to hand or rather steel to steel, the Germans were no

3rd Gurkha rifleman tries an American cigar. (Gurkha Museum)

match for the Gurkhas and after a moment of stunned and shocked surprise they broke and fled. Bhagtabahadur Gurung's section followed them a little way down the hill to overrun one of the German covering machine guns which was immediately turned to speed the unwelcome visitors.

The swiftly flowing River Sangro was swollen to a width of 100 yards, and the far bank rose gently, offering an excellent defensive position with superb all-round fields of fire. The Germans had maximized this potential by strongly fortifying the villages along the crest. The strongest of these positions was the village of Mozzagrogna. After much effort, a bridgehead had been secured over the Sangro and 1/5th Gurkhas were ordered to cross and take Mozzagrogna, while on their right 1st Battalion The Royal Fusiliers was ordered to take the large monastery to the east of the village. The attack went in at 2100 hours on 27 November in torrential rain and stygian darkness and by 0245 hours, the leading companies reported that they had taken their objectives and were consolidating.

In fact the Germans were still about, having hidden in the deep cellars to avoid the preliminary artillery bombardment. They now emerged and attacked the Gurkhas in their rear, sparking a furious battle for control of the village, with the Fusiliers coming in to help. Soon ammunition was becoming scarce; unfortunately the reserve of ammunition carried by mules had strayed into a minefield and become dispersed as the mules stampeded. As dawn broke, the battle was at its crescendo with the Germans still holding out, but with 1/5th Gurkhas and the Fusiliers slowly gaining control of the village. Without any armoured support of their own, the arrival of two German tanks tilted the battle in favour of the defenders. The tank commander of one tank unwisely stuck his head out of the cupola and was promptly shot by a Fusilier. The other sprayed all and sundry with its flame-thrower. Its commander, sticking his head out for a moment to assess the damage he was causing, was shot by Major R.W. Moreland-Hughes, commanding 1/5th Gurkhas, who had climbed the church spire to get a better view of the battle. A shell from the second tank brought him down, dusty but unhurt, in a cloud of bricks and debris and set all the bells ringing!

As the battle raged, orders were received that, because the supporting armour was held up, 1/5th Gurkhas and the Fusiliers should withdraw while a heavy artillery barrage was brought down. Major Moreland-Hughes protested strongly saying that they would soon take the village, especially as one of the German tanks had been knocked out by the Fusiliers. Brigade Headquarters however insisted and they had to withdraw in the face of German opposition.

Many Gurkhas had reached the far outskirts of Mozzagrogna and now had to run the gauntlet of intense German fire.

A Gurkha fighting patrol being briefed. (Gurkha Museum)

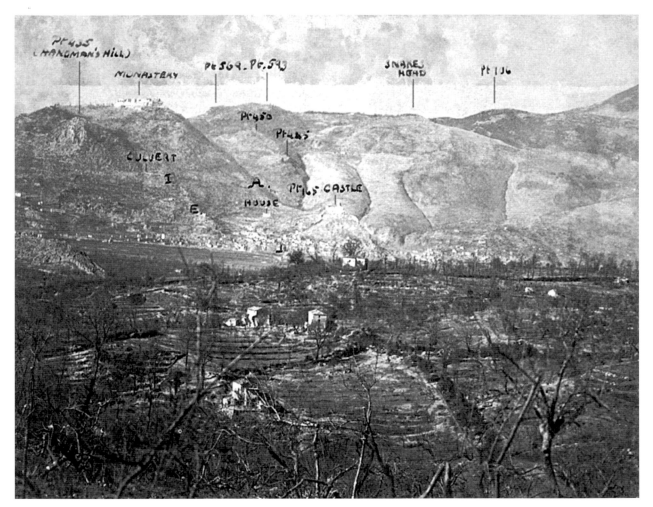

In this contemporary photo of Monte Cassino some of the much fought over key features are annotated. (Gurkha Museum)

The Fusiliers, who could have got out, very gallantly held on to cover them but the bulk of 1/5th Gurkhas, because of radio failure, were unaware they were supposed to be withdrawing and were locked in mortal combat with the Germans who were being continually reinforced.

As they fought, the British artillery barrage crashed down on friend and foe. With all the British officers dead or wounded, the senior Gurkha officer took over command of what was left of three companies and step by step they fought their way out, having held the village for six hours after the withdrawal order, which they never received, was given. Although they had suffered 36 dead and 91 wounded or missing, 1/5th Gurkhas attacked again next morning, this time supported by tanks, and broke through the Sangro defensive line. They were understandably bitter that they had been needlessly withdrawn the previous day.

After the battle, 1/5th Gurkhas now occupying Mozzagrogna, a section of Gurkhas was ordered to remove nine German bodies

from a more or less intact house selected as battalion headquarters. As the bodies were slung into a shell hole, suddenly one of the corpses sat up and started screaming. A Gurkha pulled out his kukri to silence him permanently when a nearby British soldier remonstrated. The Gurkhas looked puzzled; they had been ordered to bury nine Germans, surely the British did not want to bury one alive?!

The 4th Indian Division did not arrive in Italy until early December 1943. While preparing to attack the heavily defended mountain town of Orsogna for Eighth Army, Tuker's men were ordered instead 100 miles to the south-west across the Apennines to continue the assault on Cassino, unsuccessfully begun by the US Fifth Army in its costly push from Naples to Rome.

Arriving in the cold grey dawn of 11 February 1944, they could see the Monastery of Monte Cassino perched up on a steep hill to their left front and, directly below it, the ridge of Hangman's Hill, so called because a broken cable car pylon appeared as a gibbet. Further down and to the right was a low hill known as Castle Hill and high above that, higher than even the monastery, was Snake's Head Ridge. At the foot of this mountainous area was the once-pleasant town of Cassino with its railway station on the left and the Continental Hotel in the centre left. Gone were the happy days when the visitor arriving by rail or car could relax with an aperitif on the hotel's verandah. After weeks of bitter fighting the town was a rubble-strewn ruin and the only guests in the Continental Hotel were German paratroopers, who were in no hurry to get out!

The Americans had succeeded, after bitter fighting, in getting to the top of Snake's Head and holding it. All attempts to press on down from Snake's Head towards the monastery had been frustrated by Germans occupying the intervening Hill 593.

As well as 4th Indian Division, 78th British Division and 2nd New Zealand Division had also been moved to Cassino, all under the command of the brave and likeable New Zealander, Lieutenant General Sir Bernard Freyberg VC. Sadly General Tuker, who was tactically immensely gifted, had fallen ill and had been invalided back and so gave up his command of 4th Indian Division and its three Gurkha battalions (1/2nd, 1/9th and the reformed 2/7th). Before Tuker left, his plan had been to pinch out Cassino and, by cutting its communications, force the Germans to relinquish it. Only after the most appalling bloodshed, expended largely unsuccessfully, was his plan eventually implemented with success.

In his absence the unsuccessful American plan was to be tried again. The 4th Indian Division would attack down from Snake's Head, capture Hill 593, move on to capture the monastery and clear the slopes above the town. At the same time the New Zealand Division would directly assault Cassino town from the south. The 7th Indian Infantry Brigade, which included 1/2nd Gurkhas, was to lead the 4th Indian Division attack with two additional battalions from 5th Indian Brigade attached, 1/9th Gurkhas and 4/6th Rajputana Rifles, in all six infantry battalions.

On 13 February, 7th Brigade took over from the Americans on Snake's Head and, under continual artillery, mortar and air attack, started to move up the mountain to their assault positions. Suddenly, without any warning a heavy Allied bomber strike hit the monastery, but since there had been no attempt to coordinate this with a ground attack, much of its effect was wasted. Trying to get some collateral benefit, 1st Royal Sussex put in an attack on Point 593 but were driven back with heavy casualties. Trying again two days later they succeeded, but the Germans, having learned their withdrawal signal (three green Verey lights), tricked them into withdrawing, thus losing what they had gained at such bitter cost.

The 7th Brigade commander, Brigadier Lovett (previously commanding 1/2nd Gurkhas) now decided to use his whole force, with 1st Royal Sussex and 4/6th Rajputana Rifles, in the first wave against Point 593, and 1/2nd Gurkhas and 1/9th Gurkhas against the monastery itself. It would be a purely infantry battle. The 2/7th Gurkhas provided 22 men per company to each of the assaulting battalions to act as porters carrying spare ammunition and other vital stores. The attack on Point 593 started at midnight 16/17 February and 15 minutes later 1/2nd Gurkhas and 1/9th Gurkhas attacked the monastery itself. Let 2nd Gurkhas' history take up the tale as they topped the crest a bare 800 paces from the monastery:

Painting by Jason Askew depicting the taking of Hangman's Hill by 'C' Company 1/9th Gurkhas at the battle for Monte Cassino. (Gurkha Museum)

mines and booby traps, its outskirts threaded with trip wires. Dead riflemen were found afterwards with as many as four trip wires wound round their legs. Within 15 minutes two-thirds of B and C Companies were struck down in this deadly acre.

Despite many individual feats of extraordinary gallantry and having lost over 150 dead and wounded, 1/2nd Gurkhas had no option but to pull back and dig in. Meanwhile 1/9th Gurkhas' C and D Companies on the right received similar rough handling and after five hours of bitter fighting were recalled, having lost 94 officers and men killed and wounded. Down in the valley 2nd New Zealand Division had been unable to make any headway into Cassino town.

The plan for the next attack was somewhat different. This time 2nd New Zealand Division would attack the town again but 4th Indian Division would advance on the same axis from the south-east and attempt to seize the lower slopes of Monte Cassino and secure Hangman's Hill and then push on up to the monastery.

This time the attack was coordinated with an even greater bomber attack on the town and monastery which went in at 0900 hours on 15 March. Following shortly behind it, the New Zealand Division moved in and captured Castle Hill; and then exploited downhill into the town itself. However the bombers had created so much debris that armour could not operate and, without tanks, the New Zealanders were finding it difficult going as increasing numbers of German paratroops emerged from the ruins to dispute their advance.

The 4th Indian Division taking up the attack found it almost impossible to advance beyond Castle Hill, until 1/9th Gurkhas found a narrow way through the rubble and advanced onto the steep open slope. However, the Germans were there too and, showering D Company with grenades, caused 15 casualties. It now being night and, fearful of being caught strung out when dawn came, 1/9th Gurkhas went into all-round defence, minus C Company which had completely disappeared and with which there was no radio contact. Since 5th Indian Brigade, leading 4th Indian Division, had been able to achieve very little and was now pinned down from well-sited German positions, it was agreed to pull back while a massive artillery barrage was called down on the Germans.

Just as it was about to start, a hardly audible radio message came from C Company, 1/9th Gurkhas; they had taken the key objective Hangman's Hill! Immediately all the resources of 4th Indian Division were concentrated to exploit this company's amazing success. The remainder of 1/9th Gurkhas now started to fight their

At that instant pandemonium broke loose. Devastating fire from Spandau [machine-gun] groups on the right flank, from machine guns higher up on the crest of the spur and from posts dug in under the walls of the monastery raked the line of advance. Immediately in front the flicker and crash of grenades revealed an undetected German outpost line, hidden in the scrub which clothed the slopes. Colonel Showers' instructions had been unmistakable: 'Reach woods as quickly as possible. Do not pause for firefight or to mop-up. If enemy throws grenades rush him.' Intent on closing the leading companies leapt into a death trap. The scrub proved to be a thorn thicket sown with anti-personnel

way towards C Company on Hangman's Hill while the New Zealand Division renewed its attack on the town. The follow-up companies of 1/9th Gurkhas arrived just in time to thwart a German counter-attack onto Hangman's Hill which an exhausted and depleted C Company would have found difficult to hold.

Quickly the rest of 1/9th Gurkhas joined them and proceeded to hold out in their battered eyrie for nine days under continual bombardment from the Germans, and occasionally short rounds from British artillery. Trying to capitalize on 1/9th Gurkhas' success, General Freyberg ordered another attack but it was forestalled by the Germans counter-attacking. The 1/9th Gurkhas, short of food, water and ammunition, still hung on, with some aid from air drops, their wounded lying in rough *sangars* on the freezing hillside. Their comrades of so many battles, 1/4th Essex, had tried earlier to reach them, but were so badly mauled that only

43rd Gurkha Lorried Brigade centrepiece showing the badges of the units which served in the brigade on the base. (Gurkha Museum)

a few actually made Hangman's Hill. The 4/6th Rajputana Rifles then tried and suffered equally severely. The Germans were simply too strong and on 23 March, 1/9th Gurkhas, reduced to only 185 survivors, were ordered to withdraw with 72 all ranks of the Essex and Rajputanas who had succeeded in reaching them. Their extraordinary ordeal had become one of the epics of the Italian Campaign. On the top of Hangman's Hill, the 9th Gurkhas' badge can be found carved on a huge boulder, enduring testimony to their courage and resource.

Later, in May, Polish troops took Cassino and the monastery using virtually the same plan as had been advocated by General Tuker, coming in the rear and cutting the Germans off from their support.

In France, the Allies successfully landed in Normandy in June, but in Italy the Germans were still fighting obstinately and skilfully. In late summer 1944, another Gurkha formation arrived in Italy, 43rd Gurkha Lorried Brigade, consisting of the 2nd Battalions of 6th, 8th and 10th Gurkhas. During their short but distinguished service in Italy they were supported at various times by no fewer than six different armoured regiments, as well as their own brigade artillery, engineers and supporting services. By the time they arrived, Cassino had been taken, but the Allied advance had become stalled in the endless succession of rivers and ridges of the Apennine mountains which so lent themselves to the skilled defensive tactics of Field Marshal Albert Kesselring, the German Commander-in-Chief.

Their first big battle soon after arrival was the attack as part of 1st Armoured Division into the little independent state of San Marino which the Germans had now occupied and were strongly defending as part of the Gothic Line, their last line of defence now

Gurkhas on a Churchill tank; probably men of 43rd Gurkha Lorried Brigade. (Gurkha Museum)

they had lost Rome. The 26th Panzer Grenadier Division was strongly entrenched on top of the steep Passano Ridge, in front of which ran the swiftly flowing Fossa del Valle river. The 43rd Lorried Brigade was charged with breaking through into the German defence. Preceded by an artillery barrage of some 700 guns, 2/8th Gurkhas and 2/10th Gurkhas headed the 12/13 September night attack, supported by the 75mm tank guns of the Queen's Bays and 10th Hussars. The Germans reacted violently with a heavy counter-barrage and the attack ran into converging fire from mutually supporting Spandau machine-gun positions.

Nothing dismayed, the Gurkhas went in with sub-machine gun and kukri winkling out German positions until 2/8th Gurkhas had gained the ridgeline, closely followed by 2/10th Gurkhas. One Gurkha killed all six of a Spandau crew while others managed to put out of action two German tanks coming up in support which had unwisely left their hatches open. By dawn the vital Passano Ridge was in Allied hands. Now followed the grim race to support the Gurkha gains with the swift arrival of supporting tanks and 17-pounder anti-tank guns to quell the inevitable Panzer counter-attack. As if they anticipated such

reinforcement, the Germans shelled the temporary bridges over which the supporting armour was attempting to cross, destroying them and stopping the armour. Grimly the two Gurkha battalions held for long enough for some anti-tank guns to find an alternative way up, which decided the day in 43rd Lorried Brigade's favour – but it had been a close-run thing.

The 4th Indian Division was also involved in this battle for San Marino as it attempted a massive turning movement around the northern haunches of the mountain. Following initial success, 1/9th Gurkhas was ordered to execute a wide detour to seize San Marino town, built in terraces at the back of the mountain. At dusk on 18 September they moved forward and gained an intermediate peak without opposition. While their B Company dug in to consolidate, A and C Companies moved through towards San Marino town. Almost immediately they hit against large numbers of Germans and bitter fighting ensued with enemy artillery and mortar fire raining down. The two forward companies of 1/9th Gurkhas held on, but, without the armoured support which had bogged down crossing the river at the foot of the mountain, by dawn the situation was getting critical as ammunition ran low.

2/7th Gurkhas Bren gun team firing from a house. (Gurkha Museum)

Gurkha sniper in ruined building. (Gurkha Museum)

The artillery laid on a smoke screen which enabled C Company to be extricated, but, when it came to A Company's turn, they found themselves attacked by large numbers of enemy who swept their position with small-arms and machine-gun fire.

A young 9th Gurkha rifleman called Sherbahadur Thapa now changed the course of battle and gained the highest award for bravery, the Victoria Cross. His section commander falling wounded, he charged the enemy firing his Bren gun and broke up their attack. He then took up a fire position on a commanding knoll and brought such effective fire to bear for two hours that the enemy were unable to continue their attack and A Company was able to break clear. Sherbahadur's company commander then came to order him back but, before he would go, Sherbahadur rushed forward to rescue a wounded Gurkha in front of his position. As he and his company commander returned with the casualty they were both killed, riddled with bullets from a Spandau, as was the wounded man, 'no greater love …'.

Breaking into the Gothic Line proved to be a long and bloody undertaking in which all nine Gurkha battalions in Italy were involved. The 1/2nd Gurkhas had a desperate battle at Auditore and 2/3rd Gurkhas at Il Castello. The reformed 2/4th Gurkhas fought a magnificent battle at Monte Cedrone and the reformed 2/7th Gurkhas stormed Tavoleto by night.

Meanwhile, at last securely in possession of Passano Ridge, the Gurkhas of 43rd Lorried Brigade now prepared to attack the next German position: the Ripabianca Ridge.

At 1800 hours on 15 September, just as darkness was falling, 2/6th Gurkhas and 2/8th Gurkhas surged up the smoke-wreathed

Gurkhas fighting amongst ruined buildings in Italy. (Gurkha Museum)

2/6th Gurkhas and 14/20th King's Hussars enter Medicina, from a painting by Terence Cuneo. (The Royal Gurkha Rifles)

hillside still echoing with the tremendous preliminary bombardment. They caught the defenders reeling from its shock and unable to counter the furious Gurkha attack. German reinforcements were hurried to the scene, but the Gurkhas were ready for them and they melted away. This brilliant gain led to a belief that the Germans were cracking and two divisions were rushed in to exploit the Gurkha success. However the Germans were far from cracking and, in a devastating riposte, mauled the attacking British armour with well-sited anti-tank guns, the Bays alone losing 30 tanks.

Infantry, in this case Gurkhas, were needed to prise open the main German defence position at Santarcangelo before the tanks could try again. Attacking at 0300 hours on 23 September without artillery support, 2/8th and 2/10th Gurkhas assaulted the heavily fortified ridge position, suffering very heavy casualties. One 2/10th Gurkhas' company of over 100 Gurkhas was reduced to ten men standing. The 2/6th Gurkhas then moved up and the whole brigade, closely supported by 10th Hussars, attacked again and this

time broke through the ridgeline, and then down and across the historic Rubicon river. The Germans, licking their wounds, fell back before them.

The Allied advance now pressed on up the steep slopes and razor-backed ridges of the Apennines. It was in this terrain that the Germans planned to stop the Allies finally breaking through into the northern plains. At Monte Chicco they had a particularly strong position where the absence of any roads and the boulder-strewn slopes precluded the use of armour. It would have to be an infantry battle, and night would be best for that. At 2200 hours on 13 October, 2/6th Gurkhas crossed the start-line and were soon involved in desperate fighting especially around the 'The White House'. By dawn they were on the crest of the 1,300ft Monte Chicco, but being attacked on all sides and reduced to holding with bayonet and kukri as all ammunition was expended. The 2/8th and 2/10th Gurkhas battled up to join them and the battle raged all day until under the cover of darkness the Germans withdrew. Despite exhaustion and casualties, 2/8th Gurkhas probed forward and found an undefended crossing over the vital River Ronco. Joined by 2/6th and 2/10th Gurkhas, they then broke through the final German defences on the Apennines and by early 1945 were out onto the Emilian Plain.

The 1/5th Gurkhas, as part of 8th Indian Division on the right of Fifth Army, had also seen some hard fighting attempting to break through the Apennines and were operating towards the high feature of Monte San Bartolo, which formed the hinge between the two Allied armies and was therefore a vital objective. The 1/5th Gurkhas were ordered to patrol forward and discover how strongly the position was held. Accordingly a platoon-strong fighting patrol was sent with its objective being an intermediate ridge which joined the summit by a narrow saddle. It was known that the Germans had this saddle well defended and covered by machine guns. Rifleman Thaman Gurung was one of two Gurkhas scouting forward on 10 November and by skilful use of ground managed to get close to the saddle without being detected.

Just as they were getting near the summit, the other scout attracted Thaman's attention to two Germans in a slit trench just below the crest who had aligned their machine gun on the rest of the fighting patrol following up. Before they could fire, Thaman was on them and they surrendered without firing a shot. Working his way further up the slope he saw that it was heavily defended by Germans preparing to shower the fighting patrol with grenades. Rifleman Thaman, alone and approaching from an unexpected direction, immediately opened fire with his sub-machine gun which served to divert the Germans for long enough to allow the rest of the patrol to get into dead ground, and avoid the worst of the automatic fire to which they were now subjected. It was quite clear that the patrol could achieve no more on its own and it was ordered to withdraw, but this was easier said than done, given the closeness of many thoroughly aroused Germans.

Rifleman Thaman, although only 20 and of lowly rank, fully appreciated the situation and realized that, unless the Germans' attention could be diverted, there was very little hope for the fighting patrol being able to withdraw without being decimated. Running to the top of the crest in full view of the Germans he fired burst after burst from his sub-machine gun into their slit trenches, every German weapon was now turned on him. Running out of ammunition he threw four grenades, thus enabling most of the patrol to get clear, except those in front who were still pinned down by German fire. Running back to them Thaman took the machine-gunner's Bren gun and weaving back up the ridge he engaged the Germans with Bren fire, knowing every weapon would be turned on him. He fired two complete 30-round magazines before receiving a bullet through the throat, but the final group of the fighting patrol had now got safely away. Thaman Gurung must have known he was going to certain death but he never hesitated thereby

saving the lives of the rest of the patrol. The award of a posthumous Victoria Cross came as no surprise, even in a battalion as war-hardened as 1/5th Gurkhas, for which Monte San Bartolo became its third battle honour that year as the sole unit involved.

Among all the bloodshed and tragedy there were occasional flashes of humour without which the fighting man's life would be unbearable. The 1/5th Gurkhas, as they battled through the Apennines, suffered casualties from the anti-personnel mines of which the Germans had made much use to defend the approaches to their positions. One type that was particularly feared was the *schu* mine which although small would invariably blow the leg off whoever stepped on it. These mines were housed in little wooden boxes which made them undetectable by mine detectors; only by cautious prodding with a bayonet could they be found and disarmed. Preparing for an attack, 1/5th Gurkhas had cleared a considerable number of them from their intended line of advance and these had been stacked adjacent to the mule lines; these patient beasts being the only means of providing resupply in this mountainous country. Following the attack, on calling up the mules, they were horrified to find that one mule appeared to have eaten several *schu* mines! The animal did not appear to be displaying any signs of distress after its deadly meal but for the next week there was a marked reluctance shown for anybody to be its handler!

The 43rd Gurkha Lorried Brigade found that out in the Emilian Plain a totally different but no less deadly form of fighting was raging. The Germans, far from beaten and now within range of close Luftwaffe support, had developed the raised flood banks of the laterally flowing rivers into formidable defence positions with sweeping fields of fire. These positions were defended in depth by wide belts of mines and wire, and covered by fully concealed machine guns. The only way to breach them was to tunnel into the raised banks and then, armed with flamethrowers, literally burn the Germans out. Throughout February and early March 1945, 43rd Lorried Brigade tried every way it could to breach the Senio river defences and, by the time it was relieved, it had gained control of over three miles of the southern bank of the Senio after continual probing operations. The cost had been high; over 300 casualties. They were now equipped with 'Kangaroo' armoured personnel carriers. By 10 April the Senio, had been crossed, but not without some desperate fighting. In 8th Indian Division, 1/5th Gurkhas suffered 36 killed and 63 wounded in bitter conflict as the Germans contested every muddy yard in conditions reminiscent of 1914–18 trench warfare. Massive air support helped to slow German counter-attacks but, despite the end of the war being only three weeks away, the Germans were continuing to fight with their habitual courage.

Gurkha headstones in a Commonwealth War Graves Commission Cemetery in Italy. (Gurkha Museum)

The way was now open for 43rd Gurkha Lorried Brigade to exploit the Senio crossing and push on across the River Sillaro, which 2/10th Gurkhas achieved after some heavy fighting. The Germans, hampered by continual Allied air attack, desperately tried to reach Medicina, a key road centre 15 miles east of Bologna, before the Allies could get there. As dusk fell on 16 April the tanks of the 14th/20th King's Hussars and the 'Kangaroos' of 2/6th Gurkhas reached the town and immediately launched an attack. The German paratroops feverishly trying to organize its defence were caught on the hop. Despite desperate attempts to stem this armoured charge, in ten minutes of chaos and total confusion the Germans were completely thrown off balance. This moment is graphically depicted in a vivid diorama at the Gurkha Museum.

By dawn the next day, the dejected German defenders came out and surrendered.

Having cleared Medicina in this exemplary manner, 43rd Gurkha Lorried Brigade pushed on to the Gaiana, the next major river obstacle. To defend this river line, fed by many easily defensible drainage ditches, the Germans had brought in their elite 4th Parachute Division and the whole area was very strongly defended. An initial attempt to attack it by 2/6th Gurkhas was repulsed with many casualties The arrival of 2nd New Zealand Division triggered a massive aerial and artillery bombardment, enabling New Zealanders and Gurkhas to sweep across the river despite desperate opposition during the night of 18/19 April. Beyond the Gaiana the armour took up the pursuit, but German resistance was cracking and on 2 May 1945 all German forces in Italy surrendered.

★★★

Gurkha battalions in Italy had fought and died with incredible valour, as had their sister battalions of the Indian Army. Some very close relationships between regiments had been forged, especially between New Zealanders and Gurkhas.

General Freyberg with 2nd New Zealand Division and its band were all on the docks to bid farewell to 43rd Gurkha Lorried Brigade when it left Italy. We have seen how gallantly The Royal Fusiliers supported 1/5th Gurkhas. The relationship between 6th Gurkhas and 14th/20th King's Hussars has continued to this day, each wearing the other's badge upon their sleeves, despite their change of nomenclature to The Royal Gurkha Rifles and King's Royal Hussars.

Inevitably, from D-Day onwards the world's attention was centred on France and Germany, but now in retrospect we know just how hard the self-styled 'D-Day Dodgers' fought and, if we need reminding, we can see their carefully tended graves so far from home.

In November 1944, while the battle to break through the Gothic Line was still in progress, 4th Indian Division was withdrawn and sent to Greece where civil war was threatening as the Germans withdrew. When the Germans had conquered Greece, many of the faction backing the Greek royal family had tried to make the best of a very bad situation and came to what terms they could with their Axis occupiers. The Communists and republicans on the other hand had resisted the Germans and conducted guerrilla warfare against them. Now that Germany was clearly on the verge of collapse, the factions were actively preparing for a showdown. Churchill, who retained considerable interest and affection for Greece, and who had insisted that Britain help her militarily in 1941, was determined that the Communists should not be allowed to take over and so allow Greece to drift into the Soviet post-war sphere of interest.

The three Gurkha battalions of 4th Indian Division soon found themselves in a very tricky situation, especially in regard to the very heavily armed Communist forces, known as ELAS. The fact that they refused to be intimidated, kept the peace, despite immense provocation, and eventually disarmed ELAS, helped set Greece on a course of democracy, prosperity and peace. It was as significant an achievement as any of the more obviously martial ones of the Second World War. Perhaps this excerpt from 2nd Gurkha regimental history sums it up:

The saner Greeks realized how greatly they had been befriended. These British and Indian soldiers, foreign men of curious tongues,

who moved steadfastly about their tasks yet always found time for a grin, a chuck under the chin and a slap on the shoulder were seeking nothing for themselves nor were they the servants of any devious policy. They were in Greece to help put the house in order. They neither robbed nor raped nor flogged – unusual soldiers indeed. The hearts of the common people warmed to them and they sought to show their feelings in many ways by shy courtesies, simple gifts, timely warnings – a garland, a sheep, a flask of ouzo – small tributes meaning much.

On 7 February 1946, nine months after the war had ended in Europe, 1/2nd Gurkhas docked at Karachi. As after the First World War they were among the last Gurkhas back from a conflict the like of which the world had never seen and in which Gurkhas had played such a significant and proud part.

See Appendix 5 for a personal account of an amusing incident from the campaign, 'A Salutary Lesson', by G. P. Wheeler, Scots Dragoon Guards. Reproduced by kind permission of the Editor, Royal British Legion Journal.

The Italy Star.

CHAPTER TEN

THE SECOND WORLD WAR: MALAYA AND SINGAPORE

Let us now turn to the war with Japan which involved more Gurkha battalions than any other theatre of the Second World War in unequalled conditions of hardship and combat ferocity, where no quarter was given or received.

In the First World War, Japan had been an ally of Britain and the United States. However, her invasion of China in the 1930s and her creation of a puppet state, Manchuria, in conquered Chinese territory brought bad relations with the United States, which was a strong supporter of China and its Nationalist president Chiang Kai-shek. As a result of this antagonism, America, supported by Britain, placed a trade embargo on Japan which was particularly damaging as she had no oil supplies of her own. This in turn drove Japan to sign the Tripartite Pact with Germany and Italy. The pact did not automatically bind Japan to come in on Germany's side in the war, so she stood by and waited to see who would win. When France was defeated in 1940, Japan moved into French Indo-China (now Vietnam, Laos and Cambodia) from where she could threaten Thailand and the British dependencies of Burma and Malaya.

Burma was of particular importance as control of it would give the Japanese a stranglehold on 'The Burma Road'. This was the only point of entry left unblocked by the Japanese into China and through which a continuing stream of weapons and supplies flowed. Malaya with its tin and rubber and the Dutch East Indies

Medals of Rifleman Shiamlal Bura 2/1st Gurkhas who had already been awarded the Indian Distinguished Service Medal for an action on the North West Frontier in 1939. He was seriously wounded in the arm during the fighting in Malaya. Having amputated his arm with his kukri he plunged the stump into the creosote of a chemical toilet to prevent gangrene. After 15 days in the jungle he was finally captured by the Japanese who amputated what remained of his arm. (Gurkha Museum)

with oil and timber were also desirable targets, although the powerful British naval base of Singapore acted as a deterrent to any hostile move.

In the latter part of 1941, Japanese envoys were in almost continual dialogue with their American counterparts, seeking an agreement whereby the damaging trade embargo could be relaxed. At the same time the Nazi Foreign minister, Joachim von Ribbentrop, was trying to give the impression that the war was as good as won. Churchill, on the other hand, could plainly see that Japan was a great danger to British possessions in the Far East, but such were the military demands of the battles in the Western Desert and the naval demands of the Mediterranean and North Atlantic that no reinforcement had been possible. As the danger increased, some reinforcement took place with the second battalions of 1st, 2nd and 9th Gurkha Rifles of 28th Indian Brigade arriving in Malaya on 3 September 1941, while the modern battleship *Prince of Wales* and the battle cruiser *Repulse* with a destroyer escort were sent to Singapore. Critically they were supposed to be accompanied by an aircraft carrier to provide air cover, but accidental damage on the way made this impossible so the capital ships came without their integral air cover, an eventuality which had disastrous consequences.

Despite Japanese blandishments, America insisted that she quit China before there could be any relaxation of the trade embargo. On 7 December, without any declaration of war, aircraft from Japanese aircraft carriers launched a devastating attack on the US Pacific Fleet at Pearl Harbor on Oahu, one of the Hawaii Islands

group. Catching the battleships tied up in harbour at a stroke, the raid destroyed and incapacitated most of them. Critically, however, it failed to catch the American aircraft carriers which were at sea on exercise. Simultaneously, Japan attacked Thailand (then Siam) and Malaya, landing troops across the Gulf of Singora onto the wide beaches of the Thai and Malayan eastern seaboard.

The two British capital ships and their destroyer escort sailed north from Singapore to intercept the invasion, but were assailed by swarms of Japanese dive- and torpedo-bombers and sunk within 47 minutes of each other. Since the defence of Malaya and Singapore was predicated in a large part on sea power, this was a catastrophe indeed.

Air power which was supposed to cover the navy and obtain local air superiority was soon driven out of the skies by the more efficient and modern Japanese aircraft. Almost immediately the two main planks on which the defence of Malaya and Singapore rested were gone.

The defence plan for the Army was to push forward quickly into Thailand and seize the narrow and easily defensible neck of the Kra Isthmus. If this proved impracticable, a defensive line was to be adopted 16 miles south of the Thai frontier at Jitra.

In the event, the major push forward into Thailand never took place and the Japanese succeeded in landing at the eastern tip of the Kra Isthmus in Thailand and at Kota Bahru at the extreme north-east of Malaya. With no effective interference by the Royal Navy or Royal Air Force, the landings were successful and soon the Japanese were pushing on down south. The 28th Brigade and its three Gurkha battalions were required to defend the little town of Alor Star, as well as the airfield at Sungei Patani, and to push a force, which included 2/1st Gurkhas, towards the main defence position at Jitra in case it was needed to help. On the morning of 11 December in the midst of a tropical storm, the Japanese attacked down the road with over 20 tanks. Tanks were supposed by British planners to be unsuitable for Malaya so their sudden appearance came as a shock. The 2/1st Gurkhas gallantly managed to hold them up for a while with hand-held anti-tank weapons. Company Havildar Major Manbahadur Gurung calmly dispatched four with his .55in Boyes anti-tank rifle, but the rest broke through. The 2/1st Gurkhas were then attacked in the rear by large numbers of Japanese easily negotiating the supposedly impassable jungle and swamp.

By late afternoon all that was left of 2/1st Gurkhas were a few small groups of men trying to make their way back through the jungle. That night the Japanese succeeded in breaking through the Jitra defences which were far too spread out given the number of men available to hold them. The 2/2nd Gurkhas were then ordered back to hold Langaar just as their vehicles had moved off south. Marching through the night they reached Langaar and occupied it. While there, the remains of 2/1st Gurkhas came in; only their Commanding Officer and 200 men from an original 750. That evening the Langaar bridge was blown and the Gurkhas marched back south another 18 miles to reach the main west coast road at Jehun. Without food or sleep for two days, the men were exhausted and 2/2nd Gurkhas' Commanding Officer, Lieutenant Colonel G. H. D. Woollcombe, decided to halt and give them some sleep. As they were resting orders came to move south a further six miles to Gurun, where both 6th Indian and 28th Brigades would defend with the former on the left and the latter on the right.

Again the frontage was too great and before long the Japanese had infiltrated, wiping out 6th Brigade Headquarters in the process. The 2/2nd Gurkhas' Bren-gun carrier platoon saved the situation on 15 December by driving the Japanese out of Gurun village and forcing back their tanks, but gained only a temporary respite. A further withdrawal was ordered back to Sungei Patani and its airfield and then back again to the Muda river.

In happier post-war days Sungei Patani was to become the home of Gurkha recruit training. However at this moment it was the unedifying scene of a Royal Air Force scramble to get clear of its airfield before the Japanese arrived. The official historian of 11th Indian Division records the division's state on 16 December as it took up defence positions on the Muda river:

The Division by this time was little more than a division in name. In four days it had retreated 70 miles. Of 6th Indian Brigade 1/8th Punjabis was entirely lost. East Surreys mustered only 10

officers and 260 other ranks; 2/16th Punjabis, who had done practically no fighting, only 500 of all ranks. The three battalions of 15th Brigade totalled less in strength than one full battalion. Of 28th Brigade, only one battalion, 2/2nd Gurkhas, was intact. 2/9th Gurkhas, apart from battle casualties, had lost its 'A' Company during the withdrawal from Gurun. 2/1st Gurkhas who had been cut off three times, mustered 300 in all.

Apart from numerical losses there had been grave losses of arms, equipment, carriers and vehicles. The men themselves were dead beat, badly short of food and desperately short of sleep; their clothing torn, drenched and filthy, their boots sodden. Many were sick with fever and many more were suffering from suppurating sores on their feet and leech-ridden bodies.

In fact this report was unduly pessimistic as many stragglers and some of those cut off eventually got back, including a 70-strong 'A' Company to 2/9th Gurkhas. The last two sentences of the report reflect the normal state of troops fighting in the jungle for a prolonged period of time without relief. By contrast post-war reports showed the Japanese relieving their forward troops every 36 hours.

What was really wrong was lack of training and preparation for fighting in the jungle, which was mistakenly supposed to be impenetrable. There was a corresponding over-reliance on motorized transport, as well as poor overall senior leadership and planning that denied the troops on the ground the opportunity to occupy a strong defensive position and fight from it, using reserves to keep their lines of communication open and free from Japanese infiltration. Virtually no preparation of demolitions on bridges had taken place and other defence works were sketchy or non-existent. The 8th Australian Division was being held uncommitted in Johore but, despite pleas for its support to stabilize the situation, it was not deployed until 11th and 9th Indian Divisions, on the west and east coast approach routes respectively, were exhausted. Despite urgings from Churchill and General Wavell (now overall theatre commander) to break contact and take up a position well back in Johore, from where a prolonged resistance could have been conducted, unrealistic orders continued to emanate from the overall commander to fight for every bit of Malaya. These orders meant that the defenders were destined to fight a running withdrawal in the face of a skilful and continually reinforced foe, who had total air superiority and a network of informers and fifth columnists.

***

At a stage when the troops themselves were fought out and exhausted, an effort was made to achieve a clean break by utilizing the still working railway running down the west coast of Malaya. A new defence line was taken up on the Krian river and into this was gathered survivors from previous battles, including elements that had been holding Penang before it was evacuated. Among these elements was a squadron of armoured cars from 3rd Indian Cavalry under command of Captain Hari Chand Badhwar, who was to prove a true and valiant friend in the days to come.

In the event, fear of being outflanked by Japanese coming in from the north-eastern approach via Grik led to further withdrawals back to a strong natural defence position at Kampar, just south of Ipoh from where 2/2nd Gurkhas had originally deployed north only a fortnight before.

A period out of immediate contact with the enemy, who were being skilfully delayed by 12th Brigade further north, allowed the exhausted Gurkhas of 28th Brigade to recuperate and strengthen their position which was successfully held against increasing enemy pressure for six days, showing that given a fighting chance the Japanese could be countered. Subsequent post-war evidence from Japanese records shows their frustration at the skilful and determined defence of Kampar. However, again well-founded fears of being outflanked and cut off by seaborne landings in their rear led to the strong Kampar position being given up. The Japanese, partly using the many small boats they had captured at Penang, landed large numbers behind the defenders at Kampar on 1–2 January 1942. Although these were located and countered by a mixed force of Gurkhas and 3rd Cavalry, it was clear that eventually they would break through and cut Kampar off.

The 11th Division now ordered a withdrawal 50 miles back to the Slim river line. This line north of Slim river had considerable natural advantages, consisting as it did of heavily overgrown palm and rubber plantations pierced only by the twin corridor of the main road and railway. Although the jungle-wise Japanese infantry might well succeed in penetrating through the overgrown plantations, at least it should be possible to stop them using the road and railway. Accordingly, 12th Brigade was placed in depth along the road and railway in the area of Trolak, well forward of the river. Unfortunately, no demolitions or road cratering took place since it was felt that the road should be left open for stragglers to come back. Also such anti-tank weapons as existed were dispersed, instead of being concentrated to cover the road and railway.

The 28th Brigade with its three Gurkha battalions was placed in a rest area around Slim village, situated around the bridge over the Slim river, some five miles behind 12th Brigade. The plan was for 12th Brigade to hold Trolak for three days and then withdraw back through 28th Brigade, who would hold Slim village for probably only a day to allow 12th Brigade to get clear before withdrawing to another defence position that was being prepared further back.

On 5 January 1942 the Japanese attacked 12th Brigade at Trolak, but after heavy fighting were repulsed. Immediately Brigadier W.R. Selby, who now commanded 28th Brigade, asked 11th Division commander Major General A.C.M. Paris for permission to move his troops out of their rest area and occupy their battle positions north of the river. The divisional commander vetoed this suggestion on the grounds that another day's rest would do wonders for the men of 28th Brigade, during which time 12th Brigade should easily be able to hold the Japanese. Instead he ordered 28th Brigade to be in position by midday 7 January. This turned out to be a fateful decision.

At 0345 hours on the bright moonlit night of 7 January, the Japanese mounted 'a death drive' of about 30 medium tanks straight down the main road into 12th Brigade and, after heavy fighting, broke through. The 12th Brigade units were successively crushed one after the other, there being no coordinated anti-tank defence. While this debacle was taking place, nobody thought fit to tell the men of 28th Brigade, who according to their orders were now marching along the road north to take up their battle positions behind 12th Brigade. The 2/1st Gurkhas, who had already been cut off three times during the campaign and were much reduced in numbers, were suddenly confronted by Japanese tanks. In minutes they were destroyed and reduced to small groups trying to escape south while avoiding the Japanese.

The 2/2nd and 2/9th Gurkhas were slightly more fortunate in that most of them had already reached their new defensive positions around the road and railway when the Japanese tanks attacked. Lack of anti-tank weapons meant that the Japanese controlled the road, down which they passed lorry-loads of infantry. Frantic and gallant efforts were made to stop them. A British officer of 9th Gurkhas was last seen firing his revolver down the air vents of a Japanese tank before he fell riddled with machine-gun bullets from the tank behind. The 155th Field Artillery Regiment guns, which had supported 28th Brigade during the withdrawal, went down firing over open sights at the Japanese tanks. When dawn came, 2/2nd and 2/9th Gurkhas were still holding but the Japanese were all round them. Through them small groups of survivors from 12th Brigade, exhausted and bewildered, made their way back only to find the Japanese further beyond.

Brigadier Selby, his brigade headquarters shattered by the tanks, continued to command and direct with his customary energy and determination regardless of personal danger. Meanwhile 2/9th Gurkhas, the battalion he had commanded with such distinction, along with 2/2nd Gurkhas, fought on with increasing desperation.

Eventually the order came to break out south and retreat a further 19 miles to Tanjong Malim, the next planned defence line.

By this time the Japanese controlled the main road, the bridges over the Slim and Birnam rivers had been blown and escape was very difficult, especially as very few Gurkhas could swim. Some made their way over the twisted girders of the destroyed railway bridge which the Japanese had neglected to guard, some tried to cross the rivers using ropes of joined up rifle-slings, but many drowned in the surging current. Others headed off in to the jungle in an attempt to loop round behind the Japanese and rejoin further south; few succeeded, many dying of exhaustion, hunger and disease in the trackless jungle. Some Gurkhas disguised themselves as Malays in an effort to get past the Japanese who seemed to be everywhere.

We have a report that shows that, despite the disaster, Gurkha discipline never wavered. A large group of cut-off 2/2nd and 2/9th Gurkhas were, as explained, trying to evade the Japanese by cutting through the jungle. However the very size of the group made its progress slow and liable to discovery. It was therefore decided to split into smaller groups and 2/9th Gurkhas set off on their own. Lieutenant Emmett, attached to 2/2nd Gurkhas, records: '*Ninth Gurkhas left first, moving off section by section at one minute intervals in perfect order.*'

Sadly, few were ever seen again.

The 11th Indian Division had ceased to exist as such, its strength of 3,000 now being a quarter of its original numbers. In 28th Brigade, 2/2nd Gurkhas and 2/9th Gurkhas were reduced to less than half strength and 2/1st Gurkhas to fewer than 100 men, 28th Brigades' strength was only 600 in all. Of the amalgamated 6th/15th Brigades there were only 900 and from 12th Brigade, 415. Those that survived were exhausted many without equipment, ragged and half starving. Such had been the magnitude of the Slim river disaster.

General Wavell, coming forward to see for himself, decided that an eventual withdrawal to Singapore was inevitable. A new plan to impose some delay involved a covering force consisting of elements of 8th Australian Division and some of the reinforcing units just arriving. The remnants of 11th Division were to withdraw behind this covering force and refit and reorganize. On the night of 8/9 January 1942, 28th Brigade broke contact and were trucked back 15 miles to Serandah, only 20 miles north of the Malayan capital Kuala Lumpur. Historians of both 2/2nd and 2/9th Gurkhas give high praise to the men of 2/3rd Australian Reserve Motor Transport Company, who were waiting for the shattered men as they clambered aboard the trucks, once the final bridge over the Sungei Selangor was blown.

Without rations, troops found food foraging in the surrounding countryside while taking up a new defence position.

Detail from a picture montage painted by David Rowlands showing Gurkha POW from 2/2nd Gurkhas at forced labour in Singapore.

Subedar Hari Sing Bohra Gurkha Major of 2/2nd Gurkhas who wrote a dignified letter of protest to his Japanese gaolers complaining about the ill-treatment of his Gurkhas. As a result he was beaten so savagely that he died. (Gurkha Museum)

Some replacement weapons and transport reached them while they were preparing to hold the important bridge over the Sungei Choh river south of Serendah and the village of the same name. The Japanese were not long in arriving and, having driven in the covering troops, then tried to rush the bridge. D Company 2/2nd Gurkhas (one of the only two remaining companies) was ready for them. Holding the attack, they successfully blew the bridge before the Japanese could capture it and then skilfully extricated themselves, despite Japanese troops getting over the river and trying to get behind them. At Choh village itself a major clash took place where the now 250-strong 2/9th Gurkhas suffered a further 53 casualties in a desperate battle to avoid being cut off. The 2/2nd Gurkhas, who had moved behind them after blowing the Sungei Choh bridge, kept the road open down which the remnants of 28th Brigade streamed, having fought their way clear of Japanese encirclement.

At this stage the Johore defence line was reached and the men of 11th Division went into reserve behind the Australians and fresh troops arriving from Singapore, and received new clothing to replace their stinking rags. Their task now was to provide defence in depth and stop the Japanese landing troops by sea onto the west coast behind the main defence line.

The new defence line across Johore was soon attacked by the Japanese who tried another tank attack at the important Gemas road and rail junction in central Johore. This time the Australians had a well coordinated anti-tank defence and handled them very roughly. The Japanese lost tanks and several hundred men and could make no headway. Additionally, 50 newly arrived Hurricane fighters had been uncrated and assembled. They were now operating from airfields in Singapore, thus disputing in some small measure Japanese air superiority. Unfortunately they had originally been destined for the Western Desert and their heavy desert condition fit made them slower than the Japanese Zeros, but still a lot better than the previous Brewster Buffalo fighters which had been completely outclassed. The defence of Malaya and Singapore was predicated on there being 556 modern planes operating off 20 fully equipped airfields. In the event there were 133 obsolescent aircraft operating off four partially completed airfields in Malaya and three in Singapore. Over the two months of the campaign 650 modern fighters, Hurricanes and Tomahawks, were sent by convoy to Russia! For the infantry, fighting without any air cover, being continually bombed and strafed was a dispiriting experience and restricted virtually all movement to darkness.

Baulked for a time at Gemas, the Japanese attacked at the far west of the Johore defence line at the little port of Muar. Here they encountered the newly arrived and very raw 45th Indian Brigade and shattered it. Tremendous efforts were made to hold at Muar by rushing in reinforcements, but the Japanese penetrated and 28th Brigade was involved again, trying to contain the breakthrough at Batu Pahat. The 2/9th Gurkhas went forward to set up a roadblock while 2/2nd Gurkhas went into all-round defence in the Pontian Kechil/Pontian Besar seashore area well south towards the western tip of Johore. Here a surreal time warp had obtained, as 2nd Gurkha history explains:

> … at 0300 hours on 15 January the troop carriers rolled into another world – an ordered and civilized community where the war was still distant rather than an ever-present actuality. The anti-aircraft barrage could be heard and seen nightly as enemy air groups struck at Singapore; but at Pontian Kechil the bombs were yet to fall, the landscape unmarred by the flails of battle. Officers seeking billets found plantation owners pursuing the common round with their families still about them; at the local club there were gay frocks and dinner jackets at the sundown hour.

By 22 January the bitter fighting at Muar ended in defeat at the hands of the Japanese Imperial Guards Division. The shattered survivors staggered through the thinly spread 28th Brigade still ably and energetically commanded by Brigadier Selby. He was now commanding from a motorcycle on which by lightning journeys in extremely hazardous conditions he maintained his well-known grip on all his sub-units, especially 2/9th Gurkhas who would do anything for their old 'Commanding Sahib'. There was now no real alternative to retreat across the Johore Causeway and into Singapore Island. As the official historian of 11th Division later wrote:

> For five long weeks, alone and unrelieved our division had fought and retreated … retreated and fought again. It had delayed the advance of three Japanese divisions over 475 miles and throughout those days and nights the enemy had been supreme in the air, in full command of the sea, alone in their tanks and able constantly to replace their tired troops.

The 28th Brigade, or what was left of it, crossed the Causeway during the night of 30/31 January 1942 and deployed to the Naval Base to the immediate east of the Causeway. Behind them the Causeway was blown with a huge explosion that tore a 75-yard gap through which the sea flowed while the lock gates at the northern end were destroyed.

All three Gurkha battalions were amazed to find that far from being the island fortress they were expecting, from the north at any rate, Singapore was virtually undefended. Churchill, equally surprised and appalled, described it as 'a naked island'. Even the imposing Naval Base had no shoreward defences. As if to emphasize its vulnerability, on 2 February the Japanese bombed it and set fire to the 30 or so huge oil tanks, after which 28th Brigade worked and lived and fought in a perpetual foul-smelling sooty gloom.

Frantically they began to prepare defences, wondering why on earth nothing had been done to lay mines and wire and clear fields of fire during the seven weeks of the withdrawal. The account of Lieutenant Colonel A.M.L. Harrison, the chief staff officer of 11th Division, would be funny if it was not so pathetic. Having made his way through darkened streets in the middle of an air raid, he eventually found the officer in charge of the defence of Singapore:

> I then began to ask questions.

> 'Was there any plan for a withdrawal to a smaller perimeter in the event of the enemy breaking through on some sector of the coast?' I was told that there was no such plan.

> 'Might I have a map?' I was given a one-inch map (very small scale) on which the area of the Naval Base was a pure white blank. No details had been committed to it for reasons of security.

> 'Could I have a plan of the Base?' There was none available.

'Could I have a map showing the run of defences in our area?' There were no defences in our area.

'What was the layout of the barbed wire?' There was not a single strand of barbed wire laid in our sector.

'What would be a good place for divisional headquarters?' There had been no time to arrange details of that sort.

'How many searchlights were there available?' There were no searchlights except one or two anti-aircraft lights.

The 2/2nd Gurkhas (2/1st Gurkhas were acting as part of 2/2nd Gurkhas given their low numbers) tried to adapt the awkward shape of the Naval Base to defence by digging in along the sea wall and siting headquarters, first aid posts etc, in the bomb-proof entrances of the enormous magazines still stuffed full of naval ordnance. Meanwhile 2/9th Gurkhas were given the task of protecting the nearby airfield of Seletar. Gurkha reinforcements of five officers and 201 men (mostly only 17 years old), which had arrived on the final convoy, now joined.

Time to prepare defences was very short and on 5 February a heavy artillery bombardment started causing casualties when shells burst in the entrances of the magazines. A furious artillery duel continued until the Japanese carried out an amphibious assault on 8 February, the whole weight of their blow landing on the 8th Australian Division area to the west of the Causeway. After a spirited resistance the Australians started pulling back, unfortunately without telling 2/2nd Gurkhas on their right who suddenly found themselves totally isolated. The only clue as to where the Australians had gone was a small note in pencil handed by the last of the withdrawing Australians, indicating they were going back to the Mandai lateral road some three miles to the rear.

Soon it became clear that the Australians were now moving back south beyond the Mandai road and, when efforts to restore the situation failed, 28th Brigade were ordered to give up the Naval Base and move south. Prepared to fight to the end in their now well-defended area, the Gurkha battalions were surprised and disappointed to be ordered back. Unsettling rumours of surrender were already circulating.

By all accounts the move back south was little short of chaotic, with roads choked with refugees and military traffic. Contradictory orders circulated until eventually 2/1st and 2/2nd Gurkhas were ordered to come into 11th Division reserve, just north of the village of Nee Soon. Orders then followed to withdraw again into a tight perimeter around Singapore City. In this confined space were crammed 85,000 troops and 500,000 civilians. An eyewitness report by Major L. N. Evans of 2/2nd Gurkhas is worth quoting:

The men presented a strange and somewhat sorry sight, all dead tired and many almost asleep as they walked. They were dirty, unshaven and wearing almost every variety of head-dress and foot wear: a few, not many, in steel helmets, others in felt hats, forage caps or comforters. There was a mixture of boots and PT shoes, some even in socks or bare feet. These articles were all that remained to them after the many vicissitudes of the long retreat and numerous rapid withdrawals.

In this cramped perimeter nearly all open areas were occupied by gun positions which were continually in action. Shells falling short caused many casualties, including a platoon of 2/9th Gurkhas involved in the heavy fighting to the west of the main Singapore road, which was the Japanese axis of advance. In this last bitter struggle 2/9th Gurkhas lost heavily.

Lieutenant Colonel G.H.D. Woollcombe, Commandant 2/2nd Gurkhas, who was included in the group ordered to leave Singapore before the surrender, but was never seen again. (Gurkha Museum)

日本の陸海空軍は全部聯合国に降伏し、日本天皇陛下も二の降伏條件に御親署あらせられたので太平洋戦争はこれを以て終了した。

二の傳單の上には日本軍の捕虜となった聯合国側の兵士と抑留された聯合国人民に対する聯合国當局の指令があり、即ち日本軍抑留下にある聯合国将兵及び人民は須く各自の現位置に止まり、冷静沈着に聯合国當局の今後の命令を待つべし。

日本の衛兵諸君がこの傳單を入手した時、直ちに収容中の聯合国将兵及び人民に渡し、從事に対しては出来得べくの親切を以て取扱はれた上、この傳單諸君は二の傳單を渡した後、即時各自の宿営地に帰還すべし。

Drop'd in CHANGI T.O.W. Camp at 1750 on 28th Aug 45

IN accordance with the terms of the surrender of all Japanese forces signed by His Majesty the Emperor the war has now come to an end.

These leaflets contain our instructions to Allied prisoners of war and internees whom we have told to remain quiet where they are.

Japanese guards are to ensure that the prisoners get these leaflets and that they are treated with every care and attention. Guards should then withdraw to their own quarters.

Allied document dropped by plane telling of the Japanese surrender. (Gurkha Museum)

On 13 February, 2/1st and 2/2nd Gurkhas took up position along the Braddell Road running from the MacRitchie Reservoir eastwards to Woodleigh, close to Paya Lebar airport. This position was much better for defence and soon the Gurkhas were digging in enthusiastically, borrowing digging tools from local Chinese labourers. As they were working, an order was received to provide 20 men through the rank structure for 'special duties', the nature of which was secret. Next morning it became clear that the 'special duty' was for those selected to be sent out of Singapore so they could prepare the rest of the Army with their experience of fighting the Japanese. The selected group were gathered in the YMCA building in Singapore City and many were killed and wounded when it was bombed. The remainder, their ship having left early, tried to escape on launches, most of which were sunk by Japanese aircraft. Among those lost was Lieutenant Colonel Woollcombe who had commanded 2/2nd Gurkhas throughout the campaign.

Having prepared a strong defence position, 2/1st and 2/2nd Gurkhas were now ordered to move to another area. This was always a maddening and debilitating occurrence, when mentally prepared to fight it out from positions prepared with care and much expenditure of scarce energy, for soldiers desperately short of food and sleep. Having moved, their supply arrangements were disrupted and there was nothing to eat.

During the morning of 15 February there was very heavy Japanese bombing and shelling, but this did not stop 2/1st and 2/2nd Gurkhas moving forward to take up a new defensive position as part of 53rd Brigade, to which they had now been transferred. As they were moving forward, a dispatch rider arrived stating that a surrender would take place at 1600 hours and that secret documents but not arms and equipment should be destroyed. As it happened artillery exchanges continued until 2100 hours and units of 11th Division did destroy weapons and equipment.

The Gurkhas and especially the Gurkha officers were appalled and very reluctant to surrender, as were their British officers. All had been prepared to fight on as they had for the last ten weeks and simply could not understand what had happened. In the end nature applied her own remedy; desperately short of sleep and now out of combat, most Gurkhas simply lay down and slept the sleep of the totally drained and exhausted.

When the Japanese eventually arrived, one of the first things they did was organize a victory parade with British and Imperial troops ordered to line the route. This was filmed extensively for propaganda purposes to show the captive populations that the sun had really set on the British Empire.

Indians and Gurkhas were now separated from their British officers and put in different camps. The British officers went to Changi Barracks which was some way distant from River Valley Road where the Gurkhas were incarcerated. By various dangerous stratagems, they contrived to keep in contact and keep each others' morale up.

The Gurkhas were fortunate in Captain Hari Chand Badhwar of 3rd Cavalry, whose armoured car squadron had joined 2/2nd Gurkhas during the retreat. In him they found a valiant protector in their camp. Unintimidated by ghastly torture and deprivation, his courage blazed forth in protection of the Gurkhas in the camp against the cruel excesses of the Japanese. Suspended over 80 days in a cage in which he was unable to sit or lie down, he refused to give way to the Japanese or to cease to protect those under him. His spirit was unquenchable. Despite all Captain Badhwar could do, terrible sufferings were endured. Gurkhas were tortured and beaten for not agreeing to join the renegade Indian National Army. British officers were worked to death on the infamous Burma–Siam Railway, their sufferings vividly portrayed by the 1957 film *Bridge on the River Kwai*. To both Gurkhas and their British officers, death fighting together shoulder to shoulder was infinitely preferable to the living death to which so many were daily subjected.

Subedar Major Hari Sing Bohra, Subedar Major of 2/2nd Gurkhas, wrote a dignified letter to the Japanese camp commandant protesting against the harsh excesses of their treatment because they remained true to their allegiance to the British. He was beaten so severely that he died. There is an eventual end to all agony and, as the war progressed and Japan contemplated defeat, conditions began to improve although not in time for the many who died of disease, torture and starvation.

Returning to Singapore, on 8 September 1945 the Allies released surviving officers and men of the three Gurkha regiments. The unspeakable ordeal was over, and with joy bordering on disbelief, British officers and their Gurkhas were reunited. Many who had been taken to camps up country rejoined much later, but none quite so late as those Gurkhas, who only appeared out of the jungle during the Malayan Emergency years later, having been ordered to stay there!

One of the most touching aspects of the agony of Malaya and Singapore and its aftermath of captivity was the reception back in India of the three Gurkha battalions who had suffered so much. As their survivors landed in India they were greeted by bands and guards of honour; Field Marshal Lord Wavell, now Viceroy of India, with Lady Wavell personally greeted them. Their route was lined by the men of their own regiments who had fought in Burma, the Western Desert, Italy, Greece and on the Frontier; their path was strewn with flowers thrown by cheering crowds. All that could be done to show them honour for all they had steadfastly endured was done.

After Singapore fell the House of Commons had demanded an Inquiry into the conduct of the Malayan Campaign, but Churchill had refused it. This was perhaps wise, as in terms of its conduct there was much to be questioned. However for the three Gurkha battalions and the thousands of others who had to pay the ultimate price for these deficiencies there could be no censure. As 2nd Gurkhas' historian so rightly commented: 'In so far as the Gurkha battalions are concerned, no apology for the Malayan debacle is necessary.'

The Pacific Star awarded to troops who had fought in the Malayan Campaign of 1941–42.

CHAPTER ELEVEN

THE SECOND WORLD WAR: DEFEAT IN BURMA

Whilst British and Commonwealth forces were fighting desperately to stem the Japanese invasion of Malaya, Japan crossed over from occupied Thailand (Siam) and attacked Burma, realizing that the forces available to defend it were modest to say the least. In fact, apart from the Burma Frontier Force, which was mostly deployed in the far north and east of Burma, all there was consisted of eight battalions of the Burma Rifles and some unbrigaded Indian Army units. These were formed into 16th Brigade and included 1/7th Gurkhas. In early January 1942 they were moved to the Burma–Thai border, south of the major town of Moulmein.

In the second week of January, Headquarters 17th Indian Division, with some of its divisional troops, arrived at Moulmein to take over command of all troops in the Tenasserim area, the narrow strip of Burma running south from the Salween river to Victoria Point, sharing a common border with Thailand for some 400 miles. It was far too long an area for the limited forces available to hold in any strength. The troops deployed consisted of the newly formed 16th Brigade and four battalions of Burma Rifles. Later in January this force was joined by 46th Brigade, one of the original brigades of 17th Division, the other two having been diverted to the battle for Malaya.

The Japanese invasion of Burma started on 19 January 1942 with their 55th Division moving across the Thai border on a line

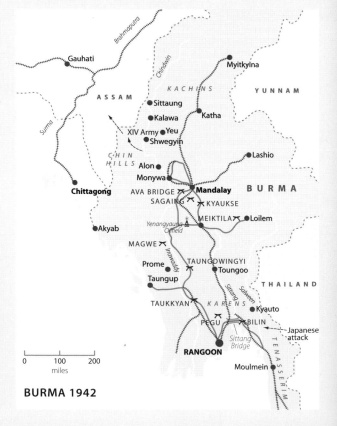

BURMA 1942

due west directed on Moulmein. At the same time their 33rd Division crossed the border further north towards the only Sittang river bridge at Mokpalin. This was a key area, for if they could secure a crossing over the major obstacle of the Sittang, then they would be able to move on the capital Rangoon, as well as cutting off all troops in Moulmein and to its east and south. Rangoon, a major port, was vital if Burma was to be reinforced; loss of it would make Burma difficult to hold, and the prospect of a long and hazardous retreat back to India through thick malarial jungle and precipitous hills could become a reality.

The 48th Brigade arrived in Rangoon from India on 31 January 1942. It consisted of brigade headquarters and three Gurkha battalions (1/3rd, 1/4th and 2/5th). On 17 February the brigade moved up to the vital Bilin area. Here a confused situation obtained: 48th Brigade lost 1/4th Gurkhas to 16th Brigade while 1/3rd Gurkhas were left to guard dumps to the rear. The 48th Brigade now took under command 1/9th Jats from 16th Brigade and 8th Burma Rifles, battalions it had never even seen, let alone trained with!

North of Bilin was 16th Brigade and to its south 46th Brigade. The 2/5th Gurkhas were used to fill the gap between 1/9th Jats and 8th Burma Rifles on the line of the Bilin river, while holding two companies further back to act as brigade reserve.

As the Japanese main force closed up to the main Bilin defensive line, they also attempted by means of infiltration to get behind the British forces and, by cutting them off, to force them to withdraw. The Japanese used all manner of ruses to achieve this, including men hiding in herds of cattle driven along the road by local drovers. There was also much use of fifth columnists and renegade Burmese National Army.

All this was very new and unsettling for the young untried riflemen of the two reserve companies of 2/5th Gurkhas. Soon however they were on top of the situation and the Japanese suffered some rough treatment at their hands. On the night of 19/20 February it was decided that 17th Division would have to fall back on Kyaukto, since 1/9th Jats were buckling under repeated Japanese attacks centred on their front, which left A Company of 2/5th Gurkhas very exposed. Marching on empty stomachs, bombed repeatedly by the Japanese and in error by the Royal Air Force, they finally harboured in a bamboo grove on the night of 21 February. They were then ordered to move with all speed to the Sittang bridge at Mokpalin, all vehicles to be sent on ahead and across the bridge. Since radios seldom worked, the message was passed on by runner to 1/3rd Gurkhas following behind. As they marched through the night, lorries from 46th Brigade passed them going west whose men spoke of their brigade in contact with the Japanese to the east.

With no guide, a single 30-year-old map and in darkness, it was difficult for the weary troops to know, when they came to the join

An aerial photo of the Sittang Bridge; the premature blowing of which led to so many Gurkhas being cut off and subsequently drowning. (Gurkha Museum)

of two major branch roads, which one they should take. Fortunately they chose the more southerly; the northerly one would have taken them straight into the path of the fast advancing Japanese 33rd Division. Arriving at Mokpalin village, 2/5th Gurkhas found the road to the Sittang bridge blocked with stationary vehicles and almost immediately came under fire from the high ground on their right. Without sleep, with very little food and having marched most of the night, 2/5th Gurkhas did not hesitate and went straight into the attack on 22 February. At the first sound of gunfire the mules carrying the 3in medium mortars and their ammunition had stampeded, so the attack on the blocking enemy positions had to be made without any covering fire other than Bren light machine-guns. Nevertheless, after three attempts the Japanese were cleared off the nearest high ground to the right of the road and 2/5th Gurkhas started to push on to try to clear the enemy positions further back. By this time their Subedar Major had managed to locate the mules carrying the 3in mortars and their ammunition, and get them into action, albeit without their sights which were still missing.

Slowly the confused situation was becoming clearer. Divisional and 48th Brigade headquarters, along with 1/4th Gurkhas, had

Detail from the painting by David Rowlands of men from the Duke of Wellington's Regiment and 3rd Gurkhas attacking Japanese, who had reached the eastern end of the Sittang Bridge.

crossed the bridge before the Japanese arrived and blocked all approaches. The rest of 48th Brigade, 16th and 46th Brigades were trapped on the east side of the huge Sittang river and unable to cross. It was vital that the Japanese, who could have only just arrived, were cleared out of the way.

On the left of the road it was believed that 7/10th Baluch Regiment was moving up to try to clear forward, so Lieutenant Colonel R.T. Cameron, commanding 2/5th Gurkhas, now prepared to attack on the right to clear the Japanese off a feature known as Buddha Hill commanding both the road and river. Using A and C Companies, the advance started well despite sniper fire. Nearing the objective the two companies became separated in the thick scrub. C Company on the left came under heavy mortar fire and started taking casualties. A Company, pushing on, met increasingly fierce opposition and, now separated from C Company, was forced back.

Meanwhile D Company, held up by enemy action, had arrived and proceeded to attack a hill on the left of the road from which fire was coming, since 7/10th Baluchis did not seem to be

doing anything about it. As they moved into the assault the whole of 1/3rd Gurkhas arrived and, immediately, Colonel Cameron briefed their Commanding Officer, Lieutenant Colonel George Ballinger, on the situation. As they were talking, two batteries of mountain artillery arrived and they decided that 1/3rd Gurkhas should attack the hill called Pagoda Hill, between Buddha Hill and the road, supported by these guns. The attack went in at 1030 hours and almost immediately 1/3rd Gurkhas were involved in bitter fighting, Colonel Ballinger being killed.

Meanwhile more Japanese were arriving from the north, attacking the hill features already secured by 2/5th Gurkhas. B Company 2/5th Gurkhas held on grimly until C Company counter-attacked to relieve them. Although some progress was made, it was not until the final reserve, 'A' Company, was put in that the Japanese were finally pushed out. The attacks by 1/3rd Gurkhas and 'D' Company 2/5th Gurkhas to try and take their respective objectives and open their way to the bridge were still in progress when Brigadier J.K. Jones, commanding 16th Brigade, arrived; his news was not good. His brigade, which included 1st and 3rd

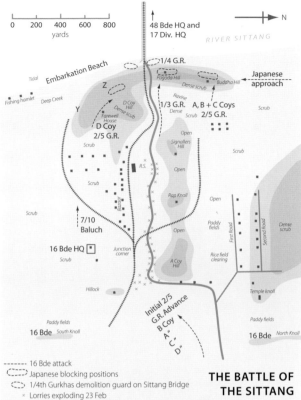

THE BATTLE OF
THE SITTANG

-------- 16 Bde attack
Japanese blocking positions
1/4th Gurkhas demolition guard on Sittang Bridge
× Lorries exploding 23 Feb

Japanese medium machine gunners in position on the eastern end of the Sittang bridge. (Gurkha Museum)

Battalions of 7th Gurkhas, had been fighting further east but had succeeded in extricating itself and was nearing the bridge area. The 46th Brigade further east had been cut off by a roadblock and after bitter fighting had been virtually destroyed as a fighting entity.

The situation at the bridge was explained to Brigadier Jones, who ordered a by-now exhausted 2/5th Gurkhas to pull back off the furthest hill they had secured and concentrate on holding their hill positions immediately to the right of the road, which were countering increasing Japanese pressure from the north. Sending 1/9th Jats forward to try and join up with D Company 2/5th Gurkhas, who had succeeded in getting close to the bridge, the rest of 16th Brigade came in behind 2/5th securing their rear. The 1/3rd Gurkhas continued to battle gallantly for their objective throughout the night.

At 0530 on 23 February 1942, just before dawn, three huge explosions were heard above the cacophony of 1/3rd Gurkhas' continuing battle. The significance was clear to everybody, the Sittang bridge had been blown and they were on the wrong side of it! This supposition was confirmed by a radio message from

Headquarters 17th Division. It was particularly tragic as 1/3rd Gurkhas had magnificently succeeded in taking their objective and were nearing 1/4th Gurkhas who were holding the eastern end of the bridge.

Part of the cause of this tragic occurrence was poor signal communications on the 108 series radio sets which, newly issued, proved almost useless. Nevertheless such a huge decision,

Major General 'Jackie' Smyth VC Commanding 17th Indian Division. (Smyth family)

involving the cutting off of two-thirds of 17th Division, should only have been taken following a personal reconnaissance by the divisional commander. This did not happen, and a terrible price had to be paid. February 1942 was an appalling month for Britain and its Gurkhas: Singapore surrendered with the loss of three regular Gurkha battalions and the Sittang bridge was prematurely blown with four regular Gurkha battalions on the wrong side.

The grim situation had to be confronted. The Japanese were now pushing hard for the bridge from the north and closing up from the east, so 6,000 men of 17th Division were virtually surrounded with a half-mile wide river between them and salvation. Added to this most Gurkhas could not swim. Desperately holding open a narrow corridor to the bridge, the wounded were got away on bamboo rafts and the few village boats that could be found. Lieutenant V.K.S. Sundaram, medical officer of 2/5th Gurkhas, was absolutely tireless and undismayed in his care of the wounded. The original plan had been to wait for nightfall before the main body attempted to cross, but it soon became clear that they probably could not hold that long and so crossing was to start immediately. Gurkhas, exhausted and famished, ate their emergency rations and prepared for 'mission impossible'.

Collecting bamboo poles for flotation from the burning village of Mokpalin, they made their way to the river. A row of exploding ammunition lorries temporally convinced the Japanese that they were under heavy artillery fire and, using this respite, the soldiers plunged into the river; many drowned or were swept away and many were later captured by the Japanese. Some kept going upriver and despite grim privations crossed and rejoined their units. Captain Bruce Kinloch of 3rd Gurkhas, with two other officers, swam the river at night and collecting a sampan, towed it back and made five crossings to rescue about 70 wounded men. It took some time to make an accurate assessment of losses as survivors continued to dribble in for some days. The 1/3rd Gurkhas had lost most of the battalion, only 221 from a total of 750 being present, 2/5th had only 227 left and the two 7th Gurkha battalions about 470 combined. Most had lost their weapons and had only what they stood up in. Altogether two-thirds of the 2,500 troops lost in this disaster were Gurkhas.

Those who made it to the other bank were collected up and moved by train to Pegu, where survivors of 3rd and 5th Gurkhas were amalgamated to form 5th/3rd Gurkhas and the two battalions of 7th Gurkhas into a single one. Fortunately there was an ordnance depot at Pegu and soldiers were reclothed and partially re-equipped. Weapons were in short supply, especially automatics. For several weeks afterwards 150 men had no personal weapons at all. There was no signal equipment, although given its inadequacy this did not prove too calamitous. In total, 17th Division numbered about a normal brigade, having lost two-thirds of its strength.

The blowing of the Sittang bridge, the only one over the river, did at least buy vital time by delaying the Japanese. This delay, short as it proved, allowed two additional brigades to reach Burma and disembark at Rangoon, now virtually bereft of any dock labour. The 7th British Armoured Brigade came direct from the Middle East and comprised two armoured regiments with Stuart light tanks and two British infantry battalions. The American tanks were obsolete, but nevertheless proved their effectiveness time and again. The other brigade, 63rd Indian Brigade, as well as two Indian battalions included 1/10th Gurkhas. Lieutenant General Sir Harold Alexander, later of Tunisia and Italy fame, had been appointed overall commander in Burma and to control all land fighting forces in Burma a I Burma Corps Headquarters was formed; to command it Lieutenant General William Slim was appointed. He had been a 6th Gurkha and had commanded a 7th Gurkha battalion and it just so happened that his two divisional commanders, Major General David 'Punch' Cowan, who had replaced Major General John Smyth VC as commander 17th Division, and Major General Bruce Scott of 1st Burma Division, were most unusually but providentially both from 6th

General 'Bill' (later Sir William) Slim, Commander 14th Army. (Gurkha Museum)

Gurkhas. Their close comradeship and friendship was to prove a tremendous asset in the grim days ahead.

As soon as the two brigades arrived they were directed to Pegu where the shattered 48th Brigade was refitting. Unfortunately, the Japanese had already reached Pegu, although not yet in strength. While 63rd Brigade commander and his three battalion commanders were carrying out an initial reconnaissance on 6 March, they were ambushed. The brigadier was seriously wounded and two of the battalion commanders killed. Lieutenant Colonel R.G. Leonard, commanding 1/10th Gurkhas, was seriously wounded and evacuated to a school where a field dressing station had been set up. The ambulance taking him back to a hospital was again ambushed and a Japanese soldier, using a captured Thompson sub-machine gun, shot at all the occupants. Fortunately for Colonel Leonard, the Japanese soldier was not familiar with his new toy and the bullets all went low smashing the slatting under the stretcher. Feigning dead, Leonard survived. Moments later a counter-attack by 1/4th Gurkhas, personally led by their Commanding Officer, Lieutenant Colonel Walter 'Joe' Lentaigne, cleared the Japanese away from their roadblock and saved Leonard.

Eventually in hospital it was discovered that Lieutenant Colonel Leonard had no fewer than 68 separate entry wounds.

Miraculously he survived and after the war became Chief Recruiting Officer for the newly formed Brigade of Gurkhas. The battle to clear the Japanese out of Pegu and resume the withdrawal north went on all night and cost both sides heavy casualties. After 1/4th Gurkhas' attack earlier in the day, 70 Japanese bodies were seen. The amalgamated 5th/3rd Gurkhas and 7th Gurkhas saw much fighting as well.

The situation was now very serious and as the Japanese were now approaching Rangoon, it was evacuated on 7 March. Since Rangoon was the only port capable of handling troopships this meant there could be no further reinforcement, unless it came all the way overland from India. The Royal Air Force, following a gallant attack on Japanese planes assembling at Rangoon airfield, was itself obliterated on the ground at Magwe and, after staging out to Akyab Island, left Burma entirely. Thereafter it was safe to assume any plane to be hostile!

The troops moving north from Rangoon were now trapped by a major Japanese roadblock 17 miles out on the road to Prome at Taukkyan which, despite determined infantry and 7th Armoured Brigade attacks, could not be broken. Failure to break through would have entailed the loss of all armour and mechanical transport with no alternative but to take to the jungle. Thankfully for no apparent reason, the Japanese lifted the roadblock. The 1/10th Gurkhas moving north at night actually crossed the rear of the Japanese roadblock moving south but did not recognize it as such. Post-war Japanese reports indicated that the roadblock had been withdrawn because the troops involved had mistakenly been ordered to attend a victory parade in Rangoon! Whatever the reason it was a major deliverance.

Reading Field Marshal Lord Slim's excellent book about the Burma campaign, *Defeat into Victory*, one gets the impression of a deliberate plan being adhered to despite reverses and disasters. However, at Gurkha battalion level, life seemed to be one of constant retreat punctuated by occasional vicious battles to remove Japanese roadblocks, or counter-attack when the situation had to be restored urgently. Decisions made instantaneously at battalion and company level often saved the day in an extremely fluid situation. Exhaustion, hunger and sleeplessness were the constants, exacerbated by further demands for action just when sleep or a meal seemed in prospect. The presence of 7th Armoured Brigade was probably a key factor in maintaining cohesion during the retreat. Not only was it the only effective counter to Japanese tanks, but a great morale-booster. Vitally, its vehicle radios were about the only ones that worked and enabled the continually embattled divisions to keep in contact with each other and Corps Headquarters.

Great hopes were entertained about the arrival of Chinese divisions from the north – after all they had been fighting the Japanese for years with some success. In the event, they were under

7th Gurkhas Vickers machine gun crew, possibly at the battle around the Yenangyaung oilfields. (Gurkha Museum)

strength and badly equipped and would attack only if they felt like it, which was not very often.

With the Chinese reluctant to advance any further south than Toungoo on the eastern north-south route, a major effort was made to hold Prome on the western north south-route so that a lateral line from Prome to Toungoo could be held across Burma. By attacking strongly south from Prome, it was hoped to halt the Japanese for long enough for the Chinese to get into action around Toungoo and push back the advancing Japanese. After the disaster at Sittang and heavy casualties at Pegu, 17th Division was really not strong enough to attack; it soon found itself in difficulties and withdrew back on Prome. The Japanese did not have it all their own way and, too boldly approaching Prome, got a very bloody reception from a well-sited 1/4th Gurkhas, who opened up at a range of 50 yards on closely packed marching troops. In spite of heavy casualties, the Japanese forced further withdrawals all the way back 100 miles to Taungdwingyi, most of which was completed on foot through waterless teak forest.

During 10–13 April 1942 the Japanese made a major assault on Kokkogwa, near Taungdwingyi. Failing to penetrate the 7th Gurkha position, they withdrew only to be caught in the open by a joint 1/4th Gurkhas–7th Armoured Brigade counter-attack. As 4th Gurkha history records: '*The plan worked well and what were not killed in the nullah were wiped out by the tanks who had called up their friends and got some 20 Brownings (machine guns) on the job.*'

Unfortunately the Japanese had managed to infiltrate round Taungdwingyi and a counter-attack by 1st Burma Division failed, so that a further withdrawal on the vital Yenangyaung oilfields

became inevitable. Retreating through Yenangyaung, the oil installations were prepared for demolition. Petrol was a vital commodity liable to be in short supply, and every container was filled to the brim. The 38th Chinese Division now joined I Burma Corps which helped to take the pressure off the disintegrating 1st Burma Division, whose Burmese soldiers were proving unreliable and deserting. Indeed ethnic Burmese were now joining the Japanese in large numbers, not only in the so-called Burma National Army but as guerrilla bands; fortunately their combat effectiveness was low.

Despite pleas by General Slim to withdraw 17th Division from its by now very exposed forward position of Taungdwingyi, the Burma Army commander, General Alexander, insisted it stay, fearing a withdrawal would lead to Lieutenant General Joseph W. Stilwell withdrawing his Chinese divisions as well. His reasoning was probably correct. In the event the newly arrived 38th Chinese Division was persuaded to attack and by so doing enabled what remained of 1st Burma Division to be extracted beyond Yenangyaung. The oilfields were now destroyed (15 April), cloaking the retreating soldiers in an aura of foul-smelling gloom, reflective of the dire situation.

Shortly after, the whole Chinese army to the east around Toungoo was shattered by a series of strong Japanese attacks and before long was making the best possible speed back to China. With an unprotected flank to the east, there was really no option left but to try and extract as many troops as possible back over the Irrawaddy river and west towards Assam, the most easterly state of India. It would be a long and testing retreat for already exhausted men.

The first thing was to secure the Ava bridge at Sagaing over the Irrawaddy before the Japanese got there first. General Slim moved his Corps back to Meiktila as a first step. Here 7th Armoured Brigade fought a brisk action to delay the Japanese so that the remaining Chinese could disengage and withdraw back to China up the Burma Road through Lashio. The 17th Division, ordered back from Taungdwingyi, now concentrated with 7th Armoured Brigade with orders to hold the Ava bridge approaches through the key town of Kyaukse. What was left of 1st Burma Division was to cross the Irrawaddy lower down by ferry and then join up with the rest of I Burma Corps, once it had crossed and destroyed the Ava bridge. Not surprisingly the Japanese had other ideas!

By 30 April, I Burma Corps were on the Irrawaddy around Sagaing. One brigade of Burma Division were across the Irrawaddy and heading north to secure the route back to India; the other two brigades were slowly making their way towards Monywa to secure a crossing over the large Chindwin river. This left 1st Burma Division Headquarters unprotected. Suddenly the Japanese attacked, and by getting to Monywa first, threatened to block the whole retreat with what would have been disastrous consequences. To try to avert a potentially catastrophic situation, 63rd Brigade from 17th Division was ordered to move by rail at night to just short of Monywa; surprisingly the railway was still in working order.

Shortly before this, the all-Gurkha 48th Brigade of 17th Division had given the newly arrived 18th Japanese Division a very rough time from its prepared positions at Kyaukse. Attacking 7th Gurkhas three times by moonlight, the recent conquerors of Singapore were repulsed with very heavy losses and, while licking their wounds, found themselves surprised by a 7th Gurkha dawn counter-attack, over 500 Japanese being accounted for the loss of ten men. This model rearguard action of 28/29 April enabled 48th Brigade to cross the Ava bridge comparatively unmolested and in good order.

Shortly before the order to move to Monywa, 63rd Brigade had also crossed the Ava bridge, 1/10th Gurkhas being the rearguard unit. Once they were over, the bridge was successfully blown on the night of 30 April, all troops having crossed the Irrawaddy.

Arriving at Monywa at dawn on 1 May, 1/10th Gurkhas found a scene of devastation and confusion. The Japanese had moved up the Chindwin river by boat and, surprising a lightly defended 1st Burma Division Headquarters, had virtually wiped it out and taken the town of Monywa itself. In fact when 1/10th Gurkhas deployed, the Japanese were still landing troops by boat, three of which were promptly sunk by the battalion's medium machine guns. The rest of 63rd Brigade now arrived and passed through the divisional headquarters which was a scene of terrible carnage and chaos. It was clear that the Japanese attack had been a complete surprise: many of the corpses had only one boot on, not having time to put on the other before they were killed. An immediate attack on Monywa by two companies of 1/10th Gurkhas, without artillery or armoured support, made no headway. It was clear that the Japanese now held Monywa strongly with at least two battalions and would take much shifting. Next day the whole of 63rd Brigade, reinforced by 1/4th Gurkhas attacked, but failed to retake the town.

That night 63rd Brigade marched round Monywa and headed north for the town of Alon in a 20-mile detour; it reached Alon the next morning. Exhausted and sleepless, 1/10th Gurkhas began digging a defensive position as the Japanese were following up fast. Destruction of all non-essentials started while remaining transport began to ferry units back to Yeu, where both divisions of Burma Corps were now attempting to concentrate, prior to crossing the Chindwin and starting the long trek back to India. It was going to be a close-run thing as the Japanese were moving fast to cut them off and the monsoon was about to break, which would make a withdrawal in any sort of order a physical impossibility.

While 48th Brigade formed a rearguard, the rest of Burma Corps prepared to cross the Chindwin at Shwegyin, having destroyed all its tanks and non-four-wheel drive transport and gone over to manpack and mules. The 7th Gurkhas guarded the vital southern approach to the so-called basin at Shwegyin where Burma Corps was by now slowly embarking on the Chindwin, and taken by six elderly steamers upstream north to Kalewa, from where the retreat to India would start. While the embarkation was slowly proceeding on 10 May, the Japanese moved a reinforced regiment upriver and suddenly attacked the 'basin'. The 7th Gurkhas stoutly held them back, but the Japanese were now causing many casualties in the crowded 'basin' with their mortars and continual air attacks. The 48th Brigade rearguard, slowly moving back to the 'basin', proceeded to plaster the Japanese with a massive artillery barrage, using all the ammunition that it would never be able to backload. This checked the Japanese for long enough to complete the evacuation over the Chindwin, and caused them to pause before following up, by which time the battered Burma Corps was on its way back to India.

After an arduous march, the troops reached India on 21 May. It had indeed been a very close-run thing as the monsoon broke a few days before they crossed the border into India. The Japanese had truly sown the wind but were now to reap the whirlwind. Before the fighting units arrived in Assam they had been preceded by fleeing administrative troops who told all sorts of horror stories about the invincibility of the Japanese. The Gurkhas knew better.

7th Gurkhas counter-attacking – note the Japanese body in the foreground.
(Gurkha Museum)

CHAPTER TWELVE

THE SECOND WORLD WAR: VICTORY IN BURMA

CONSOLIDATION AND THE FIRST ARAKAN CAMPAIGN

In the minds of most of the footsore and exhausted soldiers who came out from Burma was the thought that once they got to Assam all would be well. There they would find food and shelter, new uniforms and boots to replace rags and bare feet, and rest for shattered bodies and disturbed minds. In fact none of this came to pass and most were simply shown an area of hillside and told to bivouac on it. It never really occurred to them that Imphal, where they arrived, was one of the most inaccessible parts of India. It was served by a single-track railway, most of whose staff had disappeared following Japanese air raids. Great efforts were being made to get the wounded back and supplies and fresh troops forward, but the existing infrastructure was inadequate. Nevertheless, 2/5th Gurkhas were somewhat surprised to be told on arrival at Imphal that they would have to go on half-rations.

The 2/5th Gurkhas was now reconstituted as a battalion, but as one of the units caught on the wrong side of the Sittang bridge when it was blown, its losses in Burma had been very heavy. In all it had suffered 543 casualties, 39 Gurkhas killed in action, 75 wounded in action and the remainder missing. Of the missing, many were drowned attempting to cross the Sittang, others were killed, some captured and many simply were never heard of again. It would take time and patience to bring it and the other

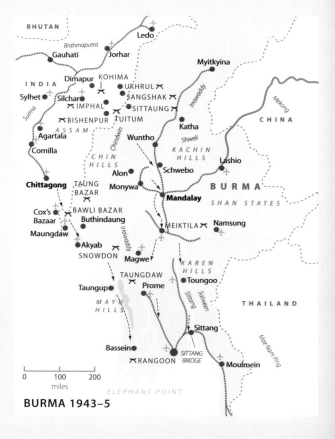

BURMA 1943–5

four Gurkha battalions that came out of Burma back to being fully operational.

Fortunately the onset of the monsoon put a brake on any further efforts of the Japanese to advance into India but, as soon as it stopped, there was no doubt that they would renew their offensive. As the shattered units of Burma Corps were slowly brought back up to full strength and effectiveness, new formations arrived; and senior commanders decided not to wait for the Japanese to attack but to regain the initiative and strike first. About the only place this could be done with any prospect of success was down the Arakan coast of Burma, astride the Mayu range of mountains. The plan called for a move down from Chittagong (in modern Bangladesh) through Cox's Bazaar and then an advance into Burma with the aim of recapturing the port and airfield at Akyab. Unfortunately arrangements for this limited offensive in July 1942 were somewhat haphazard and, after some initial success, the force was badly mauled by the Japanese and, suffering heavy casualties, was eventually forced all the way back to Cox's Bazaar by May 1943. Following this defeat, all troops in the area now came under XV Corps commanded by the able and experienced General Slim, who realized that much more preparation and training would be necessary before a further attack stood any chance of success. As his preparatory plans took shape he was promoted to command 14th Army. The Gurkhas now had their own man as their battle commander. Slim had laid down guidelines based on his experience during the fighting withdrawal through Burma and, at long last, he was in a position to see them carried out.

As soon as the monsoon ended it was expected that the Japanese would start to edge their way forward through the Chin Hills towards Imphal where 17 Division was refitting. The Chins were a proud and friendly mountain people who shared many characteristics with Gurkhas. They were also staunchly pro-British and would suffer cruel retribution should the Japanese gain control of their homeland. 17 Division's Gurkha battalions therefore pressed ahead fast with their training, drawing on all their experience during the retreat so that when the call came they would be ready.

Morale elsewhere was generally poor following the defeat in Burma and the recent lack of success in the Arakan. Something or someone was needed to restore it before the myth of Japanese invincibility took hold. This someone turned out to be Brigadier Orde Wingate. Wingate had achieved a measure of renown as commander of partisans fighting against the Italians in Abyssinia early in the war. Before that he had been in Palestine organizing the Jewish clandestine protection force known as Haganah, which was to become such a thorn in the British side in post-war years.

THE FIRST CHINDIT OPERATION

Wingate had many strong views on the use of unorthodox guerrilla warfare and its effectiveness which won over, among others, Churchill and General Wavell. The latter had previously sent Wingate and Major Michael Calvert to try and organize the hill tribes of Burma against the Japanese early in the withdrawal from Burma. This high-level support gave Wingate command of the newly formed 77th Brigade and leave to prepare it for a long-range penetration raid back into Japanese-occupied Burma. Once there, it would attack Japanese communications by blowing up railway tracks and setting road ambushes. It was felt that such activity would lead to the Japanese having to divert a disproportionate number of troops simply to guard their communications, which would harm their ability to mount another major offensive in 1943. Wingate called his men Chindits, a mispronunciation of Chinthe, the mythical half-lion, half-flying griffin guarding Burmese temples and monasteries.

One major factor would aid this long-range penetration and that was the growing power of the British and American air forces. During the retreat they had been virtually driven out of the sky over Burma by the Japanese air force, but now the balance was tilting. Large numbers of modern Allied aircraft were reaching the Far East theatre of war and the Japanese Zero, mainstay of its fighter force, was being outclassed. This meant that a measure of air supply to Wingate's columns deep in Burma was now practicable.

As a part of Wingate's force there was one Gurkha battalion, 3/2nd Gurkhas, a recently raised wartime battalion having in it many very young and inexperienced officers and soldiers, some of whom were drafted in from other Gurkha regiments. Wingate's qualities did not include understanding and relating to people and their peculiarities. If they had he would have realized immediately that Gurkhas were at their most formidable when they were working as a formed body. Instead he promptly split them up with British soldiers with whom they could neither communicate nor empathize. The other strong Gurkha traits are courage and resource in battle, so making a large number of them into mule-handlers was less than sensible.

Lieutenant D. F. Neill of 3/2nd Gurkhas records that Wingate's aloof manner, unorthodox dress and apostolic appearance failed to impress the Gurkhas. This was unfortunate in a man who was to lead them on a desperate mission 200 miles behind enemy lines. Additionally the Gurkha officers found the aim of the expedition obscure. Was it to cause real damage to the Japanese or simply prove that British troops could make their way behind Japanese lines and return, having carried out various tasks and thereby score a propaganda victory? If the latter, the whole concept was unintelligible to the Gurkha.

Brigadier Orde Wingate, the controversial commander of the two Chindit operations.

After four months of intensive training, 77th Brigade set out in seven columns on 6 February 1943. Columns One to Four were predominantly 3/2nd Gurkhas, although Gurkha mule-handlers from other Gurkha battalions were with the other columns as well. Out of a total force of some 3,000, there were some 1,289 ethnic Gurkhas. This, the first Chindit operation, was supposed to be carried out in conjunction with an attack by General Stilwell's Chinese into northern Burma. As such there would have been a good chance of major disruption of the Japanese in Burma. Unfortunately, and at the last moment, Stilwell's Chinese offensive failed to materialize, so the Chindits were on their own.

The first objective of the columns was to disrupt the Mandalay-Myitkyina railway by blowing up bridges and ambushing Japanese reaction forces. If successful, the Chindits would cross the massive Irrawaddy river and carry out further disruptive operations.

At first, reasonable progress was made and resupply by air worked quite well. The mules however proved difficult to handle and liable to bolt as soon as shooting started. On approaching the main target area, Two and Four Columns bumped a strong Japanese force and were obliged to return, but the remaining columns pushed on, reinforced by some elements of Two and Four Columns. Three Column under Major Calvert was probably most successful, causing considerable damage on the railway between the stations at Wuntho and Nankan and successfully ambushing Japanese hurrying towards the demolitions.

However, even his inspired leadership was unable to resolve the stark fact that Chindit columns were simply not strong enough to withstand determined Japanese counter-attack, and swiftly turned from hunter into hunted. From accounts of those who were present, the significant moment was the re-crossing of the Irrawaddy after quite successful operations by One and Three Columns in the hinterland around the Shweli river. While Brigadier Wingate's large group of some 700 men were re-crossing this major waterway using local boats, the bank guard on the home bank was attacked by a force of Japanese. As soon as firing broke out, Wingate ordered the whole force to ditch its heavy equipment and mules, split into small groups and make their way out to either India or China. In the view of some of those present, Wingate's column was strong enough to force the crossing and keep going as a formed body. In the event One and Three Columns did keep together for a considerable time. One Column under the 3/2nd Commanding Officer, Lieutenant Colonel L.A. Alexander, kept strong cohesion until it reached the Irrawaddy.

Since all local boats save two very small ones hidden up a creek had been confiscated by the Japanese, the Chindits had to make bamboo rafts to cross this huge river some 800 yards wide, which they did at night. When dawn came all had crossed, save the 59-strong Gurkha Brigade Headquarters defence platoon which Wingate had set adrift when he gave the dispersal order. The unit had attached itself to One Column. With dawn came the Japanese who discovered the defence platoon just casting off in its boats and rafts. Sitting ducks, all were killed except the Gurkha platoon commander and one rifleman; Colonel Alexander, waiting until the last, also fell mortally wounded. The remainder of the column then split up according to Wingate's instructions. As such they quickly became little better than fugitives. Without radio sets to call for air resupply, they were soon starving.

Very often the villages approached for food betrayed them to the Japanese, although the hill tribes such as the Kachins remained steadfastly loyal. With no other imperative the Japanese could hunt down the dispersed groups at their leisure. Knowing the difficulty small groups would have in crossing rivers, they were able to catch and destroy many trying to cross. Heartbreakingly, even groups that had got as far as the last great river, the Chindwin, were caught and destroyed although friendly patrols and observation posts on the other side saved many. These were manned by Burma Rifles units and troops from 2/5th Gurkhas; hundreds owed their lives to being picked up by their boats.

Three Column commander, Major Calvert, who had been the most successful in attacking the Japanese was loath to split up his column and many felt that under his bold leadership they might have won through together. Once split up into nine groups of 40, they too became fugitives and in common with others suffered appalling privations of hunger, exhaustion and disease, many dying of wounds or captured and subsequently murdered by the Japanese. Many hundreds simply disappeared and no record exists of what became of them. The 3/2nd Gurkhas lost 300 of the over 800 Chindit casualties. It was a disaster of appalling magnitude.

However, this was not how it was portrayed. Brigadier Wingate returned safely and quickly and captured the imagination of the world media by claiming to have vindicated his theories of beating the Japanese at their own game. His force had marched 200 miles into Japanese-occupied Burma, attacked their vital communications and then marched out again. Lionized, Wingate became a heroic world figure overnight, even as the remnants of his scattered force were being hunted down like wild animals. Those who had feared that the Japanese soldier was invincible in the jungle were now obliged to revise their ideas and, although based on hyperbole and inaccurate propaganda presentation, the First Chindit Expedition came to be regarded as a great victory and the turning of the tide against the Japanese. As we shall discover, the tide was turning, but not because of the First Chindit Expedition.

To those that survived, with few exceptions, the whole experience held a nightmarish quality that was to colour the rest of their lives. Lieutenant Neill, who later commanded 2/2nd Gurkhas, felt that his group survived only because of the Gurkhas' steadiness and ability to keep going while starving and exhausted.

Their uncanny knowledge of what jungle plants and roots could be eaten also made a vital difference to starving men. The lessons Neill learned as to what *not* to do in terms of inappropriate training, bad man-management and inadequate preparation were to serve him well in getting them all right in the latter part of the Burma campaign and in post-war conflicts.

As the starving Chindit survivors trickled in during May 1943 desperately trying to reach Assam before the onset of the monsoon, the foundations for victory were being laid. Lieutenant General Sir George Giffard, who preceded General Slim in command of what became 14th Army, had done much to put in place the administrative resources that would be needed to reopen the Arakan offensive once the monsoon ended. He had also negotiated the reinforcement of the highly experienced and battle-hardened 5 Indian Division from the Middle East and the newly arrived 7 Indian Division, both of which contained Gurkha units, many of them newly raised 3rd and 4th battalions. They were to acquit themselves with conspicuous gallantry.

THE SECOND ARAKAN CAMPAIGN

In December 1943 when all was ready, the second advance into the Arakan started. The plan was for 5 Indian Division (of which 3/9th Gurkhas formed a part) to advance down the central spine of the Mayu mountains and also to its west, while 7 Indian Division went down the east side (4/1st, 4/5th, 3/6th and 4/8th Gurkhas). Further to the east still 81 West African Division guarded the eastern flank.

At first the advance went well against light Japanese opposition until the main Japanese defence position was encountered at the Maungdaw–Buthidaung road, which crossed the Mayu range laterally through tunnels at about 1,000 feet above sea level. This was an immensely strong natural defence position which the Japanese had fortified with all their normal ingenuity. The only way to maintain an attack on such a strong position was to build a corresponding lateral road in front of the Japanese so that supplies and reinforcements could be switched between the two divisions as needed. This pass at Ngakyedauk, known by the British soldiers as the 'Okeydoke' Pass, was an amazing engineering achievement built literally under the noses of the Japanese.

The pass in full working order, 5 Indian Division opened the attack on Maungdaw bypassing the heavily fortified hill area known as the Tortoise. After some resistance the town of Maungdaw was taken on 9 January 1944 and soon its docks were back in operation. The battle for the Tortoise position now started, and this proved a very tough nut to crack. Despite heavy artillery bombardment, fighter ground-attack and close armoured support it proved difficult if not impossible to evict the Japanese from their deep and well prepared bunkers. Eventually it was discovered that the only way to shift them was for the tanks to accompany the assaulting infantry all the way, firing in succession high-explosive, delayed action and finally armour-piercing shells straight into the bunker mouth.

While this battle was grinding on it became clear that the Japanese were building up for a counter-offensive of their own. Not only were elements of two fresh Japanese divisions identified, but in the air the Japanese were making a supreme effort to wrest back air supremacy.

The blow fell on 7 Division to the east of the Mayu range when on 4 February 1944 large Japanese forces suddenly attacked its rear around Taung Bazaar, sweeping through 7 Division Headquarters and forcing it to take refuge in the main Administrative Box at Ngakyedauk. Another Japanese thrust came in even further back, heading for the newly taken Maungdaw and XV Corps Headquarters back at Bawli Bazaar near the coast.

The Japanese expected the British to do as they had always done and fall back to secure their communications. This would enable them to be destroyed piecemeal and for the Japanese to seize their abandoned rations, transport and guns. For this reason the Japanese assault was based on very tight administrative margins and had to achieve total success within a ten-day period.

General Slim had foreseen the likelihood of a Japanese offensive although its form did achieve complete surprise. Soon the whole of 7 Indian Division was put on air supply as it resolutely held firm, as did 5 Indian Division to the west. Immediately 26 Indian Division (which included 3/9th Gurkhas) moved up in support from Chittagong, to be replaced by 36 British Division in reserve. The Japanese realized they had to quickly subdue 7 Indian Division and break into the Administrative Box which served both forward divisions. This was the most vulnerable area as it had never been intended to be a defensive position and was stuffed full of

A Gurkha rifleman carrying a Bren light machine gun returns from a patrol. (Gurkha Museum)

petrol and supplies, and included mainly hospital and administrative personnel. Quickly infantry units were diverted to its defence, including two companies of 4/8th Gurkhas and one company of 4/1st Gurkhas.

Some of the most bitter fighting took place around the adjacent area known as 'Abel' manned by the remainder of the recently raised 4/1st Gurkhas. 'Abel' was the nickname of a hill feature that, with its adjacent feature 'Cain', commanded the vital Buthidaung–Maungdaw lateral pass. The Japanese needed control of this pass to sustain their offensive. However, 4/1st Gurkhas had taken both hills in bitter fighting just before the Japanese assault began and the Japanese now threw in everything they had to wrest them back.

Cut off and surrounded, 4/1st Gurkhas conceded 'Cain' but doggedly held onto 'Abel'. As casualties mounted they fought on daily rations now reduced to a mess tin of rice and *dhall* (gravy made from lentils) and occasionally a *chapatti* (unleavened bread). The wounded were passed back at night through the jungle to the hospital in the beleaguered Administrative Box, the mules and porters returning with ammunition and supplies under the noses of the Japanese.

Wounded in the day, Lieutenant 'Runce' Rooney had a lucky escape when the Japanese, indulging in their normal bestial behaviour, penetrated the Administrative Box and got into the field hospital on the night of 7/8 February. Here they proceeded to kill doctors and administrative staff and bayonet the wounded in their beds. Lieutenant Rooney had been badly wounded so, with others similarly stricken and felt liable to succumb, he was left lying in a makeshift hammock in the surrounding jungle and so was missed by the Japanese. A counter-attack swiftly drove out the Japanese, who withdrew using Indian ward orderlies as a human screen. These they promptly murdered once they had served their purpose.

Unable to break into the stoutly defended Administrative Box, or subdue 'Abel', and with 5 and 7 Indian Divisions holding firm on air resupply, the Japanese attack started to falter as fighting continued beyond its ten-day deadline.

Overhead, the decisive air battle of the Burma campaign was being fought. Japanese Zero fighters came over in scores, but were simply no match for the British Spitfires and American Mustangs and were being hacked out of the sky at a 20:1 attrition rate. Desperately the Japanese redoubled their efforts, but now they found themselves crushed between the advancing 26 and 36 Divisions and 5 and 7 Indian Divisions, which had not only held their ground but were going over to the attack. Far to the east, the West Africans were curling round the back of the Japanese. Short of food and ammunition, the Japanese fought with their usual fanatical bravery but by late February 1944, the end was inevitable as they suffered their first crushing defeat; retribution was surely at hand.

When 4/1st Gurkhas finally left the smoking hillside that they had defended with such courage and tenacity, they had suffered 52 killed and 181 wounded.

THE SECOND CHINDIT OPERATION

While the battle to finally force the Japanese out of their deep tunnels and bunkers was still in progress in the Arakan, a major British, American and Chinese operation was being planned for Northern Burma. Here the Chinese under Stilwell were to advance into Burma from China, while Wingate with an air-landed division would fly into the Japanese rear areas and prevent the enemy rushing reinforcements to counter the attack from China. Although ambitious, the plan was a practicable one and, unlike the first Chindit operation, there was a firm linkage between the Chindit operation and the Chinese-American offensive from China.

Wingate harboured misgivings about Gurkhas following the first Chindit Expedition, but these were not shared by his column commanders, especially Calvert who chose them for his brigade headquarters defence company. As a result four Gurkha battalions took part (3/4th, 3/6th, 3/9th and 4/9th). They were to earn three Victoria Crosses, a moving rebuttal of Wingate's misgivings.

The plan was for the air-landed forces to set up strongholds which would be virtually impregnable to Japanese assault. Strongholds would contain their own airstrips for resupply and would have their own fighter aircraft in situ. The Japanese would have to try to eradicate these strongholds which should enable the Chindits to hit them very hard and prevent them sending reinforcements north. Rather than just waiting to be attacked, Chindits in the strongholds would sally out and attack the Japanese wherever they could be found. Wingate's concept was a good one, but unfortunately after his death it was departed from and therein lay difficulty.

In all there were to be four codenamed strongholds all around the railway-station town of Indaw. 'Aberdeen' was 27 miles northwest; 'Piccadilly' was 40 miles northeast; 'Broadway' was 35 miles east-northeast and 'Chowringhee' was 35 miles east. Of the three brigades involved, 16th would march to 'Aberdeen', 77th would be air landed at 'Piccadilly' and 'Broadway' and 111th would be air landed at 'Chowringhee'. On 8 February 1944, 16th Brigade started its march out.

★★★

On 5 March, 77th and 111th Brigades were doing last-minute checks before getting into their gliders to set off in a great air armada. Each Dakota aircraft plane was towing two gliders, itself something of a risky experiment and for Gurkhas an entirely novel concept.

Generals Slim and Wingate had come to see them off. Suddenly with a screech of brakes a jeep arrived to deliver an air photograph showing the intended landing zone at 'Piccadilly' to be totally obstructed with newly felled trees. Wingate then threw a complete tantrum and asked that the whole operation be immediately cancelled as it had been betrayed and the Japanese were waiting for them. Slim quietly took him to one side and reasoned that if the other two zones were open, which they were, it might only be 'Piccadilly' that was blocked; anyhow 16th Brigade was already on its way and the Chindit operation was a vital contribution to Stilwell's advance. Slowly Wingate calmed down and directed that the troops destined for 'Piccadilly' were to be diverted to 'Chowringhee'. Since the latter was on the far side of the mighty Irrawaddy this was not a desperately good last-minute decision. Slim and others persuaded Wingate to opt for 'Broadway', although following this confusion, elements of 111th Brigade HQ and 3/4th Gurkhas flew to 'Chowringhee' and had to re-cross the Irrawaddy. This vignette constitutes a nice illustration of the difference between two commanders.

The 3/6th and 3/9th Gurkhas landed with Calvert's 77th Brigade at 'Broadway' and 3/4th and 4/9th Gurkhas landed at 'Chowringhee'. While Calvert's two Gurkha battalions were an integral part of his brigade, 4/9th Gurkhas were designated Morrisforce, commanded by Lieutenant Colonel J. R. Morris, whose task it was to rally the fiercely loyal Kachin warriors against the Japanese. The 3/4th Gurkhas had a difficult time crossing back over the Irrawaddy to join 111th Brigade as outboard engines refused to start and mules played up. Halfway through the proceedings, Burmese gendarmes in Japanese pay arrived by boat to arrest them and they found themselves being flown back to India for the duration!

In the event, not all 3/4th Gurkhas could cross and those that could not joined up with a separate column, Dah Force, while the remainder trudged west to meet up with the remaining two battalions that had gone to 'Broadway'; not a good start to the operation.

Landing uneventfully at 'Broadway', 3/6th Gurkhas and 1st South Staffordshire Regiment were ordered by Calvert to set up a major road/railblock at the road/railway junction near Hopin. This they did, but since it was overlooked by the Japanese they had a hard time maintaining it. Soon Japanese attacks necessitated the whole of Calvert's brigade becoming involved and a new stronghold was constructed, named 'White City' from the mass of supply parachutes hanging from the trees. This became the focus for furious attacks by 2,000 Japanese who were determined to reopen the road and railway. Casualties mounted and although supplies came in there were no reinforcements.

It was at this stage (24 March) that Major General Wingate was killed in an air crash after visiting forward units at 'Broadway'. Brigadier 'Joe' Lentaigne, whom we saw so ably commanding 1/4th Gurkhas in the last chapter, then took over.

As well as being shocked and depressed at the death of Wingate, it soon became apparent to many that, without the forceful character of their founder, the Chindits were being asked to try to do too much for their waning strength. Despite Chindit forces having held 'White City' and the Hopin block for two months, the Chinese had still not arrived from the north for all Stilwell's urgings.

By April 1944 the focus of the campaign had moved to Assam, where the battle to hold and then defeat the massive Japanese attack was swaying in the balance. Just when it had been agreed to fly the exhausted and battle-weary Chindits back to India before the monsoon broke, at Stilwell's behest they were ordered to take the fortified town of Mogaung to help the slow-moving Chinese offensive. This entailed a march of 160 miles.

As expected, 77th Brigade found Mogaung strongly held with 3,500 Japanese defending it with their usual tenacity. Captain Michael Allmand, commanding B Company 3/6th Gurkhas, a

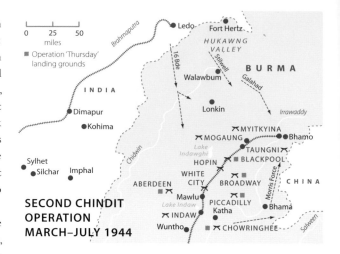

SECOND CHINDIT
OPERATION
MARCH–JULY 1944

battalion now only 230 strong, led a desperate assault on 11 June that captured a vital bridge on the outskirts of Mogaung. At the head of his men throwing hand-grenades, he seemed oblivious to the withering small arms fire from the Japanese. The capture of the bridge by Allmand's company allowed 77th Brigade to push further into Mogaung.

Now in reserve, 3/6th Gurkhas were again called forward to try to winkle out Japanese snipers hidden in the thick *lantana* bushes on a ridge surrounding the town. Again it was B Company under Captain Allmand that penetrated the virtually impassable *lantana*, killed the snipers and captured the ridge, albeit suffering several casualties.

Having entered Mogaung, the area of railway station and the 'Red House' became the key objectives on 23 June. C Company 3/6th Gurkhas was directed onto the railway station and Allmand's B Company onto the 'Red House'. The Japanese defended both doggedly and in strength. Charging a Japanese machine-gun post despite the mud and his trench foot, Captain Allmand was mortally wounded. Rifleman Tulbahadur Pun in the forward assaulting section of B Company's leading platoon suddenly discovered that half his section had become casualties. Nothing dismayed, he and the two other survivors pressed on. Moments later the other two were down and only Tulbahadur was left. Seizing a Bren gun from a wounded man he rushed the 'Red House' in full view of its defenders. Miraculously reaching it unscathed despite a storm of fire, he killed all the Japanese in the vicinity and then gave covering fire to the rest of the platoon so they could complete the capture of the objective. For this act of supreme valour, Tulbahadur was awarded the Victoria Cross as was Allmand, who died of his wounds shortly after the action at the 'Red House'. The two Victoria Crosses hang together in the Gurkha Museum at Winchester.

After the desperate battle to take Mogaung, Brigadier Calvert of 77th Brigade was unamused to hear Stilwell announce that his

Brigadier Mike Calvert and Major James Lumley 6th Gurkhas (the actress Joanna Lumley's father) in the ruins of Mogaung after its successful capture by the Chindits, an action that gained 6th Gurkhas two Victoria Crosses. (Gurkha Museum)

Chinese had taken it. His reply summed up the Chindits' attitude admirably: 'Chinese reported taking Mogaung. My Brigade now taking *Umbrage!*'

The 3/9th Gurkhas had originally been left behind to hold the landing zone at 'Broadway' and were soon fighting off heavy Japanese attacks. When 'Broadway' was abandoned, 3/9th Gurkhas were ordered to join up with 111th Brigade at 'Blackpool', commanded by Lieutenant Colonel John 'Jack' Masters of 4th Gurkhas, who was to become the celebrated writer.

Here the Japanese, desperate to break out of the tightening noose of Chinese pressing down from the north and Chindits astride their communications, frenziedly attacked 'Blackpool'. After much hard fighting, it was decided to abandon 'Blackpool' in favour of an attack on the Japanese still obstructing Stilwell's forces around Taugni. The Japanese held a high spur feature known as Hill 2171. It was decided to attack it on 9 July using two companies of 3/9th Gurkhas. One would advance directly up the jungle-covered hill while the other, Major Frank Blaker's C Company, would climb round the Japanese position and attack it from the rear.

The time to attack was synchronized so the Japanese would be taken from two directions at once. Unfortunately the going for C Company was very difficult, so when B Company attacked C Company was still some way from its objective. After a five-and-a-half hour climb, C Company walked into a Japanese machine-gun nest which opened fire at point-blank range forcing the Gurkhas to take cover. Immediately assessing the situation, Major Blaker ran towards the machine gun firing his carbine. He fell, hit by three bullets, but the impetus of his gallant charge carried his men through the Japanese position: those that did not fall to the kukri fled.

Already the holder of the Military Cross for an action causing 19 Japanese casualties in the Arakan, Frank Blaker was posthumously awarded the Victoria Cross. Beloved by his men, speaking their language with unusual fluency, he was completely identified with them; his was a grievous loss. The battle to keep this hill feature was to go on for six more days, with 3/4th and 3/9th Gurkhas battling in turn against Japanese shelling and counter-attacks.

As part of Colonel Morris's column, the 4/9th Gurkhas had some of the hardest fighting, blocking with great success the main

A 10th Gurkha rifleman looking out from his bunker on 'Scraggy', scene of some of the bitterest fighting around Imphal. (Gurkha Museum)

Bhamo-Myitkyina highway and carrying out repeated ambushes on Japanese forces endeavouring to reopen it. Coming under Stilwell's command, 4/9th Gurkhas were subject to continual conflicting orders and requests to take on attacks on strongly held Japanese positions despite having no artillery support. Gallantly rising to every request, they went on fighting until disease and casualties meant that there was hardly a company-sized force left from the whole battalion by the time the key town of Myitkyina was captured.

In mid-July, after four months incessant marching and fighting, the Chindits were flown out to India. This time their achievement was undisputed, causing the Japanese to divert large numbers of troops to try to contain their activities and clear their lines of communication, troops they desperately needed in the key battles for Imphal and Kohima which we will now turn to.

Rifleman Tulbahadur Pun 6th Gurkhas, awarded the Victoria Cross for his action at Mogaung during the Second Chindit Expedition. From a painting by G Douglas. (The Royal Gurkha Rifles)

British and Gurkha Chindits from the Second Chindit Expedition evacuated by plane. Note their emaciated condition. (Gurkha Museum)

IMPHAL AND KOHIMA

Throughout the spring of 1943, 17 Indian Division, re-equipped and restored after the fighting retreat from Burma, had been on the

Men of 3/10th Gurkhas collecting captured Japanese weapons after the successful battle to take the feature 'Scraggy' near Imphal. (Gurkha Museum)

offensive against the Japanese forces which were attempting to occupy the Chin Hills area on the Assam frontier. Clashes were of significant proportions, often involving air support and armour. In one of these Havildar Gaje Ghale of 2/5th Gurkhas, commanding a platoon of young soldiers – most of whom, like himself, had never been in action before – received the Victoria Cross for a supreme act of gallantry on 27 May. The Japanese having seized an important feature known as Basha East Hill, 2/5th Gurkhas were ordered to eject them in company with 1/10th Gurkhas. Two frontal assaults having failed, Gaje's platoon attacked. Despite being wounded by a grenade in arm, chest and leg, the Havildar led his platoon into the main Japanese position and, after bitter hand-to-hand fighting, forced the Japanese to withdraw, going on to occupy the vital position.

The Japanese master plan for the defeat of the British and the invasion of India had envisaged a successful attack in the Arakan which would draw in all British reserves. Once this had happened the main assault would go in against Assam, centring on the key high plain of Imphal and the towns of Kohima and Dimapur. A breakthrough here would allow a Japanese advance into Bengal and the heartland of India.

As we have seen, defeat rather than victory awaited them in the Arakan, and the activities of the Chindits allowed Stilwell's Chinese to advance deep into Northern Burma and capture the important town of Myitkyina. Nevertheless, the Japanese persisted with their plan for a massive attack into Assam and beyond by a complete army of three divisions.

General Slim was aware of Japanese intentions and decided to fight the decisive battle on the plain of Imphal, where he had good communications and could use his superior air power to its best advantage. Unfortunately this meant withdrawing 17 Indian Division back from the Chindwin River, and also 20 Indian Division from the Kabaw valley; 23 Indian Division, a tank brigade and 50th Indian Parachute Brigade formed the Corps reserve. Additionally, 5 and 7 Indian Divisions were put on standby in the Arakan in case they were needed.

Reluctant to withdraw 17 and 20 Indian Divisions until the Japanese attack was imminent, General Slim left it too late: suddenly, on 13 March 1944, the Japanese were attacking 17 Indian Division and threatening to cut it off, while another two Japanese divisions were fast advancing on the Imphal plain and further north towards Kohima and Dimapur.

Lieutenant General Geoffrey Scoones, the IV Corps commander and a former 2nd Gurkha officer, now sent 23 Indian Division to the aid of 17 Indian Division. Earlier he had sent forward a mixed brigade-sized force of two Gurkha parachute battalions, 152nd and 153rd (formed in 1941 from volunteers), along with the 4/5th Mahratta Light Infantry and two companies of the Nepalese Kalibahadur Regiment. This 50th Indian Parachute Brigade was supported by some artillery and Royal Air Force ground controllers to bring in fighter ground-attack support.

The 152nd Parachute Battalion, the Mahrattas and Kalibahadur Regiment went forward to Sheldon's Corner on the main Japanese axis road, while 153rd prepared a defensive position further back at Sangshak, covering the main road junction, possession of which would allow the Japanese to go either north to Ukhrul or south to Imphal. Although airborne troops, they were actually rushed forward in three-quarter-ton Dodge trucks through a scene of barely subdued panic and devastation as supply dumps were burned to prevent them falling into the hands of the Japanese; this in the fifth year of the war!

Sheldon's Corner had only ever been intended as a delaying position and was poorly sited, but from 14 to 21 March this small force held off increasingly furious Japanese attacks before withdrawing back on Sangshak. Post-war reports indicated the Japanese had lost over 400 men killed alone. One complete company of 152nd Parachute Battalion was destroyed. The Japanese, following up quickly, were soon attacking Sangshak by day and night. By day Hurricane fighter-bombers pounded the Japanese and, sadly, also, in error the desperate defenders. By night, bereft of air support, the defenders, sleepless and running out of ammunition, were hard put to keep the Japanese out.

The guns of the artillery giving magnificent support were nevertheless slowly picked off by the Japanese, while within the perimeter water had become scarce and the wounded were piling up with no means of evacuation. Still they battled on, throwing back every Japanese attack with obstinate courage, often at the bayonet's point or the kukri's slash.

17th Indian Division banner presented to 1/10th Gukhas following their gallant defence of the Tuitum Ridge during the battle for Imphal. (Gurkha Museum)

Water becoming critical, Royal Air Force Dakotas dropped it in metal canisters and, although many fell outside the 400 by 800-metre perimeter, without this timely intervention the brigade could not have held on. On the night of 25/26 March the Japanese threw in their heaviest attack on the already much-weakened 152nd Parachute Battalion and made serious inroads into the perimeter. Scraping together every fit man, 153rd Parachute Battalion counter-attacked and in desperate hand-to-hand fighting drove out the last of the Japanese and restored the perimeter.

During 26 March the brigade was ordered to break contact and make its way back to the Imphal plain. Splitting into small groups and carrying their wounded, with great skill the Gurkhas crossed the main Japanese supply line and the next day linked up with troops from 5 Indian Division just flown in from the Arakan. Their resolute defence, which delayed the Japanese sufficiently long to allow 5 Indian Division to be redeployed from the Arakan,

probably saved Fourteenth Army from serious setback if not defeat. Field Marshal Lord Slim generously acknowledged such in his book *Defeat into Victory*.

Later it transpired that the last radio message the battered defenders received before they broke out was not, as might be expected, one concerned with the breakout, but a request to submit a nominal roll of officers wishing to join the Bengal Club in Calcutta! Since of 152nd Gurkha Parachute Battalion only two out of the original 25 officers were alive and unwounded, this message was not appreciated.

The battle to extricate the cut-off 17 Indian Division was now reaching its climax. The 1/10th Gurkhas played a key role in this by first of all taking and then holding the vital Tuitum ridge under which the whole of 17 Indian Division had to pass, and the possession of which by the Japanese would have been little short of disastrous. Belatedly the Japanese realized its importance and

Japanese tanks destroyed by Rifleman Ganju Lama 7th Gurkhas for which action he received the Victoria Cross. (Gurkha Museum)

threw in attack after attack to dislodge 1/10th Gurkhas, all to no avail. As the 10th Gurkha regimental history tellingly notes: '*There was a great blooding of kukris in this small action and significantly enough, in spite of the numbers of Japanese wounded, no prisoners were brought back.*'

A grateful General Cowan, commanding 17 Indian Division, conferred the unique honour of allowing 1/10th Gurkhas to fly the famous 'Black Cat' divisional flag with their own 10th Gurkha badge superimposed on it. The original flag is on display at the Gurkha Museum. The 1/3rd and 1/4th Gurkhas were also heavily engaged in the fighting on and around the vital Tuitum ridge.

On 23 March, 1/10th Gurkhas met up with their sister battalion 3/10th Gurkhas from the relieving 23 Indian Division. One can imagine the ribald comments of the '*What took you so long? Where on earth have you been all this time?*' type that would have flashed between the two sister battalions.

The Japanese, who had confidently predicted the complete destruction of 17th Indian Division, were to be surprised and discomforted to find the 'Black Cats' ready and waiting again at Imphal. As the 10th Gurkha history makes clear, the ability of the Royal Air Force to maintain air supply when units and formations were cut off was a battle-winner, as was the immediate on-call availability of fighter ground-attack Hurricanes.

As the Japanese advanced on the Imphal plain, heavy fighting took place on the tracks and villages around its periphery. One of the hardest-fought battles was for the village of Potsangbam, which had been occupied by a reinforced Japanese battalion. The 1/3rd and 1/10th Gurkhas, with a squadron of tanks and supported by artillery, initially attacking the village on 12 May suffered very heavy casualties, not least from the shelling falling short on one of 1/10th's companies. Nothing deterred they attacked again that night, 1/3rd Gurkhas staging a feint attack whilst 1/10th Gurkhas came round the back of the Japanese. Completely out-manoeuvred, the Japanese broke and withdrew. The 1/10th Gurkhas lost over 200 men in one of the hardest infantry actions of the war.

While the fighting round Imphal swayed in the balance, the situation at Kohima was critical, the motley garrison penned into an area 500 metres square centred round the Deputy Commissioner's tennis court. The 4th Royal West Kent Regiment earned undying fame for its resolute defence, until finally relieved

Naik Agansing Rai VC 5th Gurkhas (right) holding a Japanese machine gun captured in the battle for Mortar Bluff. (Gurkha Museum)

action alone, 1st Queens and 4/1st Gurkhas lost 59 killed and 139 wounded between them. In all 20 Japanese bunkers had to be cleared.

The 4/1st Gurkhas, now commanded by Lieutenant Colonel Derek Horsford from 8th Gurkhas, were tasked with taking the so-far impregnable Basha and Nose hills, again very strongly held by the Japanese. By painstaking patrolling, 4/1st Gurkhas identified exactly where the Japanese bunkers were and whether they were occupied, always the most difficult feature of any attack. Having pinpointed the defenders, the attack was delivered with such speed and accuracy that hardly had the Japanese recovered from tank shelling and Bangalore torpedoes than Horsford's men were on them with kukri, bayonet and sub-machine gun. The taking of this key position for only 5 killed and 33 wounded was an amazing achievement and its loosening of the Japanese hold on Kohima presaged the relief of the gallant garrison.

by 33rd Indian Brigade of 7 Indian Division, of which 1st Queens and 4/1st Gurkhas were constituent battalions and together were tasked to take the vital Jail Hill feature overlooking Kohima.

The Japanese, determined to take Kohima at all costs, simply could not afford to lose Jail Hill and so the battle for it was a particularly bitter one. The Commanding Officer of 4/1st Gurkhas was killed early in a battle which involved winkling out superbly camouflaged and dug-in Japanese from virtually impregnable bunkers. Supported by a troop of four Grant tanks, 4/1st Gurkhas and 1st Queens slowly but surely took bunker after bunker in a bloody three-day battle. The Grant tanks were firing solid shot into the bunker mouths from a distance of 30 yards before the Japanese were finally subdued on 13 May. In this

Rifleman Ganju Lama VC MM, 7th Gurkhas. (Gurkha Museum)

Kohima, as General Slim admitted, had been a close-run thing. If the opposing Japanese Lieutenant General Kotoku Sato of 31 Division had contented himself with masking Kohima and gone for the virtually undefended Dimapur, he would have broken through to the Brahmaputra valley and thence into India. Instead he went on battering against Kohima until his troops were exhausted and forced to withdraw by mounting British pressure. Later, when the Royal Air Force wanted to bomb Sato's headquarters, General Slim forbade them: no replacement could be quite so stupid as Sato!

Although Kohima was relieved in late May 1944, the fighting around Imphal was still raging, with Gurkha battalions fully committed. The 2/5th Gurkhas had been heavily attacked at Ningthoukhong on 12 June by Japanese tanks and infantry after a Japanese artillery bombardment of over an hour, one of the heaviest of the whole campaign. Many of the 2/5th Gurkha defences were smashed, and so the tank attack when it came made some headway, with three tanks getting into the centre of the position and pinning the defenders. The 1/7th Gurkhas, a sister Gurkha battalion in 48th Indian Brigade, were ordered to counter-attack and restore the situation. As 1/7th Gurkhas' B Company swept in, it was held up by intense machine-gun fire which covered all approaches. Nothing deterred, Rifleman Ganju Lama crawled forward with his PIAT (Projector Infantry Anti-Tank) and calmly proceeded to dispatch two enemy tanks from within 30 yards, despite being hit in the arm, leg and wrist. As the tank crews baled out of their blazing tanks, Ganju ran forward and engaged them with hand grenades. For his outstanding gallantry that totally restored an adverse tactical situation, he was awarded the Victoria Cross which now is displayed in the Gurkha Museum.

By mid-June 1944 it was becoming clear that the Japanese offensive was reaching its crescendo with bitter fighting going on all around the Imphal plain. Gurkhas from seven regiments were

Men of the 10th Gurkhas guard Japanese prisoners. (Gurkha Museum)

Men of the 4/6th Gurkhas crossing the Irrawaddy, January 1945. (Gurkha Museum)

fighting and dying in hard-fought actions, but slowly, inexorably, Fourteenth Army was going over to the offensive.

Two actions by 2/5th Gurkhas are indicative of just how intensive the fighting had become, since both of them resulted in the award of the Victoria Cross, one posthumously. Both actions were fought over two hill features, Mortar Bluff and Water Picket, 200 yards apart in the hotly disputed Bishenpur area of the Imphal position. Permanent loss of these features would have enabled the Japanese to take Bishenpur itself and get deep into the Imphal plain. The 2/5th Gurkhas were ordered to take over Mortar Bluff from 7/10th Baluch Regiment and recapture Water Picket which the Japanese were occupying.

Having carefully sited artillery and machine guns on 25 June 1944, the Japanese attacked Mortar Bluff, held by a small force of 41 Gurkhas commanded by Subedar Netrabahadur Thapa. As stated, the Japanese had already taken the vital Water Picket the night before. Subedar Netrabahadur had only just taken over the position under intermittent sniper fire when at 1930 hours in gathering darkness the Japanese attack by a complete company came in under artillery and machine-gun cover. During the attack Netrabahadur rushed from position to position encouraging his young non-commissioned officers and riflemen and directing

Men of the 10th Gurkhas marching through Prome from which the Japanese had withdrawn after heavy fighting. (Gurkha Museum)

their fire, as well as calling for close-in artillery support to be brought down on his own position.

The Japanese, frustrated in their first attack, now used the cover of night and torrential rain to attack again, penetrating the

Gurkhas with a British officer advance on Mandalay, followed up by a Grant tank.

leading platoons pushed on until they hit barbed wire surrounding the Japanese position. It was at this point that Naik Agansing Rai stormed through the wire, destroyed the crew of a medium machine gun that had caused many casualties and then swung to his flank, silencing a 37mm anti-tank gun. At this the Japanese survivors fled.

Although Water Picket was not its original objective, C Company carried on through the Japanese position and assaulted Water Picket which, after a desperate hand-to-hand fight, was captured. It was a magnificent feat of arms by C Company but, by unanimous agreement, it was the leading section commander Naik Agansing Rai whose fearless valour made it all possible. His award of the Victoria Cross was a fitting reward.

Agansing, who was an exceedingly modest man possessed of a puckish sense of humour, later explained to the author that since his blood was up it seemed a good idea to go on and take Water

position and overwhelming the forward two sections, killing most of them. Again, Netrabahadur rushed forward throwing grenades and halted them. Radioing back to his Commanding Officer, Netrabahadur requested urgent reinforcement and ammunition resupply. Only eight men could be spared and they came up carrying ammunition. Almost immediately all became casualties. Netrabahadur crawled out and brought them and the badly needed ammunition into the bitterly fought-over perimeter. Meeting another attack with grenades and kukris, Netrabahadur fell at the head of his men, shot in the mouth, and moments later a grenade killed him. When his body was found next day, it lay alongside a dead Japanese soldier whose skull had been cleft by a kukri stroke.

Netrabahadur was posthumously awarded the Victoria Cross. Mortar Bluff fell to the Japanese after his death; only six men out of his force of 41 survived the eight-hour battle.

The 2/5th Gurkhas then had to set about recapturing both Mortar Bluff and Water Picket. The original plan was for C Company to retake Mortar Bluff and, once this was secured, for A Company to go on and retake Water Picket. Moving up for the attack, Battalion Headquarters was hit by a well-aimed salvo of Japanese artillery fire which killed the battalion second-in-command, who had only joined the morning before; three Gurkha havildars and two guides were hit, as well as a wounded survivor from Subedar Netrabahadur's group. C Company started its attack at 0950 hours and immediately came under very heavy machine-gun fire which threatened to stall the attack.

At this critical moment the reserve platoon commander, with great courage and presence of mind, ran forward onto the crest and started making hand signals to imaginary troops on his flanks. Fooled by this gallant officer, the Japanese switched their fire, allowing the attack to continue. Despite heavy casualties, the two

The Burma Star.

Picket whether it was his objective or not! It was a truly brilliant feat of arms and by such feats the Japanese were thwarted.

By common consent the fighting at Imphal and Kohima constituted some of the bitterest of the whole campaign. Despite their defeat in the Arakan, the Japanese still felt themselves to be superior and capable of defeating British forces in Assam, crossing the Brahmaputra and invading deep into India. They persisted in this attempt long after any European army would have given up. As a result, when they did at last recognize that victory was impossible, their formations were decimated and their support and administration were in tatters.

JAPANESE DEFEAT IN BURMA

As Lieutenant General Sir William Slim (he had been recently knighted) took up the advance into Burma towards the Chindwin, everywhere were sights of desolation. Abandoned tanks, guns and vehicles littered the roads going back. Field hospitals with every wounded patient neatly shot through the forehead by the departing staff stood as silent witnesses to a precipitate retreat.

In the Arakan, too, the Japanese were being driven back, albeit contesting every blood-soaked metre of ground. The XV Corps was pressing hard for the town of Akyab and its much-needed port and airfield. Possession of the latter would allow the supply Dakotas with their 250-mile range to supply up to the Irrawaddy and beyond – a vital requirement for the main attack. On 4 March 1945, 3/2nd Gurkhas were involved in a seaborne attack to occupy a hill feature called Snowdon, the possession of which would allow 82 West African Division to evacuate its mounting casualties without Japanese interference.

***

In the course of capturing the main part of the Snowdon feature, it was found that the Japanese had regained and were in strong occupation of the adjoining peak, Snowdon East. B Company 3/2nd Gurkhas was commanded by Major D.F. Neill, whom we have met before on the First Chindit Expedition. Although given artillery support, the covering fire proved to be largely ineffective, since the Japanese were deeply entrenched in mutually supporting foxholes.

As a result, when the assault went in casualties began to mount, not only from Japanese machine guns but also from snipers up trees. As a rifleman in one of the leading sections, Bhanbhagta Gurung immediately stood up in full view of the enemy and killed a sniper who was holding up the attack. Moving forward again they came under very heavy fire from two foxholes. Rushing forward alone, Bhanbhagta cleared the first foxhole with grenades and then crawled into the second foxhole and killed its occupant with his bayonet. Machine-gun fire was now being directed from

another two mutually supporting foxholes and, nothing daunted, Bhanbhagta cleared these two as well. It now transpired that the foxholes themselves were covered by a large and strongly constructed bunker further up the hill from which machine-gun fire came lashing down, causing more casualties and holding up the attack. Despite a hail of enemy fire, Bhanbhagta rushed the bunker and jumping on its roof threw in smoke grenades, having run out of HE grenades. Two Japanese came rushing out partially blinded by smoke, both of whom Bhanbhagta killed with his kukri. He then crawled into the bunker and killed the Japanese machine gunner by battering him to death with a rock. Now joined by other men from his section they opened fire on the Japanese massing for a counter-attack and drove them off.

For these amazing feats of valour Bhanbhagta Gurung was awarded the Victoria Cross. The 60-strong B Company lost 45 killed or wounded in this its last action of the war and counted 115 dead Japanese, which gives some indication of its severity. Bhanbhagta's Victoria Cross is proudly displayed in the Gurkha Museum.

During the advance from Assam, apart from the occasional desperate rearguard action such as the one at Pyingaing, in which 4/10th Gurkhas were notably involved, the Japanese were not to stand again in any strength until Slim's men reached the Irrawaddy.

***

General Slim had expected the Japanese to fight hard for the Shwebo area west of the Irrawaddy, but Major General Thomas ('Pete') Rees's 19 Indian Division hustled the Japanese out of Shwebo remarkably quickly. While so doing, 4/4th Gurkhas captured a vital Japanese map that not only showed the Japanese battle plan but also gave a disturbingly accurate assessment of British forces.

Seeing from the map that the Japanese intended fighting hard for Mandalay, General Slim immediately changed his plan and decided to pin the Japanese around Mandalay by crossings over the Irrawaddy west and north of it. He would however make his main thrust south of Mandalay to seize the vital Meiktila area, through which all Japanese road and rail reinforcement had to pass and which contained no fewer than six airfields. Slim badly needed some or all of these airfields if he was to reach Rangoon before the monsoon broke in May 1945, which would turn the whole area between the Irrawaddy and Sittang rivers into a quagmire.

Given overwhelming air power, the January/February 1945 crossings over the Irrawaddy were successfully achieved, with bridging equipment and boats being flown in from India since the Japanese had destroyed all local boats. Once across, there was a furious reaction as the Japanese did all they could to hurl their attackers back into the river. The 1/6th Gurkhas, along with their

A painting by Harry Sheldon of a Gurkha parachutist in training. Note the parachutist's helmet locally made of hessian as the proper steel parachutist's helmets were in such short supply. (Gurkha Museum)

sister battalion 4/6th Gurkhas, were in action continuously for 16 days' fighting to enlarge the bridgehead.

The 19 Division's battle for Mandalay itself was a bitter one, the Japanese resisting furiously. It was 4/4th Gurkhas who finally assaulted, taking the temple at the highest point of Mandalay Hill after a brilliant night attack that ended on 12 March with a kukri charge through the temple corridors and staircases. Meanwhile 1/6th Gurkhas was involved in the hard fighting to eject the Japanese from the immensely strong Fort Dufferin.

Once they realized 17 and 5 Divisions had taken Meiktila, the Japanese evacuated Mandalay to avoid being cut off, and threw everything they had against these two divisions in a desperate

attempt to keep open their line of retreat south. For a while the fighting swayed in the balance, but eventually the Japanese started to crack and began slowly to withdraw south.

General Slim's tactics now changed into a series of hooks designed to get behind the retreating Japanese and hold them up so that the troops advancing from the north could destroy them. In one such hook 4/8th Gurkhas were ordered to cut behind the retreating Japanese and hold a cross-track at Taungdaw. Finding their withdrawal route cut, the Japanese, over a three-day period in mid-May 1945, launched attack after desperate attack to clear 4/8th Gurkhas off their withdrawal route. The key position was held by 9 Platoon of C Company some 100 yards ahead of the main position and it was upon this somewhat isolated platoon that the main intensity of the 200-strong Japanese attacks developed very early on 13 May.

Rifleman Lachhiman Gurung was in one of the forward trenches upon which the Japanese showered grenades. As fast as they threw them, Lachhiman and his comrades threw them back until only Lachhiman was left, sorely wounded, but for four hours he continued firing his rifle despite a shattered right arm and a lost eye. The enemy never did get into his trench and no fewer than 31 bodies were found about its periphery. For this outstanding act of valour Lachhiman received the Victoria Cross.

Shortly before this action, Gurkha parachutists from a composite Gurkha parachute battalion had been dropped on Elephant Point to neutralize the coastal artillery battery guarding

Opposite: Japanese officers surrender their swords after Japan's capitulation. (Gurkha Museum)

Rangoon. This they succeeded in doing despite being bombed heavily by American Liberators in error. Once the Gurkhas had secured the coastal guns, 26 Indian Division was landed at Rangoon with only sporadic opposition and a day later, 3 May 1945, the great city was back in British hands after a little over three years.

On 8 May a victory parade was held to mark victory in Europe and the German surrender. Up-country the shattered remnants of the Japanese Burma Area Army were trying to cross the Sittang river and escape to the safety of Thailand. The Sittang was the same river where 17 Indian Division had suffered its disaster three years before. The Japanese had truly reaped the whirlwind. Sittang 1945 proved to be second only to Imphal as the most awarded Gurkha unit battle honour of the campaign.

Once the Japanese had been cleared out of Burma, preparations were made for the reoccupation of Malaya by seaborne assault, Operation Zipper. In the event, the dropping of atomic bombs on Japan and Japanese surrender made this unnecessary, although a seaborne invasion by some 100,000 went ahead anyhow. Landing unopposed in Malaya, conditions of utmost confusion were encountered. The experiences of 3/2nd Gurkhas were not untypical. Commanded by Lieutenant Colonel Philip Panton and with Major Val Meadows as their Operations Officer they had to deal with fully armed Japanese soldiery, ambivalent about surrender, gangs of heavily armed brigands intent on looting everything in sight, Thai coastal pirates swooping in on unsuspecting villages and furtive groups of renegade Indian National Army. That they achieved the restoration of calm and order and disarmed the Japanese without bloodshed is a lasting testimony to the imperturbable attitude of the Gurkha soldier..

The fighting in Burma had been some of the most bitter of the whole war. Far from being the second-class enemy that Field Marshal Lord Wavell among others had regarded him, the Japanese soldier proved to be a formidable opponent. Brave to the point of suicidal recklessness, few Japanese prisoners were taken; in general they really did fight to the last round and the last man. As soldiers their appalling and sadistic cruelty was a lasting stain on their race and it is not surprising that not much quarter was shown them when the roles were reversed.

***

Of the 45 active Gurkha battalions (not counting the 5 training and 2 garrison battalions) that served in the Second World War, 27 served in Burma, a total of 35,000 Gurkhas; that simple fact really tells its own story.

Rifleman Lachhiman Gurung VC 4/8th Gurkhas.

CHAPTER THIRTEEN

THE PAINS OF PEACE: INDIAN INDEPENDENCE, FRENCH INDO-CHINA, DUTCH EAST INDIES AND MALAYA UNTIL 1960

The ending of the Second World War should, it may be thought, have ushered in a period of peace and plenty. Instead it spawned a whole multitude of world problems. In Europe, as the shattered states started to rebuild themselves, Russia (or the Soviet Union as it preferred to call itself) turned from an ally into an enemy. As Churchill famously remarked: 'From Stettin in the Baltic to Trieste in the Adriatic an iron curtain has descended across Europe.' The Cold War had begun.

Britain, although a victor nation, was nearly bankrupt. When the last cheers of victory celebrations had died away, a period of extreme austerity was ushered in by its new Labour government. Major food rationing would continue for almost nine years after the war had ended. A pledge by the incoming government had been that all British servicemen who had served in the Far East for more than two years should be repatriated. In the final stages of the war with Japan, especially in Burma, this had significant consequences. It meant that the burden on the Indian Army was even greater as British units became, almost overnight, a shadow of their former selves.

In India, independence could no longer be delayed or political agitation suppressed. Soon the main political parties were manoeuvring for power while Field Marshal Lord Wavell, now India's Viceroy, tried desperately to hand over India as a unified state as opposed to it being split along the religious divide. Most

**INTERVENTION OPERATIONS
SOUTH-EAST ASIA 1945**

abhorrent to the returning soldiers of the Indian Army was the lionization of the traitor Indian National Army which, recruited from Indian Army prisoners of war, had fought for the Japanese. Worse still, their late leader Subhas Chandra Bose had become a sort of folk hero.

In Nepal, the powerful Rana ruler throughout the war years, Judha Shamsher, had gone into voluntary religious retreat in India. His successor, Mohan Shamsher, found his position much weakened by political agitation fanned by Nepal's King Tribhuvana, still in voluntary exile in India but helped by Indian nationalists and hankering to return to Nepal and reoccupy his throne. Despite the fact that the Ranas had supported Britain so loyally throughout two world wars, Britain now seemed unable or unwilling to do anything to help them in their hour of need.

Mohan Shamsher, Nepal's last ruler of the Rana dynasty. (Gurkha Museum)

were found to be well entrenched in strong bunkers. An initial attack was unable to take the position and the next day the enemy were evicted only after a brigade-strength attack supported by artillery and mortars. The total casualties for the two battalions of 1st Gurkhas in Indo-China were 14 killed and 28 wounded. By the end of January 1946 the French under General Philippe Leclerc were in sufficient strength to take over although they, and subsequently the Americans, were to find there was no easy way out in Vietnam.

Although Japan had been defeated and her armies were in the process of being returned to Japan, their legacy of promoting nationalism among the possessions of the colonial powers continued. Formerly defeated and occupied France and Holland were in no position to send forces to re-occupy their colonial empires and looked to Britain to do this for them. Despite her own very real post-war problems, Britain filled the power vacuum and Gurkha battalions, so recently involved in a desperate struggle with the Japanese, now gradually found themselves fighting to help re-establish French colonial rule in Indo-China and Dutch colonial rule in Indonesia, as the Dutch East Indies was becoming known.

In Indonesia, in Java, Sumatra and the Celebes, the fighting was even more severe and especially so for 3/3rd, 3/5th, 1/8th, 4/8th, 3/9th and 3/10th Gurkhas, who became involved in some very bitter conflict with Indonesian nationalists. The main task of the troops of 5, 23 and 26 Indian Divisions, having just liberated Malaya, was to safeguard the Japanese camps, which were full of Dutch and Eurasian internees. The Indonesian nationalists under Dr Ahmed Sukarno, to whom the Japanese had handed over control and weapons, were hell-bent on murdering every Dutch and Eurasian man, woman and child they could get their hands on. Efforts to get to the internee camps to safeguard them were bitterly resisted by the Indonesians and pitched battles resulted in which the Japanese, now rearmed, played a vital part in the successful outcome.

On 12 September 1945 a brigade of 20 Indian Division, under Major General Douglas Gracey, began landing in Saigon to disarm 54,000 Japanese, repatriate prisoners-of-war and civilian internees, as well maintaining order prior to the slow return of French forces. This initially humanitarian operation was bitterly resented by the nationalist Annamite (Viet Minh) organization and armed clashes became frequent. The disarmed Japanese were reluctantly employed to assist the outnumbered British forces and so, for an extraordinary three months, previously bitter enemies became collaborators. If the Gurkha officers and soldiers of 1/1st (Gracey's old regiment serving at his specific request), 3/1st, 4/2nd, 3/8th and 4/10th Gurkhas found the situation confusing, then it can be assumed that their British officers found it doubly so!

The 3/1st Gurkhas had some of the hardest fighting in the area to the south of Saigon where French captives were said to be held by the Communist Viet Minh. When encountered, the enemy

Indonesian nationalist slogan, Sumatra 1946. (Gurkha Museum)

Lord Louis Mountbatten, the last Viceroy of India, with Lady Mountbatten. (Southampton University)

In terms of intensity, some of these battles in central Java involved tanks, artillery, naval gunfire and fighter ground-attack aircraft before the Indonesians could be subdued. The 3/10th Gurkhas were involved in one such battle as were 3/3rd Gurkhas. Indeed the almost three-week Battle of Surabaya in November 1945 to secure that port-city was reminiscent of previous actions against the Japanese in Burma, with the only difference being that some of the Japanese were now fighting on the Allied side; without their help many thousands of Dutch and Eurasian internees would have been murdered. During 13 months, no fewer than 2,136 British, Indian and Gurkha officers and men were killed and wounded, including one brigade commander murdered while negotiating a ceasefire on 30 October 1945. The Indonesians matched military aggressiveness and treachery in equal proportion, as Gurkhas were to rediscover 20 years later.

Many of the Gurkhas were young soldiers hastily recruited to replace those returning home after war service. One company of 3/5th Gurkhas, while clearing a rubber plantation, came under machine-gun fire. The lead platoon commander deploying his men was dismayed to find that one of his young riflemen was unwilling to move from behind the safety of a tree. Rushing over, he berated him for cowardice. Calmly the young Gurkha replied

that he was lying on top of two fat jungle fowl that he had surprised and would come in handy at dinner, and if he got up they would fly away! In this savage little campaign there would be few such moments of humour.

After a year's conflict in Indonesia, the Dutch had arrived in sufficient numbers to guarantee the safety of their own nationals if not the continuity of their rule. The Indian Army divisions were withdrawn back to India in October 1946.

The India to which the Gurkha regiments returned was a very different one to that which they had left. As Indian independence approached, so racial tensions between Hindus and Muslims increased. Field Marshal Lord Wavell was now replaced by Lord Louis Mountbatten as Viceroy of India with orders by the Attlee Government to confer independence as soon as possible, even if it meant the partition of the country into Hindu and Muslim states. Once this had been decided upon, the slaughter began in one of the most disgraceful episodes of British Imperial history. Muslims heading in vast slow-moving columns set off for the new Pakistan at the same time as Hindus in equally vast slow-moving columns left the areas to become Pakistan for the safety of mainly Hindu India. Inevitably the columns met half way whereupon a slaughter of awful dimension resulted.

A figure of a million dead is quoted but the real figure is believed to be far in excess of that. What is indisputable is that without the steadiness of the old British-Indian Army in general and its Gurkha regiments in particular, the slaughter would have been much greater. In its last days that wonderful institution rendered its greatest service.

As the bloody path to Partition and Independence was pursued, the future of the Gurkha Regiments was now decided. Clearly any future employment of Gurkhas would have to be agreed between Nepal, their country, Britain and India. At first neither Britain nor India were sure they required Gurkhas. This attitude soon changed and an agreement was signed between the three countries which allowed Gurkhas to be recruited by Britain and India. It was called the Tripartite Agreement, was signed in November 1947 and, although never ratified, still stands at the time of writing. Its actual content is very brief but does have some important clauses and caveats protecting Gurkhas' treatment in service, their religion and their right to be discharged back to their homeland.

It was not until a few days before Independence on 15 August 1947 that the announcement was made on which regiments were going to going to India and which to Britain. The choice of 2nd, 6th, 7th and 10th Gurkhas for Britain seemed illogical. Of the ten Gurkha regiments, eight were recruited from West Nepal and only two, 7th and 10th Gurkhas, from East Nepal. The laws of numeracy and logic would have seen three western regiments and one eastern coming to Britain. In fact it later transpired that, apart from 2nd Gurkhas, who were saved for British service by the intervention of their old friends the 60th Rifles (King's Royal Rifle Corps), with whom they had held the Delhi ridge against the mutineers, the others were simply chosen because of the ease and cost-saving of transfer from Burma, where three of the battalions were serving at the time of Independence, direct to Malaya where they were to be employed. That such a momentous decision should have been decided on such paltry criteria was little short of scandalous.

Since Gurkhas were not Indian nationals, serving Gurkhas were given an initial 'opt' (choice) in August 1947, held just before

Gurkha guarding Indonesian prisoners, Java 1945. (Gurkha Museum)

Newly raised Gurkha Engineers building a bridge in Malaya. (Gurkha Museum)

Indian Independence, which allowed for very little time for consideration, but nevertheless showed most Gurkhas wishing to serve with Britain. Because of the unreasonably short timescale, this 'opt' was cancelled and held again in December 1947. Then three choices were given to Gurkhas in regiments destined to come to Britain, namely: go with their regiments to the British Army; transfer to the Indian Army; or go home. After four months of threats and blandishments by the newly independent India, and the failure by Britain to make clear terms and conditions of service in a timely manner, in the second moment of decision the figure wishing to 'opt' for Britain was very disappointing. Although 2nd Gurkhas retained most of their men for Britain, the other three regiments were significantly under strength. Gurkhas in the six regiments destined for the Indian Army were, rather unfairly, only allowed two choices: stay with the Indian Army, or go home.

As a result, when the eight battalions of the four chosen regiments eventually sailed for Malaya in early 1948, they were woefully under strength and had to be filled up with raw or partly trained recruits; not a promising start!

If times were uncertain and difficult for Gurkhas, the same held good for their British officers. Most of the Emergency Commissioned Officers who had served so courageously throughout the war and who had survived went back to Britain, leaving the surviving regular officers either to hand over their beloved regiments to India or follow their regiments into British service in Malaya. Clearly the former regulars had the most difficult and unenviable task from which they never shirked. Ordered by the British and Indian governments to leave their

regiments forthwith, they politely declined, indicating that they would leave only when the Indian officers who were to take over from them had arrived and were properly briefed and ready.

Then they went, tearful and disillusioned, from their Gurkha soldiers who had been their world and whose feelings reciprocated theirs. Most 5th Gurkha officers asked to go to 6th Gurkhas, having been co-located at Abbottabad, and, similarly, the 9th asked to go to 2nd Gurkhas, having been co-located at Dehra Dun.

At midnight on 14 of August 1947, Captain Neath of the 6th Gurkhas hauled down the Union Jack from the Red Fort at Delhi. Thus in sadness and some disarray the new Brigade of Gurkhas was born. Subsequent generations, puzzled at how spinelessly Britain had behaved in disposing of India, the 'Jewel in the Imperial Crown', have to remember the state of Britain in 1947. The threat of national bankruptcy, extreme austerity, food, fuel and clothing rationing, a flu epidemic, in 1946 the coldest winter for 50 years, the Russian Iron Curtain and, perhaps most pressing, a Labour Government totally absorbed with the changes required to set up the Welfare State. Not really sufficient excuse but after six years of total war at least understandable.

To Gurkha units arriving in early 1948, Malaya, the Brigade of Gurkhas' new home looked calm and peaceful; a place where the fledgling brigade could sort itself out in an unhurried and measured manner. Little did anyone realize that under the peaceful façade lurked a burgeoning insurrection of major proportions.

The intention of the British War Office had been for Gurkhas to form a complete infantry division in Malaya, 17th Gurkha Infantry Division; a deliberate tribute to the Burma campaign formation of the same number. As well as providing most of the infantry for the new division as for the old, it was planned for Gurkhas to provide supporting arms and services. To this end in 1948 the nucleus of what was to become The Queen's Gurkha Engineers and Queen's Gurkha Signals were formed with drafts from Gurkha infantry battalions, augmented by British specialists. Attempts to form Gurkha Ordnance, Electrical and Mechanical Engineers and Catering units never really got off the ground and the misguided idea of turning 7th Gurkhas into Gunners was abandoned after a year. A Gurkha Company of Royal Military Police, later redesignated Gurkha Military Police, was formed in 1949, and a decade later the Gurkha Army Service Corps was raised.

Early on it was decided to centralize all Gurkha recruit training at Sungei Patani in Kedah State in northwest Malaya on what was once a Second World War airfield and scene of some drama during the Malayan campaign of 1942 (Chapter 10). Gurkha Boys' Training Company raised in April 1948 was co-

located at Sungei Patani with Training Depot Brigade of Gurkhas (TDBG). Boys' Company provided educated and trained recruits mainly for newly raised Corps units.

Headquarters Brigade of Gurkhas, responsible for the non-operational management of all Brigade of Gurkhas units, was established at Seremban, just south of Kuala Lumpur. The Record Office Brigade of Gurkhas (ROBG) was set up at General Headquarters Far East Land Forces, Tanglin, Singapore.

A Gurkha Military Police company was raised in July 1949. The Queen's Own Gurkha Logistic Regiment was raised rather later, in 1958, as The Gurkha Army Service Corps.

Military music is an important facet of any military organization. The 2nd Gurkhas re-raised the only military band, whereas the 6th, 7th and 10th Gurkhas had Pipes and Drums since at least the decade before 1914. Pipes were also adopted by the nascent Corps units. In 1955 a separate Staff Band of The Brigade of Gurkhas was raised.

An early and short-lived attempt to turn 7th Gurkhas into Gunners. (Gurkha Museum)

These organizational changes needed time and patience to implement. Time, however, was not forthcoming, as in June 1948 the Communist insurgency started with the murder of British rubber planters.

In the Second World War before the surrender of Singapore a clandestine resistance organization against the Japanese was set up in mainland Malaya to harry the Japanese. This was based on the Malayan Communist Party and its helpers and in due course became known collectively as The Malayan People's Anti-Japanese Army (MPAJA). Under the impression that the MPAJA was a constant thorn in the side of the Japanese occupiers, Britain parachuted in arms and Force 136 (Special Operations Executive) advisers to support them.

While certainly carrying out some actions against the Japanese, the MPAJA, once it became clear that the Japanese were losing, were actually preparing to take over the country. As the time for the planned British invasion to reoccupy Malaya got nearer, the contacts with the MPAJA got closer, as it was hoped the guerrillas would play a significant role in disrupting the Japanese defence. As we have seen, the dropping of atomic bombs and the subsequent Japanese surrender made an opposed invasion unnecessary. After the British reoccupation of Malaya the MPAJA was paid and administered by the British and used for guard duties until December 1945, when they were disbanded, paid gratuities and expected to hand in their weapons. The problem was that nobody really knew how many weapons (largely ex-Japanese) the fighters actually had, so although the authorities paid 7,000 gratuities and received 5,000 weapons, the British had no means of knowing if that was all. In fact it was only a small proportion.

Although the MPAJA had been disbanded, the Malayan Communist Party was very much alive and, encouraged by the success of Communist uprisings elsewhere, started a series of strikes and labour disputes throughout Malaya and Singapore, often accompanied by violence and thuggery. Britain unwittingly played into their hands by tinkering with the constitution, thereby upsetting the traditional rule of the Sultans. Even though power was restored to the Sultans when it became clear British ideas of a centrally controlled Malayan Union would not work, the resultant two years of confusion and dissatisfaction enabled the Malayan Communist Party to strengthen its hand.

By 1947 Chin Peng had become Secretary General of the Malayan Communist Party at the age of 25. An able and ruthless man, he had been given the Order of the British Empire for services to Force 136 during the war. He now steered his party towards armed insurrection. Substituting the 'J' in MPAJA for a 'B' the MPAJA now became the Malayan People's Anti-British Army. As such it embraced not only the ten regiments of fighters but also

Soldiers of the Malay People's Anti-Japanese Army on parade shortly after the Japanese surrender in 1945; soon they would be fighting the British for control of Malaya. (Gurkha Museum)

their vast network of helpers, suppliers and informers. Chin Peng's battle plan was loosely based upon that adopted by Mao Tse-tung in his successful but still ongoing war against the Nationalists in China. Gradually the Communists would by terror and disruption gain control of large areas of Malaya which would become 'liberated' areas where the government writ would no longer run. Gradually the liberated areas would get larger, meld together and force the Government into reduced enclaves from where its dwindling followers would be finally ejected.

To achieve this Chin Peng had about 5,000, mainly Chinese, men and women under arms, and many times that number in the Min Yuen (People's Movement) of auxiliary helpers, informants and suppliers. To these groupings could be added thousands of Tamil rubber tappers, who were terrified into giving food and help. The armed element operated mainly from the huge swathes of jungle that then covered Malaya. The Min Yuen lived in villages and towns and in rubber plantations, appearing as bona fide citizens until called upon to assist the Communist Terrorists (CTs) as they will now be referred to.

To counter this well-organized and ruthless insurgency in June 1948, the available security forces were not as potent as their paper strengths indicated. The mainly Malay Police Force was some 11,500 strong, but about 2,000 were clerical and their intelligence-gathering capacity was small. The 17 Gurkha Division was forming with its six in-theatre Gurkha battalions, another in Singapore and one in Hong Kong, and there were three British battalions, two of which were in Singapore. We have already seen how weak most of the Gurkha battalions were on arriving in Malaya, and how desperately they needed time to train the large numbers of raw recruits who made up much of their strength.

The terrain also greatly favoured the CTs; after all, they had spent most of the anti-Japanese war in the jungle and what they did not know about living and fighting in it was hardly worth knowing. Gurkhas, too, knew a good deal about jungle as it occurred naturally in Nepal, but few had experience of jungle warfare in South East Asia since most of the first and second battalions of those regiments coming to Britain had fought in North Africa and Italy. As for the large number of young soldiers, at that stage they had hardly had time to master their weapons, let alone use them effectively in the jungle. British troops, composed mainly of young National Servicemen from urban environments, found the jungle strange and unnerving at first.

Early in the 'Emergency', as it was declared on 17 June 1948 and came to be known, the CTs held most of the cards and the Gurkha battalions took some hard knocks. In January 1949 a platoon from A Company 1/6th Gurkhas with the company commander, Major Ronald Barnes, was patrolling near the Malay-Thai border when they sighted a CT. Major Barnes immediately opened fire only to find himself caught in a well-laid ambush. Major Barnes, his Gurkha officer and nine others were killed and six wounded. One of the wounded Gurkhas was hit several times but, feigning dead, was left by the CTs and managed, despite his wounds, to rejoin his company.

In 2/2nd Gurkhas a lorry carrying 20 newly arrived soldiers to their company at Sungei Siput, north of Ipoh, was ambushed in heavy rain, ten being killed and nine seriously wounded. The CTs successfully made off with their weapons.

The Emergency, which was to continue for 12 years, was marked by certain milestones, and the first of these was the arrival of 2nd Guards Brigade from the United Kingdom in late 1948. Up until that time clothing, weapons and equipment in Malaya were unchanged from the end of the Second World War fighting the Japanese in Burma. Now the lighter Number 5 Lee-Enfield jungle carbine replaced the Number 4 rifle, and light American M1 carbines and reliable Australian Owen sub-machine guns became available. Rubber and canvas jungle boots replaced leather studded boots, and lighter radio sets replaced heavy wartime models. People in high places tended to listen to Guardsmen!

The next milestone was the arrival of Lieutenant General Sir Harold Briggs (former 1942–44 commander of 5th Indian Division), in April 1950 as Director of Operations. Briggs realized that until the security forces could break the link between the CTs and their infrastructure, the Min Yuen, ultimate success against them would be impossible. He proceeded to corral all the squatters who were aiding the CTs into defended areas called 'New Villages'. It was a long and painful task but it did in time achieve its aim of forcing the CTs to try to grow their own food deep in the jungle by breaking the link with their suppliers and helpers. There

MALAYA 1948–60

would still be dark days ahead but more than any other single factor 'The Briggs Plan', as it became known, laid the foundation for ultimate victory.

In late January 1950, Major Peter Richardson of 1/2nd Gurkhas carried out the most successful single operation against the CTs of the whole Emergency; this was in the Labis area, equidistant between the Malay capital Kuala Lumpur and Singapore. In this area a notorious platoon of CTs known as the Labis gang held sway and had recently attacked the night mail train to Singapore. A platoon of 1/2nd Gurkhas following up made contact with the gang, but was not strong enough to bring it to bay, although the platoon forced it to abandon its well-established camp, suffering in the process one killed and the company commander wounded.

Major Richardson, on receiving information from Special Branch as to where the gang had gone, moved his B Company into a rubber plantation at night where they patiently awaited the dawn, tortured by hordes of mosquitoes that for some reason greatly favoured rubber plantations in the same way as vicious red ants favoured secondary jungle. At 0630 hours Major Richardson, himself and his small headquarters in the middle, swept through the rubber plantation in extended line looking for the CTs Special Branch had indicated. Visibility was poor with morning mist

Train ambushed by Communist terrorists in Malaya. (Gurkha Museum)

hanging about the rubber trees and the rice paddy beyond. They had gone about 100 yards when they saw a man running away from a squatter's hut in the rubber. Rifleman Bombahadur Gharti in the section nearest Major Richardson opened fire.

Immediately the area came to life with CTs rushing out of the squatter's hut and firing and throwing a grenade at the advancing company. Bombahadur rushed forward firing from the hip, hitting several. Major Richardson, engaging two others, heard a dreadful noise behind him and saw a CT slashing at a Gurkha in the grass with a native *parang* knife. He shot him but not quickly enough to save the slashed man who later died in hospital.

The CTs now tried to escape the advancing company by heading east where, beyond the road, there lay the sanctuary of primary jungle. Fortunately the B Company Sergeant Major saw what they were trying to do and cut them off with the left-hand platoon. Turning back again, the CTs were caught in a deadly crossfire, some 22 being killed and found, although later it transpired that 35 had been killed. Major Richardson received the Distinguished Service Order, a rare distinction for a company commander, and second only to a Victoria Cross, while the Sergeant Major, Bhimbadur Pun, was awarded the Distinguished Conduct Medal, for which Gurkhas only became eligible in 1948.

It has to be stated that contacts with the CTs, especially of this magnitude, were few and far between. They represented the culmination of literally thousands of hours of patient patrolling in all weathers and all conditions, often for weeks at a time. It was this patient but inexorable pressure that kept the CTs on the move, never able to relax or consolidate but becoming more akin to hunted animals. To the Gurkhas and their British officers it became

a way of life, so that the jungle became their natural environment. Every few months they came out of the jungle for two weeks' rest, when jungle sores could heal up, leech bites stop suppurating, proper meals be eaten and a few cold beers enjoyed, before returning to the jungle. One can imagine that Lieutenant Colonel Walter Walker failed to make himself universally popular when, as the new Commanding Officer of 1/6th Gurkhas from 1951, he hijacked the sacred two weeks for retraining! Nevertheless his bold initiative did pay dividends in enhanced operational effectiveness, resulting in some 80 'kills' by 1/6th Gurkhas in the Kluang area of Johore, a formidable record.

The Gurkha battalion in Hong Kong was also having a busy time, as a complete division was built up in that Crown Colony to dissuade the victorious Chinese Communists from crossing the border to gobble it up. Here every day was spent in all weathers building bunkers and erecting barbed wire, the rusting remains of which can still be seen etched across the hills of the New Territories like spider's webs. Gurkha troop levels were boosted by Gurkha Engineers acting in the infantry role – rather to the detriment of mastering their primary role

Meanwhile in Nepal momentous events occurred in 1950–51. The Koirala brothers, with the tacit support of the exiled King Tribhuvana and the overt support of newly independent India, stage-managed incursions into Nepal to oust the Rana dynasty, using as their shock troops disaffected Nepalis and the sweepings of the Calcutta slums, the infamous *goondahs*. Even given the very sleepy reaction of the Royal Nepalese Army, the invasion cannot be described as a success and but, for a concurrent rising of Eastern Gurkhas, would have failed entirely. Eastern Gurkhas, mainly Rais and Limbus, many of them with military experience, were a much more formidable threat and as a result the King was reinstated in February 1951 and Mohan Shamsher obliged to step down, thus bringing to an end the 104-year rule of the Ranas.

Perhaps the reader might wonder at why Britain, thrice succoured in its hour of desperate need by the Rana dynasty, did not make some conscious effort to help them in their own hour of need? Post-war British governments could be rather remiss in helping old friends, and the Ranas had to be grateful that Britain had not actually been involved in the invasion (in which Gurkhas of the new Indian Army took part), as happened in September 1948 to the Indian princely state of Hyderabad – another old and faithful friend. In later years other old and faithful friends would suffer under Britain's newly discovered realpolitik, including, sadly, the Gurkhas who had served their employer so loyally.

Interestingly, at the time of writing, the King of Nepal and the Shah dynasty were dethroned on 28 May 2008 by a government headed by one Giriprasad Koirala. History has an uncanny way of coming full circle.

General Sir Gerald Templer, High Commissioner of Malaya and Commander in Chief, inspecting a 6th Gurkhas patrol. His outstanding leadership swung the war against the Communist Terrorists. (Gurkha Museum)

Returning to Malaya in 1951, things ostensibly appeared to be going very badly. The Briggs Plan had yet to show tangible results and its author retired to England a terminally ill man. In October 1951 the High Commissioner for Malaya, Sir Henry Gurney, was ambushed by CTs and killed and a month later the highest weekly total of security force casualties at the hands of the CTs was recorded. Actually, unrecognized at the time, another milestone was reached when General Sir Gerald Templer took over as both High Commissioner and Director of Operations in Malaya. Well did he deserve his soubriquet 'Tiger of Malaya'. Just as Sir Harold Briggs had recognized the vital importance of getting those vulnerable to the CTs into defended villages, so Templer realized the vital importance of government, police and military working closely together at all levels of command. Up until this time they had all worked separately. Police Special Branch had been sparing with their intelligence, in case the military blundered in and compromised everything. The military kept things back from the police because they felt the police were insecure and leaked information to the CTs; and nobody told the government anything.

Templer changed all this, setting up joint security committees and operations rooms throughout the whole spectrum of command. A measure of ruthlessness was necessary to overcome vested interest and prejudice; Templer provided this.

As the effects of his leadership became felt, operations against the CTs became increasingly successful. In February 1953, after ten months of constant but fruitless patrolling, 2/7th Gurkhas were briefed for an operation in conjunction with 1st Battalion The Gordon Highlanders based on information provided by an army Auster light aircraft. on a routine flight from Seremban, just south of the capital Kuala Lumpur. The pilot had spotted what looked like a CT camp hidden deep in the jungle.

Captain John Thornton, commanding C Company 2/7th Gurkhas, was to provide the area ambushes to catch the fleeing CTs, while a company of the Gordons was to assault the CT camp. Captain Thornton approached the area very cautiously, his men lying flat in their trucks to avoid being seen and debussing in darkness and rain far from the objective they were to ambush. At dawn they moved forward cautiously to set up a patrol base in deep

Gurkha recruits join in a 'Jamre' or sing-song at Dharan in the early 1950s. (Gurkha Museum)

jungle before sending out patrols to find suitable ambush positions. One of these patrols commanded by a lance corporal saw two CTs washing and deduced the main CT camp was close by. Edging forward he saw a camp with CTs moving around.

The young lance corporal then sent back a Gurkha soldier to Captain Thornton to bring up the rest of the company. Alerting the Gordons early next morning, Thornton surrounded the enemy camp with a cordon and then with a small heavily armed group assaulted the camp driving the CTs into the waiting cordon, who killed eight CTs.

Their sister battalion 1/7th Gurkhas also had a remarkable success in killing the notorious CT called Goh Sia who had terrorized the Segamat area midway between Kuala Lumpur and

Singapore. As part of a larger operation to catch Goh Sia and his gang, a Gurkha corporal, Partapsing Rai, and his section of five men waited in ambush by a CT food dump for three days. They subsisted on only water and biscuits and took it in turns to sleep as best they could, totally exposed to the elements. Despairing of anyone coming and rapidly coming to the end of their endurance, the ambushers at about 0900 on the third day saw Goh Sia and his bodyguards arrive at the food dump. Corporal Partapsing personally dispatched him, thus abruptly ending his reign of terror.

As the years passed, under relentless pressure the CTs saw the successful fulfilment of their aims pass from improbability to impossibility. They retreated deeper and deeper into the jungle, relying in some cases on the aboriginal Sakai people to supply

Newly raised Gurkha Signals operating a Brigade rear link set in Malaya. (Gurkha Museum)

To feed the embattled Brigade with a continual flow of recruits, many changes to the pre-Indian Independence system had been necessary. Before India became independent, Britain operated two recruiting depots within India close by the Nepalese border; Kunraghat for western recruiting and Darjeeling for eastern recruiting. Soon after Independence in 1947, recruiting was relocated to the nearby sites of Lehra in the west and Jalapahar in the east. In 1953 India, now a republic, objected to the retention of these two recruiting centres and an agreement was reached with the Nepalese government. This eventually resulted in the setting up of a magnificent purpose-built recruiting depot at Dharan in Eastern Nepal with its own British military hospital; and another much more basic recruiting depot, first at Paklihawa in Western Nepal, and then further north at Pokhara in the western foothills.

Since it was not then possible to fly large passenger planes into Nepal, with Indian agreement a transit camp was set up at Barrackpore, just outside Calcutta. Here Gurkhas returning on leave and pension from Malaya and Hong Kong arrived either by ship at Calcutta docks or by plane at Calcutta's Dum Dum airport; and staged at the Transit Camp prior to proceeding by train to stations on the Nepalese border, Nautanwa for Western Gurkhas and Jogbani for Easterners. Those coming back from leave, their families and recruits similarly staged at Barrackpore before boarding ships and planes.

Originally there had been some doubt as to how infantry regiments of the Brigade should be manned by British officers but the idea to man it on officers seconded from the rest of the Army was wisely dropped. From 1950 the first dedicated officers

their wants. Even then they could not be safe as Gurkhas led by talented linguists such as Major John Cross patiently won the trust of the Sakai and weaned them from helping the CTs.

All the time this slow patient process was continuing, The Brigade of Gurkhas was developing and expanding. Already The Gurkha Engineers had established a reputation for their engineering skills in the most testing conditions, their expert bridging operations facilitating many a successful operation. The Gurkha Signals were now providing rear link detachments for every Gurkha battalion as well as the whole signals network for 48th Gurkha Infantry Brigade. The doubters who had forecast that Gurkhas could never master such skills fell temporarily silent. The Gurkha Military Police had now been included in the Brigade *ORBAT* and had expanded to include a Dog Company. Rumours that their guard dogs all had flat heads from too much patting proved to be unsubstantiated!

Gurkha Army Service Corps basic driver training.

Gurkha soldier Malaya 1950. (Gurkha Museum)

had ambushed and killed a group of Malay Special Constables, all part of their campaign to terrify the local population into submission. The 2/10th Gurkhas sent two platoons of B Company to investigate. One platoon of only two sections (16 men) led by Corporal Makarpal Tamang sighted one CT moving alone through the jungle and followed up. After some time cautiously following up, the CT was seen to move up a steep hill at the top of which appeared to be a large CT camp. Sending one of his sections round the back of the hill to act as cut-offs, Makarpal led the other section up the cliff edge of the hill towards the CT camp. He succeeded in getting so close to the CT camp unobserved that when at last the CTs sighted his section, it was not possible for them to sufficiently depress their weapons from the lying position, so they were obliged to stand up if they were to engage Makarpal's section.

As they stood up they were engaged by Makarpal's Bren gunner which put them to ground again. From this position they did not see Makarpal's other section coming in from their rear, thus presenting a target that in the words of the 10th Gurkha regimental history, '*the boy with a catapult dreams of.*' Six CTs were killed and nine wounded of which three were captured; it was a brilliant operation commanded by a junior non-commissioned officer.

Meanwhile, further north around Sungei Siput, 2/2nd Gurkhas working on Special Branch information were having a string of successes, many gained by D Company commanded by Major Neill, whom we have met before on the First Chindit Expedition and again as the company commander of Rifleman Bhanbhagta Gurung VC in the Arakan. Neill personally accounted for 21 terrorists, a unique achievement.

Slowly but inexorably, the CTs were losing the initiative. Because they were deprived of the material support of the Min Yuen, now safely enclosed in defended villages, they were obliged to seek refuge deeper and deeper in the jungle. By 1954 Sir Gerald Templer felt the country was secure enough to hold an election on its future government; this took place in 1955 and was won by the Triple Alliance Party under the popular leadership of the Malay, Tunku Abdul Rahman. Templer himself, having turned the tide of the Emergency by wise policies and inspired leadership, now left Malaya's political leaders to carry on, ensuring that able British successors succeeded him separately as High Commissioner and Director of Operations, tasks that Templer had held alone as virtually a military and civilian supremo.

One of the first actions of his successors was to offer an amnesty to CTs if they surrendered. There were no immediate dramatic results despite 12 million leaflets being dropped over the jungle by the Royal Air Force. Nevertheless the amnesty did indirectly lead to a meeting between Tunku Abdul Rahman and Chin Peng, the CT leader, at Baling near the Thai border. Their

from Sandhurst were arriving, usually of very high quality as only those passing out high in the Sandhurst order of merit stood much chance of getting a place. They joined a number of National Service officers who were also of uniformly high quality.

In 1950 a Jungle Warfare School was set up by the redoubtable Colonel Walter Walker near Kota Tinggi on the east coast of south Johore state. Although this was a British Army facility many of its instructors were Gurkhas, as was its demonstration platoon.

During this formative period for the Brigade, its members had much to be grateful for in the wise and compassionate guidance of their first Major General and commander of 17th Gurkha Division, Sir Charles Boucher. It was he who had to interact with the War Office in England over a myriad of unresolved issues which were all capably and pragmatically addressed.

Meanwhile the campaign in the jungle continued with a considerable success in August 1952 by a platoon of B Company 2/10th Gurkhas in the Muar river area of West Johore. The CTs

differences were, however, irreconcilable and the war went on. Another of Templer's initiatives was now put into action which was the reverse of the CTs' plan to declare certain areas over which they had gained control 'liberated areas'. Even before the election the Malayan government started to declare certain areas 'white', which meant that the threat of CT attack was minimal. Malacca was the first area to be declared white and, by the time the elections were concluded, over half Malaya was declared white. This could only be achieved because of the unending round-the-clock pressure on the CTs by the security forces, a large proportion of which were Gurkha.

An example of this was in late 1955 in the Cameron Highlands when a strong group of CTs raided a defended village, murdered a Home Guard, cut telegraph wires and wrecked a police radio station, stealing shotguns and ammunition before making off. Major Harkasing Rai, the redoubtable commander of 1/6th Gurkhas' C Company, was sent in pursuit and having located the CT tracks eventually found them in a hut on 9 January 1956. Opening fire, four CTs were killed, but others made off under the cover of heavy automatic fire. Doggedly following up, Harkasing again ran them to ground four days later, but was seen just as his company was about to attack and the CTs made off again. A Company 1/6th Gurkhas now came in to assist and killed a further CT and wounded two more, while two more were killed by a platoon of the Malay Regiment which had also joined in the hunt. All in all it was a very successful joint operation, especially as three of the dead CTs were important Communist officials.

Later, on 31 August 1957, another milestone was reached when Malaya became an independent country within the Commonwealth. At a stroke another plank of CT dogma was ripped up and discarded. The British had handed over power to a democratically elected government and not to the terror of a successful Communist insurgency. The CTs were not yet defeated; some 2,000 were still in the jungle, over 500 in Johore alone, so the pressure by the security forces had to continue unabated. In May 1958 a very successful joint operation called 'Tiger' by 2/2nd and 2/10th Gurkhas (part of the newly promoted Walter Walker's 99th Gurkha Brigade) virtually destroyed the CT infrastructure in Johore. The CTs were hit so hard that when the 'Q' parties went in to make contact with them and offer money to surrender they got a favourable response. These 'Q' parties often consisted of young British officers and one or two Gurkhas and were highly dangerous as they never knew quite how the CTs would react. They were distasteful too, as they often resulted in rewarding those who had committed gruesome murders with large sums of money to buy them out of the jungle.

By the end of 1958 the CTs had been virtually defeated, although the Emergency was not to end officially until 1960.

The small fragmented groups of CTs that still remained were no longer a threat to the newly independent Malaya, although there continued to be occasional sightings of them, mostly in the tangled and inaccessible jungle around Grik near the border with Thailand.

So the 12-year campaign against a serious Communist insurrection ended with its defeat, in stark contrast to Vietnam, Laos, Cambodia and China itself where the Communists had been successful. That they were not successful was in no small measure due to the part played by the newly formed Brigade of Gurkhas which provided never less than a quarter of the infantry and half the military engineers deployed.

This turbulent period of history is well covered by the Gurkha Museum and includes descriptions of specific operations, as well as a fascinating diorama of a Gurkha jungle camp.

See Appendix 6 for a fascinating account of the fighting in Java 'Anone, Arimaska – The Cannon has fired' by Brigadier B.G. Hickey OBE, MC. Reproduced by kind permission of the Editor of the 5th Royal Gurkha Rifles (Frontier Force) newsletter.

General Service Medal 1918–62 (SE Asia and Malaya).

CHAPTER FOURTEEN

THE BRUNEI REVOLT
AND
INDONESIAN CONFRONTATION

The year 1960 was not only important for Malaya with the ending of the 12-year-long Communist insurrection; for Nepal, 1960 was important too.

King Tribhuvana had returned to Nepal, the Rana regime had been ousted and there were the beginnings of a democratic state. From 1950 until 1955 the country saw a bewildering succession of governments come and go, until in desperation the Crown Prince dissolved them and instituted a Council of Advisers. King Tribhuvana, long in poor health and worn out by political shenanigans, died in March 1955, and was replaced as king by the Crown Prince, who became King Mahendra Bir Bikram Shah Deva. His coronation took place with considerable pomp and splendour, and Gurkha contingents from both British and Indian armies were present. As a gesture of solidarity and friendship he was later appointed a Field Marshal in the British Army and Colonel in Chief of The Brigade of Gurkhas.

There then followed five years of political uncertainty bordering on chaos until, in December 1960, the king suspended the constitution and assumed direct rule of his country, convinced that Western-style democracy was not in the best interests of Nepal and its people. Instead, King Mahendra set up a system of *panchayats* or councils, headed by a state or *rashtriya panchayat* and running down through zones (*anchals*), districts and villages. Trekking in Nepal in the mid-1960s, travellers were struck at how

well the system seemed to work, certainly at village level. A senior and respected village personality, often an ex-serviceman, would run the village through the equivalent of our parish council. Issues affecting water and agricultural allocation were dealt with amicably and the whole village mobilized in time of emergency or natural disaster. As a result of the *panchayat* system, so ably steered through by the king, Nepal was able to enjoy some 30 years of peace and political stability. In 1961 this growing stability was celebrated by a state visit to Nepal from Queen Elizabeth II and Prince Philip. Again the Brigade of Gurkhas provided representation.

The Brigade of Gurkhas had also come to maturity with The Gurkha Engineers, Signals and Service Corps expanded to full regimental level, with squadrons deployed throughout Malaya, Singapore and Hong Kong. The early 1960s were halcyon days for the Brigade, its reputation standing at an all-time high following the successful conclusion of the Malayan Emergency. In 1959 its infantry regiments that did not have them had received Royal titles, its strength was now 15,000 and its infrastructure sound. Plans were well advanced to send an infantry battalion group, 1/6th Gurkhas, to Britain which with Gurkha elements of Engineers, Signals and Service Corps would join 51st Infantry Brigade based at Tidworth in Wiltshire, which was commanded by Brigadier Noel 'Brunny' Short, himself a 6th Gurkha.

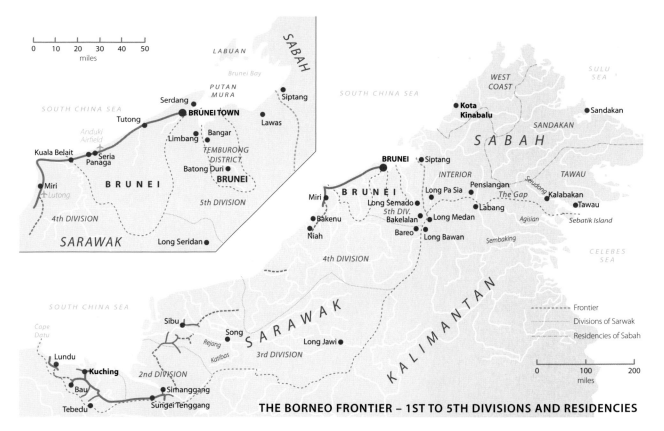

THE BORNEO FRONTIER – 1ST TO 5TH DIVISIONS AND RESIDENCIES

However, not all was as well as appeared. Unknown at the time to any but the most senior officers of the Brigade, British government plans to reduce the Brigade strength from 15,000 to 10,000 were well advanced.

Others were planning far-reaching developments too. President Sukarno of Indonesia, whom we last came across leading the nationalists against the re-imposition of Dutch colonial rule in 1945–6, was also flexing his muscles. Although he had ousted the Dutch from most of Indonesia by 1949, they still occupied the western half of the huge island of New Guinea, a region which was known as West Irian; the Australians held the other part as a trust territory. By a combination of bluff and guile, Sukarno managed to get the Dutch out of West Irian in 1962 without provoking the Australians.

Flushed by these not inconsiderable diplomatic and military successes, Sukarno planned to head a grouping of Malaya, the Philippines and Indonesia to be called Maphilindo, which as a huge Far Eastern conglomerate would exert world power influence. In May 1961, however, just as his plans were crystallizing, the Federation of Malaya announced its plans for a new political entity, Malaysia, to which Britain had given her support and blessing. At that stage Malaysia was to include Malaya, Singapore, the tiny oil-rich state of Brunei and the huge undeveloped areas of

Soldiers of 1/2nd Gurkhas emplaning at Singapore en route to quell the insurgency in Brunei. (Gurkha Museum)

British Borneo into a socio-economic grouping. Clearly this ran diametrically against Sukarno's plans for Maphilindo, and he determined to scupper it.

In fact, although implemented in September 1963, the concept of Malaysia had not really been thought through. The ruler of Brunei, Sultan Sir Omar Ali Saifuddin, had no desire for his small but immensely rich country to become subordinated to Malaysia. The mainly Chinese Singapore was frightened by the

General Service Medal 1918–62 (Brunei).

over Malaysians, Vietnamese, Thais etc. Most of the teaching staff and infrastructure were from the Brigade of Gurkhas. Both instructors and students were shortly to have a chance to test their training for real.

When Sukarno realized that Brunei was opposed to the concept of Malaysia he saw his chance. The British Protectorate of Brunei was only just over 2,000 square miles and its population was less than 100,000. Half the population were Malay, a quarter Chinese and the rest native Dyaks. Discovery of huge reserves of oil and natural gas had made Brunei fabulously wealthy. Since the Sultan ruled as a benevolent autocrat, most of the money from oil benefited him and his immediate family, although the living standards of the rest of the population were quite high. Given this rather inequitable distribution of wealth, more progressive elements of the population were agitating for democracy and a fairer share of the oil bonanza.

This agitation took the shape of an opposition political wing, the *Partai Raayat* (People's Party), allied with its militant wing the North Kalimantan National Army (TNKU), which consisted of some 8,000 semi-trained insurgents assembling in the jungles of Brunei and the adjacent Sabah and Sarawak.

Against his better judgement, the Sultan of Brunei was pressured by Britain and Malaya to make political concessions and hold elections for 16 seats in the Legislative Council, while

prospect of being ruled by Malays and in fact pulled out of Malaysia in August 1965. As for the politically naive inhabitants of North Borneo (Sabah) and Sarawak, comprising British Borneo, it is doubtful whether they really knew what was going on. However the British, who had ruled with reasonable equity and justice, assured them it was a good thing so they went along with it.

If the concept of Malaysia had flaws, that of Maphilindo was a pipe dream, yet Sukarno continued to pursue it vigorously. It helped him keep the delicate domestic balance of power between the *Partai Komunis Indonesia* or Communists, who had been the main force in expelling the Dutch, and the armed forces which were in the main nationalistic but anti-Communist. Meanwhile Indonesia herself was being wooed by both East and West. Modern Russian warships joined the Indonesian Navy, American aircraft were supplied to the Indonesian Air Force and up-to-date US arms to the Army. The British helpfully taught the Indonesians how to use their new weaponry to the best advantage by laying on courses at the Jungle Warfare School at Kota Tinggi in Malaya. Indonesian students reciprocated by generally coming out top

Gurkha escorting rebel prisoners during the fighting in Brunei Town. (Gurkha Museum)

Gurkha on guard at Tutong after it had been cleared of rebels. (Gurkha Museum)

retaining 17 seats for his own nominated representatives. The *Partai Raayat* duly won all 16 seats and the Sultan maintained his wafer-thin majority by only one. This was the signal for the TNKU to rise and capture the Sultan, who was to be used as a puppet leader of a new Borneo state comprising Brunei, Sabah and Sarawak. They also planned to attack police stations, whose weapons they wanted, as well as to kidnap 45 European executives from the huge Shell-run oilfields at Seria in the south of the country to use as bargaining chips. A.M. Azahari, the Arab-Malay leader of the *Partai Raayat*, pragmatically left for Indonesia, leaving the rebellion to be masterminded by the leader of the TNKU, Yassin Affendi.

The rebellion was launched at 0200 hours on 8 December 1962 with an attack on the Sultan's palace, police stations, the Prime Minister's house and power stations. Early on a Saturday morning did not find the reactive qualities of Headquarters Far East Land Forces in Singapore at absolutely their sharpest, and it took some time to dust off the contingency plan 'Ale', which called for two rifle companies with some engineers and signallers, all in a mainly light role, to counter civil disturbances. Unfortunately, the unit earmarked for this role, The Queen's Own Highlanders, was involved in anti-piracy duties in North Borneo, so 1/2nd Gurkhas based in Singapore, was nominated instead. Despite not being at notice for the task, 1/2nd Gurkhas responded with alacrity and were at Seletar and Changi airfields by 1230 hours as frantic efforts were made to find the Far East Land Forces map storeman, so at least 1/2nd Gurkhas should have some idea where they were going! Unfortunately, the Royal Air Force was unable to provide a transport plane until 1445, by which time there were less than four hours of daylight left. In the event the first aircraft to take off was from Changi carrying D Company, which was supposed to be the follow-up company, shortly followed by one from Seletar carrying the force commander, Major J.A. Lloyd-Williams and his headquarters, followed by others.

Initially the aircraft headed for the airfield on Labuan, a nearby island off the coast of neighbouring Sabah, in case Brunei airfield was blocked. Discovering it was in fact clear, some of the aircraft headed direct for Brunei, while the larger transports went into Labuan from whence Gurkhas were ferried into Brunei by planes with shorter landing/take-off capacity. In the event the first Gurkhas to arrive were from D Company in a Malayan Airlines plane from Labuan!

Fortunately Mr A. Outram, the Commissioner for Police of Brunei, had acted with great dispatch and resolution, securing, albeit tenuously, the safety of the Sultan, keeping the runway open and resisting the insurgents wherever possible. He was able to update Major Lloyd-Williams who, landing in darkness, his men arriving piecemeal and without accurate maps in a strange country, needed all the help he could get. Mr Outram was able to pass on the unwelcome news that the insurgents had occupied the oilfields in Seria and taken hostages, although the main local police station at Panaga was still holding out as, was the one at the little town of Kuala Belait near the border with Sarawak. What the police commissioner did not know was that the insurgents had also been active in adjacent Sarawak, capturing the riverine port of Limbang and incarcerating the Resident, Mr R.D. Morris.

Throughout that long night, despite continual resistance by the rebels, 1/2nd Gurkhas slowly but surely established control throughout Brunei Town, suffering two killed and six wounded in the process, one of the fatalities being a British officer. Major Lloyd-Williams had intended to send his C Company 60 miles down to Seria at dawn the next day to release the European hostages and settle with the insurgents. However, on receipt of a message that the insurgents were massing for an attack on Panaga police station, Captain Tony Lea, Officer Commanding C Company, set off at night in commandeered vehicles. Successfully brushing aside slight opposition they were heavily ambushed in Tutong where Captain Lea's driver and signaller were wounded. Their Land Rover crashed and, separated from the rest of their company, Captain Lea and his Gurkha Company Sergeant Major played a desperate cat-and-mouse game with the insurgents until at dawn the rest of the company rejoined and cleared the rebels out of Tutong. Dawn also brought the rest of 1/2nd Gurkhas into Brunei, one company of which was immediately sent by air to secure the airstrip at Lutong and the oilfield at Miri further down the coast from Seria in Sarawak.

Unsure what level of opposition he was facing, the Commanding Officer, Lieutenant Colonel Gordon Shakespear, who had now arrived, withdrew C Company from Tutong and completed his domination of Brunei Town, moving the Sultan out of his palace and into the main police station where he could be better protected. Several rebel attempts to reoccupy the town were severely repulsed so that, by the time Brigadier J.B.A. Glennie and his ad hoc brigade headquarters arrived, Brunei Town was secure.

Clearly the unsatisfactory situation still obtaining in Seria and the oilfields was a priority and in a daring air-landed attack 1st Battalion The Queen's Own Highlanders, just arrived via Labuan, seized the small grass airfield at Anduki, just east of Seria, and from there started to re-establish control against determined opposition from the insurgents. In this they had the support of B Company

1/2nd Gurkhas commanded by Major P.T. Bowring, who was given the task of securing Kuala Belait. With B Company reinforced by a platoon of Queen's Own Highlanders and two armoured scout cars, this task was expeditiously completed against some opposition, and several European hostages were released.

***

The situation in Brunei was now rapidly coming under control, but in neighbouring Sarawak the insurgents still held Limbang in strength and were preparing to hang the Resident, Mr Morris. His demise was forestalled by a daring dawn attack by about 100 men of Number 42 Royal Marine Commando in two ramp-powered lighters from which they stormed ashore under heavy fire. Although taking five casualties, they routed the insurgents and saved Mr Morris from an untimely fate. In Brunei Town Brigadier Arthur (Pat) Patterson, commanding 99th Gurkha Infantry Brigade, had arrived and taken over command from Brigadier Glennie and his ad hoc Brigade Headquarters. In Tutong an attempt by the insurgents to reoccupy the town by river was ambushed by 1/2nd Gurkhas with heavy casualties, 26 being killed.

Some time later the military leader of the TNKU insurgent army, Yassin Affendi, was wounded and captured by a patrol of 2/7th Gurkhas, while one of Azahari's brothers was killed and another arrested. Azahari himself never returned to Brunei although he had carelessly left his wife there and she was hospitably treated by the incoming 1/2nd Gurkhas. Various other insurgent elements took to the jungle and tried to make their way to Indonesia. Many were hunted down by friendly Dyak tribesmen under the spirited direction of Mr Tom Harrisson, Curator of the Sarawak Museum.

On 19 December 1962 Major General Walter Walker, commanding 17th Gurkha Division, arrived to take overall command as Commander British Forces in Borneo over what was to quickly turn into a long and at times intense jungle war with Indonesia. Although the Brunei revolt was successfully concluded, it had been a close-run thing. Without doubt 1/2nd Gurkhas' prompt and energetic initial deployment was the key ingredient in ultimate victory. The sad cost to 1/2nd Gurkhas was two killed and 17 wounded as against 65 insurgents killed and 783 captured or surrendered.

As the remnants of the Brunei insurgents were hunted down in Brunei and Sarawak, Indonesia started to send groups of Indonesian Border Terrorists (IBTs) into Sarawak to destabilize the somewhat fragile infrastructure. One such group attacked the little western police post at Tebedu in April 1963, killing a policeman and wounding two others. While a comparatively minor incident, it was important, as it demonstrated that Indonesia was determined to get militarily involved.

Meanwhile arrangements for the creation of Malaysia continued. Despite the failure of the Brunei revolt, President Sukarno of Indonesia was still determined on Maphilindo and seemed to be supported in this by the Philippines which claimed Sabah. To try and resolve the deadlock, the United Nations was invited to carry out a survey of the populations of Sabah and Sarawak to see if they wished to join Malaysia.

This survey was carried out in September 1963 and showed that Sabah and Sarawak were supportive of the concept. Given that the recent Brunei revolt had opened their eyes to other less palatable alternatives, the result was hardly a surprise. On 16 September Malaysia came into being. Indonesia refused to accept its creation and a mob sacked the British Embassy in Jakarta. Malaysia broke off diplomatic relations with both Indonesia and the Philippines, while Indonesia started to position regular and irregular forces along the 1,000-mile jungle frontier of Sabah and Sarawak.

Brunei, still recovering from its ordeal, declined to be a part of Malaysia and continued to strengthen its ties with Britain; ties that have kept a Gurkha battalion based in Seria, Brunei, for nearly 50 years.

Britain was now faced by the unpalatable prospect of a jungle war with Indonesia, in which the opponent appeared to hold most of the trump cards. Not only had she a huge and quite effective army, but the long open border with Sabah and Sarawak afforded limitless opportunities for covert infiltration. Within Sabah and Sarawak there was an active and dedicated Clandestine Communist Organization (CCO) with which invaders could link up and gain support and material help. At first Sukarno went through the charade of pretending that the invaders were volunteers, but he soon found that, if success was to be achieved, regular troops needed to be used and as 'Confrontation' /Konfrontasi (the policy announced by Indonesia from 20 January 1963) went on, a larger and larger proportion of regular Tentara Nasional Indonesia (TNI) became involved, as opposed to TNKU or IBT (Indonesian Border Terrorist). Initially the regulars came from marine or parachute units whose high standards fitted them for the demands of jungle warfare.

Britain did however hold some trump cards. The projected rundown of her troop strengths in the Far East had yet to start, and she still retained a very strong base at Singapore with significant naval, military and air components. Most importantly, The Brigade of Gurkhas was still at its maximum strength of 15,000 jungle-trained men. Whitehall was also fortunate as far as personalities went. The 50-year-old Major General Walter Walker had commanded a Gurkha battalion in Burma, another Gurkha battalion and a Gurkha brigade in Malaya and now the Gurkha division so was indisputably the best man for the job. Walker and the overall theatre commander,

Major General W.C. Walker, Director of Borneo Operations February 1964 – March 1965. (Gurkha Museum)

Admiral Sir Varyl Begg, got on well as he did with Sir Claude Fenner, the senior police commissioner. All British troops were theoretically under the command of the Malaysian National Defence Council, but in the event General Walker was given a fairly free hand to run the war on Malaysia's behalf.

One of General Walker's early priorities was to get information about Indonesian intentions and troop movements so as to position his limited forces in the right places. To help achieve this aim Major John Cross of 7th Gurkhas, a skilled jungle warrior and linguist, recruited young Borneo tribesmen as Border Scouts to act as 'eyes and ears' for the security forces. They were given rifles and uniforms and stiffened by a small number of Gurkha junior non-commissioned officers and radio operators. Operating on the wild, unmarked and remote border, they moved from longhouse to longhouse checking for signs of Indonesian incursion.

One of these Gurkha/Border Scout groups was operating in the area of the village of Long Jawi, in the remote headwater region feeding the mighty Rejang river in the Third Division of Sarawak (Sarawak was split into five administrative divisions and Sabah into four 'residencies'). Long Jawi was about 30 miles from

Painting by Frank Pash of the action by 1/2nd Gurkhas at Long Jawi. (Gurkha Museum)

the border and villagers crossed daily into Indonesia to trade with their fellow tribesmen across the border. The 1/2nd Gurkhas were providing the eight soldiers for this Border Scout group and Major John Burlison, who was the area military commander, visited them on 25 September 1963 to change over Gurkha personnel and resite their defensive position. What he did not know was that a group of Indonesian soldiers was watching him, hidden in a nearby hut. Three days after Burlison and his platoon had left, the Indonesians, by now heavily reinforced to about 150, attacked the unsuspecting Gurkha/Border Scout group killing a Gurkha and wounding two Border Scouts and then killing the two Gurkha and police signallers, who unaware of their impending doom, were frantically trying to communicate on their unreliable 510-type radio crystal sets in the longhouse. All hope of summoning outside help was now lost.

Nevertheless, Corporal Tejbahadur Gurung commanding the group kept his remaining four men firing back for two hours with such intensity that the Indonesians hesitated to close in and finish the job. The Border Scouts, originally 22 in number, were neither trained nor prepared for this sort of high-intensity firefight and tried to run away, but were captured by the Indonesians and ten subsequently murdered. Corporal Tejbahadur, however, was made of sterner stuff, and he and his four Gurkhas continued to battle it out until ammunition was down to a few rounds. Then the three

unwounded Gurkhas and a Border Scout, who had remained, dragged the two badly wounded men out of their trenches and into the cover of the surrounding jungle. No sooner were they in the jungle than the Indonesians attacked again and taking the position put down heavy suppressive fire in the general area which thankfully Tejbahadur's little group avoided. Tejbahadur then hid the wounded, having tended them as best he could, and made his way as quickly as possible to summon help.

Lieutenant Colonel J.B. Clements commanding 1/2nd Gurkhas was an immensely experienced jungle commander and, having weighed the situation, deployed his men by helicopter to what he considered were the likely withdrawal routes for the Indonesian force. One of the tasks of the ill-fated Long Jawi Border Scout group had been to prepare helicopter landing zones (LZ) near the border. Using one of these, Lieutenant (Queen's Gurkha Officer) Pasbahadur Gurung and 11 Platoon were winched down just in time to get to the Rejang river and ambush two boatloads of triumphant Indonesians returning to Indonesia from their successful foray. All 26 were killed and equipment and radio sets from Long Jawi recovered. A Border Scout, who had escaped murder at the hands of the Indonesians by jumping off a boat while their captive, was now able to lead the platoon towards the enemy

Gurkha 3-inch mortar crew preparing to fire. (Gurkha Museum)

camp some five miles short of the border, but it was found to be deserted; although the bodies of seven murdered Border Scouts were found, as well as five enemy graves, the latter showing that Tejbahadur and his men had given a good account of themselves.

Colonel Clements using his jungle warfare intuition continued to feed 1/2nd Gurkhas into the area. They accounted for another two of the raiders with others probably wounded. The Long Jawi incident was important for two reasons. It showed, if it needed showing, just how ruthless and dangerous the Indonesians could be; it also demonstrated, to Indonesians and locals alike, that in confronting Gurkhas any initial success was liable to be followed by swift and devastating retribution.

Another example of retribution occurred two months later in December 1963 at Kalabakan, a logging centre in Tawau, the East Coast Residency of Sabah on the Celebes Sea. Here the young and inexperienced 3rd Battalion of The Royal Malay Regiment was stationed. Its deployment there was rather more a political gesture to show Malaysian support and involvement than a reasoned military plan. As a result, an Indonesian raiding party of some 200 mixed TNI and IBT found the garrison operationally unprepared when they attacked, killing eight and wounding 19 at no cost to themselves. However they had not reckoned with 1/10th Gurkhas commanded by another able jungle veteran of Burma and Malaya, Lieutenant Colonel Edward 'Bunny' Burnett. In a two-month-long operation conducted among the labyrinthine creeks and waterways of Tawau, 1/10th Gurkhas, ably directed by their colonel, hunted down the Indonesian attackers who rebounding from ambush to ambush were steadily eliminated as they tried with increasing desperation to get back to Indonesia. By the end of this brilliant operation only 20 of the original invaders managed to return alive to tell the tale.

However even setbacks of this magnitude did not succeed in blunting Indonesia's appetite for cross-border attacks, especially in the shallower areas of Sarawak's First and Second Divisions: in First Division, for instance, the provincial capital Kuching was only some 40 miles from the border.

More worrying perhaps was the increasing involvement of high-quality regular troops from elite formations such as marines and parachutists. It was Indonesian marines (KKO) who formed the 35-strong regular element which carried out the attack at Kalabakan and it was to be paratroopers who were, in March 1964, to give 2/10th Gurkhas' A Company under Major Ian Mayman a hard battle on the rocky border ridge of the Kling Kang hill feature that runs like a huge whale's back along the road between the then company base at Sungei Tenggang and Simanggang, the provincial capital of Sarawak's Second Division.

Among the huge boulders and wet mists of the border ridge a patrol of 2/10th Gurkhas had discovered a large force of Indonesian paratroops in a strong natural defensive position among the rocks. Initial attempts by A Company to shift them failed with casualties. Next time, Mayman's company, backed by two Saladin armoured cars firing 76mm armour-piercing shells from the road, four 105mm artillery guns and two SS-11 missile-firing Royal Navy Wessex helicopters, were all used to convince the Indonesians to vacate the ridge. Even then, after an assault up the precipitous rock-strewn hillside, the Indonesians were found to have withdrawn in good order using fire and movement to cover themselves in a very professional manner.

An amusing aftermath was recorded when some time after the relieving unit, 2/2nd Gurkhas, discovered an SS-11 anti-tank missile in an armed state in the luggage bay of the provincial bus. On enquiring of its owner how it got there, the Iban replied that he had found it while hunting on the Kling Kang ridge, and carried it tied up in a jungle vine for ease of carriage to take by bus to Simanggang in hope of a reward!

Accounts of clashes with the Indonesians tend to record an unbroken string of successes, but in actual fact Gurkha units despite their natural skill as jungle fighters took some hard knocks. In June 1964 two platoons of 2/6th Gurkhas were attacked at night by a large force of Indonesians while resting in an old disused house in the village of Rasau just on Sarawak's First Division side of the border, and lost five killed and five wounded in a battle that went on for five hours. It showed that the Indonesians were far too dangerous to neglect basic precautions. In this case using a house to rest in overnight was always dangerous if sometimes unavoidable.

Yet as with any army the Indonesians were capable of making misappreciations, such as the one they made on the night of 12 June 1964 at Batu Lintang, a small border village in the Second Division of Sarawak. This village was in 2/2nd Gurkhas' operational area and had been the scene of previous incursions by Indonesian soldiers. Nearby was an Australian field artillery troop whose commander had heard a rumour that some Indonesian soldiers might slip across the border that night to watch a cock-fighting match in Batu Lintang. Determined to stop this practice, 2/2nd Gurkhas' Commanding Officer Lieutenant Colonel 'Nicky' Neill, another jungle fighter with great experience back to 1943, ordered an ambush to be laid on a likely route.

Unfortunately, such was the tempo of operations that the only platoon available and uncommitted was the numerically weak Assault Pioneer Platoon, manning the base at Sungei Tenggang. In torrential rain they made their way to Batu Lintang with just enough daylight left for their commander, Lieutenant (Queen's Gurkha Officer) Nandaraj Gurung to do a thorough reconnaissance of the area of overgrown rubber plantation and secondary jungle that surrounded the village. Laying their ambush

Detail from a montage by David Rowlands showing a Support Company 2/2nd Gurkhas action on the river Sentimo in Indonesia.

with great care in gathering gloom, the Assault Pioneers patiently awaited the arrival of several Indonesian soldiers. Actually what came was a 100-strong raiding company!

Allowing them to get well into the ambush area the Assault Pioneers opened fire, killing 11 Indonesians in the immediate killing area, all shot through the head. The Indonesians immediately counter-attacked and tried to roll up the ambush along the lines patiently taught them by their British instructors while students at the Jungle Warfare School in Malaya. In this they might have been successful but for the accurate and controlled shooting of the Gurkhas and close-in-artillery support provided by the four Australian 25-pounders, expertly controlled by Lieutenant Nandaraj. When the rest of the Gurkha company followed up the next morning they found Nandaraj's men still in their positions ready to repulse any further attack.

★★★

The 11 bodies killed in the initial opening of fire still lay on the track apart from one who had died in the nearby stream (an eventual total of 13), but there were also blood signs of many others being wounded and dragged away. Nandaraj received a well-earned Military Cross and his machine gunner, Rifleman Reshambahadur Thapa, the Military Medal.

Although the Indonesians were often repulsed, as long as they had freedom to cross the unmarked border into Sabah and Sarawak, they inevitably held the military initiative. Attempts to mark the border with tin signs demarcating it had no effect – and anyhow the signs soon disappeared, as the local tribesmen found them useful for converting into frying pans!

In fact General Walker had something much more effective as a deterrent up his sleeve, but it needed the support of a rather hesitant British government determined to try and downplay the whole 'Confrontation' affair. He realized that until his forces were able to operate against specific targets across the jungle border the military initiative would continue to lie with the Indonesians. If however he could hit specific targets inside Indonesian Borneo, then the Indonesians would have to take added precautions to defend probable targets and the lines of communication that supported them. Once forced into doing this, much of Indonesian manpower would be tied up simply implementing defensive measures, which would hurt their ability to carry out offensive operations. If this could be achieved, the initiative would pass to British/Malaysian forces.

It was a bold plan and its eventual acceptance was helped by the fact that clearance had already been given for the Special Air Service (SAS) to carry out reconnaissance patrols deep inside Indonesia. These four-man patrols had already identified several possible targets. Given their essentially intelligence-gathering role and small numbers they generally avoided contact with Indonesian troops but occasionally fighting became unavoidable.

Belvedere helicopter delivers materials for bunker construction at Biawak in 1st Division of Sarawak. (By kind permission of Norman Corbett)

Opposite: Gurkhas on patrol in thick jungle. (Gurkha Museum)

Gurkhas from 2/2nd Gurkhas constructing a deep bunker at the embattled border position at Biawak in 1st Division of Sarawak. (By kind permission of Norman Corbett)

When this occurred the Indonesians generally reacted very aggressively, so it was clear that if clearance was given such operations would be very hazardous.

Eventually the British government acquiesced to General Walker's demands and under a veil of strictest secrecy, and hedged by numerous caveats, 'Claret' operations, as they were termed, were born by May 1964. Among the more restrictive caveats was an embargo on the use of helicopters across the border either to resupply or, more critically, to evacuate casualties. Given that 12 men were required to carry and clear the way for one stretcher casualty in thick jungle this was very restrictive and inevitably led to difficulties. Not least, manhandling casualties was an incredibly slow and laborious business and the wounded might well die before the border could be reached and advanced surgery provided. Other restrictions such as the maximum range of penetration being linked to the range of covering artillery from border gun positions were sensible and easier to live with.

Another understandable but frustrating restriction was that each cross-border operation had to be cleared by the government in London. As a result a rifle company might have reached the climax of its preparedness and planning only to be told that the operation was postponed or cancelled following some shift in diplomatic perception.

If 'Claret' operations, especially ambushes, were to be carried out successfully, a maximum duration of ten days was to be aimed at. This meant carrying a huge burden of arms, ammunition, grenades, anti-personnel directional mines, heavy radio batteries, rations, some spare clothing, basic sleeping gear and first aid kit, etc, through some of the most difficult terrain in the world.

A painting by Terence Cuneo showing the action in which Lance Corporal Rambahadur Limbu 10th Gurkhas won the Victoria Cross. (The Royal Gurkha Rifles)

This task was not helped by the unsuitability of most of the equipment provided which had been designed in the main for mechanized war in Europe. British and Gurkha troops, however are great improvisers and in the case of Gurkha troops heavy tinned rations were jettisoned in favour of much lighter rice-based diets which provided a bare minimum sustenance over ten days or so. However there was simply no alternative to the heavy 7.62mm Fabrique Nationale (FN denoting its Belgian-design origin) self-loading rifle, General Purpose Machine Gun (beginning to replace the Bren gun), heavy radio sets, etc, which meant that before being stripped down for action, men resembled more beasts of burden than jungle warriors. Improvements did slowly appear but, in the time-honoured British custom, not until the campaign was nearly over!

In the very nature of such operations they nearly always fell into two categories: an ambush on enemy supply and communication routes; or an attack on a selected enemy base or position. The former were more uncertain in duration and result, as there was no way of knowing when and in what form the enemy might appear. The latter were more certain as to timing and certainty of contact, but inevitably more hazardous. In the event

Gurkha patrol being extracted by Royal Navy Wessex helicopter. (Gurkha Museum)

many started out with one aim but enemy action forced a change of plan, while others became compromised and had to be aborted.

Given the multiplicity of such operations by British, Gurkha, Australian and New Zealand troops, it will be easiest to describe each type undertaken by Gurkhas, but before so doing it might be worth looking at one of the earliest 'Claret' operations carried out by 1/6th Gurkhas which well illustrates some of the uncertainties and difficulties of these unpredictable operations. On 17 May

1964, D Company of 1/6th Gurkhas tried to set up an ambush inside Indonesia. While getting into position, it was seen by a local and was obliged to move to another ambush position to preserve the element of surprise. Seen again, it was forced to move once more. Finally in a third ambush base site, it was bumped by an Indonesian patrol and two Gurkhas were killed, as well as two Indonesians. The ambush party hurried back to its base at the sound of firing only to find four bodies, two of them Indonesians. The remainder of the ambush base group had gone back to a rear rally position as laid down by the original plan. By the time everything was sorted out, the area was fairly buzzing with Indonesian troops and the operation had to be aborted.

A month or so later the same company went on to spring a very successful ambush, but the failure of this early 'Claret' operation impressed upon everybody just how difficult it was to pull off this kind of very hazardous undertaking.

In Indonesia, opposite the Lundu area of First Division of Sarawak, the Support Company of 2/2nd Gurkhas carried out a very successful boat ambush in August 1965 that was to set a pattern of attrition against the Indonesians. After a very difficult approach march through primeval swamp, Captain (Queen's Gurkha Officer) Surendraman Gurung, who as a platoon commander in Major Jon Aslett's C Company had already been involved in several daring cross-border operations, now commanding Support Company in place of his company commander in hospital, ambushed a wide-decked assault boat carrying 12 Indonesian soldiers on the River Sentimo killing them all. They then extracted themselves successfully, covered by artillery fire directed by Captain John Masters of the Royal New Zealand Artillery. In a later operation with Support Company, Captain Masters was to save the life of a Gurkha Warrant Officer in particularly dramatic circumstances. The action is fully described in the book *Journeys Hazardous* by this author who was the Company Commander.

As soon as they were aware of what was going on, the Indonesians took positive action to counter such incursions and to try and cut them off and destroy them. On 29 August 1965, in the very active First Division of Sarawak, C Company 2/2nd Gurkhas carried out a particularly successful operation that used Indonesian cut-off plans to its own advantage. After extensive reconnaissance of the River Separan, its commander, Major G.H. Ashley, realized that in order to guard against damaging river ambushes the Indonesians had cut a wide semi-circular track through the jungle so that, hearing the sound of a river ambush, an Indonesian cut-off group would run down the track in time to ambush the ambushers as they returned.

Major Ashley therefore set two ambushes: one on the river and one on the track that the Indonesians intended to use for a cut-off

route. In due course a boat containing six Indonesian soldiers came into the river ambush and was duly dispatched. Immediately the Indonesians put their cut-off plan into effect and as the cut-off force ran down the track, they were themselves ambushed, losing a further 20 men. Given the difficulty of laying and successfully springing one ambush, to pull off two capitalizing on the Indonesians' own anti-ambush plans was no mean achievement.

A good example of a successful enemy base attack was carried out by A Company 1/2nd Gurkhas in the remote interior residency area of Sarawak's Fifth Division. Here, over the border in Indonesia, on the banks of the River Agisan, the Indonesians had a camp for about 80 soldiers, mixed marines and irregulars. A Company commander Captain Peter Duffell was ordered to destroy this camp and, in addition to his own company, was given a platoon from another company and the Reconnaissance Platoon, making some 110 men in total. His plan was to assault the enemy camp after a short but intense bombardment. The effect of the bombardment and attack would, he hoped, drive the survivors into an ambush laid by the Reconnaissance Platoon alongside the river. After a painstakingly careful approach-march and close-in reconnaissance, the enemy camp layout was identified, helped by the enticing smell of a pig which its occupants were roasting.

The short but intense mortar, rocket launcher and machine-gun bombardment initially stunned the Indonesians, although their well-sited machine guns proved difficult to subdue. The assault then went in with complete success and many of the fleeing survivors were caught by the Reconnaissance Platoon patiently

10th Gurkhas rounding up Indonesian parachutists after the abortive Indonesian parachute landings near Labis, Malaysia. (Gurkha Museum)

waiting in ambush. Later reports from inside Indonesia suggested that some 39 Indonesians were killed; it had been a brilliantly planned and executed operation.

The First Division of Sarawak and the immediate Indonesian areas on the other side of the border were some of the hardest-fought over of the campaign, especially in the complex of rivers upon which many of the Indonesian bases were sited. Captain Garry Johnson commanding D Company 1/10th Gurkhas carried out a particularly daring raid over a major river, the Koemba, onto an enemy camp the other side. Having noiselessly made camp the night before, knowing they were close to the enemy camp the next morning, they found they had only been 300 yards away! Approaching with the greatest care they found the Indonesians

cooking breakfast. Sighted by an alert Indonesian sentry, Captain Johnson and his men mounted an immediate assault and in an intense battle at 30 yards' range all 20 Indonesian soldiers in the camp were killed at the cost of two Gurkha dead.

Interestingly, but perhaps not surprisingly, both these two young Gurkha captains, Johnson and Duffell, were to become Major General Brigade of Gurkhas in succession to each other some 25 years later.

Cooperation between Gurkha units and the helicopter crews of the Royal Navy and Royal Air Force was very close, and the skill and courage of the pilots quite exceptional. Despite the embargo on evacuating casualties from inside Indonesia, such life-saving operations did take place, often in very hazardous circumstances.

A painting by Terence Cuneo of Major Haddow's company of 10th Gurkhas deploying to engage Indonesian parachutists who had dropped at Labis, Malaysia, the night before. Seconds later Major Haddow was shot dead. All the parachutists were subsequently accounted for by his Gurkhas. (10th Gurkhas Rifles Regimental Association)

The Gurkha Transport Regiment provided most of the road transport in Borneo during Confrontation as well as escorts on occasions.

Obviously, given the clandestine nature of 'Claret' operations, cooperation with fixed-wing aircraft was much less common. In December 1964 Captain B. C. Jackman's C Company of 1/2nd Gurkhas was operating out of their remote company base at Ba Kelalan in Sarawak's Fifth Division. One of his platoons lying in ambush on the border was attacked and surrounded by a numerically superior Indonesian force and, before long, began to run short of ammunition. Knowing that by the time he could reach it, the platoon would have been overwhelmed, Captain Jackman desperately cast about for some way of helping it. Eventually he appealed to the Royal Air Force for fighter ground-attack support. Although this remote area was out of range of Hunter jet ground-attack aircraft, a twin-engine Javelin interceptor jet fighter picked up the message. With commendable initiative the pilot overflew the embattled platoon, emitting a series of sonic booms. These convinced the Indonesians that they were under a bombing attack and they pulled back. Some time after this contact, Captain Jackman took the battle to the enemy in a meticulously planned

and audaciously executed attack on an Indonesian base at Long Medan, half a mile on the Indonesian side of the border, killing 32 Indonesians.

Still on aerial matters, Major John Chapple, who replaced Captain Jackman as Officer Commanding C Company at Ba Kelalan, was surprised to see an Indonesian Hercules transport aircraft suddenly appear out of the morning mist with what appeared to be Indonesian parachutists at the doors preparing to jump. With admirable promptitude, C Company opened up with everything it had and the Hercules ponderously turned and departed, only to be greeted by concentrated Indonesian anti-aircraft fire from Long Medan which obliged the parachutists to jump out of the stricken plane before it crash-landed and caught fire. It was very definitely an Indonesian own goal.

It subsequently turned out that it was an own goal in more ways than one as the elite parachutists were being concentrated at Long Medan as part of a coup against Sukarno which, as a result, was aborted.

Gurkha Bren gunner in action. (Gurkha Museum)

The operation by C Company 2/10th Gurkhas in the Serikin area of the First Division of Sarawak, which resulted in the supreme award of the Victoria Cross to Lance Corporal Rambahadur Limbu, was neither an ambush nor an attack on an enemy camp, although its final form resembled the latter. Captain Kit Maunsell, C Company commander, had been given the most difficult Claret operation of all, that of seizing a prisoner from a known enemy position over two miles inside Indonesia. It was one of those tasks set by senior commanders who have slightly lost touch with the reality of the situation on the ground, along with similar exhortations to count enemy casualties in the middle of a battle!

To try to seize a prisoner from among his generally alert comrades and get away with it unscathed was asking a great deal. Nevertheless Captain Maunsell and his much augmented company of 150 did their best and by painstaking stalking crawled very close to the enemy position unseen on 21 November 1965.

Unfortunately they were then sighted and a machine gun opened up on them wounding a man in Lance Corporal Rambahadur's section. With great courage Rambahadur ran forward and killed the machine gunner. Soon what had become a specific operation to take a prisoner grew into a full-scale encounter battle, involving all of Captain Maunsell's company group, artillery support and a light helicopter indicating targets for the guns and evacuating casualties. During this 90-minute battle, Rambahadur not only rescued two badly wounded Gurkhas under heavy fire, but also recovered a lost Bren machine gun under continual enemy fire as well as killing four Indonesians in the process.

For these and associated acts of gallantry Rambahadur was awarded the Victoria Cross, the only one awarded during the campaign. A Company suffered three killed and two wounded, and the Indonesians at least 24 killed, but without doubt Rambahadur's outstanding conduct contributed much to the successful outcome which, despite three spirited counter-attacks backed by artillery, resulted in the Indonesians quitting their previous strongly held position.

Despite continual 'Claret' incursions to harry their lines of communication, the Indonesians managed to keep up a string of their own offensive operations. In September 1964 two planeloads of Indonesian airborne troops carried out a daring parachute assault, landing in the thickly jungled area of Labis in north Johore on mainland Malaya. The 1/10th Gurkhas, supposedly enjoying 'rest and recuperation' after a strenuous Borneo tour, were deployed in a series of hard-fought actions in which a British company commander, Major Richard Haddow, was killed as well as a Gurkha Lance Corporal. The battalion eventually either killed or captured the entire force of 96 parachutists, less those accounted for by local forces. A moving and evocative painting by Terence Cuneo of Major Haddow's last moments hangs in the gallery of the Gurkha Museum in Winchester.

The parachute landing had been preceded by three Indonesian seaborne landings at or near Pontian on Malaya's west coast which were all successfully countered.

Men of The Gurkha Independent Parachute Company preparing to drop. (Gurkha Museum)

Back in Sarawak, an Indonesian company-sized attack on a Parachute Regiment base at Plaman Mapu achieved complete surprise and was only frustrated through the exceptional determination of the hard-pressed defenders and the strong construction of the base. Many of the company bases had been built to the expert design of Major Hank Bowen of the Queen's Gurkha Engineers. Generally built astride the border, they were dug underground and proof against the heaviest bombardment the Indonesians were likely to be capable of. As well as building these bases, which were continually being attacked by the Indonesians, Gurkha engineers were employed in building bridges and roads, and their contribution to final success in Borneo was fundamental.

So too was the contribution of the Gurkha Signals who manned the rear-link detachments of each of the eight Gurkha battalions as well as the signals networks of Gurkha brigades (99th in Sarawak and 48th in Hong Kong). The Gurkha Army Service Corps, redesignated The Gurkha Transport Regiment in 1965, had now come of age and manned second-line transport throughout Sabah and Sarawak, working alongside their British opposite numbers.

Some 17,000 British, Gurkha and Commonwealth troops were deployed in Sabah and Sarawak with a further 10,000 quickly available in Malaya, Singapore and Hong Kong. This major deployment in one of the world's least developed countries threw up many unique challenges, not least medical ones. Besides malaria, which was endemic, dengue fever, encephalitis, leptospirosis and scrub typhus were all present in the massive jungles and swamps. Even in defended camps unless strict hygiene was observed there could be outbreaks of intestinal disorders that could incapacitate soldiers.

One Gurkha unit in the process of taking over from a Guards battalion was proudly shown a 20-seater deep earth lavatory in immaculate order. The Guards hygiene Corporal handing over this fine edifice mentioned to his Gurkha opposite number that, once every ten days or so, it was wise to throw a white phosphorous smoke grenade down into the depths of the lavatory to flush out unpleasant creepie-crawlies. Something was lost in translation and after ten days the newly arrived Gurkha medical Corporal dutifully threw a grenade down the lavatory. Unfortunately, rather than the stipulated smoke grenade, he used a high explosive one with predictable results.

In the case of 'Claret' operations carried out up to 11.3 miles (20,000 yards) deep into Indonesia, target acquisition and direction finding were a major challenge. Although the British had made attempts to map their side of the border there were many areas completely unmapped. The Indonesians had done no mapping at all. The only map that existed of Indonesian Borneo was a small-scale Dutch one done in the 1930s which was incomplete and inaccurate. With forces often operating in huge expanses of

THE BORNEO FRONTIER – 1ST AND 2ND DIVISIONS

unmapped primeval swamp and jungle, the only recognizable features would be rivers, areas cleared for rice or maize cultivation, Iban longhouses and enemy encampments. In the absence of mapping, the only other aid was air photographs. These were mostly taken at 10,000 feet by Royal Air Force Canberra jet photo-reconnaissance missions. Unfortunately, in thickly jungled areas these were of limited use as the high jungle canopy occluded everything but the larger rivers.

For certain 'Claret' operations in this type of terrain air photographs from 5,000 feet were required. Understandably, given the Indonesian proclivity for loosing off 12.7mm anti-aircraft guns, the Royal Air Force preferred not to fly this low and special requests had to be made to get the aircraft to carry out such missions. Even then such missions were not always authorized.

The author's experience serves to illustrate this limitation, which would not occur with today's technology that can give one's exact position at the press of a button. The order was to set an ambush on a river deep in Indonesia between two large enemy camps, and 5,000ft air photographs were requested to show the target area. These were said to be unavailable, so the ambushing rifle company set off with 10,000ft images which showed little or no useful detail. As the company neared the River Separan, a Royal Air Force helicopter, wildly off course, was shot down from anti-aircraft gun positions on the other side of the river, which in any

case proved to be in spate and unusable for boat traffic. Because the air photographs showed no detail it was difficult to identify which of the two camps had shot down the helicopter. Assuming it to be the easterly one, the force moved west trying to find somewhere to cross the 65ft roaring river so as to find an interconnecting track between the two camps and lay an ambush.

Luckily that evening a place was found where a huge tree had fallen across the river which could, with a good deal of additional work, be turned into a serviceable bridge. Crossing the river early the next day, the force found the track between the two camps with a telephone wire tacked above it. Two hours later, a complete Indonesian company walked into the ambush and suffered heavy casualties at the cost of only two lightly wounded. On return, the company received the earlier requested reconnaissance photographs taken from 5,000 feet. These clearly showed the ambush to have been laid adjacent to the entrance of the westerly enemy camp. No wonder the ambush achieved complete surprise.

By early 1966 it was clear that Indonesian enthusiasm for Confrontation was waning. After a Communist attempt at a coup and the murder of several army generals it was obvious that civil war was impending in Indonesia between the Army and the Communists, with Sukarno vainly attempting to keep a balance of power between the two. Faced with this kind of internal threat, the Army were less and less enthusiastic to commit resources to what was clearly proving an unsuccessful attempt to take over Sarawak, Sabah and Brunei.

In July 1966 a final major attempt was made to insert a large force into Sarawak, heading for Brunei, commanded by one Lieutenant Sumbi, a brave if foolhardy officer. His group was relentlessly hunted by 1/7th Gurkhas and elements of the recently raised Gurkha Parachute Company which were, by brilliant tracking, the first to trace this incursion. In a major operation that went on for several weeks over mountainous jungle, 1/7th Gurkhas accounted for 46 out of the 50 that originally set out, including Sumbi himself. Details and memorabilia of this skilled operation can be found in the Gurkha Museum.

On 11 August 1966 Confrontation came to an end by a peace agreement signed in Jakarta. For the loss of 114 killed (43 Gurkhas) and 181 wounded (87 Gurkhas), Britain and Malaysia had thwarted a determined Indonesian attempt to seize Sarawak, Sabah and Brunei. Indonesian casualties were tallied at 1,583, of whom 771 were captured; even more remarkably, for a 20th century war, civilian losses amounted to 93. In his summing-up of

the campaign, the then British Minister of Defence The Right Honourable Denis (now Lord) Healey paid a special tribute to Gurkhas. There is no doubt they had borne the brunt of the three years and nine months' operations by Commonwealth ground forces. Healey's next announcement in late 1966 was to cause them pain and distress in equal measure.

In 2005, 39 years after the successful conclusion of Confrontation, in an act of great generosity, the Malaysian government awarded a commemorative 'Service to Malaysia' medal to all who had participated in the Malayan Emergency and Confrontation (during the period August 1957 until December 1966). Inside the lid of the presentation box is written:

Pingat Jasa Malaysia.

This medal is awarded to the peacekeeping groups amongst the communion countries for distinguished chivalry, gallantry, sacrifice or loyalty in upholding The Peninsular of Malaysia sovereignty during the period of Emergency and Confrontation.

General Service Medal 1962–2007.

Pingat Jasa Malaysia.

CHAPTER FIFTEEN

AN UNCERTAIN FUTURE RESOLVED

The ending of Confrontation gave the British government its long-awaited opportunity to save costs by starting the major process of withdrawing the bulk of its military presence from the Far East. With the exception of Hong Kong and possibly Brunei, with whom negotiations were continuing, it was the intention to withdraw all British military presence from Malaysia and Singapore.

As this policy was being formulated, the previous plan to reduce the Brigade of Gurkhas by a third from 15,000 to 10,000, shelved because of Confrontation, was reimposed. In the executive signal that came to all units on 12 December 1966, it was rather ominously intimated that the rundown might have to proceed below 10,000 in the future.

Since fighting in Borneo had only just stopped, the announcement of a massive reduction in the strength of those who had done so much to achieve victory was looked at askance by the Brigade. Worse still, the terms to be offered to Gurkhas being forced to retire prematurely were niggardly in the extreme – they were basically those contemplated in 1962, but with a slight cost-of-living index increase.

General (Pat) Patterson, now Major General Brigade of Gurkhas, set up a committee to assess properly the true cost of living in Nepal and represent this and Gurkha terms and conditions of service to a largely ignorant and unsympathetic Treasury. Thankfully,

in Mr Gerry Reynolds, the Labour government's Minister of Defence (Army), the Brigade found a new friend. Reynolds, convinced of the justice of better redundancy terms for Gurkhas, fought the case through Whitehall. At the time the improved terms looked reasonable, although not particularly generous. Gurkhas would be eligible for a reduced pension after 10 years instead of the normal 15; and those that left earlier would get a lump sum but no pension. For junior ranks this lump sum seems pathetically small by today's values – and even then was only enough to tide over temporarily the early stages of return to civilian life in Nepal.

General Patterson also insisted upon and got certain important undertakings as to the management of the rundown namely:

a. *Those being made redundant got a minimum of six months'
warning and a six weeks' resettlement course.*
b. *No more than 2,200 men should be made redundant every year.*
c. *Recruiting, albeit reduced, should continue, as should normal
promotion.*
d. *The Brigade should remain operational throughout.*

In the negotiations in Britain, Major John Chapple (2nd Gurkhas and later Field Marshal) was acting as General Patterson's emissary, while in Nepal, Major Colin Maddison (10th Gurkhas) spent six weeks amassing data. Together their clear findings and

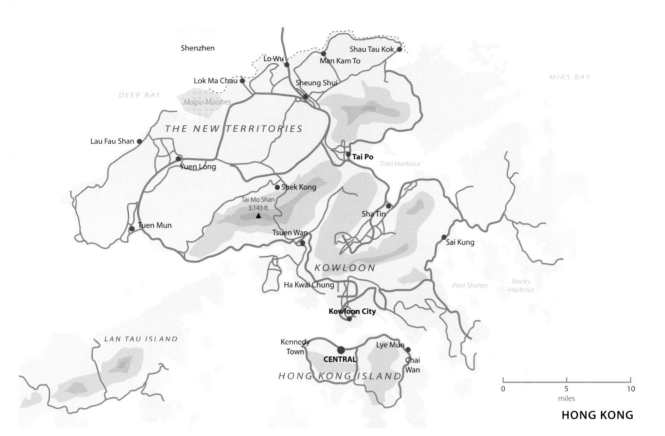

HONG KONG

reasoned arguments did much to help General Patterson sway recalcitrant government officials. However this was Headquarters Brigade of Gurkhas' first major rundown and, although it had stipulated that all units should run down at the same speed, they left it to units to decide who and in what age groups should actually go.

This proved a bone of contention: some units did all they could to protect the careers of young soldiers to try and get them minimum pensions in the future by sending out older soldiers who had qualified for pensions. Other units wished to retain older, more experienced soldiers and sent out younger soldiers without pensions. When soldiers who had joined up at the same time found on return to Nepal that they had been made redundant, but their contemporaries in other units had not, there was great distress and indignation, which often first surfaced in the less than salubrious confines of the Gurkha Transit Camp in Barrackpore on the outskirts of Calcutta.

However, given the enormity of what was happening to them, Gurkhas behaved with incredible dignity and restraint, a certain natural fatalism protecting them. There was no way that they could have known that, of those who were forced out without pensions, a large proportion would become so impoverished that without help they would have been destitute.

Gurkha Welfare Trust pensioners collecting welfare pensions. (Photo by kind permission of The Gurkha Welfare Trust)

1/2nd Gurkhas dealing with Communist-inspired riots in Kowloon-1967.

This help came from the Gurkha Welfare Trust, again set up (in 1969) by General Patterson, among others, who foresaw great distress and privation arising as a result of the rundown. If Her Majesty's Government was being niggardly, then many in Malaysia, Brunei, Hong Kong and Britain who had reason to thank Gurkhas were being correspondingly generous and money poured in; money which in later years was to do so much to succour those who had encountered real hardship. The Brigade also helped, with every officer and man giving up one day's pay towards the Gurkha Welfare Trust, as well as running innumerable fund-raising activities.

Hardly had the rundown started, than early in 1967 the British government produced its Defence Review which presaged the major withdrawal from the Far East (more generally 'East of Suez') and called for further reductions to the Brigade of Gurkhas, cutting it to about 6,000 by 1971; after this its future, if any, would be decided. This, coming so soon after the first announcement, was a shattering blow to the Brigade and out of a total of 180 British officers, 80, including some of middle rank, seeing no future, left the Army while three transferred to British units.

As long lines of soldiers, many decorated for gallantry in Borneo or Malaya, waited patiently outside their commanders' offices to be told their futures, life went on. In Malaysia and Brunei,

where a Gurkha battalion paid for by the Sultan was permanently based, counter-insurgency warfare was all the rage. Gurkhas dressed as Viet Cong or North Vietnamese Army acted as enemy in numerous Five Power (Australia, Malaysia, Singapore, New Zealand and the United Kingdom) exercises; and tried hard not to disillusion hopeful observers that reinforcing troops from Britain could manage splendidly in the jungle without in-country acclimatization.

If exercises in Malaysia were make-believe, then events in Hong Kong were brutally realistic. Mao Tse-tung's internal Cultural Revolution had been launched with the intention of re-establishing revolutionary principles and correcting those who had strayed from the true path. Clearly the presence of two capitalist outposts, Hong Kong and Macao, was an affront to such principles and China was determined to humble them.

Encouraged by Portuguese submission in Macao, the authorities in Canton bordering Hong Kong decided to apply the same treatment in the hope of obtaining a similar result. In the sweltering heat of May and June 1967, China engineered major industrial unrest and rioting in both Kowloon and Hong Kong Island, and Gurkha riot squads deployed alongside police to counter an escalating spiral of violence and destruction. There were over 8,000 reported bomb incidents, 16 people were killed and 340 injured. A battalion of 7th Gurkhas was flown in from Malaysia as reinforcements. Temporarily diverted to the United States Air Base of Clark Field in the Philippines to refuel, the Americans there were surprised to see, in their own words 'Hundreds of little brown men with damned great knives sitting on the runway!'.

If the situation in Kowloon and Hong Kong Island was serious then the situation on the border had become critical. On 8 July rioters from across the border opposite the little border town of Sha Tau Kok attacked its police post. A police reserve company marching forward in crowd-dispersal box formation was accurately fired on by a Chinese militia medium machine gun from across the border and suffered two killed and five wounded. The 1/10th Gurkhas D Company commanded by Major Christopher Pike immediately deployed, backed by two armoured cars, but was not allowed to proceed further than the main police station one and a half miles behind the border, while the Hong Kong government tried to decide whether to commit 10th Gurkhas or not. Further firing inflicting more casualties on the

police clinched that decision and D Company, now joined by A Company, coordinated by the Commanding Officer Lieutenant Colonel Ronald McAlister, started to leapfrog tactically towards the by-now beleaguered police. They immediately came under machine-gun fire but, protected by the armoured cars, pressed on with one rifleman wounded. By 1700 hours the confrontation, which had teetered on the brink of full-scale battle, had finished, and 10th Gurkhas were evacuating the five dead and 11 wounded police from the police post and the nearby rural committee building. The battalion had behaved with admirable restraint tempered by soldierly efficiency.

This major incident was only the beginning of weeks of insult, violence and provocation towards the security forces. In one incident the Chinese managed to seize some weapons from Gurkhas in a surprise attack in order to make a political point. When the District Officer, the Commanding Officer and a senior policeman went forward to negotiate their return, they were also were seized. The 1/10th Gurkhas were not standing for this sort of thing and prepared to do battle despite a company of Chinese

10th Gurkhas at Sha Tau Kok, scene of a Communist machine gun attack on Hong Kong police. (Gurkha Museum)

7th Gurkhas at Man Kam To where several of the most serious border incidents in 1967 took place. (Gurkha Museum)

regular army ready and waiting behind the demonstrating civilians. Just as Major Bruce Niven's C Company were moving up to free, if necessary by force, the Commanding Officer, the Chinese released those captured.

Again it had been a close-run incident. Attempts to control the border crossings with barbed wire-covered 'knife rests' invariably led to more violence coordinated by and watched over by the People's Liberation Army. The 1/10th Gurkhas however were up to every challenge.

A major attack was staged against the two adjoining border crossings of Man Kam To and Lo Wu, with professional rioters armed with axes, cargo hooks and knives trying to pull down the barbed wire barricades, while behind them the Chinese army stood ready, occasionally firing bursts of machine-gun fire over the heads of the Gurkhas. For three hours 1/10th Gurkhas companies blocked the rioters, dispersing them with CS chemical irritant gas rounds and, when these proved ineffective, white-phosphorous smoke grenades. In the end the Gurkhas prevailed and the rioters pulled back. Although similar events went on for several weeks it

was dawning on the Chinese that there was going to be no 'Macao solution' with Hong Kong. That there was not was due in no small measure to the Brigade of Gurkhas.

★★★

By 1971 all Gurkhas had been withdrawn from Malaysia. In independent Singapore, however, the British-officered Gurkha Police Contingent was retained by the Singapore authorities and continued to be commanded and officered by ex–Brigade of Gurkha officers, both British and Gurkha. It acted as a riot-control two-company reinforcement to the normal police and its recruiting and recruit training was undertaken on its behalf by the Brigade of Gurkhas.

In Brunei, the Gurkha battalion in Seria had now become a semi-permanent fixture as part of the treaty between the Sultanate and Britain. Although the battalion continued as part of the British Army, all its expenses were paid for by the Sultan. To a perennially cash-strapped British government this had to be a good deal, allowing as it did a continuing presence in the Far East with all the influence that allowed without incurring costs. For Brunei, too, it represented a very worthwhile insurance policy against further Indonesian attempts at encroachment. Gurkha battalions on two-year roulement (military rotation) in Brunei also benefited from the excellent jungle training facilities, as did the British Army generally when a jungle training wing was set up. The Sultan also started his own paramilitary Gurkha Reserve Unit. This was initially commanded and officered by ex-Brigade of Gurkhas British and Gurkha officers, and gave a valuable employment opportunity to many good young soldiers being forced out on premature redundancy.

In 1971 the rundown that had started in 1966 finally stuttered to a halt. Since 1969, British troops had been deployed to Northern Ireland in ever-increasing numbers, and the commitment seemed to be a permanent one which put huge additional demands on British Army manpower. It was decided to deploy a Gurkha battalion to Britain to help with this overstretch so, with a requirement for one battalion in the United Kingdom, one in Brunei and three in Hong Kong, five Gurkha battalions would be needed. All-up Brigade strength settled at 6,700. The rundown stopped just in time to save 2nd Battalion of the 2nd Gurkhas which was reprieved for another 21 years. The three Gurkha Corps Regiments had also been significantly reduced in size as part of the run down, whilst the Gurkha Military Police and Gurkha Independent Parachute Company had been disbanded and the bands of 2nd Gurkhas and Brigade of Gurkhas had been amalgamated.

10th Gurkha rifleman carrying confiscated Greek Cypriot weapons. (Gurkha Museum)

***

In 1972, 7th Gurkhas were deployed to England and housed in an ex-wartime hutted camp at Church Crookham, near Fleet in Hampshire. It was to become a Gurkha base for the next 25 years.

Although ex-soldiers who had served in the Second World War alongside Gurkhas remembered them with affection, the majority of Britons knew little if anything about them. This was understandable as, since the end of the war, British Gurkhas had served almost exclusively in South East Asia and the Far East with the exception of the Gurkha battalion group which had served in UK between 1962 and 1964. With the arrival of 7th Gurkhas all this changed as Gurkhas were seen not only in Fleet but also mounting guard outside Buckingham Palace and participating in other largely ceremonial public events. In the home-based army, too, the men from Nepal became a familiar sight, particularly as they provided demonstration troops at the Royal Military Academy Sandhurst and at the School of Infantry at Brecon in Wales. Soon after arrival, they ran and administered the Regular Army Skill-at-Arms Meeting at Bisley, Surrey, and continued to do this on a regular basis.

While Gurkha battalions served in Britain, they received the same rates of pay as their British counterparts which were considerably in excess of the Gurkha rates of pay received in the Far East. This factor as well as the different military challenges made United Kingdom service very popular. The only downside was that initially they served without their families, although this was partially compensated for by receiving a higher proportion of the married quarters available on return to Hong Kong. Thus a roulement of two years in Britain, followed by four in Hong Kong, two in Brunei, two more in Hong Kong and then back to Britain came into being. The Gurkha Corps regiments also established small and dispersed detachments in the UK which eventually grew into squadron sized units for The Queen's Gurkha Engineers and Queen's Gurkha Signals.

***

The 10th Gurkhas which had taken over as United Kingdom battalion in March 1973 was destined for an exciting intervention in Cyprus where, after years of aggravation between Greek and Turkish Cypriots, in July 1974 Turkey had invaded following an attempted

Cyprus 1974. 10th Gurkhas deploy in Ferret armoured cars. (Gurkha Museum)

coup by the Greek National Guard. The 10th Gurkhas had been preparing to exercise in Cyprus when the orders were changed to an operational role to guard the two British Sovereign Base Areas. These were threatened by the fighting between the invading Turks and the Greek National Guard. In a remarkably efficient move, Lieutenant Colonel Christopher Pike and his battalion flew into Cyprus on 11 August and were almost immediately involved as they tried to disarm Greek National Guard units fleeing into the British Sovereign Base area near Larnaca.

With fighting all around them, 10th Gurkhas patiently but firmly demonstrated to Greek and Turk alike that the Sovereign Base Areas would remain inviolate. This led to some highly charged eyeball-to-eyeball situations from which the Gurkhas never flinched. One particular situation nearly escalated into violence when, after Archbishop Makarios had returned to Cyprus in December 1974, his Prime Minister, Clerides, while visiting a Greek refugee camp heard that the Turks had captured a Greek shepherd. This was too much for the refugees who in a fury rushed the Turkish soldiers who had abducted the shepherd. Major Michael Allen's B Company of 10th Gurkhas, supported by armoured cars, swiftly interposed themselves between indignant refugees and Turks thereby avoiding certain bloodshed. This

10th Gurkha checkpoint, Cyprus 1974. (Gurkha Museum)

incident typified 10th Gurkhas' watchful, sensitive but very firm attitude to both invaders and invaded.

As a result they received accolades from all involved for their conduct. Major General Corran Purdon, the British commander in Cyprus, was to write: '*Operationally they are outstanding. We will*

206

miss 10 GR greatly, they have set the highest standard.' Perhaps equally importantly, the British High Commissioner Sir Stephen Oliver wrote: *'They have as usual impressed everybody with their efficiency, determination, good behaviour and personal charm … you will remember that certain reservations had to be overcome before a final decision to send out a Gurkha battalion … they have been so effective that I would like to record my views.'*

Foreign and Commonwealth Office nervousness about deploying Gurkhas was apparent in 1978 when 6th Gurkhas were sent at very short notice to Belize (previously British Honduras) in Central America to counter a perceived threat from neighbouring Guatemala. Guatemala was asked before their deployment whether she had any objections. Not having a clue as to who or what Gurkhas were, the reply was opaque. The 6th Gurkhas, well used to the jungle, deployed immediately without the hitherto obligatory acclimatization and training period and, after two weeks, the Special Air Service asked to be withdrawn from the border area, as there was nothing that could not be equally effectively done by 6th Gurkhas. So successful were they that Belize subsequently became a regular deployment area for Gurkha battalions based in Britain.

At long last the period of uncertainty seemed over and the Brigade of Gurkhas had a definite role and the necessary strength and organization to discharge it. It had also gained a powerful and fearless ally in General (later Field Marshal) Edwin Bramall. He had first come into contact with Gurkhas while commanding 2nd Royal Green Jackets in Borneo. Much impressed by them, the relationship blossomed when he became Commander British Forces in Hong Kong in 1973. Accepting Colonelship of 2nd Gurkhas, Bramall became an avid supporter and powerful protagonist for Gurkhas as he made his way inexorably up the ladder of preferment to Chief of the General Staff and then Chief of the Defence Staff. The Brigade of Gurkhas, which had been conspicuously bereft of any senior patron since the departure of General Sir Walter Walker, now had its own 'White Knight' who unhesitatingly rode forth to do battle on its behalf. Without his intervention, Gurkhas would have never gone to Belize nor, as we shall see in the next chapter, to the Falkland Islands. 'Dwin' Bramall's influence also secured a reasonable future for them and removed, albeit temporarily, the threat of complete disbandment and enabled the retention of a fifth battalion.

Gurkha observation post at Man Kam To on the Sino / Hong Kong Border. From a painting by Ken Howard. (By kind permission of Major G.L. Davies)

CHAPTER SIXTEEN

CRISIS IN HONG KONG
AND THE
FALKLAND ISLANDS CAMPAIGN

The Crown Colony of Hong Kong had always been a haven of refuge for those fleeing from China. When the Japanese moved on Shanghai in 1937, many thousands of Shanghai businessmen and entrepreneurs fled to Hong Kong, as well as a number of White Russians who had originally fled to Shanghai from Russia as the victorious Bolsheviks gained control. After the Second World War and Chinese Civil War, thousands of Chinese Nationalists fleeing the Communists took permanent refuge in Hong Kong. As a result, Hong Kong regarded itself as a haven for the oppressed of China and it made it easy for those crossing the flimsy border fence to settle.

As we have seen in the last chapter, a new belligerence from China led to military deployment on the border and a tense stand-off. In the face of a heavy military presence on both sides of the border, few mainland Chinese attempted to cross and seek a new life in Hong Kong. However, by 1970 the situation on the border with China had calmed down, the Royal Hong Kong Police had taken back responsibility for the border and on the other side the Chinese military had decreased their presence. Very soon a trickle of refugees were making their way into Hong Kong and joining an ever-lengthening queue at the government immigration office at Yuen Long in the New Territories.

The death of Mao Tse-tung, Communist China's 'Great Helmsman', in 1976 led to a power vacuum which had a paralyzing effect on local authorities in adjoining Kwantung Province. As a result thousands of refugees started crossing the border fence every night, threatening to overwhelm Hong Kong's ability to cope. By 1975, the British garrison was deployed and by 1978, every Gurkha

Gurkhas rounding up some of the thousands of Illegal Immigrants (IIs) trying to cross the Sino-Hong Kong border by day and night. (Gurkha Museum)

6th Gurkhas and Royal Hong Kong Volunteer Regiment dog handlers escorting an illegal immigrant caught in the Maipo marsh area of the Sino-Hong Kong border. (Gurkha Museum)

unit was spending virtually all its time arresting illegal immigrants, or IIs as they came to be known. If the Army succeeded in catching the IIs and handing them back to the Chinese by 1100hrs, then they were not in a position to apply for refugee status.

Not only did the IIs come over the land border, but they also swam and rafted over adjoining bays and inlets. The author can do no better than reiterate the words he used at the time to describe the situation:

> *After dark the majority of our manpower deployed to coves, inlets*
> *and vantage points to help counter the flood of illegal immigrants*
> *who tried to break in. They swam, came crammed in little boats,*
> *pushed sledges and scooters over the mud and floated in as*
> *hopeless corpses killed by cold or sharks. Women looked much the*
> *same as men, bedraggled, wet, mud-stained creatures in blue*
> *denims with bare feet bleeding from rocks and shells. Some came*
> *carrying children, others heaved aged relations; all were*
> *determined to try again even if caught.*

To help control the situation, reinforcement infantry units were flown in from Britain and elements of 10th Gurkhas from Brunei. The Queen's Gurkha Engineers set up highly efficient boat troops of high-speed 'Rigid Raiders' to patrol the bays and inlets while the Army Air Corps fitted special scramble nets to its helicopters so it could pluck IIs off the muddy tidal reaches. The Hong Kong government spent vast sums building a highly sophisticated double-tier fence across the land border.

Significantly for the Brigade of Gurkhas, the need for more manpower to cope with the border situation was recognized with the re-raising of 2nd Battalion of 7th Gurkhas in 1982. Initially formed as a mixed unit with reinforcements from across the spectrum of the Brigade, it was stationed in the old and scenic barracks at Lyemun at the north-east end of Hong Kong Island. In addition a Gurkha Engineer squadron was also raised for service in the UK.

Eventually the Hong Kong government, after much soul-searching, decided to give up its 'touch base' policy which allowed those successfully evading the security forces to remain in Hong Kong. To this decision was added the Chinese authorities' growing determination to deploy more of their own army units on the border to stop the IIs trying to cross in the first place. Slowly all these measures took effect, so that by 1983 the worst was over and the crisis averted. Gurkha units had been involved from first to last in an exhausting sometimes dangerous and always unhappy task to the exclusion of almost every other military activity. The people of Hong Kong recognized this as they had recognized Gurkha fortitude on the border and in the streets during the Cultural Revolution.

Meanwhile in Britain, 1/7th Gurkhas had taken over as the Gurkha battalion in Church Crookham near Aldershot. Its parent formation, 5th Infantry Brigade, had been given a new role as an 'out-of-area' brigade. Its task would be to use one or both of its two parachute battalions to seize an airstrip, and then for the Gurkha battalion to be flown in to protect the seized airstrip while the parachute battalions exploited further afield to rescue hostages, topple warlords or whatever the mission required. 'Out of area' simply meant out of the North Atlantic Treaty Organization (NATO) area, probably in some Third World country. When 1/7th Gurkhas joined 5th Infantry Brigade, its planning, organization and possible tactical deployment were still evolving.

When Argentina invaded the Falkland Islands on 2 April 1982 she did so under the firm impression that Britain would not go to war to recover them. This view had been encouraged by British defence cuts and the announced withdrawal of even a token Royal Naval presence in the area. Indeed, the initial reactions of British

ministers were much along the lines the Argentines expected; vigorous protests but no military response. However, they reckoned without a Prime Minister like Margaret Thatcher or a First Sea Lord like Admiral Sir Henry Leach, who assured her that, if she so requested, a naval task force could sail in short order to recover the Falkland Islands and South Georgia.

The land warfare element of the naval task force was 3rd Commando Brigade consisting of three Royal Marine commandos, each of a comparable size to an infantry battalion, with all the necessary integral artillery, engineer, light helicopter and service support. To 3rd Commando Brigade were added the two Parachute Regiment battalions of 5th Infantry Brigade, leaving only 1/7th Gurkhas of the brigade's original infantry component.

It then became apparent that additional ground forces would be needed, if not to fight, then to garrison the Falklands once the Argentines had been ejected. It was felt that the role of simply garrisoning the Falklands was the most likely option. Given objections on the use of more NATO-assigned troops it was decided, somewhat illogically, not to use available specialist trained and equipped NATO-roled formations. Instead 5th Infantry Brigade was selected and brought back up to strength by adding two Guards battalions, The Scots Guards and The Welsh Guards.

Political objections then arose to deploying a Gurkha battalion, it being felt that Nepal would be bound to object. The Defence Attaché in Kathmandu, Lieutenant Colonel Keith Robinson, himself a 7th Gurkha, quickly scotched this supposition by ascertaining that neither King nor government would have any objection. Remaining objections were removed when General Sir

A painting by Terence Cuneo showing soldiers of 7th Gurkhas at The Tower of London during the Ceremony of the Keys. (The Royal Gurkha Rifles)

Edwin Bramall, now Chief of the General Staff, strongly backed the inclusion of 1/7th Gurkhas in the Task Force. On informing the Prime Minister that a Gurkha battalion would sail with the task force she is reputed to have replied 'What, Dwin, only one!'

It was one thing to decide to send 5th Infantry Brigade, but an entirely different thing to implement it. Since the original concept of the brigade was as a light air-inserted intervention force, it had only the minimum of supporting elements; for instance, it had only a single artillery battery to support it rather than the normal whole regiment. Even in this light role, a recent brigade exercise had brought to notice wide divergences of opinion as to how it should operate and be equipped. Now it had only one of its original battalions, 1/7th Gurkhas. Of the two recently added Guards battalions, The Scots Guards had only just come off public duties in London and had done virtually no collective military training for some time – they had not even got any standard operating procedures, which lay down the actions a battalion takes when tasked to go to war. They wrote them with some urgency.

In order to bring this divergent brigade together, an exercise in Wales was laid on so that the units could practice jointly. While useful, the exercise did tend to show that there was a very long way to go before the formation could be considered battleworthy, especially in brigade command and control aspects. The 1/7th Gurkhas, commanded by the capable and experienced Lieutenant Colonel David Morgan, clearly demonstrated themselves to be well trained and ready for war, having specialist skills, such as that of operating the General Purpose Machine Gun in the sustained fire role, which the two Guards battalions, through no fault of their own, had hardly ever carried out. As the exercise ended, news of the decision to send 5th Infantry Brigade to the Falklands filtered through and soon a bonanza of arctic kit started to become available to the now much-enlarged brigade.

One aspect of the preparatory period and exercise had been an unqualified success, and that was public relations. The media literally had a field day and soon pictures of Gurkhas wielding kukris and uttering bloodthirsty screams were being studied somewhat uneasily in Buenos Aires and all points south.

In a remarkably short period of time, 5th Infantry Brigade, 3,150 strong, had been embarked in the converted ocean liner *Queen Elizabeth 2* (QE2) and on 12 May 1982 she sailed from

Southampton to a rapturous farewell. Colonel Morgan used the long voyage south to the best advantage, getting his men used to all the new equipment they had received, such as the highly effective Milan anti-tank launchers, and .50 Browning heavy machine guns, both very effective for 'bunker busting', as well as sophisticated Clansman radios. He was lucky in having a very experienced and capable set of company commanders and this strong unified team did much to see the battalion through the testing times ahead. Even as 5th Infantry Brigade sailed, its exact employment in the Falklands was uncertain, but what was definite, or what was thought to be definite, was that once it reached Ascension Island the troops would have a chance to disembark themselves and their equipment and organize themselves for immediate action on arrival.

As *QE2* neared Ascension on 21 May, the initial landings of 3rd Commando Brigade took place at San Carlos Water, a large inlet on East Falkland. The order was then received for 5th Infantry Brigade to head as quickly as possible for the battle area with only a very brief stop at Ascension, insufficient to properly organize and re-stow equipment. It was the first of the many order, counter-

order and ensuing disorder-type decisions that the unfortunate 5th Infantry Brigade, always the poor relation to 3rd Commando Brigade, was to suffer in the weeks ahead.

The *QE2* now made for Gritvyken in South Georgia where 1/7th Gurkhas trans-shipped to the P & O ferry *Norland* and then, in freezing temperatures and howling gales, made their way to San Carlos Water. Gurkhas from land-locked Nepal have always been indifferent sailors and suffered agonies of sea-sickness as they were tossed this way and that by heaving 70-foot waves. A subsequent press report describing them disembarking like 'heat-seeking ferrets' was probably more indicative of their wish to get off *Norland* and on to dry land than to grapple immediately with Argentines.

After landing on 1 June, 1/7th Gurkhas, in the absence of any other instructions, spread out and awaited orders. One company was ordered to defend the southern perimeter of the bridgehead while the remainder was moved in dribs and drabs by the one surviving Chinook helicopter to Goose Green, scene of the 2nd Battalion The Parachute Regiment's (2 Para) recent remarkable victory. They had taken 67 casualties including their Commanding Officer killed and were understandably exhausted, with many down with trench foot. Nevertheless, rather illogically, the victors of Goose Green were moved forward to the next phase of the battle while the fresh 1/7th Gurkhas were left to clear up the shambles and administer 500 Argentine prisoners fearful of being emasculated or eaten by 'Los Barbaros Gurkhos'.

Concurrently orders were received to dominate Lafonia, which constituted the southern half of East Falkland. To achieve this, 1/7th Gurkhas were to carry out short, sharp, helicopter-inserted patrols to root out groups of Argentines said to be acting in an anti-helicopter role armed with hand-held anti–aircraft missiles. A British Gazelle helicopter carrying the brigade signals officer was suspected of having been shot down by one such group. Before undertaking these patrols, 1/7th Gurkhas were assured that there were no friendly forces in or near the crash site so any military encountered would be Argentine and could be engaged as such. The first task given was for a Gurkha officer and a small patrol to make their way to the helicopter crash site and guard it. Accordingly Lieutenant Belbahadur Limbu and his patrol set off and on nearing the crash site heard voices. Assuming them to be Argentine, he prepared to attack.

Before ordering the attack, Lieutenant Belbahadur went forward himself to see the situation. There were indeed voices but they were speaking English! The speakers turned out to be members of 5th Infantry Brigade re-broadcast station who were being visited by the brigade signals officer when he was shot down. A tragic blue on blue ('friendly fire') situation was thus narrowly avoided by the professionalism of 1/7th Gurkhas. This

From a montage by David Rowlands. The much improved Sino-Hong Kong border fence completed in 1981 which helped stem the flood of illegal immigrants over the land border.

7th Gurkha on Public Duties at Buckingham Palace. (Gurkha Museum)

7th Gurkha with pintle-mounted GPMG in anti-air role at San Carlos Bay shortly after landing in the Falklands. (Gurkha Museum)

sort of confusion was symptomatic of 5th Infantry Brigade's lack of opportunity to work together and become a team before deployment.

While other Commanding Officers in 5th Infantry Brigade were to take powerful issue on such occasions, this recourse was simply not open to Colonel Morgan. Like all Commanding Officers of United Kingdom-based Gurkha battalions before him, he knew he was carrying the banner for the whole Brigade of Gurkhas and how it was generally perceived. This in turn would inevitably bear on its future, as always threatened by the Damocletian sword of total disbandment swaying ominously on a very slender thread. What others achieved by direct confrontation, he achieved by tact, good sense and total loyalty, attributes sometimes stretched to near breaking point.

A further patrol did encounter an Argentine group armed with anti-aircraft missiles which on sighting a drawn Gurkha kukri immediately surrendered. After the war the kukri in question was auctioned for £1,300 and the proceeds given to Army charities.

By now 5th Infantry Brigade, headed by a re-brigaded 2 Para, had leapfrogged forward and, virtually unopposed, captured the

important area of Fitzroy and Bluff Cove on 3 June. The 1/7th Gurkhas were ordered to send forward a company to act as a brigade patrol company. D Company was selected and made the journey by sea in the elderly Falklands Island coastal steamer *Monsunen*. A second voyage was to take elements of Headquarters and Support Companies of 1/7th Gurkhas forward. Ordered by the brigade commander to move immediately in daylight, both Colonel Morgan and second-in-command Major Bill Dawson, who was in charge of the group, realized that given the high level of enemy air activity the rickety steamer proceeding with agonizing slowness up the coast in daylight would be easy meat. Displaying considerable tact, they ensured that by 'hastening slowly' Major Dawson's group did not actually set off until darkness was falling.

Given what happened to the Welsh Guards in the landing ship *Sir Galahad* earlier on 8 June at Fitzroy, theirs was a wise precaution. Nevertheless the whole move still nearly ended in disaster when the crew of the *Monsunen* tried to take in tow a disabled landing craft met on the voyage. In the process of this manoeuvre a rope became entangled in *Monsunen*'s propeller and the two craft began to drift without power in stormy seas. By the time the rope was disentangled, there were insufficient hours of darkness left to complete the voyage and reluctantly they turned back.

It was fortunate that at that juncture sufficient helicopters became available to move 1/7th Gurkhas forward, as the British Broadcasting Corporation, always a rogue element, had already announced to the world that the Gurkhas were being transported in the *Monsunen*.

As British forces closed on Stanley, the capital, several plans were made, only to be discarded as events overtook them. The final battle plan was a three-phase one with 3rd Commando Brigade seizing Mount Longdon, Two Sisters and Mount Harriet, followed by the Scots Guards taking Mount Tumbledown, and the 1/7th Gurkhas taking Mount William, with 3rd Battalion The Parachute Regiment under 3rd Commando Brigade taking Wireless Ridge. Finally, the latter brigade would break into the area of Stanley Common and then on to Stanley itself. Suffice to say 3rd Commando Brigade achieved all its Phase One objectives despite bitter fighting.

On 10 June, Brigadier Tony Wilson, the 5th Brigade commander, briefed his Commanding Officers on their Phase Two objectives and, following the briefing, 1/7th Gurkhas marched forward to their designated assembly area. By this stage both Colonel Morgan and the Commanding Officer of the Scots Guards realized that the brigade attack timetable was too optimistic and asked for a delay of 24 hours. This was a difficult one for Brigadier Wilson as he was being urged to attack as soon as possible, as 3rd Commando Brigade were coming under continual and effective fire from the Phase Two objectives. Confusion over the securing of 3rd Commando Brigade's Phase One start-line had also exacerbated relations between brigades. Nevertheless 5th Brigade commander loyally insisted on the delay which was reluctantly agreed. Meanwhile in their assembly area 1/7th Gurkhas were being heavily shelled, sustaining four

Above: 7th Gurkhas in freezing conditions on a rocky hillside shortly before their advance on Mount William. (Gurkha Museum)

Right: 7th Gurkhas entrenched position. (Gurkha Museum)

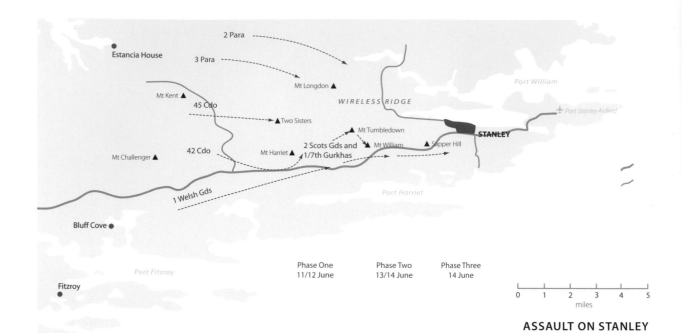

Estancia House

2 Para

3 Para

Mt Kent ▲

45 Cdo

Mt Longdon ▲

WIRELESS RIDGE

Port William

Port Stanley Airfield

Two Sisters ▲

Mt Tumbledown ▲

▲ Mt William

STANLEY

Mt Challenger ▲

42 Cdo

Mt Harriet ▲

2 Scots Gds and
1/7th Gurkhas

▲ Sapper Hill

1 Welsh Gds

Port Harriet

Bluff Cove ●

Port Fitzroy

Phase One
11/12 June

Phase Two
13/14 June

Phase Three
14 June

Fitzroy ●

| 0 | 1 | 2 | 3 | 4 | 5 |

miles

ASSAULT ON STANLEY

wounded, one of whom was a Gurkha officer. Major D.R.d'A. Willis, A Company commander, had a lucky escape when his trench was destroyed with all his equipment while he was away at an orders group. Colonel Morgan and the Commanding Officer of the Scots Guards now carefully coordinated their attacks so that 1/7th Gurkhas followed beneath the line of the Scots Guards attack to take their objective, Mount William, from the north. The move would take place in darkness covered by not only artillery and Royal Navy gunfire support, but also by 1/7th Gurkhas' Milan missile-launchers and 0.50-inch Browning machine guns with which they were expert. Nevertheless they were aware that their approach route would probably be mined and to counter this they were preceded by a Parachute Regiment three-man clearance team from 9 (Parachute) Squadron Royal Engineers.

Unfortunately, the Scots Guards attack, ultimately brilliantly successful, fell way behind schedule, thus forcing 1/7th Gurkhas to

Left: Men of the 1/7th Gurkhas with a captured Argentinian anti-aircraft gun. (Gurkha Museum)

7th Gurkhas occupy Goose Green. (Gurkha Museum)

1/7th Gurkhas march through Fleet on return from the Falklands.

make their hazardous approach march in daylight on 14 June. In clear view of the Argentine defenders, they suffered a further eight men wounded by artillery fire; nearer the objective 'A' Company 1/7th Gurkhas Royal Artillery Forward Observation Officer, Captain Keith Swinton, was shot in the chest but miraculously survived. As 1/7th Gurkhas crossed their start-line to attack, the Argentines began to surrender, streams of them heading for the Scots Guards, no doubt apprehensive of what the bloodthirsty 'Gurkhos' would do to them. It was a bitter moment for 1/7th Gurkhas, baulked of their prey at the last after all they had endured. Their reputation had preceded them; the Argentines had no stomach to face men made supermen in their minds by unending propaganda.

Soon after the surrender, 3rd Commando Brigade and the two Parachute battalions were on their way home to a heroes' welcome; 5th Infantry Brigade remained for a time to clear up the mess and garrison the islands. It was during this period that 1/7th Gurkhas suffered its only fatality when at Goose Green a Gurkha Lance Corporal's shovel hit a grenade as he was filling in a trench. Ninety-five days after their departure 1/7th Gurkhas received a rapturous welcome home by the good citizens of Fleet and Church Crookham. They had done all that had been asked of them and more. Unfortunately, like the unlucky Number 40 Commando left to garrison West Falkland as the other two Commandos earned the laurels of victory, the final accolade of a victorious engagement was denied them. Such are the fortunes of war.

Lieutenant Colonel Morgan later wrote: 'If we can win wars through our reputation who wants to kill people?' He certainly had a point.

The South Atlantic Medal 1982.

CHAPTER SEVENTEEN

A DIFFICULT DECADE: 1983–1993

Although the Falklands War had captured the headlines in Britain, life in Hong Kong for the majority of the Brigade changed little. Long periods were still spent on the border rounding up illegal immigrants, to which was added the additional burden of dealing with boatloads of Vietnamese boat people who braved treacherous seas to make their way to Hong Kong and a new life, as well as sophisticated smugglers using powerful speedboats. These duties captured no headlines but were vitally necessary to the stability of Hong Kong. The long periods of static observation in very basic conditions, lack of sleep and the monotony of repetitive tours on the border would have worn down any less resilient organization.

To this was added uncertainty. After much deliberation the Prime Minister, Margaret Thatcher, had made it clear that given certain safeguards Hong Kong would be handed back to China when the lease expired in 1997. Where would that leave The Brigade of Gurkhas? In Europe the spirit of 'glasnost' (openness), emanating from the Soviet Union's President Mikhail Gorbachev, showed every sign of breaking down the antagonisms of the Cold War which had dominated the continent for so long. Already people were talking about a 'Peace Dividend' which would inevitably mean a major reduction in the strength of the British armed forces.

In Nepal, too, things were changing. The *panchayat* system which had worked well for Nepal was now seen to be discredited and demands for democratic elections were becoming difficult for King Birendra to resist, despite his reservations based on previous experimentation with Western-style democracy. In 1990 he was obliged to hold elections which the Congress Party won convincingly. However the agendas that aspiring politicians put forward were totally unrealistic and, when they inevitably failed to deliver them, there was discontent and disillusion throughout the country.

In previous times of uncertainty Gurkhas had looked to their senior British officers for reassurance and guidance. Unfortunately the post of Commander British Forces Hong Kong was now automatically linked to that of Major General Brigade of Gurkhas, thus allowing the senior and most important post in the Brigade to be filled by an officer having no or, at best fleeting, experience of Gurkhas. In itself this was not critical providing that other key posts such as Brigadier Brigade of Gurkhas and Commander 48th Gurkha Infantry Brigade were filled by permanent-cadre Brigade of Gurkhas, officers who knew and understood their men. Unfortunately this did not always happen. Within the regiments, too, the best British officers were being encouraged to get out into the wider Army to seek preferment, their places being taken by ever-increasing numbers of seconded officers from British regiments who were, in some cases, just looking for a pleasant break of three years in the tropics.

Men of The Gurkha Transport Regiment in Saracen Armoured Cars patrolling the streets of Kowloon, Hong Kong. (Gurkha Museum)

All these factors inevitably bred uneasiness in the minds of serving Gurkha soldiers and the carapace of unquestioning obedience to orders and awesome discipline based on mutual respect started to waver.

Small changes in conditions of service subtly assisted this process. Hitherto, unmarried British officers throughout the Army had received free accommodation within barracks to which strict conditions of occupancy were attached. Once officers were obliged to pay for their accommodation no such conditions could be attached and inevitably a much more laissez-faire attitude prevailed. This tended to destroy the close companionship and shared life of British and Gurkhas in the same environment, especially as Gurkhas were expected to continue exactly as before. As a result, the unique relationship of mutual trust and respect was becoming eroded.

This was to manifest itself in some serious disciplinary cases. In one battalion a British officer was murdered by a booby trap laid by a serving or recently retired Gurkha who was never identified. In another battalion, while on a 1986 overseas exercise in Hawaii, a company-sized mutiny broke out in which one British and one Gurkha officer were injured and other British officers manhandled. It led to 120 Gurkhas being dismissed the service.

Another battalion saw a Gurkha officer killed by a frenzied kukri attack while on border duty in Hong Kong. In Britain, the battalion based in Church Crookham had six men arrested at Heathrow trying to smuggle in drugs. These incidents, especially the one in Hawaii, led to considerable press comment and speculation on the future of Gurkhas in the British Army. As is the way of the media years of loyal and blameless service were conveniently overlooked.

In 1987 Major General Garry Johnson took over as Commander British Forces Hong Kong and Major General Brigade of Gurkhas. Before transferring to the Royal Green Jackets, Johnson had spent his formative years in 10th Gurkhas and we have met him before in these pages as a young company commander in Borneo. His background made him particularly suited to see what was ailing the Brigade and how it might be put right, and for that reason it is worth quoting his address to the Brigade of Gurkhas conference in autumn 1987 in full:

> The movement towards modernization, which began a
> decade ago, was undoubtedly necessary and the benefits
> are obvious. But I do get the strong feeling that the process

The Queen's Gurkha Engineers operating a minelayer. (Gurkha Museum)

has become an end in itself; that the machine is in full gear towards turning Brigade units into replicas of British ones and cheap ones at that. The motivation is, of course, survival, but I ask you to consider whether this is the best or only way to survive. It is my strong conviction that we can never be the same as British units. Our strengths are not their strengths, our weaknesses are not their weaknesses, and if we could be the same, I'm afraid we would only be turning ourselves into 'second class Brits' and I for one will not sign up to a second-class future which degrades our long history of excellence. So if we cannot and should not be turned into *goras* (white soldiers) what is it that we can offer the Army that will make it worth its while employing us, at a time when money will be tight as always and when calls for further reductions in the size of the Army can be expected?

I suggest to you that we can only sensibly capitalize on our innate strengths rather than on our acquired skills, at those things which we are better at doing than our British equivalents. And to define these strengths I can do no better than to go back to the words of that greatest of Gurkha soldiers, Field Marshal Bill Slim, who said:

The Almighty created in the Gurkha an ideal infantryman, indeed an ideal rifleman, brave, tough, patient, adaptable, skilled in fieldcraft, intensely proud of his military record and unswerving loyalty. Add to this honesty in word and deed, his parade perfection, and his unquenchable cheerfulness…

This is not in any way to disregard the skills and the success of the Corps units, but I have to say to you that, in the UK, the pool of clever boys to make into technicians is far deeper now than is the pool in which you fish for good infantrymen. This poses a number of questions: will the raw material be there – not just in 1997 but in 2007 and 2017, for we must surely be looking into long-term viability? Are we placing too much emphasis on education and course gradings as qualifications for promotion and not leaving COs enough latitude to promote leaders? Is our discipline as tight as it should be? And it turns the spotlight on officers too. Are we sending too many officers away to further their careers at the expense of manning battalions? Are officers as close to their men as they should be? (And don't forget that the times when Regiments of the Indian Army, past and present, and of the British Army too, have faltered have been when the

H.M. The Queen visits 2nd Gurkhas in Belize.

officers began to take their men for granted.) Are we sure we want to discard the QGO [Queen's Gurkha Officer] rank structure, with the Gurkha Major at its head, for something new and untested, just because the rest of the Army finds it different, and just when the real strain will be placed upon us? I know I am digging up discussions you have had before but these are fundamental issues on which I want you to reflect during the week and be prepared to discuss with me so that I can come to my conclusions. You will, I dare say, have realized that my inclination is not to rush headlong down the high road of modernization as we are presently heading but nor do I think it is possible to revert back to the low road. There must be a middle way: it is the degree to which the tiller needs touching that I wish to define.'

There is no record of whether the assembled officers agreed or disagreed with General Johnson's analysis but he had spoken to them as one Gurkha officer to another, something that his two predecessors, through no fault of their own, had been unable to do. In retrospect his analysis was very accurate and, coming so soon after the demise of 2/7th Gurkhas, a particularly fine battalion, provided a much needed tonic to a Brigade badly in need of reassurance.

This trend was greatly assisted by a statement by the Secretary of State for Defence on 22 May 1989 which clearly charted a long-term future for the Brigade. This statement, based on a study done by Major General Morgan Llewellyn, who had previously commanded 48th Gurkha Infantry Brigade and was Colonel of The Gurkha Transport Regiment, saw a Brigade of 4,000 men consisting of four infantry battalions, a squadron each of engineers, signals and transport and a small headquarters and recruiting element. Clearly reductions would be necessary to reach this reduced establishment but at least all the historic cap badges would be preserved and, more importantly, an assured future beyond 1997 seemed to beckon.

Well might the Brigadier Brigade of Gurkhas, Brigadier Miles Hunt-Davis (later Sir Miles Hunt-Davis, personal assistant to the Duke of Edinburgh and Colonel 7th Gurkha Rifles) point out that the parliamentary decision opened the way for several key achievable aims, namely:

a. A worthwhile role within the mainstream of the Army
b. The centre of gravity of the Brigade being in Britain.
c. The retention of all Gurkha cap badges.
d. The achievement of a viable Gurkha force.
e. Recognition that in some areas the Brigade would be
significantly different to the rest of the Army; namely

Gurkha on patrol in the Brunei jungle. (Gurkha Museum)

Men of The Queen's Gurkha Engineers in mine clearance training. (Gurkha Museum)

The Queen's Gurkha Officer ranks, its terms and conditions of service, Nepalese citizenship, religion and custom.

As, in December 1989, General Johnson handed over as Commander British Forces Hong Kong and Major General Brigade of Gurkhas to Major General Peter Duffell (2nd Gurkhas), another long-serving Gurkha, it seemed that the future of Gurkhas after 1997 was assured. With such nagging doubts now dispelled, the Brigade threw itself into its various tasks and commitments in Hong Kong, Britain and Brunei with its usual élan and enthusiasm. Hopes that Gurkhas would be actively involved in the war against Iraq, which had invaded Kuwait in 1990, were only partially fulfilled with the formation of the Gurkha Ambulance Group based upon 28 (Ambulance) Squadron GTR and which included The Band of The Brigade of Gurkhas and some Gurkha signallers. This was the first occasion that Gurkhas had served on operations in the desert since WW2. A few British officers were also able to participate, calling upon affiliations with British regiments to involve themselves. Deployed along the casualty evacuation chain, The Gurkha Ambulance Group capability was fortunately only tested in the handling of Iraqi POW casualties.

The Gurkha Transport Regiment was called upon again to provide a transport squadron to serve with the UN force in Cyprus. So began a new era in military operations for Gurkhas where they served as part of an international or coalition force across the globe. In recognition of The Gurkha Transport Regiment's service in the Gulf and Cyprus and its loyal service since being formed in 1958, it too was granted a Royal Title in 1992; that of The Queen's Own Gurkha Transport Regiment.

Pipers of Queen's Gurkha Signals being inspected by HRH The Princess Royal on the occasion of the presentation of her personal pipe banner, 13 May 1980. (Gurkha Museum)

allowed Headquarters Brigade of Gurkhas to drop its previous objections and fight desperately for a continued if limited existence at 2,500.

Help in this battle came from an unexpected quarter. The Governor of Hong Kong, Sir David Wilson, made it clear to the British government that, while he would have no objection to British troops replacing Gurkhas in Hong Kong, the Hong Kong government could not be expected to pay any more money towards the Defence Costs Agreement. Since British troops were at that time paid a lot more than Gurkhas when serving in Hong Kong and cost more to administer, British troops replacing Gurkhas would have incurred considerable extra costs to the British government. Since the whole point of 'Options for Change' was to save money, anything that would cost more was vetoed by the Treasury. Option A, immediate disbandment, was accordingly dropped.

This still left Option B, running on the Brigade until 1997 when Hong Kong was to be handed back to China and then disbanding it. Major General Duffell as Major General Brigade of Gurkhas argued that this was an unreasonable option and that it would be difficult, if not impossible, to retain morale over such a vital period, if at the end of it Gurkhas knew they would be disbanded. In this he was backed by General Sir John Chapple who was a long-serving 2nd Gurkha and was now, as Chief of the General Staff, the senior soldier in the army. Thus, after much agonized discussion, it was decided to run on a Gurkha force of 2,500 for an unspecified time after 1997 based in Britain and Brunei. The determination of Brunei's Sultan to continue to have a Gurkha battalion based in his country did much to sway the eventual decision, especially as he was picking up all its costs.

The decision to continue with Gurkhas, albeit cut by over 70 per cent, did not please British infantry regiments who, from the Director of Infantry downwards, had adopted the mantra of no cuts to British infantry until all Gurkhas were disbanded. This was a rather depressing commentary on over 150 years of shared comradeship, especially as the British infantry reduction would only be 24 per cent as opposed to 70 per cent in the Gurkhas.

While the battle for limited survival was won, the future profile of this much-reduced Gurkha Brigade needed to be addressed, as did the negotiation of terms for Gurkhas made redundant. Both Major General Duffell and his Brigadier Brigade of Gurkhas, Brigadier Bullock, had been adjutants of their battalions when the first big rundown of the late 1960s occurred and immediately realized the importance of getting fair terms for all Gurkhas being made redundant.

First contacts with the Director of Personal Services at Ministry of Defence were not propitious, the outgoing director being firmly of the opinion that the retention of any Gurkhas was

However, unbeknown at the time, this new confidence in the Brigade's future was to prove misplaced. A new fundamental reassessment of Britain's defence capabilities following the collapse of the Warsaw Pact was now under way, seeking a major 'Peace Dividend' in terms of reduction in numbers and capability. This process, innocuously named 'Options for Change', was to throw the whole future of British Gurkhas back into the melting pot. All waited with bated breath to hear how the Brigade would be affected. When the news came it was little less than catastrophic. Fundamentally the Brigade was faced with three options namely:

a. *Total disbandment now.*

b. *Disbandment in 1997 on Hong Kong reverting to China.*

c. *The retention of a Brigade of about 2,500 for an unspecified period of time in Britain and Brunei.*

The figure of 2,500, although offering a slender lifeline, was difficult for Headquarters Brigade of Gurkhas to accept as it had already gone on record as saying that any figure below 4,000 was unsustainable, in view of the unavoidable overheads of recruiting in Nepal and the recruit training organization.

Fortunately, however, Colonel Christopher Bullock (2nd Gurkhas and 6th Gurkhas) had done a comprehensive study on the whole recruiting and processing organization in Nepal during 1986 and this pointed the way to economies of scale which, while painful, would provide an efficient organization still capable of meeting Brigade requirements. The implementation of this study

The Gurkha Transport Regiment in Iraq, 1991. (Gurkha Museum)

an aberration. Fortunately, his successor Major General Mike Jackson (later Chief of the General Staff) was far more supportive and being a Parachute Regiment officer realized what it was like to be an endangered species. After many discussions and staunch support from Major General Jackson and General Sir David Ramsbotham, the Adjutant General (later Lord Ramsbotham, Her Majesty's Inspector of Prisons), the Treasury agreed to what were to be the most generous redundancy terms ever given to Gurkhas. Pensions were given to Gurkhas after a minimum of four years service, which meant that everybody who had to go out would get one. Armed with such satisfactory terms it made it much easier for regiments to select men for redundancy – indeed, there were many volunteers.

If the path of getting fair, even generous, redundancy terms had been smoother than anticipated, the path of planning and agreement on the future form and composition of the Brigade was to be very stony. A 2,500 ceiling would only allow of two infantry battalions and three squadrons, one each of engineers, signals and transport, a small headquarters and training element and a minimum recruiting and resettlement organization in Nepal.

As a result of the Bullock report, the organization in Nepal was being drastically slimmed; the large headquarters and recruiting depot in Dharan in Eastern Nepal was closed in 1990 and, along with its well-equipped hospital, released back to the Nepalese authorities. In the capital Kathmandu, where all air trooping was now directed, a new and much smaller headquarters and transit accommodation was built, replacing the rather dilapidated Rana palace that had been utilized when the transit camp in Calcutta had been closed in 1978. All recruiting was now centred on a newly built camp just outside the Western Nepal hill town of Pokhara, to where recruits from Eastern Nepal were bussed in some discomfort along the grandiosely named East-West highway.

An early challenge to the planned 2,500-man order of battle came from The Queen's Gurkha Engineers who argued with some justification that the need now was for supporting arms and not infantry. With Queen's Gurkha Signals personnel then

The new British Gurkha Centre at Pokhara, Western Nepal, rebuilt after the closure of the HQ and recruiting depot at Dharan in Eastern Nepal. (Gurkha Museum)

HM The Queen inspects a 6th Gurkha guard of honour on arrival in Hong Kong in 1986.

being deployed from their UK base at Blandford to Northern Iraq (supporting a United Nations-protected enclave for Kurdish refugees from Saddam Hussein in spring 1991), this seemed a reasonable argument. Nevertheless the infantry requirement was for one battalion in UK and one in Brunei, so objections were overruled.

Headquarters Brigade of Gurkhas' original plan had anticipated the two Western regiments 2nd and 6th amalgamating to form 2nd/6th Gurkhas (the two battalions of 2nd Gurkhas having amalgamated in 1992) and the two Eastern regiments forming 7th / 10th Gurkhas, thereby retaining the historic titles. However the Colonels of the Regiments concerned thought otherwise and decided to go for an entirely new regiment 'The Gurkha Rifles' which being duly honoured became 'The Royal Gurkha Rifles'. Vexatious but secondary issues such as order of amalgamation, dress and accoutrements, etc, were settled by animated discussion in the smoke-filled conference rooms of various London military clubs.

Finally, on 1 July 1994, in circumstances of great sadness but huge dignity, the old regiments marched into history and 2nd/6th Gurkhas became First Battalion The Royal Gurkha Rifles, 7th Gurkhas The Second Battalion and 10th Gurkhas The Third Battalion. The second and third battalions amalgamated in 1996 to bring the Gurkha infantry order of battle down to the agreed two battalions. All this involved not only large numbers of Gurkhas being made redundant but a massive reallocation of manpower. That all this was done with comparatively little fuss and on time is a lasting testimony to the dedication of unit redundancy officers who so efficiently, but compassionately, implemented the plans of Headquarters Brigade of Gurkhas. Some of the adverse effect of these reductions was ameliorated by the requirement to raise three Gurkha reinforcement companies to bolster under-strength British infantry battalions.

As rifle regiments, the previous regiments had not carried colours but 2nd Gurkhas, the oldest regiment, had proudly carried their 'Queen's Truncheon', presented to them by Queen Victoria to mark their bravery and loyalty during the Indian Mutiny. The new regiment showed no wish to continue this tradition, even had the Trustees of the 2nd Gurkhas been willing, so the Truncheon was laid up in a touching ceremony at The Royal Military Academy Sandhurst in June 1993. The new regiment also decided against wearing the distinctive red piping or 'lali' round their collars as 2nd Gurkhas had done. Interestingly both traditions were re-introduced some years later at the express wish of the serving officers and with the agreement of 2nd Gurkha Trustees.

In spring 1992, Major General John Foley took over as Commander British Forces and Major General Brigade of Gurkhas. Although a Royal Green Jacket, he had spent much of his service close to Gurkhas, first in the Special Air Service in Borneo and then as Brigade Major 51st Infantry Brigade in Hong Kong, which had a Gurkha battalion under command. Not having served in a Gurkha regiment turned out to be something of an advantage, as General Foley could truly be regarded as neutral in any inter-

regimental dispute. His wise and far-seeing tenure of command, allied to his excellent relations with the new and last Governor of Hong Kong, The Right Honourable Christopher (now Lord) Patten, helped smooth the very real difficulties the Brigade was confronting. In this Foley was much helped by his Brigadiers Brigade of Gurkhas, first Bullock and then Brigadier S.M.A. Lee, who as a Gurkha signaller was able to ensure that the interests of the Gurkha Corps units were not neglected. So as the troubled decade ended, the Brigade, having looked down the abyss of complete disbandment, determinedly faced an uncertain future with its customary aplomb and innate optimism.

A Gurkha sentry surveys the Tolo Peninsula, New Territories, Hong Kong ... 'Guardians of the Hong Kong border for over 40 years'. (Colonel B.M. Niven)

CHAPTER EIGHTEEN

A NEW HORIZON

While General John Foley was Major General Brigade of Gurkhas, he commissioned a paper entitled 'New Horizons' which endeavoured to chart the way forward for a much reduced Brigade post-1997. Nobody, however prescient, could have foreseen the unexpected turn of events that completely upset the planning assumptions of the Ministry of Defence. Instead of the expected 'Peace Dividend', following the end of the Cold War, a variety of new and potentially explosive issues engulfed not only Europe but also Africa and the Middle East.

The collapse of the Soviet Union released an upsurge of nationalistic feeling in those countries in Europe which had so long been held in the straitjacket of the Eastern Bloc, and in nowhere were these tensions more marked than in Yugoslavia. When Gavrilo Princip murdered Archduke Ferdinand of Austria in Sarajevo in June 1914, not only did he precipitate the First World War, he also, by extension, caused the end of the Austro-Hungarian Empire that had for so long ruled, with varying degrees of efficiency, the jumble of countries and ethnic groupings that made up the Balkans. Here the tide of Ottoman invasion had lapped so that, as well as ethnic differences, the populations were religiously divided into Christian and Muslim. After the First World War and the collapse of the Austro-Hungarian Empire, these diverse countries were welded into a new country called

THE BALKANS

Yugoslavia (United Slavs), with close cultural ties to their fellow Slavs, the Russians.

After Hitler bombed Belgrade, invaded Yugoslavia and then Russia, the Yugoslav partisans under the Communist leader Tito rose up and conducted a bitter guerrilla campaign against the occupying Germans, sporadically helped by British special forces parachuted in. Other parts of the Balkans helped the Germans so that, after the war, there were not only the old religious tensions but also fresh hatreds, the legacy of the Second World War. Fortunately in Marshal Tito, as he had become, Yugoslavia had a

The Queen's Own Gurkha Transport Regiment at the end of their UN tour in Bosnia.

leader of exceptional strength and ability who ruthlessly suppressed any internecine strife, as well as keeping his country prosperous and independent although nominally Communist.

With Tito's death in 1980, it was truly a case of *après moi le deluge*, and very soon his federal republic collapsed into vicious civil war as Serbia, the most powerful of the constituent states, tried to dominate its Croat and Muslim neighbours by war and genocide. The United Nations having shown itself powerless to stop the fighting, NATO was obliged to step in to halt the massacre of defenceless people.

In Africa, the withdrawal of the colonial powers had resulted in some areas to a return to the *status quo ante*, namely tribal conflict made more lethal by the easy availability of modern weaponry. There soon developed a continual need for United Nations intervention and observers, backed up where necessary by British troops prepared to fight.

In the Middle East, Saddam Hussein, leader of Iraq, although driven out of Kuwait by coalition forces, still exercised a latent threat to the region which America's new President, George W. Bush, intended to exorcise once and for all.

Therefore, rather than benefiting from the optimistic assumptions of a peace dividend, the British Army, now significantly reduced, found itself over-committed. More ominously, even its much-reduced establishment continued to be under-implemented because of poor recruiting. Additional manpower became a pressing requirement.

The Brigade of Gurkhas meanwhile faced a bewilderingly complicated set of objectives. It had to reduce its strength by over 70 per cent, move out of Hong Kong, its base for the last 35 years, relocate its command and control and recruit training to Britain, implement the planned changes to its recruiting and resettlement functions in Nepal, and still remain operationally effective. If ever an organization was required to manage change, the Brigade was so challenged from 1994 to 2000. That all this was achieved was due not only to first-class leadership and the selfless devotion of long-serving British and Gurkha officers, but above all to the incredible flexibility and innate cheerfulness of the Gurkha soldier, be he an infantryman, engineer, signaller or driver. Instead of being daunted by the challenges, the Gurkha relished them and threw himself into overcoming them with his customary enthusiasm and good humour, thereby confounding his critics who said he would never cope outside the comfort zone of the Gurkha-dominated Far East.

In June 1994, the post of Major General Brigade of Gurkhas, which was also that of Commander British Forces Hong Kong, ceased and in Major General Sam Cowan (later General Sir Sam Cowan), the Brigade received its first Colonel Commandant. A Gurkha Signaller, Sam Cowan had served with Gurkhas over many years, knew them well and was to lead them through this turbulent period with wisdom, courage and unquenchable optimism.

In 1993, Her Majesty The Queen became the Affiliated Colonel in Chief of The Queen's Gurkha Engineers and Her Royal Highness The Princess Royal was appointed the Affiliated Colonel in Chief of the Queen's Gurkha Signals and The Queen's Own Gurkha Transport Regiment. The appointment of Affiliated Colonel in Chief is unique to Gurkha Corps Regiments. The following year, His Royal Highness Prince Charles, The Prince of Wales, was appointed Colonel in Chief of the new regiment The Royal Gurkha Rifles. All four regiments now enjoyed Royal patronage. The post of Brigadier Brigade of Gurkhas was downgraded to Colonel and Colonel D.R. d'A. Willis now had the unenviable task of establishing Headquarters Brigade of Gurkhas in Church Crookham, co-located with the United Kingdom Gurkha battalion. With the move back to Britain, the post of Liaison Officer Brigade of Gurkhas, carried out for 45 years in London advising the Ministry of Defence on Gurkha matters, now closed and its staff also moved to Church Crookham.

To this, by now, very busy barracks came the 1995 intake of recruits under the watchful eye of their commander, Major Gordon Corrigan. Inevitable difficulties in transposing and setting up recruit training in Britain were all successfully overcome, but not without continual improvisation on a large scale. Corrigan's account of having to beg, buy, borrow and occasionally extract from the back of a truck the equipment necessary to train the recruits would be funny were it not so poignant. Despite all the seemingly insuperable obstacles, this massive reorganization was achieved at no cost to operational efficiency.

In the Far East, The 1st Royal Gurkha Rifles, the last Gurkha infantry battalion in Hong Kong, moved its location to Malaya Lines which had housed the Training Depot Brigade of Gurkhas. Queen's Gurkha Signals Headquarters and one squadron moved into Headquarters British Forces at HMS *Tamar* (the Royal Navy Hong Kong shore establishment). The 67th Squadron The Queen's Gurkha Engineers moved into the old 48th Gurkha Infantry Brigade Headquarters at Sek Kong, in the heart of the New Territories. All was flux and movement.

Meanwhile in the UK, the two resident Gurkha Corps squadrons relocated; 69 Gurkha Engineer Squadron to Maidstone in Kent, where it joined its new parent regiment 36 Engineer

Gurkhas training before deployment to the Balkans as part of the Stabilisation Force (SFOR). (Gurkha Museum)

Men of The Royal Gurkha Rifles patrolling a destroyed railway line in Bosnia. (Gurkha Museum)

Regiment, and 250 Gurkha Signals Squadron to Bramcote where it formed part of 30 Signal Regiment. They were joined by the Gurkha-manned 28 Transport Squadron which moved from Hong Kong to form part of 10 Transport Regiment in Colchester.

★★★

However, no sooner than Gurkhas had arrived in Britain than they started to be operationally deployed. The first unit to deploy was the newly arrived 28 Transport Squadron forming part of the British logistic battalion deployed to the former Republic of Yugoslavia with the UN Protection Force (UNPROFOR).

The signing of the November 1995 Dayton Accords, which called for the disarming of the warring Balkan factions, required a massive NATO presence prepared to use force if necessary, something the United Nations had never been prepared to do. Suddenly soldiers from The Royal Gurkha Rifles, The Queen's Gurkha Engineers, 250 Squadron Queen's Gurkha Signals were moving to follow in the footsteps of men of 28 Squadron The Queen's Own Gurkha Transport Regiment, with their huge Demountable Rack Off-loading and Pick-up System (DROPS) trucks, and getting involved in this messy, unpredictable and dangerous internecine warfare.

Everywhere they served throughout the Balkans, Gurkhas became a byword for cheerful efficiency and high standards. Also noted was their ability to get along easily with the local people of these war-torn provinces who immediately warmed to them. As Hindus or Buddhists, the Gurkhas' religious credentials were impeccably neutral in an area where much of the fighting was across the Christian/Muslim divide. In the case of the Corps units, the traditional Brigade of Gurkhas' ethos of being infantrymen first and specialists second ensured that the troops could effectively act as infantrymen when the need arose, as it frequently did.

Men of 28 Squadron, The Queen's Own Gurkha Transport Regiment with their DROPS fuel vehicles in Bosnia. (Gurkha Museum)

Queen's Gurkha Signals satellite communications team in Kosovo. (Gurkha Museum)

A rifle company of 3rd Royal Gurkha Rifles had a particularly tense stand-off. Major James Robinson's A Company had been ordered to verify that the Bosnian Serb Army had moved its air defence weapons from the Vrbas Military Academy near Banja Luka to an IFOR (NATO Intervention Force) approved air defence weapons-storage site. On inspecting Vrbas Academy, Robinson found that the weapons had not been moved as requested and his company prepared to remove them, by force if necessary. The Serbs for their part showed every sign of preparing to fight to retain them. Major Robinson duly reported the situation to Major General Mike Jackson (later General Sir Mike Jackson) commanding the British contingent, who worked out a face-saving solution with the Serb general commanding the Vrbas Military Academy.

The Queen's Gurkha Engineers were also having a busy time when 69 Squadron from Maidstone and elements of 67 Squadron from Hong Kong were rushed to Nepal which was inundated by floods. There, in record time, they built emergency bridging brought in by huge Russian Antonov and American Galaxy transport aircraft. Theirs was a meticulously planned and executed operation in very difficult conditions, carried out in conjunction with Nepalese army engineers.

Even as they were receiving the accolades of Nepalese government and people, in the remote western hills of Nepal Maoist guerrillas were starting their campaign of intimidation and coercion. The Maoists soon gained a following against a background of poor economic conditions and discontent at the failure of democracy to address many areas of social injustice.

At Bisley, where the annual army Skill-at-Arms meetings were held in Britain, Gurkhas continued to dominate. Lieutenant (Queen's Gurkha Officer) Dharmendra Gurung of 6th Gurkha Rifles and later The Royal Gurkha Rifles achieved the then unique distinction of winning the coveted Queen's Medal for the best shot in the Army for the third time.

The 3rd Royal Gurkha Rifles now moved to Brunei, where it amalgamated with the Second Battalion, being replaced in Britain by the First Battalion from Hong Kong, leaving the colony without a Gurkha infantry battalion for the first time in 45 years. As if to right the balance, Headquarters Brigade of Gurkhas, after considerable reorganization, formed two full-strength infantry companies to reinforce The Royal Scots and The Princess of Wales's Royal Regiment, both of which were significantly under strength. This requirement was in addition to a continuing requirement to provide a permanent demonstration company for the Royal Military Academy Sandhurst and a demonstration platoon, soon to be expanded to a company, for the School of Infantry at Brecon in Wales.

The reinforcement companies became a regular feature on the military landscape for some time to come, thereby easing the pressure on the Gurkha rundown and providing much needed additional manpower for the rest of the Infantry. However the next requirement, to provide a parachute-trained company for The Parachute Regiment, was felt by some to be asking a little too much. Here they were proved wrong when Major Simon Gilderson

A Gurkha in Bosnian winter conditions. (C. Schulze)

Men of The Royal Gurkha Rifles training Government soldiers in Sierra Leone. (Gurkha Museum)

Opposite: Joanna Lumley leading the Gurkha protest for right of abode in UK. (Times)

triumphantly brought his fully parachute-trained and qualified Gurkha company into The Parachute Regiment's order of battle. Far from being unable to cope with European soldiering as their detractors had forecast, there seemed there was nothing that Gurkhas could not do given proper training and preparation.

The same held good for the Corps regiments. As if to make a point, Gurkha signallers were flown in to war-torn Angola to provide communications for United Nations peacekeepers and then into Zaire/Congo to provide communications during the evacuation of British nationals.

The British government which came to office after a landslide electoral victory in May 1997 showed from the start a very welcome impression of wanting to give Gurkhas a fair deal and reassure them as to their future within the British Army. It was

A Combat Engineer Tractor of The Queen's Gurkha Engineers. (C. Schulze)

unfortunate that just as this supportive attitude was helping the Brigade overcome all the difficulties of relocation to Britain, a new and vocal Nepalese ex-servicemen's association should be making its presence felt. GAESO (Gurkha Army Ex-Servicemen's Organization), claiming to represent Gurkha ex-servicemen, initiated legal proceedings for Gurkhas, whenever they served, to be given an automatic right to settle in the United Kingdom, and to receive British Army pensions.

To understand the complex issues involved, one has to go back to the Tripartite Agreement of 1947 between Nepal, Britain and India which governed the employment of Nepalese citizens in the British and Indian armies following Indian independence. Among other requirements, the agreement called for similar rates of pay and conditions of service for Gurkhas in both the British and Indian armies. Very soon it became clear that this requirement was impracticable because the cost of living for Gurkha soldiers employed by Britain in Malaya and Hong Kong was far higher than for those serving in India. Rather than renegotiate the whole treaty, Britain simply paid a cost of living allowance over and above the basic Indian pay rate. Pensions, paid after 15 years service, were similar in both armies because both Indian- and British-employed Gurkhas returned to Nepal where the cost of living was not only very low but the same for both. As the years passed, the British Government added incremental pension increases to cover medical treatment and travel, while India gave its pensioners free medical treatment in Indian military hospitals.

As far as pensions were concerned, although the Gurkha soldiers' pension was smaller than the British soldiers' pension, he got it much earlier, after 15 years rather than 22, with those made redundant in the 1990s getting a reduced pension as early as after four years' service, unheard of elsewhere in the British Army. Also, whereas all Gurkhas stayed long enough to get a pension, comparatively few British soldiers did so, mainly for personal reasons. For those British soldiers that did not serve for 22 years, monetary recognition came in the form of a preserved enhanced pension when they were 60 or 65.

***

At the time of writing, the British government through the Ministry of Defence has been prepared to allow Gurkhas serving between 1997 (ie since the return of Hong Kong to China) and 2007 to opt either for British Army pensions or the Gurkha pension scheme. Those retiring after 2007 automatically come on to the British Army pension scheme. In a separate but interlinked decision the Home Office (Immigration Authorities) have granted indefinite leave to remain in United Kingdom (ILA) to all retired Gurkhas who have completed four years' service. This concession allows them to start to qualify for UK citizenship. Under the original Tripartite Agreement there was never this

option, as all Gurkhas were expected to settle in Nepal where the hard currency of their pensions directly benefited Nepal's fragile economy.

The point at issue is that although the previous 15-year Gurkha pension gave, by Nepalese standards, a generous retirement pension to a retired soldier settling in Nepal, it was inadequate for a Gurkha wishing to retire in Britain. In recent times, often because of Maoist threats, many who retired before 1997 had moved or wanted to move to Britain, and this situation predicated the case to allow Gurkhas to settle in the UK and to have their Gurkha pensions upgraded to British ones to finance such a move. These are complicated issues with difficult legal implications. The ruling in April 2009 allowing certain categories of ex-Gurkhas retiring before 1997 to remain in Britain did not end the debate, especially as it was followed by a Government defeat on the issue. Joanna Lumley, the actress and presenter, who had made the Gurkha right of abode cause her own went on to have personal interviews with the Prime Minister as a result of which further concessions on right of abode were announced on 21st May 2009. These included the permanent right of abode in

The Royal Gurkha Rifles mounting guard at Buckingham Palace for the first time.
(Soldier Magazine)

the UK for all who had served in the post-war Brigade of Gurkhas for four years or over as well as their immediate families including all children under eighteen.

The Brigade of Gurkhas were indeed fortunate to have had the steady hand of Colonel David Hayes on the tiller during these momentous days.

Whereas the present controversy centres on right of abode in UK and the upscaling of pensions, soldiers who were made redundant without any pension in the late 1960s and whose plight is explained in Chapter 15 remain the worst affected as they have no pension at all.

Additionally, it should be noted that over the years there have been continual improvements to Gurkha terms and conditions of service (TACOS) so that today they mirror those of their British counterparts. Certain special-to-Gurkha aspects such as free travel to Nepal at the beginning and end of a soldier's service and on compassionate leave are now all that differentiate them. As far as welfare is concerned, The Gurkha Welfare Trust continues to look after our Gurkha ex-soldiers in Nepal, while service charities such as The Soldiers, Sailors, Airmen and Families Association (SSAFA), The Royal British Legion and The Army Benevolent Fund (ABF) increasingly help those in UK.

Importantly these ongoing improvements included permission for Gurkha families to accompany their serving menfolk who, while in Britain, had initially served unaccompanied, then with a proportion getting their families with them and, later, with every married man with over three years service being accompanied. The family is of paramount importance to Gurkhas who still see their wives as being central to family, the guardians of hearth and home, rather than career-seekers.

The unveiling of the Gurkha statue outside The Ministry of Defence, Whitehall.
(Gurkha Museum)

In the past, the overall lower costs of Gurkhas when compared to British soldiers helped to ensure their retention at critical times, such as when their whole future was threatened in 1993. Clearly their newly acquired terms and conditions of service identical to British troops increase their costs, but their 100 per cent retention rate still make them very cost effective when compared with their British counterparts who have a perennially low retention rate, thus necessitating continual re-recruitment and re-training. Overall, their acknowledged effectiveness and full manning now make cost considerations far less significant, but the seemingly unending litigation that now accompanies Gurkha service in itself could constitute a new threat to their attractiveness as soldiers. So much for developments on terms and conditions of service, pensions and immigration between 1997 and 2009. Let us now return to our historical narrative.

2nd Royal Gurkha Rifles with The Queen's Truncheon on parade during the alliance parade with The Royal Brunei Land Force in Brunei on 18th September 1998.
(Gurkha Museum)

Late 1997 was a good time for the erection of some long-overdue memorials to Gurkhas in Britain. In November 1997 a Gurkha Memorial Garden was set up at Sir Harold Hillier's famed gardens near Ampfield in Hampshire. The money for this was generously provided by the Kadoorie Foundation in memory of Sir Horace Kadoorie, a well-known Hong Kong philanthropist who had done much to assist Gurkha ex-servicemen through improvements to their animal breeding stock as well as infrastructural support to their hill villages. Money for the regimental crests carved in Portland stone around a central *chautara* or Nepalese resting place was raised by the regimental associations. The project was coordinated by the Gurkha Museum and the Sir Harold Hillier Gardens as a joint memorial to Sir Horace and The Brigade of Gurkhas. The memorial garden was opened in November 1997 by The Honourable Mrs Rita McAulay, Sir Horace Kadoorie's niece. Now the surrounding plants and shrubs have matured it has become a place of great beauty and tranquillity and is regularly visited by Brigade of Gurkhas members.

Above: Mrs Margeret Neill opens 'Bhanbhagta VC' block, the newly constructed Gurkha training wing at Catterick. To her left is Colonel D. G. Hayes, Colonel Brigade of Gurkhas. Mrs Neill is holding a picture of Bhanbhagta VC. (Gurkha Museum)

Left: Gurkha from 1st Royal Gurkha Rifles on patrol in Kosovo – note the burnt out house in the background reflecting the bitter inter-communal violence. (C. Schulze)

Men of 3rd Royal Gurkha Rifles preparing to deploy by helicopter in the Balkans.

Whereas the Gurkha Memorial Garden is hidden away in the depths of the Hampshire countryside, the Gurkha Memorial Statue occupies a pivotal position opposite the entrance to the Ministry of Defence in Whitehall, London. The statue was based on one of a Gurkha in the Foreign and Commonwealth Office (itself a copy of the Gurkha War Memorial at Gorakhpore in India close to the Nepal border) and was sculpted by Philip Jackson. The site was chosen through the good offices of Field Marshal Lord Bramall who, as Her Majesty's Lord Lieutenant of Greater London, prevailed upon Westminster City Council to make it available.

The large sum of money necessary to fund the project was raised through a public appeal and grants from regimental associations. The project, which was four years in gestation, was steered through by a committee of government and ex-Brigade of Gurkha officers, among whom Brigadier Miles Hunt-Davis, Chairman of the Gurkha Brigade Association, was prominent. The statue was unveiled by Her Majesty The Queen on 3 December

1997, with many Gurkha officers and men present. It bears the final lines from Professor Sir Ralph Turner's famous dictum about Gurkhas (quoted in full in Appendix 10), as well as the names of all major Gurkha units which have served the Crown since 1815, including where they have served.

The year 1999 ended the millennium in dramatic fashion, as matters in the Balkans reached a critical stage. The 5th Airborne Brigade, which included 1st Royal Gurkha Rifles, deployed to Macedonia in June, and after moving to an assembly area near Skopje were preparing to enter Kosovo when its orders were suddenly changed.

The brigade was now ordered to move to Pristina airport, which had been seized by 250 Russian paratroops in a pre-emptive road move designed to show their support for their fellow Serbs. With the overall American NATO Commander ordering General Jackson to retake Pristina by force, the potential for a major conflagration was suddenly apparent, and the world's media closed in.

The 1st Royal Gurkha Rifles and 1st Parachute Regiment were standing by their helicopters on 11 June, ready to deploy to Pristina. As the chronicler of The Royal Gurkha Rifles wryly remarked: 'The gravity of the situation was reinforced when Kate Adie [a well-known BBC trouble-shooting reporter] arrived in her body armour!' Meanwhile General Jackson, understandably reluctant to precipitate a Third World War, demurred from giving the executive order to retake Pristina. While frantic high-level discussion took place in Moscow, Brussels and Washington, the Gurkhas and Paras sweltered in their full battle equipment waiting for the order to go. It never came, and after hours of waiting on tenterhooks, they were stood down.

The same night, 1st Royal Gurkha Rifles were ordered up to the border, where they were opposed by armed Serbian Ministry of Interior Police. In the full glare of the world's media, in a tense and unpredictable situation, they disarmed the police, and The Queen's Gurkha Engineers cleared the mines obstructing the defile leading to Kosovo. Their operation successfully completed, it was now clear for the Kosovo Intervention Force (KFOR), headed by 4th Armoured Brigade, to enter Kosovo. The 1st Royal Gurkha Rifles, having spent an uncomfortable night huddled on the road verge while the whole of KFOR roared through, were flown to Lipljan, southwest of Pristina, where they dominated the area and monitored the disarming of the Kosovo Liberation Army, a task requiring endless patience and a good deal of sang froid.

They also had the responsibility of protecting the Serbs who, having oppressed the Kosovans, were now on the receiving end. Despite continual attempts at armed violence and arson, the Gurkhas kept the peace in a thoroughly professional and fair manner, managing an amazingly complex and volatile situation with calm efficiency. In late August, they were relieved by a Finnish battalion and flown back to Britain with the rest of 5th Airborne Brigade. If people had not heard of Gurkhas before they certainly had now!

Meanwhile, on the other side of the world, Tactical Headquarters and a company group of 2nd Royal Gurkha Rifles in

Soldier from 2nd Royal Gurkha Rifles on patrol in Dili, capital of East Timor, as part of the intervention force (INTERFET). (Gurkha Museum)

Land Rover patrol of 2nd Royal Gurkha Rifles in Dili, East Timor; note heavy Browning machine gun mounted on the Land Rover. (Gurkha Museum)

Brunei found themselves flown to Dili, capital of East Timor, in a joint intervention operation with the Australians designed to restore peace to a shattered and abused island country. The Indonesians had invaded East Timor in 1975 shortly after its colonial rulers, the Portuguese, had left, having giving it independence. Despite having 100,000 of their population murdered by the Indonesians, the armed guerrillas fighting for independence kept resisting the Indonesians until, in 1999, Indonesia agreed to let the East Timorese decide between independence or local autonomy.

Determined that the East Timorese should not seek independence, the Indonesians sponsored violent militias, which included soldiers disguised as militia, to wreak terrible damage on those wishing to vote for independence. Citing a breakdown of law and order, the Indonesian Army (TNI) intervened directly, which led to a withdrawal of United Nations observers and the deployment of an international intervention force (INTERFET), coordinated by the Australians. The 2nd Royal Gurkha Rifles acted as part of INTERFET and on arrival on 19 September immediately deployed into Dili, the war-torn capital of East Timor.

Despite the risk of direct confrontation with the TNI, soon Gurkhas were disarming the militias, cleaning up Dili, removing dead bodies, distributing aid and encouraging terrified householders to return to their homes. As normality returned to the capital, 2nd Royal Gurkha Rifles began to dominate outlying areas where fighting and atrocities were still continuing. With the withdrawal of the Indonesian army, the tension eased and Gurkhas

were able to concentrate more on the humanitarian aspects of the operation, where their natural compassion and cheerful reassurance worked their usual magic spell on the bewildered and terrified population.

This operational deployment from Brunei represented an important milestone in the status of the Brunei-based Gurkha infantry battalion. Hitherto it had been felt that since the Sultan was paying for the battalion, it should not be operationally deployed outside Brunei territory. The East Timor deployment, carried out with the agreement of the Brunei authorities, now created a precedent that left the door open for further operational deployments throughout the area.

The high-profile, swift and successful operations in Kosovo and East Timor carried out by both Royal Gurkha Rifles battalions – as well, in the case of Kosovo, by Gurkha Engineers, Signals and Transport – sent out a clear message to the rest of the Army and the British public and media that Gurkhas could not only cope but were, in terms of speed of reaction and military professionalism, difficult to equal. Clearly the vital ingredient to this success story was the Gurkha soldier himself who had adapted so ably to overcome every challenge. The leadership given to him by his British officers was also an important ingredient. Lieutenant Colonel S.D. Crane commanded 1st Royal Gurkha Rifles in Kosovo and Lieutenant Colonel M.M. Lillingstone-Price commanded 2nd Royal Gurkha Rifles in East Timor.

Sadly, there were also casualties. During a 69 Squadron The Queen's Gurkha Engineers unexploded ordnance-clearing operation in Kosovo, the Brigade suffered its first fatalities when Lieutenant G.J.M. Evans and Sergeant Balaram Rai were killed on 21 June 1999, trying to clear a local school of spent NATO munitions, some of which exploded.

Back in Britain, Gurkha recruit training was about to move to the Infantry Training Wing at Catterick. There a purpose-built block, 'Bhanbhagta VC' block, was fittingly opened by Mrs Margaret Neill, the widow of Colonel D.F. (Nick) Neill, who had been Bhanbhagta's company commander in the Arakan in Burma when he won his Victoria Cross.

After 28 years in Queen Elizabeth Barracks, Church Crookham, the United Kingdom Gurkha battalion was about to move to its new home, Sir John Moore Barracks, Shorncliffe, Folkestone, Kent. Here, under the watchful eye of the project officer, Major G.L. Davies (6th Gurkhas and The Royal Gurkha Rifles), a rather run-down junior leaders' battalion barracks was being transformed into a top-quality Gurkha infantry battalion barracks. As part of the development, Major Davies earmarked a deconsecrated chapel for a visitors' centre. This was developed by the Gurkha Museum to tell the Gurkha story.

Headquarters Brigade of Gurkhas, the coordinating headquarters for all things Gurkha, was itself also on the move to Airfield Camp, Netheravon, Wiltshire. There, in its windswept Portakabins, it continued under, first, Colonel David Hayes and then Colonel William Shuttlewood and then Colonel Hayes again, to oversee the massive changes that were affecting the Brigade of Gurkhas as it established itself in the mainstream of the British Army. As the new Ministry of Defence 'Strategic Defence Review' started to take shape, the welcome requirement for more Gurkhas, rather than fewer or none, became clear, in contrast to the previous 'Options for Change'. Soon plans for increasing Gurkha Corps units by an additional squadron each were being discussed and implemented, while The Queen's Own Gurkha Transport Regiment was to soon change its name to The Queen's Own Gurkha Logistic Regiment to reflect its expanding role in supply and distribution, as well as assuming the responsibility for the provision of Gurkha chefs throughout the Brigade.

More ominously, back in Nepal, the Maoist insurgency was no longer confined to remote areas in the far west but had now spread over virtually the whole of central and western Nepal.

NATO Medal Former Yugoslavia.

Australian International Force East Timor Medal.

CHAPTER NINETEEN

A NEW MILLENNIUM

In 2000 at his annual audience with the King of Nepal, General Sir Sam Cowan, Colonel Commandant Brigade of Gurkhas, was able to report many satisfactory achievements and developments. These included operational successes in Kosovo, East Timor and Sierra Leone, as well as organizational increments in the form of the addition of second squadrons to all the Corps units and the continued requirement for three Gurkha reinforcement companies for the rest of the British infantry.

The King, Birendra Bir Bikram Shah Dev, by now had a number of concerns to contend with. The Maoist insurgents now controlled almost all the outlying areas of Nepal with the government secure only in Kathmandu and the larger towns. As yet the 70,000-strong Royal Nepalese Army had not been deployed against the Maoists, but it was becoming increasingly clear that the armed police were incapable of resolving the situation. The King, to whom the Army was absolutely loyal, was reluctant to see it deployed, fearing an escalation of violence. By nature a conciliator, he desperately wanted a peaceful solution. Additionally he was only too aware that the Maoists represented, in part at least, widespread popular disillusion with political parties who had promised so much and delivered so little. The King had perhaps been correct in distrusting the suitability of Western-style democracy for Nepal. Nepalese politicians seemed not to comprehend the principle of public service without personal

King Gyanendra Bir Bikram Shah Dev – the last King of the ancient Shah dynasty whose short reign ended in abdication in 2008. (Gurkha Museum)

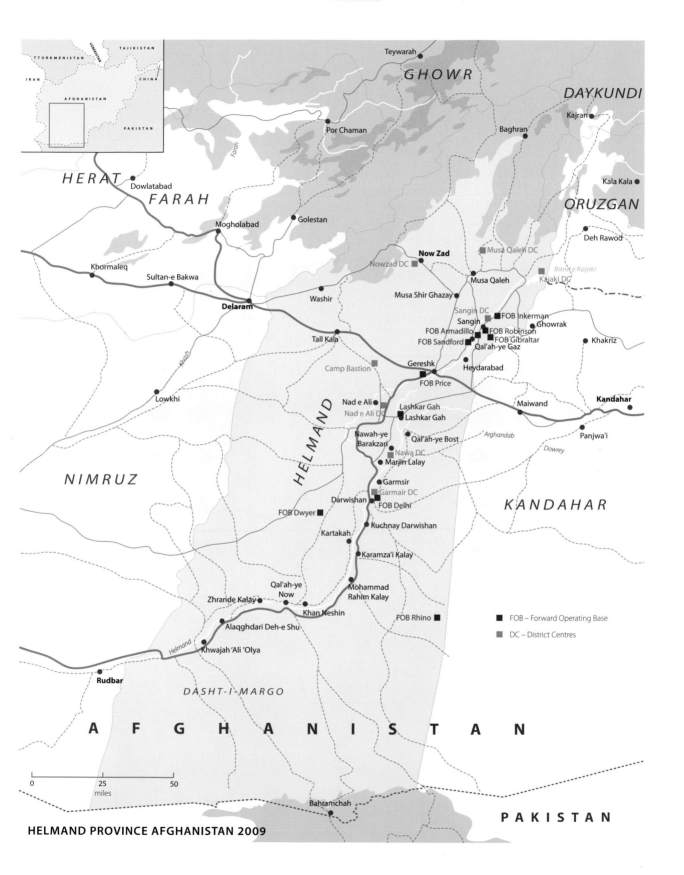

HELMAND PROVINCE AFGHANISTAN 2009

■ FOB – Forward Operating Base

▨ DC – District Centres

advantage, with the result that there appeared to many to be an unfortunate mix of inefficiency, continual bickering and the suspicion of venality; all of which tended to play into the hands of the Maoists.

Brigade of Gurkhas ex-servicemen living in the hills now found themselves the target for Maoist extortions and threats on the basis that, because of their pensions, they were able to pay. More and more of them, fearful of the Maoists, left the hills and sought the comparative safety of the towns. In their absence, the Maoists simply levied accumulative fines payable on pain of death which effectively meant that they could never return. In the towns, although safe from the Maoists, the ex-servicemen were open to GAESO 'fundraising'.

As the Maoist threat increased, so tourism, Nepal's biggest foreign-currency earner, began to dry up. It was against this deteriorating situation that disaster unfolded. On 1 June 2001, the Crown Prince, Dipendra, armed with a variety of automatic weapons, shot dead his father and mother and nine other royal relations at a family get-together. He then shot himself. He technically ruled Nepal for two days in a brain dead coma before dying. Dipendra's reason for this mass murder appeared to be his parents' opposition to his marriage to a half-Indian girl. It seemed that he was affected by drink and drugs at the time and used the weapons lent him by the army to evaluate since he was keen on all things military.

The murdered King Birendra was succeeded by his brother Gyanendra who, fortunately for himself, had been away in the country at the time and thus not at the family gathering. Later his detractors were to insinuate that he had some foreknowledge of what was to take place on 1 June, but in retrospect that would seem to be most unlikely.

King Birendra had been a very popular monarch and had embodied national conceptions of rightful grandeur and semi-divinity. He was felt to be sensitive to Nepal's problems and to have a genuine concern for its citizens. Gyanendra appeared a much more assertive personality, not averse to using what powers he had as he felt appropriate. His son, Paras, was widely disliked as being brash and arrogant and was said to have been involved in the death of a popular Nepalese female film star. Gyanendra was not slow to show his power when in October 2002, he sacked the elected government and, taking power, ruled through a succession of administrations appointed by himself. At the same time he deployed the Army in an all-out campaign to defeat the Maoists. King Gyanendra may have been encouraged to take this hard-line approach following 9/11, reasoning that America and Britain

would be bound to support his fight against the Maoists, given their own war on terror. If so, he miscalculated.

On 5 November 2002 a very symbolic act took place when, for the first time in its short history, The Royal Gurkha Rifles had the honour of presenting The Queen's Truncheon to Her Majesty The Queen. It had been presented five times to Her Majesty by the 2nd Gurkhas, the first time being in 1953 shortly after The Queen's coronation, but this was the first time for their successor regiment. After each royal presentation a commemorative silver band is added.

All in The Brigade of Gurkhas were deeply shocked by the murder of King Birendra, but life had to go on and the Brigade, by now a key element in the deployable strength of the Army, was soon on the move. Elements of 1st Royal Gurkha Rifles were deployed from Brunei to Sierra Leone on Operation 'Silkman' (late 2001) which was designed to disarm warring elements and then, having brought them together into a unified command structure, train them to a reasonable level of proficiency – a task 2nd Royal Gurkha Rifles had already been involved in. D Company of 1st Royal Gurkha Rifles was charged with protecting the International Military Advisory and Training Team while Support Company got on with the actual training; something of a challenge when the students, who had been running around with lethal weapons for years, had no concept of an aimed shot! As ever in this sort of situation, Gurkhas did a first-class job, showing compassion and sensitivity but standing no nonsense from anybody.

Just back from Operation 'Silkman' in sunny Sierra Leone, 2nd Royal Gurkha Rifles were deployed to the bitter Balkan winter on Operation 'Palatine' as part of a battle group including Household

A Queen's Gurkha Engineer in Iraq constructing a P.O.W. cage.

Opposite: Prince Charles, Colonel in Chief of The Royal Gurkha Rifles inspects The Queen's Truncheon. (Soldier Magazine)

Reinforcement Company with 2nd Battalion The Parachute Regiment (2 PARA) having handed back all its special-to-arm equipment was preparing for its disbandment parade when it was deployed at short notice with its parent battalion on Operation 'Bessemer' in Macedonia in the Balkans. Here internecine war between Albanian rebels and the Macedonian authorities was threatening to break out. The battle group's task was to guard the specialist teams relieving the Albanians of their weapons and to generally maintain security. This the Gurkhas did with their customary firmness and good humour (despite being fired at during some close confrontations with recalcitrant rebels) and succeeded in collecting over 3,300 weapons, including a T-55 tank.

On return to Britain, the Gurkha Parachute Company again prepared for its disbandment parade after handing in all equipment. Suddenly it was warned to accompany 2 Para to Afghanistan and frantically redrew its equipment and started training on new equipment such as the Minimi machine gun and

Operation Fingal, deployment to Afghanistan. Gurkha officer from C (Gurkha) Company The Parachute Regiment next to the gravestone of Major John Cook VC of the 5th Gurkhas. (Gurkha Museum)

Cavalry equipped with Scimitar tracked armoured vehicles and Royal Artillery equipped with the new self-propelled AS 90 guns. In Bosnia they took over security in the British area of operations as well as that of the departing Czech contingent. This involved patrolling to dominate the area and confiscating illegally held weapons, as well as reassuring the war-torn locals. A measure of their success was that by the end of their tour of duty, they had collected in over 2,000 weapons and half a million rounds of ammunition. Concurrent with military duties, the battalion found time for several 'hearts and minds' projects, including helping build hospitals and refurbish schools, as well as providing security for the safe distribution of the new Euro currency.

Since British Army recruiting appeared to be improving, the Ministry of Defence had decided to phase out the three Gurkha reinforcement companies. The parachute-trained Gurkha

Personal Role Radios. Given their ability to communicate linguistically with the Afghans, one platoon of Gurkhas was attached to each company of 2 PARA which now started to patrol the capital Kabul, as well as organising training courses for the Afghan Army. The training courses were visited by important dignitaries, including the immaculately dressed Hamid Karzai, leader of the interim Afghan administration. Despite random shooting incidents, Afghan conceptions of discipline, and earth tremors during lessons, the training was adjudged to be a considerable success. Time was also found to visit some of the sites around Kabul where Gurkhas had fought and died in years gone by, including the grave of Major John Cook, 5th Royal Gurkha Rifles (FF), who won a Victoria Cross in the Second Afghan War. This remarkable company of Gurkha parachutists eventually disbanded on 25 May 2002.

Meanwhile the Corps units were equally occupied on operational deployments: The Queen's Gurkha Engineers and The Queen's Own Gurkha Logistic Regiment in Kosovo, where the latter was required to drive and maintain a bewildering variety of vehicles in sub-zero conditions, and Queen's Gurkha Signals in Sierra Leone and, in 2004, in Kosovo. Whereas ten years ago one campaign medal would have been rare to see, now, given the

Top: Men of C (Gurkha) Company The Parachute Regiment reinforcement company bundling captured weapons in Macedonia. (Gurkha Museum)

Left: General Sir Hew Pike greets men of C (Gurkha) Company The Parachute Regiment reinforcement company. (Gurkha Museum)

Next page: Operation Telic, the invasion of Iraq, a soldier of D (Gurkha) Company with 1st Royal Irish. (Gurkha Museum)

frequency of National and NATO medal issues, most soldiers had three or more.

In March 2003, a number of Gurkha units took part in the Coalition invasion of Iraq. D (Gurkha) Company, the reinforcement company with 1st Battalion The Royal Irish Regiment, was preparing to disband when it was warned to accompany its parent battalion on Operation 'Telic', the invasion of Iraq. After a training period in Wales, Gurkha Company accompanied 1st Royal Irish to Kuwait, crossing the border into Iraq on 21 March 2003. Their first task was to secure the vital oilfields at Rumailah and ensure there were no enemy forces still in the area, as well as conducting vehicle checkpoints around the periphery of Basra. The Gurkhas and their comrades were then ordered to push on up the River Euphrates to El Medina and Al Amarah, following the footsteps of their predecessors 87 years before. There, in spite of harassment and abuse, by continual patrolling they restored order and stopped looting. By the time the Gurkhas left three months later, they had instilled sufficient confidence in the local police to be able to conduct joint patrols with them. On return to Britain they disbanded and the personnel returned to their parent units.

The 69th Field Squadron of The Queen's Gurkha Engineers was also deployed to Iraq where, among other area tasks, they built blast-proof protection for the Kuwaiti port of Shaiba, a 200-bed military hospital, a small-arms range and prisoner-of-war cages for the large number of Iraqi prisoners. The 70th Support Squadron, some elements of which had been deployed to Afghanistan, was now redeployed to Iraq where it joined 69th

Men of The Queen's Gurkha Engineers using their Rough Terrain Tractor to good effect in Iraq. (Gurkha Museum)

Squadron in construction tasks. The newly reformed 246th Squadron of Queen's Gurkha Signals also moved to the area, where it provided the communications for the final preparatory joint service exercise before the invasion and, once the war had started, rear-link communications back to Britain, two vital, technically sophisticated and high-profile tasks. The only Gurkha operational unit to have taken part in the Gulf War of 1991, 28 Transport Squadron was extensively employed in the build-up phase and subsequent operations of Operation Telic.

Although the three reinforcement companies had now come to an end, the requirement to re-raise third squadrons in Queen's Gurkha Signals and The Queen's Own Gurkha Logistic Regiment, as well as the additional Gurkha manning requirement to staff a Jungle Warfare School in Brunei, kept the overall Gurkha strength constant at 3,100 and the recruit intake steady at 230 a year.

With the Maoist insurrection now paralyzing life in the hills and provincial towns, recruiting became a hazardous undertaking fraught with continual threats and harassment. The Chief Recruiting Officer, Lieutenant Colonel Adrian Griffiths, and accompanying staff were kidnapped and their fate for some time was in doubt. However with great coolness they prevailed upon the Maoists to release them and went on with their tasks, thus ensuring that the recruits kept coming in, representing as they did the Brigade's lifeblood.

King Gyanendra, having taken personal control of the country and dispensed with even an appointed government, unleashed the full strength of the Army on the Maoists with inconclusive results. Some 15,000 people, many totally innocent, were said to have been killed in this upsurge of fighting between the Army and the Maoists. Finally in January 2003, a shaky ceasefire was negotiated but broke down in August of the same year, with fighting soon renewed. The King, having instigated a raft of repressive measures, including the imprisonment of politicians and the closing down of mobile phone and computer networks, found himself increasingly alienated from his own people and at odds with his natural allies in Britain and America.

On top of requirements for the invasion of Iraq, the tensions in former Yugoslavia demanded continual tours of duty in that troubled area. The 1st Royal Gurkha Rifles were back in Bosnia in early 2004 and, just as their tour of duty was ending, B Company and Tactical Headquarters were rushed to Kosovo where serious fighting had again broken out between Kosovan and Albanian Serbs. As ever, unfazed by the bitter ethnic tensions, the Gurkhas restored calm, arrested troublemakers, collected in weapons and restored public confidence.

Immediately before them, from June until December 2003, A (Gallipoli) Company, the Gurkha reinforcement company with 1st Highlanders (now The Highlanders, 4th Battalion The Royal

'C' Company 1st Royal Gurkha Rifles removing captured weapons in extreme weather conditions on Operation Commercial in Bosnia. (Gurkha Museum)

Regiment of Scotland) was deployed to Bosnia where it carried out patrols, cordons and searches for illegal weaponry, seizing three buried howitzers and some 30 tons of ammunition. It also provided security for the visit of the Pope; no mean task given the number of illegally held ground-to-air missiles and the willingness of some locals to use them. At the conclusion of their tour, A (Gallipoli) Company was the last of the three Gurkha reinforcement companies to be disbanded.

The negotiations and accompanying litigation that accompanied the various changes in Gurkha terms and conditions of service involved Headquarters Brigade of Gurkhas in a huge amount of extra work. Colonel W.F. Shuttlewood was retiring to run the Gurkha Welfare Trust and Colonel D.G. Hayes, who had originally handed over the Headquarters job to Colonel

Shuttlewood, was to take up the reins there again in 2004. For Colonel Hayes to do the same job twice was unusual, but had the great advantage of continuity, allowing someone who totally understood all the complicated issues and could provide expert advice to ministers and the Ministry of Defence.

Since 1994 General Sir Sam Cowan had been Colonel Commandant Brigade of Gurkhas and had piloted the Brigade through very choppy waters with wisdom and moral courage. In June 2003 he handed over to Lieutenant General Philip Trousdell (later Sir Philip Trousdell), who had commanded 48th Gurkha Infantry Brigade in Hong Kong before becoming General Officer Commanding in Northern Ireland. Trousdell was also Colonel of The Queen's Own Gurkha Logistic Regiment, so in every way was a very suitable successor.

A montage of The Band of The Brigade of Gurkhas by Alix Baker showing their new badge which was finally approved in 2002. (Gurkha Museum)

The Band of The Brigade of Gurkhas plays in the National Stadium in Kabul, Afghanistan. (Gurkha Museum)

Whereas the Gurkha Welfare Trust had been set up specifically to help Gurkhas in Nepal, a new scheme was needed to help Gurkhas settling in UK. This is being done through existing service charities, particularly the Army Benevolent Fund, the Royal British Legion, and the Soldiers, Sailors and Airmen and Families Association.

Aware of all the changes and improvements to their terms and conditions of service over this period, Gurkhas continued to serve with distinction in many theatres but increasingly in Afghanistan, where the American-led NATO deployment strove to back the Afghan government, at the same time as combating a resurgent Taliban and a still-menacing Al-Qaeda. The level of fighting continued to spiral upwards in intensity as 2nd Royal Gurkha Rifles were to discover when they were deployed in autumn 2003, having only just arrived in Brunei from Britain.

They were given three separate tasks to carry out, all very demanding. The first was for training assistance to the Afghan National Army which Major F.M. Lawrence coordinated. Since

the Afghans had a completely different concept of discipline, weapon safety and general soldierly behaviour, initial impressions were of 'a mission impossible'. However as Major Lawrence touchingly wrote:

During my time away from Regimental Duty I had forgotten, however, just how rewarding our Gurkhas can be to work with. Humour, an innate sense of what is achievable, and an irrepressible desire to succeed are just some of the characteristics that make them special. The gauntlet had been thrown down and we were going to surpass every expectation.

This they certainly did, 'leaving the Americans, Afghans and other coalition forces in Afghanistan in no doubt that the Royal Gurkha Rifles were the most professional soldiers that they had or would ever come across.'

Commanded initially by Lieutenant I.N.A. Thomas and then by Lieutenant Colonel I.A. Rigden, 2nd Royal Gurkha Rifles

A member of a Gurkha training team with the Afghan army in 2005.

quickly settled down to their other two key tasks; those of providing the Kabul Patrols Company and the Provisional Reconstruction Team.

The Kabul Patrols Company task was given to C Company 2nd Royal Gurkha Rifles, initially commanded by Major F.J. Rea, later by Major M.H. Reedman, and this company was augmented by two platoons of British Territorials, initially from The West Midlands Regiment and then from The Rifle Volunteers. Almost as soon as they arrived, they were handed a complicated snatch operation to catch a well-known terrorist who had long evaded capture. Skilfully conducted, the operation was a success and sent a clear message to friend and foe alike that the Gurkhas had arrived.

For the next six months, through increasingly bitter weather conditions, C Company kept up a relentless pressure on Afghan terrorists despite being continually subjected to rocket attacks and

explosive devices, one of which caught a Rifle Volunteers platoon, killing one and wounding several others. During this time the Gurkhas carried out several successful snatch operations, removing very dangerous terrorists from circulation as well as much of their weaponry. As importantly, they instilled growing confidence in the civil population who implored them not to leave.

The Provisional Reconstruction Team (PRT) manned by 2nd Royal Gurkha Rifles was one of 12 deployed across Afghanistan. Their task was to improve the general stability of the region by keeping the lid on the Taliban and promoting confidence in the Afghan government. A fairly tall order for 51 (later 70+) Gurkhas. The PRT was deployed in Military Observer Teams (MOT) of five in two Land Rovers, accompanied by an interpreter and a medical orderly. They would be led by a British or Gurkha officer or senior Gurkha non-commissioned officer and would patrol out into their province, which was the size of Scotland, for ten days at a time. In the event these teams found their main task to be to try and stop serious internecine warfare between heavily armed rival warlords.

The main confrontation appeared to be between two well-known warlords who, having fought the Taliban, were now preparing to fight each other with the not inconsiderable weaponry at their disposal. The MOTs, with considerable courage, would interpose themselves between the opposing factions and, having given a clear picture of what was happening to their superior headquarters, then attempt to negotiate local 'ceasefires'. In this they were generally successful, although occasionally they had to request overflights by ground-attack aircraft to convince the Afghans that they meant business. As a result of their negotiating skills and cool courage, local 'ceasefires' were turned into a general 'ceasefire', thereby saving considerable bloodshed and dispersion of effort from the main task of fighting the Taliban. Heavy weapons were also removed under the supervision of MOTs and collected into designated dumps under coalition control.

Operating in some of the remotest and wildest areas of Afghanistan, the PRTs would search out areas of community life that would most benefit from local support schemes, including infrastructural assistance, and then put such help in hand. Given the volatile nature of the situation and the historical hazards of working with Afghans, it was no wonder that the Gurkhas in the PRT felt a definite sympathy with their forebears who had played Kipling's Great Game. As their Officer Commanding Major J.C. Murray wrote: '*I have noted that Gurkhas have a real cultural empathy with Afghans and they and us like what we see.*'

While 2nd Royal Gurkha Rifles were heavily involved in Afghanistan for a demanding six-month tour, 1st Royal Gurkha Rifles were back in the Balkans covering both Bosnia and Kosovo, the first infantry battalion to attempt to maintain security over such a wide geographical area. Here the demands on them were becoming ever more complicated, with the tracking down of war criminals and profiteers becoming reliant on the confiscation of computer hard drives and credit card histories. However the modern Gurkha was up to this kind of demand and soon successful arrests were being made.

Soon they would need all their resourcefulness as the role in Afghanistan intensified.

The Iraq Medal.

NATO Medal Kosovo.

CHAPTER TWENTY

INTO BATTLE

Although the Brigade had been involved in a numerous campaigns in recent times, none of them, even the Falklands, had actually involved hand-to-hand fighting. In fact, for actual infantry combat one would have to go back to the Borneo campaign of the 1960s, some 40 years before.

All this was about to change in Afghanistan where so many of the Gurkhas' forebears had fought and died. Like so many past armies, the NATO coalition were finding that it was easier to get into Afghanistan than to get out and also that the Taliban, far from being beaten, were getting more aggressive and formidable by the day as their strength was augmented by co-religionists and like-minded fighters from many other countries.

As far as Gurkhas were concerned, the first intimation of a much higher tempo of operations in Afghanistan was the deployment of D (Tamandu) Company of The Royal Gurkha Rifles to Afghanistan in April 2006. This company was specially formed as a Gurkha reinforcement company for 16th Air Assault Brigade during their deployment to Afghanistan on Operation 'Herrick 4', forming up in Sir John Moore Barracks, Shorncliffe, in January 2006. Personnel for the company came from both battalions of The Royal Gurkha Rifles and even included some Gurkha soldiers just out of recruit training in Catterick. Initially its commander was Major J.C. Murray, followed by Major Dan Rex.

Royal Gurkha Rifles rifleman as part of the international force in Afghanistan. (Gurkha Museum)

Royal Gurkha Rifles deployed on operations in Afghanistan. (Gurkha Museum)

On arrival in Afghanistan, D Company went to Camp Bastion in the barren terrain of the Dasht-e Margo or 'Desert of Death', deep in Taliban country (see map page 245). Initially the company's task was to hold Camp Bastion, the new British base in Helmand Province, under the direct command of 7th (Parachute) Regiment Royal Horse Artillery and soon the Gurkhas settled into a routine of surveillance, guards and patrols in the searing heat and dust. In May the company received orders to send one of its platoons to Now Zad and another to Sangin, both towns and districts far to the northeast, to support 3rd Battalion The Parachute Regiment (3 PARA) by relieving its C Company, while the third platoon commanded by Lieutenant P.R. Hollingshead were tasked to provide an outer cordon to a 3 PARA cordon-and-search operation.

The platoon at Sangin under Warrant Officer Class 2 Trilochan Gurung was initially deployed out of its base to assist, if necessary, with the deployment of the Kandak Battalion of the Afghan National Army (ANA), and then redeployed some six kilometres (4 miles) east of Sangin to a small position called Combat Outpost Robinson. Once there, the Gurkhas were immediately tasked with providing protection for a mixed team of

Royal Artillery and Afghan Army which was going to recover the remains of an unmanned spy plane that had crashed, hopefully before the Taliban could get to it. Finding that in fact the Taliban had got there first, on return they themselves were ambushed by a large group of Taliban and a gunner was wounded. Fighting its way out of the ambush, the Gurkha platoon secured a helicopter landing site and oversaw the safe evacuation of the casualty before darkness fell. During the night the Gurkhas were repeatedly attacked by the Taliban, but successfully holding them off, were relieved at dawn by a quick-reaction force from 3 PARA. This successful little action represented the heaviest infantry combat the Brigade had experienced for 40 years; there was plenty more to come.

Very soon after, the same platoon, still under command of Warrant Officer 2 Trilochan Gurung, became involved in another battle when it went to the rescue of a patrol which had suffered two killed at the hands of the Taliban. Told to move to a point east of Sangin, the Gurkhas were then to link up with the beleaguered patrol and help extricate it. As they approached the rendezvous they came under very heavy Taliban fire and were forced to stop and go into all-round defence, one of their Land Rovers being destroyed. Warrant Officer 2 Trilochan then called for artillery and air support but, despite receiving both, it was three hours before repeated attacks by missile-firing Apache attack helicopters forced the Taliban to withdraw and allowed 12 Platoon to make contact with the patrol and extricate it and the two casualties back to safety.

Caught in a very difficult situation, Warrant Officer 2 Trilochan Gurung's leadership, allied to skilled and swiftly executed battle procedures and effective and prompt artillery and air support, saved them from what could have been a disastrous situation.

Meanwhile the remainder of D Company were at Now Zad, some 65 kilometres north of Camp Bastion, where Number 11 Platoon had relieved Number 10 Platoon in the District Centre. Now Zad, which was surrounded by mountains, consisted of a typical Afghan bazaar with its warren of narrow alleyways, high-walled compounds and mudbrick houses. Through the town north to south ran a single metalled road. The District Centre itself lay to the southwest of Now Zad and consisted of a 200-metre square compound containing an office building, a mosque, a prison and an accommodation block. It was overlooked by a hill one kilometre to its south known as ANP (Afghan National Police) Hill which was routinely occupied by Afghan soldiers of doubtful allegiance. The compound itself was protected by six sandbagged *sangars* and D Company had its operations centre in the central office building which was topped by an observation tower. Grouped with D Company, presently reduced to Company Headquarters and Number 11 Platoon, were 20 ANA soldiers of dubious loyalty under Captain Bartholomew and his training team from the Black Watch (3rd Battalion The Royal Regiment of Scotland), an air controller, a medical officer, a Royal Electrical and Mechanical Engineers vehicle mechanic and a military policeman.

Corporal Nagen Rai waves goodbye from a helicopter after completing a six-month tour of duty in Northern Helmand. (Times)

Gurkhas of The Royal Gurkha Rifles coming under fire in Helmand province, Afghanistan. (Gurkha Museum)

Soon after taking over, D Company noticed a significant change in the pattern of behaviour in Now Zad. The normally busy bazaar became quiet and locals started to leave the town. It became clear that the Taliban were infiltrating into the town and preparing to attack the district centre and ANP Hill. From 12 to 22 July, D Company was under prolonged and heavy attack by the Taliban by day and night, despite repeated protective air strikes by American A10 ground-support aircraft. Apart from the reinforcement of ANP Hill by two 81mm mortars and two machine guns from 2nd Battalion Royal Regiment of Fusiliers, this small garrison, otherwise unreinforced, beat off continual rocket, mortar and small arms attacks by day and night, inflicting significant casualties on the Taliban for the cost of three wounded in D Company.

In August and September 2006, D Company provided the infantry component for joint armoured, artillery and infantry Mobile Outreach Groups, not dissimilar in concept to the Long Range Desert Group in the Western Desert during the Second World War. The aim was to conduct long-range patrols into the north of Helmand Province. These patrols tried to disrupt and interdict the Taliban and so stop them attacking the district centres, as well as reassuring the local Afghan population. The Taliban in turn strove to ambush and mine the patrols. Number 12 Platoon,

A member of 2nd Royal Gurkha Rifles Provincial Reconstruction Team, Northern provinces, Afghanistan. (Gurkha Museum)

still under Trilochan Gurung, had several brushes with the Taliban on these patrols, thus disrupting attacks on security forces in the district centres. When D Company was relieved in Afghanistan in early October 2006, it had probably seen more continuous action than the Brigade had experienced since 1945. Throughout

Tracking Training Course, Labi Jungle Reserve, Brunei. (Gurkha Museum)

traditional Gurkha martial qualities had asserted themselves; qualities that were well noted by both friend and foe.

★★★

When Lieutenant General Sir Philip Trousdell made his annual report to King Gyanendra in 2005, probably neither he nor the King realized that it was to be the last such meeting and that the 2006 report would be to the veteran Prime Minister Giriprasad Koirala. The King had played a very high-risk strategy in dissolving his government, imprisoning ministers and ruling by decree. Analogies with Charles I of England do not seem too far-fetched and the end result was not dissimilar. Had all these and many other repressive measures resulted in the defeat of the Maoist insurrection, then the ends may have justified the means and the king would have kept his crown. As it was the Royal Nepalese Army was unable to defeat the Maoists and a military stalemate resulted with both army and Maoists resorting to reciprocal atrocities, so that life in the hill villages became a living nightmare as army and Maoists alike visited vengeance killings on mainly innocent civilians.

By spring 2006, the King had been obliged to release the politicians and hand back power to them and they in turn negotiated a United Nations-supervised ceasefire with the Maoists, a condition of which was the inclusion of the Maoists in Government. Since the Maoists had always insisted on the abdication of King Gyanendra, the days were clearly numbered for both the 250-year-old monarchy and for Gyanendra himself, the 12th in its line. The insistence on the Colonel Commandant's traditional speech to the throne being given to the prime minister was but one manifestation of the removal of the monarchy. Other more obvious signs were the deletion of 'Royal' from the title of the

28 Squadron The Queen's Own Gurkha Logistic Regiment deploy by RAF helicopter to the Iraq / Iran border on Operation Vedette. (Gurkha Museum)

army and the national airline and the dropping of the loyal toast at dinners and other gatherings.

Early in 2008, the Nepalese Parliament voted by a large majority to abolish the monarchy and in July 2008, Nepal officially became a republic; 'Mr Shah', as he had now become, kept his head, but lost his crown and most other privileges. These developments were deeply unsettling for the Brigade, but at least the ten-year civil war in Nepal was over and all looked forward to the return of some sort of normality in their homeland.

The adoption of British terms and conditions of service, while conferring many advantages, also brought some problems and anomalies. The difficulty in the British infantry was to retain soldiers, with many leaving after only four or five years' service, a continual haemorrhaging of trained manpower. With Gurkhas the problem would be quite the opposite, with all wanting to serve to the maximum of 22 years. Clearly if the Brigade was to retain a balanced age rank structure this would be impossible, so what was to happen to those that were no longer needed? Obviously, one solution was for them to go as individuals to British units that were under strength. This however would conflict with the previously oft-stated principle that Gurkhas should only serve in formed

Gurkhas from Mandalay Company, the Gurkha Demonstration Company, with the Infantry Battle Centre in Wales fight floods in Tewkesbury in June 2006. (Gurkha Museum)

During the 150th Anniversary of the Siege of Delhi at RMA Sandhurst, a painting by Jason Askew of an action during the siege was presented by the President of The Sirmoor Club to The Colonel of The Royal Gurkha Rifles. Left to right: The artist, Jason Askew, Lieutenant General Sir Peter Duffell, President of The Sirmoor Club, Lieutenant General Peter Pearson, Colonel of The Royal Gurkha Rifles and Field Marshal Sir John Chapple. (Gurkha Museum)

Gurkha units. If, on the other hand, they were prematurely forcibly discharged, then they would have no pension until they reached the age of 65 so arguably would have been better off with a Gurkha pension after 15 years.

Adoption of British terms and conditions of service also meant the loss of the Queen's Gurkha Officer (QGO) rank and its substitution by the Late Entry Commission of four years in the rank of captain. The old QGO commission, which had its roots in the Viceroy's Commission of the old British-Indian Army, traditionally provided all the lieutenants to command infantry platoons. If the Late Entry Commission started at captain, where would all the platoon commanders come from? The backbone of a British unit was its Warrant Officers' and Sergeants' Mess, while that of a Gurkha had always been the Queen's Gurkha Officers' Mess. Now that the QGO commission was no more, where would the power lie? At the time of writing it is too early to answer these questions, but indications are that these changes have made the Gurkha infantry battalions far more like their British counterparts, in the same way as Gurkha Corps units had already become.

Before finally adopting British terms and conditions of service, in the spirit of the Tripartite Agreement it was necessary to consult closely with the Nepalese Government As a result of these negotiations five principles which safeguard the Brigade's structure in law were enshrined:

a. *Only Nepalese citizens should be recruited into the Brigade with the exception of British Direct Entry (DE) Officers required as part of the officer structure.*

b. *The recruiting and selection of new Gurkha recruits should take place in Nepal.*

c. *Gurkhas should serve only in formed Gurkha units, at least for a minimum mandatory period of five years.*

d. *The command structure in formed Gurkha units should continue to include Gurkha (Nepalese) officers.*

e. *Current arrangements for separate appropriate initial training for Gurkhas should continue for the time being.*

In 2007 Lieutenant General Sir Philip Trousdell handed over as Colonel Commandant Brigade of Gurkhas to General Sir David Richards, and in him the Brigade was again very fortunate. Although a Gunner rather than a Gurkha, he had commanded Gurkhas in East Timor, Sierra Leone and most recently in Afghanistan, and had struck up a strong rapport with them, which was warmly reciprocated.

Soon his genuine interest and conscientiousness made him a well-known, popular and much respected Colonel Commandant, whose distinguished service now included Commander-in-Chief Land Command, the top operational job in the Army. This was followed by that of the professional head of the Army, Chief of the General Staff (CGS) in August 2009. There would continue to be many internal problems for the Brigade to sort out, but in General Sir David Richards it had just the right person to oversee their resolution.

While the centre of operational focus shifted to Afghanistan, Gurkhas were enduring some very tough conditions in Iraq where the British presence in Basra was coming under ever increasing pressure by the Shiite militias. Here, Queen's Gurkha Signals and The Queen's Own Gurkha Logistic Corps units had been continuously deployed on repeated short tours. Continually harassed by mortar, machine gun and sniper fire, they set enviably high specialist standards in particularly hazardous circumstances. For the Gurkha logistic drivers delivering stores or recovering broken-down vehicles, the threat from ambush and explosive devices laid on the roads was particularly acute, and resulted in continual woundings and fatalities among their predecessors. However by never lowering their guard and keeping alert at all times, they were able to repeatedly return from Iraq with the same number of men as they set out with.

The Queen's Gurkha Signals were additionally tasked with the key responsibility of providing secure communications for the British military headquarters in Baghdad. Initially some doubt was expressed as to whether they would be up to such a vital task.

*Colour Sergeant Kajiman Yakso of B (Gallipoli) Company, 2nd Royal Gurkha Rifles in South Kohistan, Afghanistan, during Operation Mandalay as part of the Provincial Reconstruction Team. (*Soldier *magazine)*

69 Squadron The Queen's Gurkha Engineers preparing to deploy to Afghanistan. (Gurkha Museum)

General Sir Sam and Lady Cowan say farewell to his regiment Queen's Gurkha Signals as his tour as the first Colonel Commandant Brigade of Gurkhas comes to a close. (Gurkha Museum)

The doubters need not have worried, for in a few days everyone was saying that the standard of communications had never been bettered.

The 1st Royal Gurkha Rifles deployed to Afghanistan on Operation 'Herrick 7' in September 2007. The battle group was accompanied by 69 Squadron The Queen's Gurkha Engineers, Queen's Gurkha Signals rear-link detachment and The Queen's Own Gurkha Logistic Regiment drivers and cooks. It was given two distinct assignments, with the bulk of the force forming Regional Battle Group South, covering the provinces of Kandahar, Uruzgan, Zabul and Helmand, while B Company, arriving later, was detached under command of the Household Cavalry Regiment to Garmsir, also in Helmand.

Since the Royal Gurkha Rifles battle group had relieved only a company-strength force, greater numbers allowed it to be more aggressive and proactive, constituting a flexible manoeuvre force

Gurkhas from A (Gallipoli) Company, 1st Battalion, The Highlanders searching for hidden weapons in Bosnia. (Gurkha Museum)

Queen's Gurkha Engineers in Iraq on Operation Telic. (Gurkha Museum)

rather than simply being tied down to defending district centres. Additionally the battle group had access to an awesome variety of supporting weaponry, including artillery, light armoured vehicles, fighter ground attack and missile-firing helicopters; all would be needed.

Their tasks were the traditional complementary ones of defeating the Taliban and winning the hearts and minds of the local people. On arrival from Brunei, the Gurkhas were immediately given the task of pushing into the notorious 'Green Zone' flanking

Gurkha vehicle patrol from The Queen's Own Gurkha Logistic Regiment guarding distribution points in Iraq.

the River Helmand between Gereshk and Sangin. The Taliban immediately reacted with improvised explosive devices, killing a Royal Engineer.

The main attack on the Taliban in the area started with a feint by the Warrior armoured vehicles of 1st Battalion The Scots Guards which suppressed Taliban fire allowing two companies of Gurkhas, led by a Queen's Gurkha Engineer bridging party, to cross a wide canal and enter the 'Green Zone' undetected. At dawn they started to clear Taliban-held villages and were soon coming under sniper fire. This they suppressed using fire and manoeuvre and calling in air strikes. Once the Taliban had been cleared out of the villages, the Gurkhas could then concentrate on reassuring the locals, which they attempted to do over the next ten days. However without a permanent presence, the Taliban would always return. Of this action the Commanding Officer, Lieutenant Colonel Jonny Bourne, wrote:

When I addressed the battalion the afternoon before we broke into the 'Green Zone' I was struck by the veil of apprehension evident

on almost all of the faces looking back at me. This was entirely understandable; for the majority this was the first time they were going to be in combat. By the end of the operation many had been in contact and had prevailed, they had seen comrades go down but successfully evacuated and all had witnessed the benefits of their various training. There was a real buzz as we gathered up the force for recovery to Kandahar airfield.

Sadly 1st Royal Gurkha Rifles were to suffer their only operational fatality on the move back to Kandahar when an improvised explosive device set off under a Land Rover killed Major Alexis Roberts, a talented and popular officer who during his time as an instructor at the Royal Military Academy Sandhurst had His Royal Highness Prince William as a cadet in his platoon. He left behind not only saddened comrades but a wife and young family.

B Company, which had arrived a month later, now moved to their outpost at Garmsir, while the rest of the battalion prepared to assist the Dutch contingent in a clearance operation in the Baluchi valley flanked by steep mountains. In this area the Taliban had been

Gurkha recruits Passing Out Parade at The Infantry Training Centre, Catterick.

very active, destroying police posts and generally making life difficult for security forces. Determined to gain surprise, the battalion deployed by helicopter to the rear of Kala Kala, one of the disputed villages, the landing zone having been secured in advance by the Australian Special Air Service (SAS). Having achieved surprise, the Gurkhas were able to keep the initiative despite a strong Taliban reaction. Sadly, in one of the resultant firefights, an Australian SAS sergeant was mortally wounded despite his being recovered under fire by Gurkhas. Their brave and immediate rescue attempt endeared them to the Australians, who had fought on so many occasions alongside Gurkhas.

Once the attack had been successfully concluded, much of the Taliban infrastructure was uncovered, including a medical facility and a defensive bunker system. Reassured, the villagers started to return. The Gurkha's ability to move on foot carrying all his needs, to live off the land, to communicate with the locals and be a formidable fighter were all adding to his reputation as each day passed.

With very little time for rest and reorganization, 1st Royal Gurkha Rifles were again deployed, this time to the Chernatu valley, where the Taliban had a stronghold. Pretending they were simply reinforcing the incumbent Dutch garrison, once night fell they struck off into the mountains and after a gruelling climb came in to the rear of the Taliban position, so surprising the insurgents that they pulled out without a fight. It had been a textbook operation brilliantly executed and proved the old adage of 'Sweat saves blood'.

Gurkha from The Gurkha Police Contingent, Singapore Police, guarding a high-risk location. (Gurkha Museum)

Gurkha recruits visit the British War Cemetery at Ypres where many of their forefathers lie. (Gurkha Museum)

Next, A Company was flown up to the key area of Sangin where the Taliban were reported to be massing. Under cover of darkness the company fanned out, meeting the enemy attack head on. The resultant battle went on for some ten hours and a number of Gurkhas were wounded, but the Taliban were successfully thwarted.

Meanwhile, C Company was deployed to help a Canadian operation west of Kandahar and got into some hard fighting with the Taliban, who were eventually shifted by a combination of outmanoeuvring and air strikes. As the area became stabilized, it was possible to construct police posts and generally pacify the area where much evidence of Taliban activity was found, including bomb-making equipment. As a result of this joint operation, a close working relationship was formed with the Canadians which was later recognised by a Canadian Defence Citation. A subsequent clearance operation led to a Land Rover being blown up and one Gurkha losing a leg and two others being badly injured.

As winter set in the weather became bitterly cold, but 1st Royal Gurkha Rifles continued to carry the battle to the Taliban who increasingly avoided them, allowing the Gurkhas to concentrate on restoring confidence in the local population so

long cowed by the Taliban. In an operation near the site of the disastrous Battle of Maiwand during the Second Afghan War, a Chinook helicopter carrying Gurkha assault troops hit the ground hard on landing, injuring several. The momentum however was sustained and another successful foray into what had been Taliban-dominated territory completed.

At Garmsir, B Company was grouped with artillery and armoured vehicles of The King's Royal Hussars, to whom The Royal Gurkha Rifles are affiliated and with whom Gurkhas had long historical connections stretching back to the Battle of Medicina in 1945. This force was under continual fire from the Taliban and life was very hazardous. His Royal Highness Prince Harry was with B Company acting as an Air Control Officer from December 2007 to February 2008 bringing down air strikes on the Taliban. He made the point that he always felt very safe with Gurkhas, a feeling shared by generations of British officers about their soldiers. Determined not to simply hunker down in the face of continual incoming fire, B Company mounted clearance operations, thereby extending the area controlled and forcing the Taliban further and further away from the perimeter, thus reducing the effectiveness of their fire.

Working unafraid for peace. A British officer of The Royal Gurkha Rifles in Afghanistan. (The Royal Gurkha Rifles)

At the end of their time in Afghanistan, 1st Royal Gurkha Rifles had firmly re-established the Gurkha fighting reputation, which for so many years had lain dormant on the far-flung borders of Hong Kong, proving without any doubt that the present-day Gurkha was in no way less brave or aggressive than his predecessors. He was however much more skilled – he had to be if he was to master the complex weaponry and communications of 21st century warfare.

The fact that the Gurkha has successfully done all that has been asked of him in regard to technological advance, but not lost his traditional qualities of hardiness, courage and fortitude is his great and lasting achievement, be he infantryman, sapper, signaller or logistician. During their six-month deployment in Afghanistan, 1st Royal Gurkha Rifles had shown that with first-class leadership and utilizing to the greatest degree the innate toughness of the Gurkha soldier, it was possible to beat the Taliban at his own game, whatever the terrain or climatic conditions. The Gurkhas' ability to carry huge loads over inhospitable terrain enabled the battalion

to surprise the Taliban time after time and thereby tilt the operational balance in favour of the coalition forces. These achievements were not lost on either friend or foe, and many were the accolades from coalition partners and the rest of the British Army.

Very soon after the return of the 1st Battalion from Afghanistan, 2nd Battalion The Royal Gurkha Rifles (Lieutenant Colonel Chris Darby) deployed to Helmand province. Soon after deployment, 2RGR was involved in high intensity operations involving heavy weapons used to break into Taliban strongholds which had previously remained undisturbed. The first major operation was called Operation Mar Nono 1 from 4–5 November 2008. This was a major attack using a range of armoured vehicles into the Dagyan area and, while 5 Platoon (Lieutenant Oli Cochrane) of B Company (Major Ross Daines) was manoeuvring in the open, fire was opened on them by hidden Taliban and Rifleman Yubraj Rai hit. He was recovered under heavy fire but tragically died, the first ethnic Nepalese to be killed in action in

Keeping cheerful whatever is round the corner, Afghanistan. (The Royal Gurkha Rifles)

Afghanistan. The attack however proceeded and on finally taking the enemy positions, blood trails were found indicating that the Taliban had suffered casualties. Also bomb-making equipment was recovered. A subsequent operation, Mar Nono 2, was carried out into the Green Zone to interdict Taliban ambushes placed between areas mined with improvised explosive devices. This time a large deception force was used to convince the Taliban that it was the main force and so fix them in place. Meanwhile a mixed force of 2nd Royal Gurkha Rifles and the Afghan Army approached on a circuitous route by night so taking the Taliban by surprise. This attack, again led by B Company, met with complete success and not only evicted the Taliban from their heavily fortified positions, but also led to the subsequent capture of a number of high-profile Taliban commanders. Sadly a second Gurkha was killed in the course of these operations when Colour Sergeant

Krishnabahadur Dura, Officer Commanding the 2nd Royal Gurkha Rifles sniper platoon, was killed when the Warrior armoured vehicle he was travelling in was blown up by a Taliban improvised explosive device.

★★★

Further to the south in southern Helmand province, D Company group (Major Jody Davis) was tasked with advancing into Taliban-held areas to deal with selected targets and to neutralize areas rendered untenable by improvised explosive devices. In a joint operation with B Company 1st Battalion The Rifles, they advanced into a heavily defended Taliban area and, having baulked

Lieutenant Colonel Jonny Bourne addresses members of 1st Royal Gurkha Rifles shortly after arrival in Afghanistan. (The Royal Gurkha Rifles)

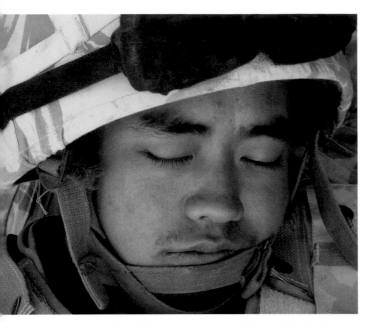

A moment of welcome oblivion during operations in Afghanistan. (The Royal Gurkha Rifles)

with villagers, something at which Gurkhas proved themselves particularly adept.

★★★

While operations continued in Afghanistan, as ever with The Brigade of Gurkhas, the sword of Damocles continued to sway precariously on its frail thread, threatening its continued existence in various ways. The recent Prime Minister of Nepal, Pushpa Kamal Dahal or Prachendra 'The Fierce One', erstwhile leader of the Maoists, has gone on record as stating his intention to end all foreign employment of Nepalese citizens, including Gurkha soldiers. India of course has far more Gurkhas than Britain, some 33 battalions, but many of her Gurkhas come from Gurkha stock domiciled in India so the effect on them would be less marked. Also some 450,000 other young Nepalese men and women work abroad, mainly in the Middle East. It may well be that with the recent resignation of Prachendra, the realties of office for his successor and stern economic imperatives will demand a more realistic policy.

a Taliban counter-attack by saturating the area with fire, a team led by Lieutenant Crawley went in and painstakingly identified a whole complex of interconnected improvised explosive devices, all of which were subsequently destroyed, thus allowing unfettered access to the area with the resultant withdrawal of the Taliban.

As operations of this type continued, 2nd Battalion Royal Gurkha Rifles were able to maintain a defensive 'envelope' of territory from which Taliban influence was removed and local people could once more return to tend their fields and livestock without continual harassment from the insurgents. To achieve this between 8 November 2008 and 30 March 2009, no fewer than 206 Taliban attempts to break in to the 'envelope' had to be thwarted, thus wresting the initiative away from the Taliban. The initiative once held by the Gurkhas was maintained by continual forays into Taliban-held areas outside the securely held 'envelope'. As ever in these type of operations, it was vital that military success was accompanied by winning back the hearts and minds of local Afghans. This was achieved in the main by Major Toby Jackman's Fire Support Company, which carried out a vital reconstruction role combined with psychological reassurance, liaison and the gathering and collating of intelligence.

As 2nd Battalion The Royal Gurkha Rifles' efforts within the coalition improved the security situation, so normality returned with the re-emergence of Afghan government, education and justice – all of which had ceased under Taliban depredations. Reassurance of the local population had to be continually worked at by a variety of measures which required constant interaction

Operational Service Medal (Afghanistan).

'Under their watchful eye...' (The Royal Gurkha Rifles)

Gurkha ability to recruit is the opposite to ethnic British under-recruitment and has led to a recent requirement for up to four Gurkha reinforcement companies to be re-raised. However in raising such companies, Colonel Commandant Brigade of Gurkhas, General Sir David Richards, has been emphatic that they are to be deployed as formed bodies under their own officers, which has always been part of the Brigade 'credo'. This top level endorsement of how the Brigade operates and deploys has provided tremendous reassurance at a time when so much of the Brigade is on active service.

The first of these reinforcement companies, 'F' Company made up from men of The Royal Gurkha Rifles, has recently deployed to Afghanistan with 19 Light Brigade. Within a short time of arrival, it had suffered its first fatality as a result of an improvised explosive device detonated in a busy market square, which killed 18 people, including two soldiers, one a Gurkha. To paraphrase Turner's historic words 'Their unwavering lines continue to disappear into the smoke and wrath of battle.'

For the present however we can leave Britain's Gurkhas as an integral and much valued and respected part of the British Army, having successfully overcome all the many and often high hurdles in their path from 1948 to the present day. That they have managed to achieve this is mainly due to the amazing determination of the individual Gurkha to succeed at all costs and against all odds.

Jai Gurkha!

GLOSSARY OF TERMS

CHAPTER ONE

Nagri – Nepali script.

CHAPTER TWO

Swami – Holy One or religious mendicant.

CHAPTER THREE

Shikari – Nepalese for 'hunter of game'.

Plus ca change – First part of French saying 'Plus ça change, plus ça la même chose' (The more things change the more they stay the same). Used now to denote 'no change in practice despite the lapse in time'.

Chota peg – Indian Army expression to denote a measure of alcohol.

Kshatriya – The traditional Brahmin warrior class of Nepal drawn from the direct descendants of the Rajputs who fled India for Nepal to escape the Mogul invasion.

Kiranti – The hill tribes of East Nepal.

CHAPTER FOUR

Panji – Sharpened bamboo stake which when laid in lines provided a formidable barrier. Alternately it could be placed at the bottom of camouflaged pits where it made a deadly booby trap.

CHAPTER FIVE

Kalo pani – literally 'black water'. Nepal being completely landlocked at the time of the First World War, few Gurkhas would have ever seen the sea.

CHAPTER SIX

Dum dum – A bullet that has had its tip cut off thus making it expand on impact, causing far more serious wounding than a normal bullet.

CHAPTER SEVEN

Status quo ante – The situation as it existed before, in this case before the First World War.

Unzeroed – Zeroing is a process whereby rifles and other weapons are test fired on a range to assess their accuracy and altered to fit the individual firer's aim pattern.

Desi – Term used by Gurkhas to describe Indians.

Contra mundum – Literally 'Against the world'.

Khud – Nepali meaning 'steep hillside'.

Rakshi – Nepali term for strong home brewed spirit made from millet for the best brew, rice or maize for rougher but equally powerful concoctions.

Sarkar – Nepalese term to describe the British Indian Government.

CHAPTER EIGHT

Urdu – The Indian language used throughout the British Indian Army.

Nepali – The language of the Nepalese used throughout The Brigade of Gurkhas after 1947 with its written form being romanized for ease of use.

CHAPTER NINE

Sangar – A fortification made of piled stones or boulders. Often erected in rocky areas where the ground is too hard for trench digging.

Schu mine – Type of German anti-personnel mine housed in a wooden box to avoid finding by mine detectors. It invariably blew off the leg of anybody unfortunate enough to tread on it.

Kangaroo – Sherman tank turned into armoured personnel carrier by removal of turret.

CHAPTER TWELVE

Dhal – Gravy made from lentils.

Chapatti – Unleavened bread.

Lantana – A thickly growing spiny shrub with a distinctive odour.

Umbrage – 'Taking Umbrage' – A colloquial expression of the forties and fifties meaning 'taking offence'.

CHAPTER THIRTEEN

Parang – Long slashing knife used throughout Malaysia and Indonesia

Goondahs – Murderous gangs found in the slums of Calcutta and other Indian cities.

ORBAT – Army abbreviation for 'order of battle'.

CHAPTER SEVENTEEN

Glasnost – Openness.

Laisser faire – Leaving matters to take their own course.

CHAPTER EIGHTEEN

Apres moi le deluge – Literally 'After me the flood'. Famously used by General de Gaulle on his resignation in disgust at French politics after the war.

Status quo ante – A return to the situation existing before any particular event.

Chautara – Stone resting places found throughout the hills of Nepal traditionally shaded by a Banyan and a Pepul tree.

CHAPTER TWENTY

Bazaar – Term used throughout the Indian subcontinent to describe a market or shopping area.

Credo – Belief or article of faith.

(Photo opposite by kind permission of Major Robin Adshead)

CHANGES IN TITLES OF GURKHA REGIMENTS

SPELLINGS OF REGIMENTAL TITLES:

In the early days there was little general agreement on the correct transliteration of words and place names from the local dialects, and much of it was phonetic. This led to a number of variations in spelling in the titles of regiments (e.g. Nusseree/Nusseri; Huzara/Hazara), and none more so than in that of 'Gurkha'. In its earliest form it is found spelt 'Gorka', followed, at various times, by 'Goorkah', 'Goorka' or 'Goorkha'.

In 1891 the form 'Gurkha' was adopted as the official spelling to be used in British service and still remains as such. The Indian Army, after Independence in 1947, adopted the official spelling 'Gorkha' for the regiments in its service to conform to the spelling used in Nepal. The spelling of the titles in this Appendix reflects those in current use at the time shown.

1ST KING GEORGE V'S OWN GURKHA RIFLES (THE MALAUN REGIMENT)

1815	1st Nusseree Battalion
1823	6th, 1st Nusseri (Gorkha) Battalion
1824	6th, 1st Nusseri Battalion
1826	4th, 1st Nusseri Battalion
1830	4th Nusseree Battalion
1845	4th Nusseree (Rifle) Battalion
1850	66th, or Goorka, Regiment, of Native Infantry
1851	66th Regiment of Native Infantry (Goorkas)
1857	66th or Goorka Regiment
1858	66th or Goorka Light Infantry
1861	11th Regiment, Native Infantry
1861	1st Goorkha Regiment
1886	1st Goorkha Light Infantry
1891	1st Gurkha (Rifle) Regiment
1901	1st Gurkha Rifles
1903	1st Gurkha Rifles (The Malaun Regiment)
1906	1st Prince of Wales's Own Gurkha Rifles (The Malaun Regiment)
1910	1st King George's Own Gurkha Rifles (The Malaun Regiment)
1937	1st King George V's Own Gurkha Rifles (The Malaun Regiment)
1947	Remained in Indian Army

2ND KING EDWARD VII's OWN GURKHA RIFLES (THE SIRMOOR RIFLES)

1815	Sirmoor Battalion
1823	8th, Sirmoor (Gorka) Battalion
1824	8th, Sirmoor Battalion
1826	6th, Sirmoor Rifles
1845	6th, Sirmoor (Rifle) Battalion
1850	Sirmoor (Rifle) Battalion
1852	Sirmoor Battalion
1858	Sirmoor Rifle Regiment
1861	17th Regiment, Native Infantry
1861	2nd Goorkha (The Sirmoor Rifle) Regiment
1876	2nd (Prince of Wales' Own) Goorkha Regiment (The Sirmoor Rifles)
1886	2nd (Prince of Wales's Own) Goorkha Regiment (The Sirmoor Rifles)
1891	2nd (Prince of Wales' Own) Gurkha
1901	2nd (Prince of Wales' Own) Gurkha (Rifle) Regiment (The Sirmoor Rifles)
1901	2nd Gurkha Rifles (Prince of Wales' Own) (The Sirmoor Rifles)
1903	2nd Prince of Wales' Own Gurkha Rifles (The Sirmoor Rifles)
1906	2nd King Edward's Own Gurkha Rifles (The Sirmoor Rifles)
1936	2nd King Edward VII's Own Gurkha Rifles (The Sirmoor Rifles)
1948	2nd King Edward VII's Own Gurkha Rifles (The Sirmoor Rifles) The Gurkha Regiment
1948	2nd King Edward VII's Own Gurkha Rifle (The Sirmoor Rifles) The Brigade of Gurkhas
1950	2nd King Edward VII's Own Gurkha Rifles (The Sirmoor Rifles)
1994	Amalgamated to form The Royal Gurkha Rifles

3RD QUEEN ALEXANDRA'S OWN GURKHA RIFLES

1815	Kemaoon Battalion
1816	Kemaoon Provincial Battalion
1823	9th, Kemaoon Battalion
1826	7th, Kemaoon Battalion
1850	Kemaoon Battalion
1861	18th Regiment, Native Infantry
1861	3rd Goorkha (The Kemaoon Regiment)
1864	3rd (Kumaon) Goorkha Regiment
1887	3rd Goorkha Regiment
1891	3rd Gurkha (Rifle) Regiment
1901	3rd Gurkha Rifles
1907	3rd The Queen's Own Gurkha Rifles
1908	3rd Queen Alexandra's Own Gurkha Rifles
1947	Remained in Indian Army

4TH PRINCE OF WALES's OWN GURKHA RIFLES

1857	Extra Goorkha Regiment
1861	19th Regiment, Native Infantry
1861	4th Goorkha Regiment
1891	4th Gurkha (Rifle) Regiment
1901	4th Gurkha Rifles
1924	4th Prince of Wales's Own Gurkha Rifles
1947	Remained in Indian Army

5TH ROYAL GURKHA RIFLES (FRONTIER FORCE)

1858	25th Punjab Infantry or Huzara Goorkha Battalion
1861	7th Regiment of Infantry (or Hazara Goorkha Battalion), Punjaub Irregular Force
1861	5th Goorkha Regiment (The Hazara Goorkha Battalion) attached to the Punjaub Irregular Force
1886	5th Goorkha Regiment, The Hazara Goorkha Battalion
1887	5th Goorkha Regiment
1891	5th Gurkha (Rifle) Regiment
1901	5th Gurkha Rifles
1903	5th Gurkha Rifles (Frontier Force)
1921	5th Royal Gurkha Rifles (Frontier Force)
1947	Remained in Indian Army

6TH QUEEN ELIZABETH'S OWN GURKHA RIFLES

1817	The Cuttack Legion
1822	Rungpore Local Battalion
1823	Rungpoor Light Infantry
1823	10th, Rungpoor Light Infantry
1826	8th, Rungpoor Light Infantry
1828	8th, Rungpore Light Infantry
1828	8th, Assam Light Infantry
1844	8th, 1st Assam Light Infantry Battalion
1850	1st Assam Light Infantry Battalion
1861	46th (1st Assam) Light Infantry
1861	42nd (Assam) Light Infantry
1864	42nd (Assam) Regiment of Bengal Native (Light) Infantry
1885	42nd (Assam) Regiment of Bengal (Light) Infantry
1886	42nd Regiment, Goorkha (Light) Infantry
1889	42nd (Goorkha) Regiment of Bengal (Light) Infantry
1891	42nd Gurkha (Rifle) Regiment of Bengal Infantry
1901	42nd Gurkha Rifles
1903	6th Gurkha Rifles
1948	6th Gurkha Rifles, The Gurkha Regiment
1948	6th Gurkha Rifles, The Brigade of Gurkhas
1950	6th Gurkha Rifles
1959	6th Queen Elizabeth's Own Gurkha Rifles
1994	Amalgamated to form The Royal Gurkha Rifles

7TH DUKE OF EDINBURGH'S OWN GURKHA RIFLES

1902	8th Gurkha Rifles
1907	7th Gurkha Rifles
1948	7th Gurkha Rifles, The Gurkha Regiment
1948	7th Gurkha Rifles, The Brigade of Gurkhas
1950	7th Gurkha Rifles
1959	7th Duke of Edinburgh's Own Gurkha Rifles
1994	Amalgamated to form The Royal Gurkha Rifles

8TH GURKHA RIFLES

1st Battalion

1824	16th or Sylhet Local Battalion
1826	11th or Sylhet Local Battalion
1827	11th or Sylhet Local Infantry
1861	48th (Sylhet) Light Infantry
1861	44th (Sylhet) Light Infantry
1864	44th (Sylhet) Light Infantry
1885	44th (Sylhet) Regiment of Bengal (Light) Infantry
1886	44th Regiment Goorkha (Light) Infantry
1889	44th (Goorkha) Regiment of Bengal (Light) Infantry
1891	44th Gurkha (Rifle) Regiment of Bengal Infantry
1901	44th Gurkha Rifles
1903	8th Gurkha Rifles
1907	Became 1st Battalion, 8th Gurkha Rifles

2nd Battalion

1835	Assam Sebundy Corps
1839	The Lower Assam Sebundy Corps
1839	1st Assam Sebundy Corps
1844	1st Assam Sebundy Regiment
1844	2nd Assam Light Infantry Battalion
1861	47th (2nd Assam) Light Infantry
1861	43rd (Assam) Light Infantry
1864	43rd (Assam) Regiment of Bengal Native (Light) Infantry
1885	43rd (Assam) Regiment of Bengal (Light) Infantry
1886	43rd Regiment Goorkha (Light) Infantry
1889	43rd (Goorkha) Regiment of Bengal (Light) Infantry
1891	43rd Gurkha (Rifle) Regiment of Bengal Infantry
1901	43rd Gurkha Rifles
1903	7th Gurkha Rifles
1907	2nd Battalion, 8th Gurkha Rifles

Both Battalions

1947	Remained in Indian Army

9TH GURKHA RIFLES

1817	Fatehgarh Levy
1818	Mynpoory Levy
1823	1st Battalion, 32nd Regiment of Bengal Native Infantry
1824	63rd Regiment of Bengal Native Infantry
1861	9th Regiment of Bengal Native Infantry
1885	9th Regiment of Bengal Infantry
1893	9th Gurkha (Rifle) Regiment of Bengal Infantry ~
1901	9th Gurkha Rifles
1947	Remained in Indian Army

10TH PRINCESS MARY'S OWN GURKHA RIFLES

1766	14th Battalion of Coast Sepoys
1767	The Amboor Battalion
1769	11th Carnatic Battalion
1770	10th Carnatic Battalion
1784	10th Madras Battalion
1796	1st Battalion, 10th Regiment Madras Native Infantry
1824	10th Regiment Madras Native Infantry
1885	10th Regiment, Madras Infantry
1890	10th (Burma) Regiment of Madras Infantry
1891	10th Regiment (1st Burma Battalion) of Madras Infantry
1892	10th Regiment (1st Burma Rifles) of Madras Infantry
1895	10th Regiment (1st Burma Gurkha Rifles) Madras Infantry
1901	10th Gurkha Rifles
1948	10th Gurkha Rifles, The Gurkha Regiment
1948	10th Gurkha Rifles, The Brigade of Gurkhas
1950	10th Princess Mary's Own Gurkha Rifles
1994	Amalgamated to form The Royal Gurkha Rifles

11TH GURKHA RIFLES

1918	11th Gurkha Rifles
1922	Disbanded
1948	Re-raised in The Indian Army

THE ROYAL GURKHA RIFLES

1994	The Royal Gurkha Rifles

THE QUEEN'S GURKHA ENGINEERS

1948	Royal Engineers Gurkha
1954	Gurkha Royal Engineers
1955	Title changed to 50 Field Engineer Regiment RE
1955	Gurkha Engineers
1960	The Gurkha Engineers
1977	Queen's Gurkha Engineers
1977	The Queen's Gurkha Engineers

QUEEN'S GURKHA SIGNALS

1948	Royal Signals Gurkha
1954	Gurkha Royal Signals
1955	Gurkha Signals
1977	Queen's Gurkha Signals

THE QUEEN'S OWN GURKHA LOGISTIC REGIMENT

1958	Gurkha Army Service Corps
1965	The Gurkha Transport Regiment
1992	The Queen's Own Gurkha Transport Regiment
2001	The Queen's Own Gurkha Logistic Regiment

GURKHA MILITARY POLICE

1949	Royal Military Police (Gurkha Regiment)
1957	Gurkha Military Police
1965	Disbanded.

BATTLE HONOURS AND BADGES OF GURKHA REGIMENTS

Note: Those regiments that remained as part of the Indian Army, post-August 1947, have been shown as having battle honours up to that date only, ie won while serving the British Crown.

1ST KING GEORGE V'S OWN GURKHA RIFLES (THE MALAUN REGIMENT)

Bhurtpore, Aliwal, Sobraon, Afghanistan 1878-80, Tirah, Punjab Frontier, Givenchy 1914, Neuve Chapelle, Ypres 1915, St Julien, Festubert 1915, Loos, France and Flanders 1914-15, Megiddo, Sharon, Palestine 1918, Tigris 1916, Kut-al-Amara 1917, Baghdad, Mesopotamia 1916-18, North-West Frontier, India 1915, 1917, Afghanistan 1919, Jitra, Kampar, Malaya 1941-42, Shenam Pass, Bishenpur, Ukhrul, Myinmu Bridgehead, Kyaukse 1945, Burma 1942-45.

2ND KING EDWARD VII'S OWN GURKHA RIFLES (THE SIRMOOR RIFLES)

Bhurtpore, Aliwal, Sobraon, Delhi 1857, Kabul 1879, Kandahar 1880, Afghanistan 1878-80, Tirah, Punjab Frontier, La Bassée 1914, Festubert 1914-15, Givenchy 1914, Neuve Chapelle, Aubers, Loos, France and Flanders 1914-15, Egypt 1915, Tigris 1916, Kut-al-Amara 1917, Baghdad, Mesopotamia 1916, 1918, Persia 1918, Baluchistan 1918, Afghanistan 1919, El Alamein, Mareth, Akarit, Djebel el Meida, Enfidaville, Tunis, North Africa 1942-43, Cassino I, Monastery Hill, Pian di Maggio, Gothic Line, Coriano, Poggio San Giovanni, Monte Reggiano, Italy 1944-45, Greece 1944-45, North Malaya, Jitra, Central Malaya, Kampar, Slim River, Johore, Singapore Island, Malaya 1941-42, North Arakan, Irrawaddy, Magwe, Sittang 1945, Point 1433, Arakan Beaches, Myebon, Tamandu, Chindits 1943, Burma 1943-45.

3RD QUEEN ALEXANDRA 'S OWN GURKHA RIFLES

Delhi 1857, Ahmed Khel, Afghanistan 1878-80, Burma 1885-87, Chitral, Tirah, Punjab Frontier, La Bassée 1914, Armentieres 1914, Festubert 1914, 1915, Givenchy 1914, Neuve Chapelle, Aubers, France and Flanders 1914-15, Egypt 1915-16, Gaza, El Mughar, Nebi Samwil, Jerusalem, Tell, Asur, Megiddo, Sharon, Palestine 1917-18, Sharqat, Mesopotamia 1917-18, Afghanistan 1919, Deir el Shein, North Africa 1940-43, Monte della Gorgace, Il Castello, Monte Farneto, Monte Cavallo, Italy 1943-45, Sittang 1942, Kyaukse 1942, Imphal, Tuitum, Sakawng, Shenam Pass, Bishenpur, Tengnoupal, Meiktila, Defence of Meiktila, Rangoon Road, Pyawbwe, Pegu 1945, Burma 1942-45.

4TH PRINCE OF WALES'S OWN GURKHA RIFLES

Ali Masjid, Kabul 1879, Kandahar 1880, Afghanistan 1878-80, Waziristan 1895, Chitral, Tirah, Punjab Frontier, China 1900, Givenchy 1914, Neuve Chapelle, Ypres 1915, St Julien, Aubers, Festubert 1915, France and Flanders 1914-15, Gallipoli 1915, Egypt 1916, Tigris 1916, Kut-al-Amara 1917, Baghdad, Mesopotamia 1916-18, North-West Frontier, India 1917, Baluchistan 1918, Afghanistan 1919, Iraq 1941, Syria 1941, The Cauldron, North Africa 1940-43, Trestina, Monte Cedrone, Italy 1943-45, Pegu 1942, Chindits 1944, Mandalay, Burma 1942-45, Bishenpur, Shwebo.

5TH ROYAL GURKHA RIFLES (FRONTIER FORCE)

Peiwar Kotal, Charasiah, Kabul 1879, Kandahar 1880, Afghanistan 1878-80, Punjab Frontier, Helles, Krithia, Suvla, Sari Bair, Gallipoli 1915, Suez Canal, Egypt 1915-16, Khan Baghdadi, Mesopotamia 1916-18, North-West Frontier, India 1917, Afghanistan 1919, The Sangro, Caldari, Cassino 11, Sant'Angelo in Teodice, Rocca d'Arce, Ripa Ridge, Femmina Morte, Monte San Bartolo, The Senio, Italy 1943-45, Sittang 1942, 1945, Kyaukse 1942, Yenangyaung 1942, Stockades, Buthidaung, Imphal, Sakawng, Bishenpur, Shenam Pass, The Irrawaddy, Burma 1942-45.

6TH QUEEN ELIZABETH'S OWN GURKHA RIFLES

Burma 1885-87, Helles, Krithia, Suvla, Sari Bair, Gallipoli 1915, Suez Canal, Egypt 1915-16, Khan Baghdadi, Mesopotamia 1916-18, Persia 1918, North-West Frontier, India 1915, Afghanistan 1919, Coriano, Santarcangelo, Monte Chicco, Lamone Crossing, Senio Floodbank, Medicina, Gaiana Crossing, Italy 1944-45, Shwebo, Kyaukmyaung Bridgehead, Mandalay, Fort Dufferin, Maymyo, Rangoon Road, Toungoo, Sittang 1945, Chindits 1944, Burma 1942-45.

7TH DUKE OF EDINBURGH'S OWN GURKHA RIFLES

Suez Canal, Egypt 1915, Megiddo, Sharon, Palestine 1918, Shaiba, Kut-al-Amara 1915, 1917, Ctesiphon, Defence of Kut-al-Amara, Baghdad, Sharqat, Mesopotamia 1915-18, Afghanistan 1919, Tobruk 1942, North Africa 1942, Cassino I, Campriano, Poggio del Grillo, Tavoleto, Montebello Scorticata Ridge, Italy 1944, Sittang 1942, 1945, Pegu 1942, Kyaukse 1942, Shwegyin, Imphal, Bishenpur, Meiktila, Capture of Meiktila, Defence of Meiktila, Rangoon Road, Pyawbwe, Burma 1942-45, Falkland Islands 1982.

9TH GURKHA RIFLES

Bhurtpore, Sobraon, Afghanistan 1879-80, Punjab Frontier, La Bassée 1914, Armentieres 1914, Festubert 1914, 1915, Givenchy 1914, Neuve Chapelle, Aubers, Loos, France and Flanders 1914-15, Tigris 1916, Kut-al-Amara 1917, Baghdad, Mesopotamia 1916-18, Afghanistan 1919, Djebel el Meida, Djebel Garci, Ragoubet Souissi, North Africa 1940-43, Cassino I, Hangman's Hill, Tavoleto, San Marino, Italy 1943-45, Greece 1944-45, Malaya 1941-42, Chindits 1944, Burma 1942-45.

8TH GURKHA RIFLES

Burma 1885-87, La Bassée 1914, Festubert 1914, 1915, Givenchy 1914, Neuve Chapelle, Aubers, France and Flanders 1914-15, Egypt 1915-16, Megiddo, Sharon, Palestine 1918, Tigris 1916, Kut-al-Amara 1917, Baghdad, Mesopotamia 1916-17, Afghanistan 1919, Iraq 1941, North Africa 1940-43, Gothic Line, Italy 1943-45, Coriano, Santarcangelo, Gaiana Crossing, Point 551, Imphal, Tamu Road, Bishenpur, Kanglatongbi, Mandalay, Myinmu Bridgehead, Singhu, Shandatgyi, Sittang 1945, Burma 1942-45.

10TH PRINCESS MARY'S OWN GURKHA RIFLES

Amboor, Carnatic, Mysore, Assaye, Ava, Burma 1885–87, Helles, Krithia, Suvla, Sari Bair, Gallipoli 1915, Suez Canal, Egypt 1915, Sharqat, Mesopotamia 1916–18, Afghanistan 1919, Iraq 1941, Deir ez Zor, Syria 1941, Coriano, Santarcangelo, Senio Floodbank, Bologna, Sillaro Crossing, Gaiana Crossing, Italy 1944–45, Monywa 1942, Imphal, Tuitum, Tamu Road, Shenam Pass, Litan, Bishenpur, Tengnoupal, Mandalay, Myinmu Bridgehead, Kyaukse 1945, Meiktila, Capture of Meiktila, Defence of Meiktila, Irrawaddy, Rangoon Road, Pegu 1945, Sittang 1945, Burma 1942–45.

11TH GURKHA RIFLES
Afghanistan 1919

THE ROYAL GURKHA RIFLES

Amboor, Carnatic, Mysore, Assaye, Ava, Bhurtpore, Aliwal, Sobraon, Delhi 1857, Kabul 1879, Kandahar 1880, Afghanistan 1878-80, Burma 1885-87, Tirah, Punjab Frontier, La Bassee 1914, Festubert 1914, 15, Givenchy 1914, Neuve Chapelle, Aubers, Loos, France and Flanders 1914-15, Helles, Krithia, Suvla, Sari Bair, Gallipoli 1915, Suez Canal, Megiddo, Egypt 1915-16, Sharon, Palestine 1918, Shaiba, Kut-al-Amara 1915, 17, Ctesiphon, Defence of Kut-al-Amara, Tigris 1916, Baghdad, Khan Baghdadi, Sharqat, Mesopotamia 1915-18, Persia 1918, North West Frontier India 1915, Baluchistan 1918, Afghanistan 1919, Iraq 1941, Deir es Zor, Syria 1941, Tobruk 1942, El Alamein, Mareth, Akarit, Djebel el Meida, Enfidaville, Tunis, North Africa 1942-43, Cassino I, Monastery Hill, Pian de Maggio, Campriano, Poggio Del Grillo, Gothic Line, Tavoleto, Coriano, Poggio San Giovanni, Montebello-Scorticata Ridge, Santarcangelo, Monte Reggiano, Monte Chicco, Lamone Crossing, Senio Floodbank, Bologna, Sillaro Crossing, Medicina, Gaiana Crossing, Italy 1944-45, Greece 1944-45, North Malaya, Jitra, Central Malaya, Kampar, Slim River, Johore, Singapore Island, Malaya 1941-42, Sittang 1942, 1945, Pegu 1942, 1945, Kyaukse 1942, 1945, Monywa 1942, Shwegyin, North Arakan, Imphal, Tuitum, Tamu Road, Shenam Pass, Litan, Bishenpur, Tengnoupal, Shwebo, Kyaukmyaung Bridgehead, Mandalay, Myinmu Bridgehead, Fort Dufferin, Maymo, Meiktila, Capture of Meiktila, Defence of Meiktila, Irrawaddy, Magwe, Rangoon Road, Pyabwe, Toungoo, Point 1433, Arakan Beaches, Myebon, Tamandu, Chindits 1943, 1945, Burma 1942-45, Falkland Islands 1982

THE QUEEN'S GURKHA ENGINEERS

QUEEN'S GURKHA SIGNALS

THE QUEEN'S OWN GURKHA LOGISTIC REGIMENT

BIBLIOGRAPHY

Regimental Histories

PETRE, F. LORAINE, OBE, *The 1ˢᵗ King George's Own Gurkha Rifles. The Malaun Regiment, 1815–1921,* The Royal United Services Institution, 1925.

BELLERS, BRIGADIER E.V.R., *The History of the 1st King George V's Own Gurkha Rifles (The Malaun Regiment),* Volume II, 1920–47, Gale & Polden Ltd, 1956.

SHAKESPEAR, COLONEL L.W., *History of the 2nd King Edward's Own Goorkha Rifles (The Sirmoor Rifles),* Volume I, Gale & Polden Ltd, 1912.

SHAKESPEAR, COLONEL L.W., CB CIE, *History of the 2ⁿᵈ King Edward's Own Goorkhas (The Sirmoor Rifle Regiment),* Volume II, 1911–21, Gale and Polden Ltd, 1924.

STEVENS, LIEUTENANT COLONEL G.R., OBE, *History of the 2nd King Edward VII's Own Goorkha Rifles (The Sirmoor Rifles),* Volume III, 1912–48, Gale & Polden Ltd, 1952.

WOOD, COLONEL D.R., MBE, *History of the 2ⁿᵈ King Edward VII's Own Goorkhas, (The Sirmoor Rifles),* Volume IV, 1948–94, D.R.Wood, 2003.

WOODYATT, MAJOR GENERAL NIGEL G., CB CIE, *The Regimental History of the 3rd Queen Alexandra's Own Gurkha Rifles, 1815–27,* Philip Allan & Co Ltd, 1929.

BARCLAY, BRIGADIER C.N., CBE DSO, *The Regimental History of the 3rd Queen Alexandra's Own Gurkha Rifles,* Volume II, 1927–47, William Clowes and Sons Ltd, 1953.

MACDONELL, RANALD, CBE, and MACAULAY, MARCUS, *A History of the 4th Prince of Wales's Own Gurkha Rifles,* Volumes I and II, 1857–1937, William Blackwood & Sons Ltd, 1940.

MACKAY, COLONEL J.N., DSO, *A History of the 4ᵗʰ Prince of Wales's Own Gurkha Rifles,* Volume III, 1938–48, William Blackwood & Sons Ltd, 1952.

MOLLOY, LIEUTENANT COLONEL and Officers of The 5ᵗʰ Royal Gurkha Rifles (F.F.), *History of the 5th Royal Gurkha Rifles (Frontier Force),* Volume I, 1858–1928, Gale & Polden, 1929

OFFICERS of The 5ᵗʰ Royal Gurkha Rifles (Frontier Force), *History of the 5ᵗʰ Royal Gurkha Rifles (Frontier Force),* Volume II, 1928–47, Gale & Polden Ltd, 1956.

RYAN, MAJOR D.G., DSO, STRAHAN, MAJOR G.C., OBE, and JONES, CAPTAIN J.K., *Historical Record of the 6th Gurkha Rifles,* Volume I, 1817–1919, Gale & Polden Ltd, 1925.

GIBBS, LIEUTENANT COLONEL H.R.K., *Historical Record of the 6th Gurkha Rifles,* Volume II, 1919–48, Gale & Polden Ltd, 1955.

MESSENGER, CHARLES, *The Steadfast Gurkha, Historical Record of 6ᵗʰ Queen Elizabeth's Own Gurkha Rifles,* Volume 3, 1948–82, Leo Cooper, 1985.

LUNT, JAMES, *Jai Sixth!, The Story of the 6ᵗʰ Queen Elizabeth's Own Gurkha Rifles 1817–1994,* Leo Cooper, 1994.

MACKAY, COLONEL J.N., DSO, *History of 7ᵗʰ Duke of Edinburgh's Own Gurkha Rifles,* William Blackwood & Sons Ltd, 1962.

SMITH, E.D., *East of Katmandu: The Story of The 7ᵗʰ Duke of Edinburgh's Own Gurkha Rifles,* Volume II, 1948–73, Leo Cooper, 1976.

The Autumn Years, History of the 7ᵗʰ Duke of Edinburgh's Own Gurkha Rifles, Volume III, Spellmount, 1997.

HUXFORD, LIEUTENANT COLONEL H.J., OBE, *History of the 8th Gurkha Rifles, 1824–49,* Gale & Polden Ltd, 1952.

POYNDER, LIEUTENANT COLONEL F.S., MVO OBE MC, *The 9th Gurkha Rifles, 1817–1936,* The Royal United Services Institution, 1937.

STEVENS, LIEUTENANT COLONEL G.R., OBE, *The 9ᵗʰ Gurkha Rifles,* Volume 2, 1937–47, 9ᵗʰ Gurkha Rifles Regimental Association (UK), 1953.

MULLALY, COLONEL B.R. *Bugle and Kukri: The Story of The 10ᵗʰ Princess Mary's Own Gurkha Rifles,* William Blackwood & Sons Ltd, 1957.

MCALISTER, MAJOR GENERAL R.W.L. CB OBE, *Bugle and Kukri: The Story of the 10ᵗʰ Princess Mary's Own Gurkha Rifles,* Volume Two, The Regimental Trust 10ᵗʰ Princess Mary's Own Gurkha Rifles, 1984.

PEARSON, BRIGADIER P.T.C., *Bugle and Kukri: The Story of the 10ᵗʰ Princess Mary's Own Gurkha Rifles,* Volume III, 10ᵗʰ Princess Mary's Own Gurkha Rifles Regimental Trust, 2000.

PEROWNE, MAJOR GENERAL L.E.C.M., CB CBE KStJ, *Gurkha Sapper: The Story of The Gurkha Engineers 1948–70,* Cathay Press Ltd, 1973

BOWEN, BRIGADIER D.H., OBE, *Queen's Gurkha Sapper: The Story of The Royal Engineers (Gurkha), The Gurkha Engineers, The Queen's Gurkha Engineers 1948–96,* Unwin Brothers Ltd, 1997.

DEXTER, MAJOR A.C., *The Queen's Gurkha Signals. Forty Years,* Queen's Gurkha Signals, 1994.

CAWTHORNE, COLONEL J.R., *The Queen's Own Gurkha Logistic Regiment: A Short History,* The Regimental Association, The Queen's Own Gurkha Logistic Regiment, 2003.

In addition to the regimental histories listed above, the following books afforded me great assistance:

ALLEN, CHARLES, *The Savage Wars of Peace,* Michael Joseph, 1990.

ALLEN, LOUIS, *Burma: The Longest War,* Dent, 1984.

BARTHORP, MICHAEL, *The North West Frontier,* New Orchard Editions, 1986.

BIDWELL, SHELFORD, *The Chindit War,* Hodder & Stoughton, 1979.

BIGGS, MAURICE, *The Story of Gurkha VC's,* The Gurkha Museum 1993.

BULLOCK, CHRISTOPHER, *Journeys Hazardous,* Square One, 1994.

CALVERT, MICHAEL, *Prisoners of Hope,* Jonathan Cape, 1952.

CARVER, FIELD MARSHAL LORD *The Turkish Front 1914–1918,* Sidgwick & Jackson, 2003.

CHAPPLE, FIELD MARSHAL SIR JOHN, *The Lineages and Composition of Gurkha Regiments in British Service,* Gurkha Museum, rev. edn, 2009

CHURCHILL, WINSTON S, *The Second World War (Volumes 1–6),* Cassell, 1952.

COLEMAN, A.P. *A Special Corps: The Beginnings of Gorkha Service with the British,* The Pentland Press, 1999.

COLLETT, NIGEL, *The Butcher of Amritsar, General Reginald Dyer,* Hambledon, 2005.

CORRIGAN, GORDON, *Sepoys in the Trenches,* Spellmount, 1999.

CHANT, CHRISTOPHER, *Gurkha,* Blandford Press, 1985.

CROSS, J.P. and BUDDHIMAN GURUNG, *Gurkhas at War,* Greenhill Books, 2002.

DALRYMPLE, WILLIAM, *The Last Mughal,* Bloomsbury, 2006.

DAVIS, PATRICK, *A Child at Arms,* Hutchinson & Co, 1970.

DICKENS, PETER, *SAS, The Jungle Frontier,* Arms and Armour, 1983.

ELLIOT, MAJOR GENERAL J.G., *The Frontier 1839–1947,* Cassells,

FARWELL, BYRON, *The Gurkhas,* Allen Lane, 1984.

FERGUSSON, BERNARD, *Wavell: Portrait of a Soldier,* Collins, 1961.

GAYLOR, JOHN, *Sons of John Company,* Spellmount, 1992.

GOULD, TONY, *Imperial Warriors,* Granta Publications, 1999.

GRENFELL, RUSSELL, *Main Fleet to Singapore,* Faber and Faber Ltd, 1951,

JAMES, HAROLD, *Across the Threshold of Battle,* The Book Guild, 1993.

JAMES, HAROLD and SHIEL-SMALL, DENIS, *The Gurkhas,* Macdonald, 1965

A Pride of Gurkhas, London, Leo Cooper, 1976.

HASTINGS, MAX, *Nemesis,* Harper Press, 2007.

HEATHCOTE, T.A., *The Afghan Wars 1839–1919,* Osprey Publishing Ltd, 1990.

HICKEY, MICHAEL, *The Unforgettable Army,* Spellmount, 1992.

MAGNUS, PHILIP, *Kitchener – Portrait of an Imperialist,* John Murray, 1958.

LEWIN, RONALD, *Slim: The Standard-Bearer,* Leo Cooper, 1976.

MASTERS, JOHN, *Bugles and a Tiger,* Michael Joseph, 1956.

MOOREHEAD, ALAN, *Gallipoli,* Hamish Hamilton, 1956.

NEILD, ERIC, *With Pegasus in India: The story of 153 Parachute Battalion.* Jay Birch & Co (Pte),

NEILL, COLONEL D.F., OBE MC, *One more river,* Personal typescript account of the First Chindit Expedition.

NEILLANDS, ROBIN, *A Fighting Retreat 1947–97,* Hodder and Stoughton, 1996.

PALMER, ALAN, *Dictionary of Twentieth Century History,* Penguin Books, 1979.

PEMBLE, JOHN, *The Invasion of Nepal,* Oxford, Clarendon Press, 1971.

POCOCK, TOM, *Fighting General,* Collins, 1973.

PRAVAL, K. C., *The Red Eagles,* Vision Books, 1982.

RAMBAHADUR LIMBU, VC, *My Life Story,* Gurkha Welfare Trust,

REID, CHARLES, *Delhi Centenary. The Diary of Charles Reid,* W.G. Kingham (Printers) Ltd 1957.

ROBSON, BRIAN W., *The Road to Kabul,* Arms & Armour, 1986.

SLIM, FIELD MARSHAL VISCOUNT, *Defeat into Victory,* Cassell and Co, 1956.

SMITH, E. D., *Britain's Brigade of Gurkhas,* Leo Cooper, 1973.

Battles for Cassino, Ian Allan, 1975.

Battle for Burma, Batsford, 1979.

Malaya and Borneo – Counter-Insurgency Operations, Ian Allan, 1985.

Johnny Gurkha, Leo Cooper, 1985.

Victory of a Sort. The British in Greece 1941–6, Robert Hale, 1988.

Valour – A History of the Gurkhas, Spellmount, 1997.

War Brings Scars, R J Leach and Co, 1993.

SMYTH, SIR JOHN, VC, *Milestones – A Memoir,* Sidgwick & Jackson Ltd, 1979.

TUKER, LIEUTENANT GENERAL SIR FRANCIS, *Gorkha, The Story of the Gurkhas of Nepal,* Constable, 1957.

VAN DER BIJL, NICK, BEM, *Confrontation: The War with Indonesia, 1962–1966.* Pen and Sword Military, 2007.

VAN DER BIJL, NICK, BEM, and ALDEA, DAVID, *5th Infantry Brigade in the Falklands,* Leo Cooper, 2003.

WALLACE, LIEUTENANT GENERAL SIR CHRISTOPHER, *Rifles and Kukris, Delhi 1857,* The Royal Green Jackets Museum Trust, 2007.

In addition, I have consulted copies of *The Kukri,* The Journal of The Brigade of Gurkhas, published since 1949 by HQ, Brigade of Gurkhas.

A SALUTARY LESSON

BY G.P. WHEELER, ROYAL SCOTS DRAGOON GUARDS

(Reproduced by kind permission of the Editor, Royal British Legion Journal)

All that month we had crawled forward with maddeningly frustrating slowness, but now there was an end to frustration and frayed temper. Over the ridge before us – 1,100 yards distant by my gunner's estimation – was the valley of the river Po.

Our squadron of tanks had been ordered to halt to allow the division on the right to close up. While we had been floundering blindly through the dust from ridge to ridge, they had been sweating and scrabbling in a slow, dirty, infantryman's battle through the maze of seaside chalets south of Rimini.

The squadron was deployed in line behind the crest of the ridge, the crews squatting round a clutter of brew cans and mugs under the rear engine doors of their tanks. The commander of each tank, beret or cap well down over his eyes, lounged on top of his turret studying, with varying degrees of interest, the final obstacle – the ridge we should attack tomorrow.

Mingled among the tanks were the infantry of the Brigade we were supporting. My own tank was at the junction of the forward positions of the two battalions in the line. To my left was a Gurkha Battalion, to my right British infantry of the line. Both, in their own fashion, were making themselves comfortable for the night.

The Fusiliers finished first. A shallow hole, quickly scratched out, groundsheet and greatcoat flung into the bottom of it, the owner cocooned in his grey blanket wormed under the greatcoat – and that is Fusilier Atkins for the night, or, anyway, until his turn for guard.

Such a simple routine required little supervision from the platoon commander, and he and his sergeant, having posted their sentries, climbed up on my turret for a night-cap from the bottle in my grenade rack and a gossip. Mug in hand they surveyed, with the gently patronising air with which the British infantry of the line customarily regard the soldiers of any other nation – in this case the efforts of their brothers-in-arms, the Gurkhas – to prepare themselves for the night.

This was a more elaborate process than that favoured by the Fusiliers. The Gurkha platoon had formed up, sentries had been posted and each man allotted a site for his slit trench. The little square men had quickly dug their trenches to a uniform depth with the soil neatly piled round the head and sides of the trench and camouflaged with turf. The Platoon Sergeant, a grey veteran, impeccably turned out despite four weeks of battle, inspected each trench unhurriedly. As he finished his inspection at the trench closest to my tank, he turned to look at the mists settling on San Marino and sniffed at the gentle breeze which stirred the limp pennants on our tank aerials.

He gave an order. Half the platoon, rifles slung, doubled down into the little valley behind us, returning shortly with great armfuls of dry reeds. These were distributed to each trench and every man at once began to make a little steep thatched roof over his trench, pinning the lower ends of the bundles of reeds into the ground with short forked sticks and securing them with turf. This done, the whole platoon, sitting outside their little shelters, cleaned their weapons and washed their clothes and themselves. Finally clutching their rifles with the bayonet fixed, they disappeared like so many rabbits into their holes, securing the entrance with a fold of their groundsheets. All this was done under the stern gaze of the eternally inspecting platoon sergeant.

As the last light faded behind the mountains and the last Gurkha disappeared into his burrow, the sergeant marched smartly away towards the centre of his company position. He returned in a moment, reappearing beside my tank with the unexpectedness of a genie. Saluting with grave solemnity both the platoon commander of the Fusiliers and myself, he addressed the former in lisping, clipped English: 'Sergeant Nambahadur Thapa, seven platoon Gurkha rifles, reporting, sahib. All is well. Permission to dismiss?'

Somewhat taken aback by the formality of this address, the platoon commander rose awkwardly from the turret, returned the salute and stammered out the required permission.

'Thank you, sahib. I wish good night to the sahibs.' And with a final immaculate salute the Gurkha sergeant disappeared again into the dusk.

The platoon commander sank back again onto the turret with a short embarrassed laugh. 'Jolly smart they are,' he said. 'Funny little men, bit primitive really.' He drained his mug. 'Practically barbarians, you know' he added with all the authority of his nineteen years. 'Shouldn't wonder if it rained tonight,' he said moving off. 'It would lay this damned dust.'

I watched while they moved silently over the ridge to the sentries' position on the forward slope. They came back as silently to the centre of their platoon position and subsided with muffled grunts into the same shapeless heaps as the rest of the platoon.

The wind felt colder and stronger and my rubber-soled boots slipped on the smooth glacis plate of the tank, wet with the first splashes of rain the wind was bringing. My crew had spread their bed-rolls on the engine hatches and had lashed the tarpaulin to cover them and the engine hatches. I squeezed under the corner of the tarpaulin and into my cupola, closing the hatch after me.

It was warm in the turret. I switched on the festoon light and the wireless and tuned the receiver to the BBC. My crew had unrolled my bedding, correctly appreciating that not even I would be so stupid as to try to sleep outside on my camp bed in the rain which was rattling on the tarpaulin. It was dry and still warm with the heat of the engines. I opened the whisky again, listened to the dance music and pitied the infantry.

The platoon commander's prediction was fulfilled. It rained hard all night with a cold wind which blew the rain under the edges of the turret hatches. I was awakened by a collection of steady drippings along the whole length of my huddled form. I opened the pistol port and peered out. It was still dark and the wind and rain hissed in a chilly chorus. I ducked back into my blankets, stiff and cold – there's nothing quite so cold as the turret of a tank in the early morning – and longed for dawn. It came as the wind died and the rain drizzled its last fitful dregs. A sentry banged his Sten on the side of the tank and made the customary muffled blasphemous appeal to my crew to stand to. The daily overture of groans, coughs and assorted oaths followed, ending with the rattle of the tarpaulin being pulled off the turret. The operator's hatch swung open with a squeak of wet hinges. A hoarse Scots voice said 'We've some hot water oot here sir,' and a pair of muddy boots dangled over my head.

It was still barely light, but the cold raw air woke one thoroughly in no time at all. My gunner and I crouched at the back of the tank in the hot engine draught, sipping scalding tea and scraping at our whiskers reflected dully in the top of a biscuit tin which served as a communal mirror.

The rising sun quickly dispersed the remaining rain clouds, and now shone on the green ridges around us bright with the polish of the rain and the brown faces of the mountains, their heads still wreathed in golden and silver mists. It was a lovely morning.

So I thought as I sat on my turret, eating bacon and fried bread from a mess tin and listening to the early morning news from the BBC. My attention was distracted from my breakfast by the appearance of the platoon sergeant and the platoon commander of the Fusiliers at the front of my tank – a pitiable sight. Soaked, filthy, haggard, unshaven, unwashed and apparently unfed, they epitomised the British attribute of never failing to be caught out by a drastic change in the weather.

It appeared that the whole platoon had been washed out of their weapon pits, and had spent the night vainly trying to keep themselves and the platoon equipment at least partially dry. Every stitch they had was sodden, including their blankets and greatcoats, and they couldn't get a fire going because the kindling was wet and the company cookers awash. Could the platoon please dry themselves off in our exhaust draughts and could we please let them have some hot water? My crews quickly had tank cookers and petrol fires heating a variety of water containers, and the platoon came in relays to stand half naked, shivering and chattering in groups at the back of the tanks, while the exhaust draughts tore at their wet clothes and their blankets and greatcoats steamed on the engine hatches. The platoon commander and sergeant climbed up on my tank and stood, still dripping disconsolately, on the engine hatches and sipped steaming mugs of tea and rum. From this vantage point they were able dejectedly to compare the shambles of waterlogged holes which formed their own platoon positions with the well ordered lay-out of the Gurkha platoon with its simple but apparently effective reed shelters, around which drainage ditches had now been dug. They could also remark on the contrast between their own sodden and dishevelled – but by no means dejected – soldiery and the Gurkha platoon, who, clean and dry, fastidiously flicked specks of mud from their puttees and hose-tops as they moved about repairing the reed thatch on their shelters and clearing the drainage ditches.

Embarrassment loomed like a thundercloud around my tank as the British infantry of the line was metaphorically rammed into the mud of their own waterlogged weapon pits. The unintentional agents of their embarrassment were naturally far too generous and well mannered to remark on it, even by the most sidelong of glances. But the knife was not to remain unturned in the wound.

Picking his way carefully through the platoon position, his boots and puttees spotless, his drill trousers and grey flannel shirt neatly pressed, and the brim of his slouch hat stiff and level, with chin strap gleaming, came the Gurkha platoon sergeant. Having inspected his positions thoroughly he approached my tank, halted and saluted smartly first me and then the platoon commander of the Fusiliers – whose drooping figure in its dripping, mud-besmeared groundsheet, slightly steaming now in the heat rising from the tank engines, reminded me of nothing so much as of a long dead and decaying carrion crow dangling on a keeper's vermin gibbet.

'Good morning, sahib,' said this primitive from the backwoods, smiling politely. 'A lovely morning, sahib,' said this helpless barbarian.

Editor's note

1/5th RGR(FF) were brigaded with the Fusiliers at the crossing of the River Po. I think, therefore, that this story can rightly be attributed to them.

'ANONE, ARIMASKA
– THE CANNON HAS FIRED'

The sun shone brightly that October morning as C and D Coys disembarked from the LST at Batavia, the rest of the Battalion having arrived the previous day.

3/5 RGR had left Malaya on consecutive days earlier that week, having boarded two Landing Ships Tank at high tide off a beach near Port Dickson. They had just completed their task of rounding up two Japanese Battalions (Habu Butai and Kobiashi Butai) in the Kuala Pilah / Ladang Geddes area, with the surrender parade taking place on the Bahao golf course. This was phase 2 of Operation 'Zipper' which followed 37 Brigade's unopposed landing three weeks previously at Sepang on the west coast.

The Brigade Commander, Brigadier N. Macdonald CBE DSO (Mac, of 4/5th fame), met the Battalion on its arrival and briefed the officers on the operational situation. The CO was Peter Sanders and his rifle company commanders were the following: Cameron (A), Gouldsbury (B), Hickey (C) and Buchanan (D).

The picture was not a rosy one. All reports from the interior showed that Dr Soekarno had lost control over the extremists who were terrorising the countryside and roving about in bands lusting after blood and plunder. The Japanese were in the process of being disarmed. On the surface there was little to show that the Indonesian Independence movement was Jap inspired, but those better acquainted than the ordinary soldier with Japanese methods saw clearly the product of a policy which aimed at leaving the United Nations a legacy of disturbance as the immediate aftermath of the war. The Dutch were in a state of impotence and unlikely to be able to provide a peace-keeping force from the Netherlands for another nine months.

As the briefing continued it became increasingly evident that 23 Div (The Fighting Cock) was virtually on its own and about to be spread thinly over a densely populated area covering 400 miles from west to east. Deployments, and thus the likely flash points, we were told, were to be as follows:

Batavia–1st Brigade–1st Seaforths, 1/16th Punjabis, 1st Patiala
Bandoeng–37th Brigade–3/3rd Gurkhas, 3/5th Royal Gurkha Rifles (FF) and 3/10th Gurkhas

Surabaya–49th Brigade–4/5th Mahrattas, 6/5th Mahrattas, 5/6th Rajputana Rifles (Centre)
3/10 GR, in Coy detachments, was to join an ad hoc force being hurriedly formed to cover Semarang, Megalang and Ambarawa, to the north of the island.
49 Bde (4/5 Mahratta, 6/5 Mahratta and–Surabaya (East) 5/6 Rajputana Rifles)

THE LULL BEFORE THE STORM

The Battalion moved by train to Bandoeng, a major hill station about a hundred miles to the east. The men were favourably impressed by the country which in many parts was so like their own. The hillsides were terraced almost to their summits with vivid green rice fields. The stations were placarded with anti-Dutch posters and the people, though not openly hostile, were obviously resentful of the passage of troops. We moved into the former Dutch barracks within a surrounding wall. The men were well content with their accommodation, although it was insufficient for the whole Battalion. Some of us, therefore were sent out to protect the Dutch residential areas in company or platoon detachments.

In order to keep this narrative within reasonable bounds, I must now restrict my comments, in general, to the activities of C Coy. The Gurkha seemed to have difficulty in getting his tongue round certain words. One day my orderly, who was very keen, reported to me that there was a Dutchman waiting outside: 'Sab, eota Duck a'achha,' he said.

We were billeted in the Juliana Ziekenhuis (hospital) adjacent to the Pasteur Institute complex and a large quinine factory, our task being to patrol the area by day and by night with a view to preventing the mayhem caused by rampokkers (raiders) armed with parangs, who would break into the up-market Dutch-owned houses, killing or wounding the occupants, destroying the furnishings and looting whatever they could carry away.

My telephone extension was 16 ('anamblas', in Indonesian); J was pronounced Y and the letter R invariably rolled. In the early hours of the morning the call would inevitably come, with a frantic Dutchman at the end of the line: 'Is that anamblas spe-cial? Is that the Mayor? Is that Mayor Heeki? Please send the Goorkhas quickly, my huis is being rampokked, the rampokkers have come, my dogs have been killed and I am under the bed.' Inevitably the 'quick reaction section' would arrive after the birds had flown.

A change of tactics was clearly called for. Night patrols were replaced by a platoon's worth of two-man ambushes deployed over a wide area, moving out stealthily after dark into previously reconnoitred positions in the shrubberies of selected homes. The results were spectacular. The rampokkers were picked off with stenguns at close range and the buzz soon got round. The warning notices on every gate-post along the boulevards, proclaiming Awas Anjing (beware the dog) were rapidly replaced by their owners with Awas Goorkha!

THE STORM CLOUDS DARKEN

3/10 GR were heavily engaged with fighting off the marauding hordes hell bent on overrunning the RAPWI camps (Released Allied Prisoners of War and Internees) in the Ambarawa area, already bulging with Dutch and Eurasian refugees, while the news from Surabaya was very bad indeed. 49 Bde (some 4000 troops) were widely dispersed in a heavily built up area, many of them in isolated company and platoon posts. The whole town seemed to rise up in arms against them, a fanatical mob over 140,000 strong, 20,000 of them Japanese trained, whipped up to an uncontrollable frenzy and armed to the teeth. The bestial scenes that followed in the name of freedom rivalled the vilest moments of the French revolution. The troops stood their ground bravely but the casualties were appalling, the Brigade Commander (Mallaby) being among the dead. The Rajputana Rifles suffered more killed and wounded in three weeks than during the whole of their time in Burma.

The storm clouds rolled westwards towards Bandoeng. We were already too thin on the ground throughout Java, with no reserves. In response to an urgent appeal from the Theatre Commander, back came a signal from Mountbatten: 'No reinforcements available. Rearm the Japs and take them

under command.' It was an Alice in Wonderland situation. Bandoeng garrison was increased within a week by 1,500 armed Japanese, much to the relief of Brigadier Mac, already short of one battalion (3/10th).

I was allocated 100 Japs, formed into an ad hoc coy, with instructions to weld my force into a battle group in the face of the increasing threat. No fraternisation was the order of the day! This was easy as far as the Burma veterans were concerned, but for the large number of young reinforcements it was a different matter – they were already impressed by the apparent efficiency and discipline of our new 'allies'. Control was exercised through an interpreter, Capt Hiro Namazawa, a diminutive artillery officer with glasses. His looks belied him: when he cracked the whip his troops jumped to it. His English was rudimentary, although his comprehension was good and he enforced my instructions to the letter.

Things were hotting up in the C Coy area just then, the enemy having occupied the quinine factory in platoon strength, erecting roadblocks along Kininaweg (Quinine Road) within the factory walls. I was ordered to clear them out. The Bn IO [Intelligence Officer], Gus Ashby, joined me in the leading armoured car, a left-hand drive Marmon-Harrington from the Dutch stockpile with a Gurkha driver. CHM Hastabahadur Gurung manned the Vickers MMG mounted through a hole in the roof of the vehicle. We were followed closely by an escort of 20 Gurkhas in two Japanese trucks with Japanese drivers. We took a tremendous risk, but it paid off. The element of surprise prevailed as we burst through the barricades, the whole force penetrating the defences before the enemy was able to react. There followed a fierce exchange of fire and grenades were thrown from the top floor, resulting in 2 killed and 3 wounded on our side. Hastabahadur then stood up in full view of the enemy and emptied a belt of long sustained fire at a group of 15 Indonesians preparing to counter attack. He killed 12 and escaped unscathed. The remainder surrendered. It was all over within an hour and Hastabahadur was awarded the IDSM.

Bandoeng was now on 'red alert' with both Battalions fully committed. The town was divided by the main railway line which ran east-west, the southern half being described by the Dutch as the Native Quarter, consisting mainly of Indonesians and Chinese, the northern half (our side) being the European residential area, which included two hotels and a number of department stores.

Despite our earlier efforts on behalf of the RAPWI to evacuate the Eurasians and the Dutch still living in the southern sector, many of them had refused to leave their homes for the secure Camps to the north. By now of course there were over a hundred of them held hostage and we were ordered to rescue them. The task overall was given to the 3/3rd, with my Coy Group under command. The CO (Arthur Greenway) gave me as my objective the Zuider Zee, an area of semi high-rise flats to the east of the southern sector, where many of the hostages were known to be held. I marked my town plan accordingly, having consulted my Eurasian sleuth who knew the specific buildings. I was to operate independently, with two Jap tanks in direct support together with two Jap 150mm howitzers, the gun position being a mile further back near 'Chhattari Ghar', an umbrella-like house well known to us all. In order to achieve surprise D Day was to be December 25th!

I gave out my orders on Christmas Eve, the 'O' group including Capt Namazawa and two other Jap officers, with specific instructions as to the artillery fire plan and the targets (known strongholds away from the flats). We would attack in two phases, Phase 1 being a frontal attack by the Japs! H Hr: 0530 Hrs (dawn).

Our axis of advance was to be Slachthuis Weg (Abattoir Road), with the FUP to the north of the railway embankment and the Start Line the railway line itself. We moved forward (160 strong) in complete silence, the Japanese "discipline" being remarked upon later by my GOs. At H minus 5, Capt Namazawa, who was also the FOO [Forward Observation Officer], with his radio headset clamped firmly over his cloth cap, spluttering with excitement and forgetting that this British officer did not understand Japanese, exclaimed: 'Anone, Arimaska! the Canon has fired.' As the shells whined over our heads and crashed down accurately on the selected targets, the injunction not to fraternise with the Japs was momentarily forgotten.

To keep matters simple, the success signal following Phase 1 was to be a live Japanese head sticking out of each of the line of windows in the nearest block of flats visible to me, whereupon C Coy would take over.

The two light tanks rumbled down the street to the left, machine-gunning indiscriminately anything that moved, and silencing a strong bunker position 400 yards ahead with it's 6 pounder gun. Everything went according to plan, out popped the Japanese heads and C Coy went through (Phase 2). There followed some fierce close quarter fighting and heavy Indonesian casualties, our own losses being 2 killed and 7 wounded (Gurkhas); 2 killed and 5 wounded (Japs). 95 hostages were rescued, the remainder, sadly, being killed in the cross fire.

EPILOGUE

I left Bandoeng on a month's leave in the UK in March 1946. When I returned to the Battalion to take over second-in-command, they had already moved down to Krandji and Klenda near Batavia. The worst was over, mopping up operations being the order of the day. It had been a tough year for 3/5 RGR, after the exhausting Burma campaign, and we had suffered over 50 casualties including a BO [British Officer] and a GO [Gurkha Officer] numbered among the dead. Nevertheless morale remained high, thanks to the outstanding leadership of GPVS [The Commanding Officer – Lieutenant Colonel Peter Sanders].

B.G.H.

HOLDERS OF THE VICTORIA CROSS FROM GURKHA REGIMENTS

NAME	REGIMENT	YEAR	CAMPAIGN
Lieutenant J. A. Tytler	1 GR	1858	Indian Mutiny
Major D. Macintyre	2 GR	1872	Looshai
Captain G. N. Channer	1 GR	1875	Perak
Captain J. Cook	5 GR	1878	Afghanistan 1878–80
Captain R. K. Ridgeway	8 GR	1879	Naga 1879–80
Lieutenant C. J. W. Grant	8 GR	1891	North East Frontier 1891
Lieutenant G. H. Boisragon	5 GR	1891	Hunza 1891
Lieutenant J. Manners-Smith	5 GR	1891	Hunza 1891
Captain W. G. Walker	4 GR	1903	Somaliland
Lieutenant J. D. Grant	8 GR	1904	Tibet 1904
Rifleman Kulbir Thapa	3 GR	1915	France
Major G. C. Wheeler	9 GR	1917	Mesopotamia
Rifleman Karanbahadur Rana	3 GR	1918	Palestine
Subedar Lalbahadur Thapa	2 GR	1943	Tunisia
Havildar Gaje Ghale	5 RGR	1943	Burma
Lieutenant (Acting Captain) M. Allmand	6 GR	1944	Burma (Chindit campaign)
Rifleman Ganju Lama MM	7 GR	1944	Burma
Rifleman Tulbahadur Pun	6 GR	1944	Burma (Chindit campaign)
Jemedar (Acting Subedar) Netrabahadur Thapa	5 RGR	1944	Burma
Rifleman (Acting Naik) Agansing Rai	5 RGR	1944	Burma
Captain (Temporary Major) F. G. Blaker MC	9 GR	1944	Burma (Chindit campaign)
Rifleman Sherbahadur Thapa	9 GR	1944	Italy
Rifleman Thaman Gurung	5 RGR	1944	Italy
Rifleman Bhanbhagta Gurung	2 GR	1944	Burma
Rifleman Lachhiman Gurung	8 GR	1945	Burma
Lance Corporal Rambahadur Limbu	10 GR	1965	Borneo

Gurkhas, in common with the rest of the Indian Army, only became eligible for the Victoria Cross in 1911.

MAJOR GENERALS AND COLONELS COMMANDANT OF THE BRIGADE OF GURKHAS

MAJOR GENERAL

1948–50	Major General Sir Charles Boucher KCB CBE DSO
1950	Major General R.E. Urquhart CB DSO
1950–52	Major General R.C.O. Hedley CB CBE DSO
1952–55	Major General L.E.C.M. Perowne CB CBE
1955–58	Major General R.N. Anderson CB CBE DSO
1958–61	Major General J.A.R. Robertson CB CBE DSO
1961–64	Major General W.C. Walker CB CBE DSO
1964–65	Major General P.M. Hunt DSO OBE
1965–69	Major General A.G. Patterson CB DSO OBE MC
1969–71	Major General D.G.T. Horsford CBE DSO
1971–75	Major General E.J.S. Burnett CB DSO OBE MC
1975–77	Major General R.W.L. McAlister CB OBE
1977–78	Lieutenant General Sir John Archer KCB OBE
1978–80	Major General Sir Roy Redgrave KBE MC
1980–82	Major General J.L. Chapple CBE
1982–85	Major General D. Boorman CB
1985–87	Major General T.A. Boam CB CBE
1987–89	Major General G.D. Johnson OBE MC
1989–92	Major General P.R. Duffell CBE MC
1992–94	Major General J.P. Foley CB OBE MC

COLONEL COMMANDANT

1994–2003	General Sir Sam Cowan KCB CBE ADC Gen
2003–07	Lieutenant General Sir Philip Trousdell KCB
2007	General Sir David Richards KCB CBE DSO ADC Gen

Words of Professor Sir Ralph Turner MC, 3rd Gurkhas, at the end of the preface to his English/Nepali dictionary, written after the First World War and the last sentence now inscribed on the Gurkha War Memorial in front of the Ministry of Defence.

'As I write these last words, my thoughts return to you who were my comrades, the stubborn and indomitable peasants of Nepal. Once more I hear the laughter with which you greeted every hardship. Once more I see you in your bivouacs or about your fires, on forced march or in the trenches, now shivering with wet and cold, now scorched by a pitiless and burning sun. Uncomplaining you endure hunger and thirst and wounds; and at the last your unwavering lines disappear into the smoke and wrath of battle. Bravest of the brave, most generous of the generous, never had country more faithful friends than you.'

Following pages: The Gurkha Memorial Garden at Sir Harold Hillier's Gardens and Arboretum, near Romsey, Hampshire. (Gurkha Museum)

(Photo opposite by kind permission of C. Schulze)

THIS CHAUTARA WAS ERECTED
TO THE MEMORY OF
SIR HORACE KADOORIE
1902-1995
BENEFACTOR TO GURKHAS
AND THEIR HOMELAND

IN MEMORY   IN MEMORY   IN MEMORY   IN MEMORY   IN MEMORY   IN MEMORY   IN MEMORY

INDEX

LIST OF SUBSCRIBERS

This book has been made possible through the generosity of the following subscribers:

Grant Abernethy
Alfred John Abraham
John L Ackroyd
Lieutenant James Logan Adair
Gordon Adams
Iorwen Adams
Peter J Adams
Captain B L Addison, Royal Signals
Eric Addison
Michael T Ainsworth
Mrs P W Akrigg
Mrs J Alda
Colin W Alderman
Major Prembahadur Ale MVO QGE
John Allan
Maureen Allen
Don Allen (Darby)
Wing Commander H Allen
Brian and Emma Allkins
John Allkins
Christopher Allmand
Mr Victor H Allport
Laurence Allum BEM
Sheila McGregor de Alonso
Carol Edwina and Erik Andersen
Miss C Anderson
David C and Marjory I G Anderson
J R and R P Anderson
Brigadier John Anderson
John C Anderson
Major John T Anderson
R A L Anderson
Damian N Andronicus
A L Andrews
Geoff Andrews
Jason Andrews
John Andrews
Archie Angus
Robert B Ansell
M J Aplin
George Appleby, Gwent
Mr M J R Appleby

Peter Appleby
Captain John Russell Archibald QGE
Alan R Armstrong
Sqn Ldr R L Armstrong, RAF (Retd)
Alain Arnot
Mrs P Asher
Major G H Ashley
Miss B V Ashton
F G L Askham
G H and V A Asquith
E H Aston
William J Aston
Major G M Athey RAEC
J L Attridge
Patricia M Attrill
M S J Attwater
Major T Attwood
David W Auchterlonie
Derek C Austin
John (Bill) Ayres
F H E Baaj-Sterkenburg
John T Bach
Janie Bacon
Frank Baggaley
Ian M M Bagshaw
Barbara K Bailey
Mr Simon P Bailey
Errol Baker
Geoffrey Baker
William (Harry) Baker
Yvonne Baker
Derek James Baldry
Peter B Blair
John Graham Ball
Virginia Ball
Derek Latham Ballantyne
Ann A Bannister
Mr Gordon Bannister
Laxmi Bhakta Bantawa MBE
J M Barber
Mrs Marjorie Barber
Shelagh Barber
Tony Barker
D R Barnard
Clive Barnes

Robert W Barnes
Dennis Barnfield
Leslie Barrett
Lieutenant Colonel M C Barrett OBE
John B Bartlett
Michael Barton
Mrs I Barwick
Michael Bassano
John Bateman
Tony Bateman
Colin Bates
Anthony Batten
Lieutenant Colonel Frank Batten MBE DL
Steve and Barbara Bayes
A R A Beadle
Marina Beadnell
Alistair Beard
Mrs S Beaton
Vernon Beauchamp
Hugh Beckett
Peter Beckwith
Joan Beddow Roberts
Graham R Bedford
Alistair Begg
Alan Belcham
Adam M D Bell
Colonel G N Bell
Jeff Bell
Major (Retd) G A Bennett QGE
Gary Bennett
Mike Bennett
W T Bent
Charles R Beresford
ARMR SSGT A Berkley TDBG 1981–3
Brigadier A E Berry
I C Berry
Mrs E Best
James R Bevan
P Bevis
Lieutenant Colonel Willie Bicket
V C Bignell
Michael Binder
B S Binstead
Lieutenant Colonel G D Birch
Major J N B Birch

Derek W Bird BEM

Brian D Birdseye

Eunice Birt

Lewis Birt

Mungo Bisset

Mr C Stan Blackburn

Jessie Blackburn

Cedric B Blacker

Allan F Blacklaws OBE

M H Blackmore

Elizabeth Blaine

Jason Blake

Mr J R Bland

Colonel and Mrs C D A Blessington OBE JP DL

R I Blois (née Farebrother)

Donald and Carole Boag

Andrew Boakes

John Bolam

Alan A Bolland

John Bolton

Stephen F Bond

Leroy Bonifas

Roy W Booth

The Booton Family, Shropshire

K Borch

Mrs M M Bostock

Paul William Bostock

Vera I Botham

Arthur Bourne

M J Bourne

Philip Bowdler

Major (Retd) A D Bowen

John Bowlby

George F Bowles

Mr and Mrs W Neville Bowen

Percival Bowpitt

F C Bowtell

Major M A L Bowyer

P D C Bowyer

Dr M Walter J Boyd

Brian Thomas Bradbury-Pratt

Eleanor Brade

Jeremy Brade

Karen Brade

Woodren Brade

Cllr Derek L Bradley

Major General P E M Bradley

Mr William Bradwell

Ms Janet Brady

Sean Brady

Colin M J Brand

Peter H W Bray

Alec and Jean Braybrooke

H F J Brayne

Major (Retd) L Brazier

June Brebner

Tony Brennan CB

Chester Brett

Brigadier J S Brewer CBE

Eric Brice

Brigadier L H J Bridgeford, 178 Field Regt RA

Lieutenant Colonel A L Bridger OBE

D L Bridger Esq

M W Bridger Esq

Mike Bridges

K Bridgewater

D J Brittain

Mr Valentine Bromley

Mrs Eve Brooke

Martin Brooks, 7th DEO Gurkha Rifles

Major A V Brown

Ivy D Brown

Lieutenant Colonel P J Brown

R E Brown

Dr Robert Brown

Ronald Brown

Sandy Brown

St John Brown

Tom Brown

Major John Browne

Keith Brownhill

Paul Anselme Bruchez

S/Ldr Morton Bruckshaw

Derek Bruton

David H Bryant

Mrs Margaret Bryant

P R Buchanan

Captain Allan Buck

Julian Buckeridge

John Milne Buckner

Jocasta Bullock

Mrs A K Bullock

Elizabeth Bullock

Neil Bullock

Frank H Burbidge

J A Burd

Chris Burdekin

Thomas Edward Burden

Bruce H Burgess

F J Burgin

Catherine O Burns

R T (Bob) Burns

Ted and Connie Burren

James Burrows Flockton

Mr and Mrs Brenda and Richard Burton

Mr F and Mrs D Burton

John Bush

George A Butcher

B R R Butler

David Butler

Roger Butt

Alfred E J Butterworth

Mr J J C Byrne

Edgar Caddick

Mr and Mrs I Caffin

Jim Cain

Mr J S Caldwell

L G Calvert

Stuart Cameron

Mrs M M Campbell-White

John Campbell

K A Carey

Major General Sir Michael Carleton-Smith CBE DL

Lieutenant Colonel G P T Carpenter

James Carr

Richard and Elizabeth Carrington

David Carswell

Colonel (Retd) A F Carter MBE QG, Signals

Brian C Carter

Mr D A Carter

Peter G Carter

R E Carter

R S M Carter

Peter Stewart Cartwright

Mr R D Cartwright

Maureen Casey

David Casher Soffe

Martin Castle

Julian P Cavey

John Cawood RJE

Annabel Cessford

Ken Chadwick

William J Chadwick

Mrs M E Chalker

G H Challis

Fiona Chaloner

Dr W B Chamberlain

N G S and N M Champion

A C M Chanin Chandrubeksa

Michael Channing

David Chapple

Brian Chellingworth

Olive L Chesworth

Mr Fred Chew

James S Cheyne

Bharat Singh Thapa Chhetri

James Chirrey, Ex QO HLDRS ATT 99 Gurkha BDE, Singapore

Chris Chirscoli

N Chitticks

Kenneth B Christie

Mrs Sylvia Christmas

Michael Chu

Lord Clifford of Chudleigh

Derek Yeo Yong Chun

Leslie A Clack (Devon)

E Claremont

Marie Claridge

Dr Gordon A Clark

Mike Clark

Paul Moir Clark

Mr Richard D Clark

H D Clarke

Captain J C Clarke, RADC
Lieutenant Colonel J H Clarke
Michael J Clarkson
Dorothy Clay
Peter Cleary
W N Clegg
Air Commodore and Mrs A J B Clements
The late Lieutenant Bridget M Clifford
   QARANC
Robert L Clifford MBE
Major Peter Cobb
Roger W Cobbett
Mr and Mrs J Cochran
Amanda Cochrane
Mr and Mrs K W Cockburn
A K Cockerill
Maurice Coe
Ian Coff
Jamie Stephen Cole
Nigel Coleman
Mr R G Coleman
Lieutenant Colonel N A Collett
Mrs V Collett
Charles Henry Collicutt
Chris Collier
Sally Collins
Stephen Collins
Mike Colson
Rupert Connell
Mr Cook
C J Cook
H A Cook
Mr Henry George Valentine Cook
Eric R Cooke OBE
Mr K G H Cooke
Michael J Cooke
Oliver W Cooke
Michael Cooper-Evans
Mr A L Cooper
Mrs Dorothy Cooper
Ian D Cooper
Mr M J Cooper
D J Cope
Alan and Mary Coppin
Major N T Corbett
Paul Cordle
Derek Corke, Royal Navy
R L B Cormack
Gordon Cornell
Major J G H Corrigan MBE
Revd Ivan Cosby
Tony Cossey
Nigel Cotton
John Coughlan
James C Counsell and family
Alex Coupar
Mrs C E Courtney
J V Courtney, RAF

Lieutenant Colonel P L G Covernton
General Sir Sam Cowan
N Cowley
Mark F Cox
A J A Coxson
N Crabtree
John R Cracknell
Jackie Craig
Stuart B Craig
Joyce Craufurd-Stuart
James Crawford
Leslie Crawley
Colin P Creasey
Mrs J Credland
Dr and Mrs Ronald K Crisp
Stephen Croad
Captain J H Crompton
J P Cross
D Crossan
Miss Jenny Croucher
Mrs Doreen Crowther
George Cruickshank
M M Cruickshank of Auchreoch
J Culshaw, 17/21 Lancers
Vera C Cumming
Ann Cumming
Anthony M Cupper
Liam D Curley
Jim Curran
C S Currie
Keith Currie
Norman G Currie
C G Curtis
Colonel D J Cutfield
Mr Michael George D'Arcy
Mr J Dack
Godfrey V J Daffurn
Mrs B J Dales
Dona Dales
Paule Dalrymple
A Daltry-Cooke
G W Dancer
Captain Roy Dand, 1/10 Gurkha Rifles
Janet Dangar
Mrs K J Daniel
Arthur 'Danny' Daniels
B T A Darby
John O R Darby
J D Darkin
K W Darley
Arthur Davenport
G J Davenport
Mr J and Mrs E Davenport
Wildred Davey
David Davidson
Sir Frank Davies
Major G L Davies
Colonel (Retd) Graham Davies

Dr Howard G Davies
J P Davies
Mrs K Davies
Anne-Marie Davis
Les Davis
Richard I Davis
Mr George William Davison
W J Dawson
Mrs Marguerita L Day
Patricia Day
Mrs Basil De Ferranti
A M Deakin
Jeremy N Deane
Major John Deane
Mr Colin Dearman
Philip W Deegan
J S Deeley
Monica Deeley
Edward Deere
William Dell
John A Denton
Roger and Christine Dettmer
Patrick Devey
The Earl of Devon
S Dewan BEM
Major (Retd) Tikendra Dal Dewan
Ian D Dewar
Mrs Shirley Dickinson (née Dykes)
David G Dicks
Major J Dicksee
David Cranstoun Dickson
Leslie Cranstoun Dickson
J Dillon-Godfray
Steve Dillon
Pamela J Dinneen (née Hoare)
Major David J Dinwiddie
John Dixey
Mr D A Dixie
Major Anthony Dixon RE
Group Captain Bob Dixon
James Robert Dixon
Dr Peter L S Dixon
Cy Dobson
Mr B Dodd, Ex RM
James (Jim) Domm
D S Donachie
Mr Thomas I Donaldson
Robert Eric Donnison
G E Dorrington
Mrs Iris Dorset
Malcolm Dougal
G E Douglas
E T Dowber
Jean Cameron Dowine
Mr Hilary Brian Downer
Robert J Downie
Mr and Mrs C I Dracott
Michael J Draper

Denys Drayton
Reg J Drew
Edwin Dring
Mrs E B Driscoll
Elizabeth Driver
Robert Driver
Frances Drummond
Ross Drummond
Roger F Dubber
Peter Duckworth
Simon Duerden
Lieutenant General Sir Peter Duffell KCB CBE
   MC
Sydney William Duke
John D Duncan
John Ernst Duncan
R S M Ron (Dally) Duncan, Royal Corps of
   Signals
Mrs Ella Duncum
Roy A Dunlop
Barnaby Durrant
Charlotte Durrant
Mrs Sylvia Dyche
Major L J Dyde
John M Dyer
Nigel A Dyer
Arthur and Beryl Eabry
Barry N Earp
G L Eccleshall
Mr and Mrs J G H Eckersley
Mary Ede
John Edson
Mrs J Edwards-Heathcote
Adrian Edwards
Andy Edwards
Charles Edwards
Colin Edwards
Richard Edwards
Penelope Elias
John Elliot
N A Ellis-Leagas
George L Ellis
Mr Richard Elms
Andrew C England
David C Erickson
James Erksine-Ure
Frank Esaw
Iain Esslemont
M P Ethelston
Albert William Evans
Mr J E Evans
Colonel Jimmy Evans
K M Evans
Mrs Madeleine Evans
P V Evans
Pamelia J Evans
Sam Evans
Eileen and Alan Everett

Flt Lt (Retd) DV Eves RAF
Mr John Fairgrieve
S J Farrington
Colonel W H Farrington
Brigadier A S J Fay
Thomas Fender
Anthony Fenn
George Irwin Fenton, Ex RAMC Wartime
Shirleyann Fidler
Michael J Fielding
Captain Raymond J Fields MN-MC
Mrs Sheila Finch
Brigadier C A Findlay CBE
T Alastair Findlay
Tony Fine
Alexander Finnie
Colonel A J Fisher
David Fisher
Eliot J H Fisk
Ian B Fisken
Kenyon B Fitzgerald
John Flanagan
Patrick S Fleming
David and Kate Fletcher
Leslie H Fletcher
P C Flory
R R Flynn BEM
David James Fobister
James Forbes
Barry Ford
Jill Ford
Hamish C Forrest
Robin Foster
J W Foulds
A J H Fowler
Trevor Fox
T C Frame, Ex REME ATT 2/2 GR
Mr and Mrs F J Francis-Smith
Patrick J Franklin
Major Mike Fraser
Major Tom Fraser
Major William Macduff Fraser, 9th Gurkha Rifles
Revd Eric Freeman
Robin Freeman
Simon Fresson
Martin Frewer
Michael Frewer
John Friberg
Betty Frost
Harry James Fuller
Dennis Fullwood
Michael Fullwood
Charles Furness
P J Furse
Jack Furtado
Tettamanti Gabriele
T T W Gadsby
G E Gaines

Maud C Gall
Mrs Elizabeth Galt
Anthony P Gammie
Denys George Gardiner
Margaret A Gardiner
R W K Gardiner
A E D Garnett
P J Gautrey MA
Mrs H C Gay
Major (Retd) P H Gay
A R and S H M Gedge
Peter Frank Gentil
Heather and Michael Gerrard
Paul Gerrish
Cdr (Ret) George R Gibson RN
Michael J Gifford
Mrs M Gilderson
Charles D M F Giles
I A Giles
Michael Alan Giles
Peter Giles
Lieutenant Colonel P A C Gilham
John Reginald Gill
Wilf Gill
Mr J Gillespie
C Paul Gillett
Ian Gillies
David Gim
William Gittus
David Glaisyer
T M Glaser
Angus G Glass
Captain G P St C Glendinning BA
Myra Godsmark
Norman Goldsmith RVM
Lieutenant Colonel S G Goodall DL
John Henry Goodman
Adrian C S Gordon
Joan Maxwell Gordon
Ian Gosling Esq
Miss Jane Gostynska
Howard L Goy
Miss Barbara May Grabham
C W Graham
Peter Granger
John George Granville Lockwood
F C Graves OBE DL
Andrew R Green
Colonel Stuart Green
William Green
John P Greener
W T Greenfield
Ian Greenhedge
Iris Greening
Brigadier J B K Greenway CBE JP
Major General R A Grey AO DSO
Henry A Grierson
M Griffin

M J Griffin
Lieutenant Colonel A P M Griffith RGR
J M Miles Griffiths
J W A Griffiths
John R Griffiths
Margaret and Denis Griffiths
Mr Terence Grimmond
Philip Grimshaw
L S Grose
Mr G A Groves
W L S Guinness
Mr and Mrs W Gumbrell
Dr Yvonne Gunn
Gurkha Fine Foods
Mr Anthony Owen Hawker Gwynne
Pamela Hadley
R F Hale
Alan Hall
Albert J Hall
Lieutenant Colonel Bill Hall
F J J Hall, 8th Gurkhas
Jim Hall
Ken Hall
P M Hall
R Hall and M Hall
S M Hall
John Harvey Hallam
Anne Hamilton
K F Hamilton
Nicholas Hamilton
Stephen M Hamon
B H Hampson
Margaret Hanchet
Mrs W Hancock
John Hancock
Col Helen B Hannah L/RAMC
Magnus Harcus
Claude Harden BEM
D F Harding
John Harding
Margaret Harding
Sally Harding
Mr Gerard Hardman
Wilfred Hardy Esq MBE
T W Hares
Alan Harford
Dr David Harkness
Sq. Ldr Ken Harman, RAFVR
F G Harper
A J Harradine
A J Harris
Family of Bill Harris
Mr and Mrs J E Harris
Colin Harrison
George Brian Harrison, Sergeant RAOC
H C Harrison
Nigel J Harrison
Ron Harrison

Major T Harrison MBE KStJ TD
William Michael Harrison
Major J R Harrop
John C Hart
Robert Hart
Dick Hartley
Susan Hartley
The late Lieutenant Colonel A S Harvey OBE
    MC, 2/6th Gurkha Rifles
Alma Harvey
Daphne G Haskard
Commodore Sir Robert Hastie KCVO CBE RD
E A Hatch
Mr Winston Hathaway
Mrs Zena Hawkin
John Hawkins
H Hawksworth
J W Hay
Kenneth Hayden-Sadler
Antony Hayes
Colonel D G Hayes CBE
Mr V W Hayes
Mrs E Haynes
Brigadier Nigel Haynes
Mrs R E Heale
Tom P Healy
Alexander Heddleston
Alan Heginbottom
George and Judith Heller
K S Helps
Mr 'John' Hemsley, 9 GR
Joseph Tat-Yong Henderson-Tang
J T Henderson
Michael G D Henderson
William Henderson
Peter John Hentage
Lieutenant Colonel P C Hepherd
Tim Hepplewhite
T Heron
Bob Herring
Lieutenant D G Hessey RN
John and Alison Hewat
Mrs Sandie Hewer
Pauline J Hewitt
Rosemary Hibberd
B G Hibbert
Geoff Higgins
Robert Higgins
Ian Highley
A J Hill
Charles John Hill
Ernest Hill
Geoffrey R M Hill
Colonel John Hill OBE TD
Ken Hill, 1/Seaforth
Peter Arthur Hill
T L Hill
William J Hill

F G J Hillier
K W Hilton
Jack Hinde
Eric Hinds
Colonel N J H Hinton MBE
Christopher Lawrence Hiscox
Philip Hobday
John Hobson JP
Catherine Hocknell
Benjamin Hodges
David Hodgkiss
S W Hodgson BVSc MRCVS
T E Hodgson
Derek Hogg
E Higg
J Holbrook
Mr M G Hole
Jean Holland
John Holland
Laurence E Holland
Mr R G Holman
Dr A Holmes Pickering
Philip Holmes
E J C Homewood, Ex 3/3 GR
Ian C Hood
Thomas H Hood
Douglas F Hooper
Lieutenant Colonel D A Hooper
Victor Edwin Hooper
Gwyneth Hope
Duncan J Hopkin
Glyn C Hopkins
Raymond J Hopkins
G T Horn
Gerald W Horne
Pauline E Horsbrough
Lieutenant Colonel Elliot Horsford
Mrs Gilly Horsford
Rick H Horton
George Houguez, I/P 47
John Houseman
J B Houston
H G Houston
Patrick Howard
Alex C Howat, Ex RSF
Ted Howell
Captain M J Howitt, Royal Navy
Audrie and Peter Howland
Jean Howman
Keith Howman OBE
J R Howorth
Ronald and Winifred Hubble
B Hudson
Captain Esdaile Hudson FRSA
David Hughes
Mrs Dilys Hughes
F E C Hughes
Jeremy Hughes

Mr John Hughes
Ted Hugo
R J Hulbert
Mrs Vera M Hulley
Roger F Humm
Mr P F Humpherson
Peter W T Humphreys
Major D H Humphries
Brigadier Sir Miles Hunt-Davis KCVO CBE
Derek Harold Hunt
N H Hunter OBE
P D Hurford, Lt Cdr RN (Retd)
Richard G Hurley
Edwin J Hutchinson
F J Hutt
J M Hutton, ex 11th Hussars
J M G Hutton
Miss Ivy Teresa Hutty
Keith H Hyatt
Flight Lieutenant Bernard Hyde AE★ and Mrs
    Marian Hyde
Stephen Richard Ingram
Captain J M N Irens
Scott James Irving
Tareq Islam
Dennis W Isles
Brigadier B C Jackman OBE MC
Canon Derek Jackson, Ex 4GR
Mrs Maureen R Jackson
Mr Stanley Arthur Jackson
Stephen Jackson
Sylvia J Jackson
Mrs Georgina Jacobs
Ted Jacomb-Hood
Joan Jacques
Harold James MC
Mr J James
Major Jimmy James MBE
Norma James
P A E James MBE
Margaret Jamieson
R Jarratt BEM
Colonel A M Jenkins MC
Ieuan Huw Jenkins
Mr D H Jennings
F A Jenning
Mr David R E Jenson
Dr Malcolm Jenyon
Paula Jervis
Mrs Ann Jewell
Norman L Job BEM
Ronald Job
James W Jobson
A G Johnson
Mr D Johnson
General Sir Garry Johnson KCB OBE MC
J A Johnson
Dr John C Johnson

Mrs Joy Johnson
Mary Ethel Johnson
Mrs P Johnson
Peter Johnson
P L Bowyer Johnson
Stephen Johnson
A Johnston
Mervyn Johnston
Barbara E Jones
Charles W Jones
Dr David A Jones
Dr Donald Jones
Brigadier G R Jones OBE QVRM TD
Glynn C Jones
Corporal Gordon Jones, Royal Corps of Signals
John Hedley Jones
Michael Geoffrey Jones
Mrs Moira Jones
Peter F Jones
Ray Jones
Rhidian H B Jones
Robert Cyril Jones
Trevor Jones
N F Jose
Mr M F C Joslin
Mrs P Juden
Kitto Juleff
John Karle
George D Kay
Mr Johnny Kaye
Ronald Kaye
John Keal
Graham Keeley
Barry Keen
Frederick Keen
Geoffrey H Kellock
Bernard D Kelly
Lieutenant Colonel J N Kelly
Lieutenant Colonel (Retd) P Kemmis Betty
Malcolm Kemp
M Kendal
Jean Kennedy
Dennis R Kennerley
William Kent
Michael L J Kernan QFSM
E W L Keymer MC
Mike Kidd
Colonel Peter W E Kidner
B A Kilpatrick
I C A King-Holford
Geoffrey Kenneth King DFC
Roy L King
Steve Kingshott
Mike Kinrade
Jonathan Kitchen
Richard and Margery Kitchener
Colonel (Retd) John Kitching
Barry S Kitson

Major (Retd) D W Knight
Major J R Knights, 6GR
K W Laming
A Lancaster
Mr I G Lancefield-Walker
James Ernest Lane
Captain N J Lane
Stephen G Lane
Lieutenant Colonel A M Langlands OBE
Mrs Susan F Laniado
W B Lappin
Lieutenant Colonel D R Large
Lieutenant Colonel R C Larking MBE TD
F/Lt R L C Lasham DFC and Bar
John G Laskey
Mr H R M Lau
John Nicholas Lauderdale
Colonel Christopher Lavender
Colonel J O Lawes LVO MC 2GR
P C Lawrence
Clive Lawry
W/Bombardier Clifford Lawton
T J Laybourn
Mr W Lebeter
Colin and Lee Lee
David H Lee, COLDM GDS
Mrs P Lee
R J Lee
Brigadier S M A Lee OBE
Michael J Legg
Dr W J J Legg
M J Leigh
Dr Margaret Leigh
Mr R W Lemon
David Leslie
William Allan Leslie
Major P H Lewis-Jones
A David Lewis RM
Kathleen D Lewis
Esmé Leworthy
Joel Linacre, WO2 RAMC Retd
J V Lindley
Horace George Linton
Mr Dominik Lipnicki
Brigadier P A Little
John Livingston
Dr John Stuart Livingstone
Lieutenant Colonel James Lloyd-Bostock
Carnegy Major Richard Lloyd 9th Gurkha Rifles
    1894–1911
Gerard Lobo OBE
Dr Rupert Lobo
Norma M L Logan
T Logan
J E Lomas
Ana London
T R W Longmore
J T Looke

S L Lord
Adrian Clary Lorrimer
F J Loveless
Bernard P Lovelock
P D Lowndes, Lt Cdr RN
John Luby
C J Lumb of Exley
Joanna Lumley
Mr and Mrs D W Lydford
W Lyne
T Lyness
Kenneth William Lynn
Anthony W Lyon
Eion MacDonald
Ian and Patricia Macdonald
Dr J S Macdonald
S J Mace
John Macfarlane
Ann MacGilchrist
Hector G Macgregor
Mr C C Mack
Edward Mackaness
Colonel Hugh Mackay
Mark MacKenzie-Charrington
Ewan MacLeod
Mr Robert Macnab
Michael Fenwick Macnamara
D J Maddison-Roberts
Robert J Maddocks
J C A Madgwick
Bryan D Maggs
Dr Ian Mair
R J Makepeace
Major Philip Malins MBE MC
James Malpas
Alan Manger
Richard and Ann Manning
Joyce M Mapletoft
Mr S C Marcandonatos
Donald Sydney Marriner
J G Marsden TD
Keith E Marsh
Charles Alan Marshall
Ernest Marshall OBE
Mr and Mrs G E D Marshall
Arthur R Martin
Eric Martin MBE
Mr Howard Martin
I C D Martin
David C L Marwood
Carol Mason
E B Mason, Ex RAF Ex CHINDIT
P G and A J Mason
Perry Mason RMP
Stewart Mason
Lieutenant Colonel M Massam RAMC
G D Masters
John Masters

Raymond Mather
Lieutenant Colonel Guy Mathews
Heather W Mathews
Ian J Mathieson
Ken Matthews (New Zealand)
Shirley Ann Matthews
I M Ikey May and Eric May MC
Peter May
Karl Mayers
Peter and Sheelagh Mayes
Major I Mayman DL
B McAllister
Richard McAllister
Miss J F McAra
Elizabeth McBeath
Cobby and Sisse McCall
R L S McCartney
The late T S McConnell
Major Winnie McCracken
D McCutchan
Mr M F McDonald
David M McFarlane BDS
Rory McGregor
Sheriff D W M McIntyre, 2/6 GR
Maureen Mcintyre
Norman McIver
Don McKay F/LT
Martin McKay
Bob McKean, Queens Gurkha Signals
Graham McKenzie
James McKeown NI
Mr George S McKinley
R B McLachlan
Mr J B Mclaughlin
Hugh H McLean
J K McLean
James F McLean
William McLean, Major Coldstream Guards
Ian McLetchie
M C McManus
Major (Retd) R A McNaughton
Arthur McPhee
Malcolm and Eileen McSporran
Patrick McVeigh DCM
Sonia Meaden OBE
Mrs Val Meadows
Mr R E P Medway
Richard P Mellon
Doug Meredith
R E Meyer
Christopher Miles
Dr Alan E Mill
Mr Roger Millar
Beryl Miller
Mr H R Miller
John Miller
Olga Orr Miller
Captain Robert C Miller, 1/9th Gurkha Rifles

Captain P J Millington
Major H J Millman
Frank Mills
Dr K L M Mills
V M Mills
Mrs Pamela Milne
Ronald Milne
Lawrence W M Milner
Lieutenant Tony Mirfin 6GR
Thornton Mitcalfe
Alex B Mitchell
Mrs C Mitchell
James Andrew Mitchell
James H F Mitchell
Mr J D Moir OBE
Richard Moir
Major Jolsen Mole
Tony Molyneux
Mr S D Moncaster
Michael Montgomery-Buick EGC
George David Monument
Dr Jean Mooney
A E Moore CBE
A E W Moore
Jolyon Christoper Moore
Lieutenant Colonel M P Moore
N E Moore
Major and Mrs P V Moore
Pony' Moore, ex CPO SPTI RN
F D M Moores
Stephen Morant
James More
Major James More-Molyneux OBE DL
Brigadier David Morgan
G H and R E Morgan
Mr K Morgan
Stuart Morgan
W H and G M Morris
Frank T Morley
Anthony Morpeth
Fred A Morphew
Mr R Morris-Shaoul
Major B W M Morris
P and J Morris
William H Morris
Cyril Morrison
Malcolm Morrison
S R Morrison MIET
Mrs Vanessa Morrison
B J Morton
David Morton
John Ringer Moss CB
Andrew A Moyes Matheou
Aileen M Moyes
Dr Marjorie Mudge
Peter Muggeridge
Mr J F Muirhead
Brian Muirhead

Kathleen E Mumford
E J Murphy
Edith M Murphy
Marguerite Murphy
Mary-Rose Murphy
Gordon Reid Murray
Ian P Murrin
Tim Musgrave
Oliver Musgrave
Major (Retd) M H Myers MBE,
    Royal Pioneer Corps
David G Naish
J G Nancollas
Major Nov Nanovo, RLC 10 QOGLR
Elisabeth Napier-Munn
A R Nash
Sheila Nash
Alexander David Nasmyth
Lieutenant Colonel R C Neath OBE
D Neaverson
V Neeves
Margaret Neill
Ronald W Neilson
William Nellies
Henry Nelson
Alex P R Nevill, ex 7GR
Stan New
Harry Newby
Charles Newcomb MC
D J Newey FACCA FCT
Lieutenant Colonel David Newton
Roger Newton
Sir Wilfrid Newton CBE
Mark Niblock
Lt Cdr J U Nichol
G T Nicholls
John Nicholls
David A P Nicholson
D Nicholson BEM
P J Nicholson
Allan Nicoll
Edward Noden
Doreen Elizabeth Nolan
D G W Norris
William F North
Ephraim John Northfield
John Nott
Miss June A L Nunn
R Nuttall GP Capt OBE
Mrs Olga Sweeney
Lieutenant Colonel Brian O'Bree, 6GR
David John O'Brien
Kevin H O'Brien
Gerald O'Callaghan
William J O'Connell
Doris O'Connor
Shane O'Neill
Molly O'Shea

John Buckley Ogden
Brian Olof
Mr Alan Charles Osborne
Anthony E Otway
Mr Jack Otway
R A B Ouwens
Major David Owens
Christopher L Packham
Richard John Page
Mr and Mrs Stirling Page
Tony Page AMA
Alfred and Josiane Pain
Mr H L and Mrs E B Painter
Antony Palmer
Christopher Palmer
Derek Palmer
Lieutenant Colonel J C Palmer
Mrs N M Palmer
P H R Palmer
R E Palmer
Edward Pank
Mrs E Papanicolaou
Cynthia G A Pardy
Major John Parfect
Henry and May Park
Brian James Parker
Guy Parker
Mr Michael N Parker
Samuel Thomas Parker
Mr E M and Mrs J M Parkin
David Parnall
Mr G Parrish
CFN J Parrish REME
Tony Parrott
Howell Parry
Ian Parry and Marie Parry
Mrs T F Parry
Lieutenant A J Parsons
Roland Hill of Parsonby
Mr Ernie Parsons
Pat Parsons
John Lewis Partridge MBE
John and Durga Patchett
David M Patton
Mr Richard Payne
Anthony W Pazda
Michael E P Peach
John G Pearce
Mrs Sheila Pearce
W (Peter) Pearce
General Sir Thomas Pearson
Christopher A Peckham
Harry Peckham
David Penrice
Mr and Mrs M G W Pepper
Alf Perkins
Clive Perkins
Miss Barbara Perrott

Sydney Perry
Mark Pessell
The late Gordon Petty
A M Phelps
Lieutenant Colonel Fred Phillips Comd. St John
    TD DL
Jeff Phillips
Captain (Retd) P Phillips
Mrs Doreen Pickard
J R Pigeon
Lester and Susan Piggott
Mr Brian Pill
Kenneth J Pink
Malcolm J Piper
Suzanne Piper
Ian A Pirie
Barbara Plummer
Patricia Poel
Ivan Pogue
Michael C Pointer Esq
The late Captain Alec Pollard (Burma)
E P J Pollard
Jim Pollock
Mrs Marion Pont
Eric S Poole
Irene Porteous
Valerie Porter (Molesworth)
Geoffrey R Potten
Eric Potton
Elizabeth M Powell
Mr J Pratt
John L Pratt
W G Preece
John Pressney
Presteigne Royal British Legion
Dennis Charles Price
Mr Edward Graham Price
Lyndon Price
Sam F Price
G Prince
Major R Prismall
E M J Procter
Ian Purvis
Major P R Quantrill
John A Rabley
David Rackham
A J Raffray
Lieutenant Colonel (Retd) J R Rahilly
Bala Mogan Raja-Gopal
Taff Randall
Duncan R Ranger
Eileen A Ranger
Valerie E Ranger
Terry Rann
Mr Ronald Leslie Ransom
Harry Rawlings
Captain J S Rawlings
Mr and Mrs N W Raworth

A J A Rea
Peter C Read, PWO 3/4 G.R.
Cyril and Sandra Rebak
Gordon Reddin, Flt Lt (Rtd) RAF
John Redfern
Mr C P Redford
J Lumsden Redpath
Bernard Redshaw
Joan Reed
Joanna S Reed
P A Rees-Boughton
Major William Michael Regan
Desmond Reid
Bill Reynolds
Lieutenant Colonel Ralph Reynolds
Peter Rhodes
Derrick Richards
D R Richards
Paul Richards
Charles Richardson-Bryant
Colin J Richardson
Stanley Richardson
W N B Richardson DL
Sally J Rider
Viscount Ridley
Colonel I A Rigden OBE, late RGR
Kenneth Riley
Jane Ritchie
Brian S Robbins
Mr Roberts
Adrian L N Roberts
Elsie Robertson
James Robertson
Michael Robertson
Major Patrick Robeson, 6GR
J M Robinson
John Robinson
Keith Robinson
Paul A Robinson
Roland Robinson
Captain Mike Robson
Henry J Rockley
L F Rodgers
Carol Boyd Roffey
Mr Robert Rogers
Mrs Gladys (Babs) Rogers
Major D A A Ronaldson
Major A F Roney-Dougal
Margaret Rook
Major General Oliver Roome
John and Eileen Rose
A E R Ross
Christine Ross
Miss Myrtle Ross
P D G Ross
Sinclair A Ross
C J Rothery
Major (Retd) K J Rowbottom

William John Rowe
Colonel Stephen Rowland-Jones
Geoffrey Rowland
John Rowlands
Dr John K Rowlands
Mr and Mrs J A S Royals
Mrs Y M Royle
Dr A Rozkovec
J N P Rudd
Brian Ruffell-Ward
Edward Ruscoe
Jeremy Russell QC
John Rylance
D I Rymell
Mr A N Sainsbury
Cherry Salisbury
Christopher Sampson
Nicholas J R Sanceau
John A Sanderson
Brigadier D M Santa-Olalla DSO MC
Neville Sarony QC
Captain K J H Saxton
Mr Kenneth Sayce
Margaret J Schofield
Philip Schofield
Mr F D Scotson
John Scott-Oldfield
Anthony B Scott
Barry D Scott
Dr Frank Scott
Peter R Scott
Thomas Scott
Mrs P M Scroop
Mike Seabourne, Ex GMP
Miss Anne N Seagrim
D J S Seaman
Victor Searle
Peter McCormick Seddon, RSM Corps of
    Military Police
Colin Sedgwick
Robert Seeley
Roger Stanley Selwood
Andrew M G Sharpe
Stuart Sharpe
Arthur Shaw
Mrs Elizabeth Shaw
R W Shaw
Dr Trevor Shaw
Mrs Catherine Sheldon
Mike Shepherd
George Shields
Martin Harper Shields
Colonel Ted Shields MBE
H A Shippey, CHINDITS 77 Brigade
George Shorrock
Mrs R W Shorthouse
Barbara Shuttleworth
Mrs D Siburn

David Side
Geoffrey Sides
Mr W C Sievewright
Mary E Silva
Clive Simpson
John Simpson
Mr M N Simpson
Robert A Simpson
Michael Sinden
Richard Brenton Sinker
Sir Walter Gilbey Memorial Co Ltd
W E D Skinner
G L Skinner
Gordon Skivington
James Slater
Gp Captain F W Sledmere
Miss M Sleeman
Major (Retd) Royston J Smart
Lieutenant Colonel A J M Smetham
J W M Smiles
Robin Smiley
Andrew D Smith
Arthur N Smith
Lt Cdr (Retd) C A Smith RNR
Donald Reuben Smith
E N M Smith
Mrs F E Smith
G M K Smith
Gordon A Smith
Graham Smith
Henry Arthur Smith
John A Smith
John and David Roland Smith
John Vernon Smith
John W Smith
Joshua Michael Smith
K L and J Smith
Keith E O Smith
Margaret Smith
Matthew James Smith
Mrs Marion Smith
Michael G Smith
Philip Smith
Reg Smith, Manorbier
S Phillip Smith
Eric Smithson
W J Smyly
Charmian Sneath
Paul Snook MBE
Kenneth H Southam
Mr John A F Spalding
Richard Sparshatt
J E Speight
Major David Spencer
Denis G Spencer, RAF (Retd)
J J P Spillane
G H Spink
Bob Splaine, Ex RAMC

K Spriggs

P A Springett

Bruce Spurr

Mrs Janet Squires

K Stacey

Peter R G Stainsby

Mr Leonard Standen

Peter J Stanford

Mrs Susan Stanislas

J L Stanley

Mr and Mrs K D Stanworth

G W Stark

Mark W Starr

R I Steawart

Cyril Steel

Mrs June M Steele

Mr Terence A Steele

John Stephany

Mr Paul Stephens

Eric Stephenson

Major General John Stephenson

Victor J Stephenson

Brian D N Stevens

D H J Stevens

James Stevenson

Mark L Steward

Mr David Stewart

Lieutenant Colonel (Retd) T H Stewart RE

Iain P A Stitt

Keith Stobbs RN

Arthur Stock

E A Stocks

George and Ruby Stoddart-Stones

Graham H Stokes

Neville W Stokes

Thelma D Stollar

Mrs E D Stone

D Stonell

Capt Jack H Storer OBE

Kenneth M F Stott

P H Strange

Barbara L G Street

Mrs N Strickland Cooper

Anthony Strong

T W J Strutt, Royal Navy II WWL/ Stoker Mec, D/KX158963

M M Stuart

A L Stubbs

Surgeon Captain K H Sugars RN

E Douglas Summers

Mark Summers

Neil Summersgill

D T Sumner

Mr Alexander Sutherland

Major Eric R M Sutherland TD Royal Signals

Mr R L Swayne

John Sweet

Anthony Tabbinor

Mr and Mrs Bernie and Maureen Taffs

James C E Tainsh

Eddie Talbot

Mr M Taylor

Beatrice Taylor

Brian Taylor CBE

Lieutenant Colonel C D Taylor

The late Captain D J Taylor, 9th Gurkha Rifles 1942–6

Doug Taylor

Mr Douglas John Taylor

Edith Taylor

George E Taylor

George W Taylor

Iain S Taylor

Ian and Fiona Taylor

Jack Taylor

John E Taylor

Colonel K G Taylor

R F Taylor

Colonel Raymond A Taylor

Pamela E Tebbutt

Audrey Tee

Brian Temperley

Jon Terry

G T Thackray

Karnabahadur Thapa, KAAA BGN

The Army and Navy Club Library

Captain D Thirkill

Major David Thomas MBE

Elwyn Thomas

Ian Thomas

James Thomas

Malcolm K Thomas

Noel B Thomas

Richard H Thomas

Tobyn Thomas

Mr Brian Thompson

Colonel Brian Thompson MBE L/RAVC

Lieutenant Colonel Sir Christopher Thompson BT

Robin Thompson

Samuel Paul Thompson

Douglas Thomson

John Ireland Thomson

Mr Jonathan Thomson

Major J Thornbee

J A W Thornton FRICS

Major (Retd) M E Thorp

Matthew Threapleton (RIP)

Miss S Thurlow

E J Tideswell

Mark Tidmarsh

David Frederick Tillett

G H G Tilling

G J Tinkham

David C Tipney

David A Tipple

Joe Tobin

Gordon Tomlinson

Captain S W Tough MBE

Margaret Towart

Bill Towill

Alan Townley

Jim Townsend

Major D J Tregenza

Mr and Mrs W D Trevarthen

Ron Trevitt

E B Treweek

Mrs Joan Tribe

John G Trimmer

Ian Tring ISO

The Trodd Pomeroy Family

Mike Trueman

Adrian Tubb

N R Tubbs

Colonel J J H Tuck

Nigel Tuck

Louis N Tucker

Andrew Tuggey, Gurkha Engineers QGE

Revd D F Tunbridge BA HCF

Rodney J Turk

Mavis J Turnbull

Lieutenant Colonel D J Turner GTR

Mr David B Turner

Peter W Turner MInst LM

Trevor Turner and The Brothers of Charterhouse

A P Turrall

Ann G M Turton

Owen Twigg

Dr Alison Twigley

David W Tyler

Simon R Umfreville

George Underwood

George Upton

S A Uren

F Urquhart

Johan Ursing

John and Gillian M Usher

Christopher Ussher

Mr Lewis Vanstone

William 'Willy' Vatcher

Captain N G Vaughan MN

Nicky Veitch

Victor Howard Venables

Mr Richard M Venning

Paddy Verdon OBE

Professor Martin Vessey

David Campbell Vetch

James L Vickers

Mrs Betty Vincent

Keith (Jake) Wade

Major P G Wade

David Wadey

Walter Wake

Robert M R Wakefield

Tom Waldron

Brian Grant Walker
George R Walker
Ivor H Walker
Colonel M P Walker
Alice E M Walklett
Mr Kenneth Gordon Wall
Leo Wall
A D M Wallace-Cook
Janetta W Wallace
Alan L Waller
Geoffrey C Wallinger
Captain R S J Wallington, 4th Hussars
Peter S Wallis
John Ashley Wallis
Jane 'Moose' Walters
Mr R E Wand
Patricia Wanning OBE
David Wansbrough
Major Bruce H Ward
David Sean Ward
John and Shirley Ward
James Marshall Wardrop
Colonel D B Warne
Nick Warrell
Mr N H Watkins
L J Watkins
James Watling
David Watson
Lieutenant Colonel G A Watson RAMC
Ian Watson
John Barton Watson
R N Watson
Mrs Rosemary Watson
Peter G Waymouth
Alma Wearing
N F Weaver
Captain Michael Webb
Trevor H Webb OBE
Sally Weekes
Anthony Welch
J B P Wells
Mr Richard Wells
Sydney E Wells
V A Werrett BEM
Anthony Wheatley
Geoffrey Wheatley
Gerald Wheatley

Marg Wheeler
James H Whent MBE
Lieutenant Colonel Peter Whitaker
Mrs Anne P S White
Brian White
John A White
J F White MBE MIMECH.E
Michael J J White
Roy White
R K White
L H Whitehead
Mrs Michael Whitehead
Peter Whiteley
Linda K N Whitfield
Eric Whitford
David J Whitmore
Simon Whitmore
Floyd Whitney
Roy Whittaker
T F and Mrs B J Whittaker
Mr R J Whittaker
A R Whittle
Marion Wierszycki
Major Bill Wiggett RE
Barry J Wigzell
Pamela H Wilcock
Mr Stephen Wild
John Wilkes
Anthony M Wilkinson
D I Wilkinson
David Wilkinson
Major Roger Wilkinson
Dave Willacy
The Williams Family, Norfolk
A R Williams
David A Williams
Derek Williams
Dr F Williams
Haydn John Williams
Gp Captain (Retd) R E Williams RAF
Terry C Williams
David Soulsby Williamson
Peter Williamson
D R d'A Willis
M J R Willis
Reginald Sidney Wills
Colonel and Mrs R F Willsher

John Wilmot
Roy F Wilsher
Trooper Wilson, Queens Bays
Brian Victor Ernest Wilson
D J M Wilson
David T Wilson
Edward Wilson
James W M Wilson TD
Ron Wilson, Catterick Garrison
Ronald James Wilson
T Peter Wilson
Captain A L Wiltshire, 4th POW Gurkha Rifles
Harry and Marian Windsor
Leon Winnert
Mr J B Winter
Anthony Peter Winter
Colonel K S B Wintle CBE
C Ian C Wishart
Alan Wood
Peter B Wood
Cliff Woodhead
Charles Woodings
L D Woodley Esq
Lieutenant Colonel T G W Woodman MBE RLC
Dennis Woods-Scawen
Margaret Woolcott
Godfrey Woolf Gunners 4th Indian
Mr John Edmund Woolley
Mike W Woyen
Dr John Wratten
Christopher Wrigglesworth
Major D A Wright TD
Mr M H Wright MBE
Colonel M J Wright late QGE
Nick Wright
Mrs Shirley Wright
Major N D Wylie Carrick MBE
Francis Wynd
Elizabeth Wynne
Sir Eric Yarrow MBE DL
Mrs J M W Yeomans
Professor F J L Young OBE
R L Young
Ronald C Young
Mrs S L H Young